Anderson Guide to
ENJOYING
GREENWICH

Connecticut

An insider's favorite places

Seventh Edition

Anderson Associates
Greenwich Real Estate Specialists

with illustrations and maps
by Vanessa Y. Chow

Avocet Press

Anderson Guide to
Enjoying Greenwich, Connecticut
An insider's favorite places

Written by
Carolyn Anderson &
Anderson Associates, Ltd.
www.greenwichliving.com
164 Mason Street, Greenwich, CT 06830
203.629.4519

Illustrations and maps by Vanessa Y. Chow

Published by
Ickus Guides, Avocet Press Inc
19 Paul Court, Pearl River, NY 10965
www.avocetpress.com

Find updates at www.greenwichguide.com

ISBN 978-0-9677346-3-7

Anderson Guide to
ENJOYING GREENWICH

Connecticut

An insider's favorite places

The Anderson Guide is a treasure trove of information about Greenwich. Solid Gold and five stars!!!!!! Hats off to Anderson Associates.
— Joan Roome

No household should be without one! As I read it, I am learning new things about our town. It is a great gift for new neighbors and friends.
— Betty Deming

The Guide just keeps getting better and better. I keep all of the editions.
- Livvy Floren

Your Guide is so informative, that within the first few minutes of perusing it, we came upon the perfect Christmas gift idea for our son.
— Lou & Barbara Hardvall

I am thrilled with the new edition of the Guide. It is the book I reach for instead of the telephone directory. I truly appreciate all of the effort that goes into it.
— Linda Taylor

Your restaurant reviews are accurate and we rely on them.
— Kathleen and Steven Gray

Your book is so helpful in every way. We have found all kinds of fun activities and trips in the children's section.
— Susan Schuller

Anderson Guide to
ENJOYING
GREENWICH
Connecticut
An insider's favorite places

WHAT KIND OF
GUIDE IS THIS ?

The Guide is a list of our favorites...simply that. It is not a book of advertisements. No place mentioned in the Guide had any idea that it would be included. We never accept favors as a result of including someone. Establishments and programs are listed because we like them. Although the Guide is about enjoying Greenwich, you will note many selections are outside of Greenwich's town limits. These easy-to-reach places complement our many in-town resources .

Initially, many years ago, our first Guide was prepared for our real estate clients. Then the calls came in—their friends needed a copy. The owner of a local book store saw it and said we must publish it. That is where it started. Our initial reason for writing it has not changed. We know finding favorite spots takes a while. We have lived in Greenwich for many years and we hope the resources in the Guide will help everyone moving into town feel right at home.

The new edition has 180 restaurant reviews. Jerry and Carolyn anonymously visit each one at least twice before writing the review. We are looking at the whole experience: food, ambience and service. If the restaurant is disappointing in too many ways, we do not include it. Restaurant reviewing is a professional responsibility. We have a great deal to do with a restaurant's success or failure. We have extensive food and restaurant experience. Carolyn is the author of the *Complete Book of Homemade Ice Cream* and several other cookbooks. For a number of years we owned and operated a small vineyard. Tasting foods and wines and knowing how they are prepared is greatly helpful in reviewing. Carolyn is a professional member of the American Society of Interior Designers. Before devoting full time to real estate, she designed restaurants. Many people remember the popular restaurant, Morgan, open for many years in Greenwich, which she designed. Knowing the requirements of good restaurant design is helpful in reviewing. We love discovering new "finds." We hope our readers of the Guide will enjoy them too.

We are grateful to so many residents for their support and enthusiastic appreciation of the Guide. We hope you will find this 7th edition useful, too! The Greenwich Library keeps copies at their information desk to help people with questions. The Historical Society has copies of our past editions in their archives. We are pleased to be documenting our town's many events, restaurants, shops and tips about the Greenwich way of life.

Please let us know what you think of this Guide or of the restaurants, stores or services we reviewed. We love your comments and suggestions! Please send your comments to Carolyn@GreenwichLiving.net or call Carolyn at 203.629.4519 x 18.

Sincerely,

Carolyn and Jerry Anderson
Amy Zeeve
and all of us at Anderson Associates.

With a special thanks to Lynn Chimblo, Laura Davis and Victoria Lincoln for tireless editing.

Greenwich Guide Website

The Guide website, www.greenwichguide.com has the index of Restaurants and Stores (without reviews) together with mapping to out-of-town locations. We hope this will make it easier for Guide owners to find their favorite restaurant or store. Because stores and restaurants change so frequently, we will post changes and new reviews on the Guide website.

Disclaimer

The purpose of this Guide is to educate and entertain. Every effort has been made to make this guide accurate; however, it should not be relied upon as the ultimate source of information about Greenwich or about any resource mentioned in the Guide.

There may be mistakes both typographical and in content. We have done our best to lead you to spots we hope you will like. This is by no means a complete guide to every resource in Greenwich. Unfortunately, even the best are not always perfect. If you have tried one of our favorites and are disappointed, if we have missed your favorite, or if we have made a mistake in a description, please let us know: fill out the feedback form in the back of the book and send it to us.

A note about "Hours"

The hours and days of operation are intended as a guide, but they should not be considered definitive. Establishments change their hours as business dictates. In addition, many change their hours for winter and summer and during holidays. Finally, just about every establishment takes a vacation.

CONTENTS

CONTENTS

CONTENTS

CONTENTS

CONTENTS

CONTENTS

CONTENTS

CONTENTS

CONTENTS

CONTENTS

CONTENTS

CONTENTS – TIPS

CONTENTS – TIPS

GREENWICH

at a glance

- Median age: 40
- Median household income: $112,041
- Average residential price: $2,652,238
- Assessed value of all residences: $18 billion
- Assessed value of all real estate: $32 billion
- Population: 61,101 (2000 census)
- Number of households: 23,569 (2000 census)
- 47.8 square miles
- 1,500 acres of public parks
- 32 miles of shoreline
- 150 miles of riding trails
- 37 houses of worship (34 churches, 3 synagogues)
- 9 yacht clubs, 8 country clubs and 1 tennis club
- 98 special interest organizations
- 11 garden clubs
- 38 languages spoken
- 17% of public school students come from non-English speaking homes
- School system rated #1 in Connecticut
- Rated safest community in Connecticut
- Town of Greenwich budget: $361,455,462
- Town of Greenwich capital budget: $63,575,000
- Town of Greenwich Mill Rate: 7.449

Information based on data from the CERC Town Profile, Greenwich Multiple Listing Service, United Way and the Town's Budget presentation to the RTM.

GREENWICH

rated best town in Connecticut

Time and again, Greenwich is rated as Connecticut's number one place to live. Greenwich is the premier town along what is called the Connecticut Gold Coast. The town's unique beauty has been preserved by very careful town planning and zoning. Like Beverly Hills, Greenwich has the rare distinction of being one of those recognizable names. But unlike Beverly Hills, which is a 5.7 square mile enclave, Greenwich extends over fifty square miles with rolling hills, woodlands, meadows and 32 miles of gorgeous shoreline bordering the Long Island Sound. Greenwich is not isolated—it is a real community and a wonderful place to raise a family.

Although Greenwich conjures up thoughts of stately country homes and waterfront estates reserved for the select few, Greenwich is much, much more. As you will discover, Greenwich offers diversity, not only in real estate and architecture, but also in residents. Greenwich is home not only to a cosmopolitan group of executives, but to a great variety of professionals, artists, writers, diplomats, actors, and sports figures.

In addition to being rated number one in safety and education by *Connecticut Magazine*, Greenwich is rated the number one city in Connecticut for quality of life. Greenwich has a vast array of attractions. Whether you look at the picturesque shopping areas, the personal service provided by its mix of elegant shops, its fantastic library (the most used in Connecticut), its ultra modern hospital or its fifty fabulous restaurants, Greenwich has it all. *Connecticut's Best Dining Guide*, which covers the entire state, gave 19 of Greenwich's restaurants top honors. Of the 20 best restaurants in the state, 4 were located in Greenwich. *The New York Times* declared that Greenwich has more Very Good and Excellent restaurants *per capita* than any other community in Connecticut. One of the many unique things about Greenwich can be found on Greenwich Avenue every day between the hours of 8 am and 6:30 pm: the police officers at the street corners directing traffic. These officers help to preserve the feeling of a small town and, of course, also help keep the town's crime rate low.

GREENWICH

town facilities

Greenwich is still 25% green. It has 32 miles of coastline, with its main beaches at Greenwich Point (147 acres), Byram Beach and the two city-owned islands (Captain's Island & Island Beach). Greenwich has 8,000 acres of protected land, over 1,000 acres of town parks, 35 town tennis courts (not including the YWCA Courts), an indoor ice rink (open only to residents), 14 public marinas and a 158-acre, 18-hole golf course (open only to residents). Music lovers enjoy the Greenwich Symphony, while the Bruce Museum appeals to everyone and is rated one of the best museums in Connecticut.

education

Greenwich public schools (eleven elementary, three middle and one high school) are rated number one in Connecticut: 40% of the graduates go to the "Most Competitive Colleges." The school budget is approximately 113 million dollars. The average class size is twenty and 90% of the teachers have masters degrees. In addition, Greenwich has thirty independent pre-schools and nine excellent private and parochial day schools. For details, see section SCHOOLS.

TIP: 100 THINGS TO DO

The Greenwich Post publishes two excellent guides. The 100 Things to Do guide has many of the fascinating places to visit in our region. In the spring, they publish 100 Things to Do for Kids. For parents or grandparents, this is a great resource. These guides are available online at www.acorn-online.com

GREENWICH

fire department

15 Havemeyer Place Nonemergency phone: 622.3950
To report a fire dial 911
The Greenwich Fire Department is a combination fire department that consists of uniformed career firefighters and professional volunteer fire fighters who work together to preserve life and protect property in Greenwich.

Our fire department responds to over 4,000 emergency calls per year, ranging from minor fire alarm activations to structure fires, motor vehicle accidents, and even hazardous materials incidents. Equipment consists of 14 Engine Companies, 3 Ladder Companies, and 2 Rescue Companies. The Fire Department operates this equipment out of 8 fire houses within Greenwich (and Banksville, New York) with the help of nearly 100 uniformed career firefighters, and over 150 well-trained and dedicated volunteers.
See NUMBERS YOU SHOULD KNOW for a complete list of fire stations and their telephone numbers.

police department

11 Bruce Place
Nonemergency phone: 622.8000, emergency number: 911
www.greenwichpolice.com
The Greenwich Police Department is a group of helpful, kind and competent professionals. They are charged with the protection of life and property, the preservation of public peace, the prevention and detection of crime, the apprehension of offenders and the enforcement of state and local laws and ordinances, as well as the countless calls for service that the Police Department handles on a daily basis. In a typical year they respond to over 40,000 calls. The department offers a ten-week Citizen Police Academy program, allowing residents the opportunity to get a behind the scenes look at police operations.

crime

Greenwich is rated the safest community in Connecticut and one of the safest in the country—and it's no wonder: with 14 police cars on the road at all times, traffic downtown directed by police officers, and with a force of 156 dedicated police officers, the average response time to a call is less than 4 minutes.

GREENWICH

library — Greenwich

www.greenwichlibrary.org

The Greenwich Library is a special treasure used by young and old alike. In a typical year the library loans 675,000 customers an average of 4.5 books per minute. It is no wonder the library has been rated the best in the country. The library received a $25,000,000 bequest from Clementine Peterson. Based on this bequest and funds raised by the Friends of Greenwich Library, Architect Cesar Pelli designed the 31,000 square foot addition as well as renovations to the original building. In addition to the Main Branch, the library has marvelous branches in Cos Cob and Byram. Old Greenwich has its own superb independent library, Perrot. For more information on our wonderful libraries see LIBRARIES AND BOOKS.

hospital

Greenwich Hospital
5 Perryridge Road, 863.3000
www.greenhosp.org
The 160-bed Greenwich hospital is an affiliate of Yale University School of Medicine. It is a world-class hospital, providing the town with excellent health care. Patients from all over Fairfield and Westchester seek treatment at Greenwich Hospital. The hospital has a state of the art cancer center (Bendheim) as well as a $129,000,000 expansion to make it a high tech diagnostic and healing center without the austere look, normal delays and "red tape" often associated with hospitals. With the new $98,000,000 expansion "The Watson Pavillion", Greenwich residents have a completely new hospital with the best of services and amenities. For more information on the Hospital and other medical services, see HEALTH.

TIP: TEDDY BEAR CLINIC
Once a year (usually in September), the Greenwich Hospital invites young children and their teddy bears to learn about surgery, ambulances and health check-ups. Each teddy bear is given its own ID bracelet. Call 863.3627 for more information.

GREENWICH

Greenwich Town Hall
101 Field Point Road, 622.7700
Call this number for any town department
www.greenwichct.org
See NUMBERS YOU SHOULD KNOW for a complete list of departments, their hours of operation and meeting rooms.
Post Offices and Zip Codes are listed under their own heading.
www.GreenwichPost.com

location

Greenwich is in the southwest corner of Connecticut, providing residents with the convenience of being close to a big city, while living in the comfort and security of the country. Greenwich has an excellent transportation system and is just minutes from Westchester Airport, which makes trips to nearby cities such as Boston or Washington convenient. Greenwich is only 29 miles from Times Square (43 minutes by one of the 78 trains that operate daily between New York City and Greenwich). There are 4 train stations conveniently located throughout the town. U.S. Route 1, the historic Post Road, is the main commercial artery. Locally, it is named Putnam Avenue. In addition, Interstate 95 and the Merritt Parkway traverse Greenwich, giving it excellent regional accessibility. It takes about 10 minutes to drive to Stamford, about 60 minutes to Danbury and approximately 15 minutes to White Plains. Limousines provide easy and quick access to New York City's international airports: La Guardia Airport is about a 45-minute drive, Kennedy Airport is about a 60-minute drive. The Merritt Parkway, built in 1935 for cars only, was placed on the National Register of Historic Places in 1993. For more information, see TRAVEL.

GREENWICH

population and housing

The population of Greenwich grew until about 1970. Since 1970, the resident population has been more or less stable. This has been accompanied by the construction or conversion of more dwellings to house the same number of people. In 1950, the population of 40,835 lived in 10,524 households, with an average of 3.9 persons in each. In 1990, the population of 58,441 persons lived in 23,515 households, with an average of 2.5 persons. Presently the population is 62,236 living in 23,569 households with an average of 2.6 persons. Two-thirds of Greenwich homes are for single families, mostly detached, one to a lot. The town's residential zones provide a wide variety of housing types, from small condominiums to single family homes of more than 10,000 square feet on 4 acres or more. Greenwich is divided into several strictly enforced zoning areas. In or near town, the density is high as a result of condominiums and apartments. Further from the center of town, the zoning changes to 1 acre per family, then to 2 acres per family and north of the Merritt Parkway it is a minimum of 4 acres per family. The population of the town continues to be diverse. One sixth of all public school students, with 38 different first languages, are learning English as a second language.

jobs and income

Greenwich is a job center where 35,278 people are employed. More people now come to work in Greenwich than go to work elsewhere. As a result of the many offices moving to the suburbs, Greenwich has become a net provider of jobs during the past twenty-five years. At the same time the median household income in Greenwich has been growing steadily. In 1979 it was $30,278. Ten years later, in 1989, it was $65,072. Today it is over $100,000.

taxes

The Town of Greenwich operates on a "pay as you go" basis and does not carry debt. This allows Greenwich to keep property taxes low while maintaining a budget of over $300,000,000. Real estate taxes are based on assessments limited by statute to 70% of market value, at present 7.449 per thousand of assessed value (mill rate). There are no separate school taxes. There is a personal property tax on cars equal to the mill rate. There is no town income tax. The state has an income tax of 5%.

Greenwich is in the largest metropolitan area of the United States, and is fortunate in its location, natural features, and historic development. Within the New York metropolitan area, Greenwich is the most desirable place to live. The migration of business and jobs from New York City to White Plains, Greenwich and Stamford has increased the demand for housing here. Greenwich intends to keep its place as the premier town to live in. To maintain control of its future, Greenwich has developed a Plan of Conservation and Development. This plan, filled with maps and information on the town, is very influential in preserving the town's goals. It can be purchased from the Planning & Zoning Commission at Town Hall, 622.7700. Greenwich has a Geographic Information System (GIS) which allows the town and residents to access information such as property boundaries, assessments and building lines. The GIS map request form is online at www.greenwichct.org/planningzoning/planninzoning.asp.

TIP: LOCAL GOVERNMENT IN ACTION

The best way to understand how our town can be run so efficiently by the largest legislature in Connecticut (The RTM or Representative Town Meeting) is to attend some of their meetings. Meetings are open to the public and are held in the beginning of most months at the Central Middle School auditorium. Ask the Town Clerk (622.7700) for a schedule of their meetings and for an agenda, "The Call," or find it on the website at : www.greenwichct.org/rtm.
Guests always sit in the last rows.

GREENWICH

government

Unlike many towns and cities, there is a great feeling of community here. Greenwich is run primarily by volunteers, not politicians. The town is governed by a Board of Selectmen (one full-time and two part-time) who are elected every two years. Although town departments are staffed by paid professionals, except for the Selectmen, all town boards (such as the Board of Estimate and Taxation, which serves as the town's comptroller) and the Representative Town Meeting, are made up of unpaid citizen volunteers. In addition to the volunteers in government offices, Greenwich depends on many residents who serve in unofficial capacities. The volunteer network supports and supplements the work of town departments and gives the town its unparalleled cultural and social values.

representative town meeting

www.greenwichct.org/rtm

Greenwich still retains the traditional New England Representative Town Meeting (RTM). The RTM consists of 230 members selected by the voters in the town's 12 districts. It is larger than the State's House and Senate combined. Candidates run on a non-partisan basis and serve without compensation. As a result, the composition of the RTM is very egalitarian. The RTM serves as the town's legislative body and most issues of importance, including appointments, labor contracts, town expenditures over $5,000, town ordinances and the town budget, must be approved by the RTM. Any town issue may be brought before the RTM by a petition of twenty registered voters. Because many of the RTM members are quite successful in business and other careers, the town is run efficiently, honestly, conservatively and in the interest of its citizens. RTM meetings are held at night about once every month. RTM meetings are open to everyone and are a good source of information about the town.

The League of Women Voters (352.4700) is very active and is a great way to get involved. They publish an informative guide on Greenwich Government, "People Make it Happen."

GREENWICH

history

Greenwich is the tenth-oldest town in Connecticut. Named after Greenwich, England, the town began as a temporary trading post founded by Captain Adrian Block in 1614. Greenwich was settled in 1640 when it was purchased from the Indians as part of the New Haven Colony, with allegiance to England. The settlers grew restless under the Puritan influence and, in 1642, withdrew their allegiance to England and transferred it to the more liberal Dutch. At this time, the Cos Cob section of Greenwich was occupied by the Siwanoy Indians and a toll gate was set up between them and the central part of Greenwich, called Horseneck. In 4 years the town was forced back under the domination of the New Haven Colony. Greenwich supported the British during the French and Indian War, but during the Revolution the town was sacked several times by the King's troops. The advent of the New Haven Railroad in 1848 began the transformation of Greenwich into a residential community. This period saw many wealthy New Yorkers, including Boss Tweed, building summer homes. In the twenties, the town began to grow rapidly and land values began to soar. By 1928, Greenwich led the nation in per capita wealth. In 1933 the town had grown so large that it had to abandon open town meetings and adopted the Representative Town Meeting (RTM). Although the population growth has abated (because of the scarcity of buildable land) the property values have continued to climb.

TIP: GREENWICH LIBRARY ORAL HISTORY

www.glohistory.org

The Greenwich Library and The Greenwich Historical Society have developed an Oral History of Greenwich. This program records the memories of residents who were influential in the town's development or who observed important events in the town's history. Volunteers have compiled 700 interviews into 131 books. Books are also for sale at the Oral History office.

GREENWICH

areas and villages

Greenwich is made up of a number of small villages and neighborhoods, each with its own character and charm. The largest of these are Byram, Banksville, Back Country, Central, Cos Cob, Mianus, Old Greenwich, Glenville, and Riverside. All parts of Greenwich share the same government, school system, property tax rate and access to public facilities.

main streets

The central street connecting the main part of Greenwich with the Riverside, Cos Cob, and Old Greenwich sections is Putnam Avenue (a.k.a. Post Road, US 1). It runs essentially east to west through the town (of course out-of-town maps show US-1 running North/South from Stamford to Port Chester). Greenwich Avenue, the main shopping street, is the dividing line between East and West Putnam Avenue. Sound Beach Avenue on the eastern end of Putnam Avenue is the main shopping street for Old Greenwich and runs to Greenwich Point Beach (Tod's Point).

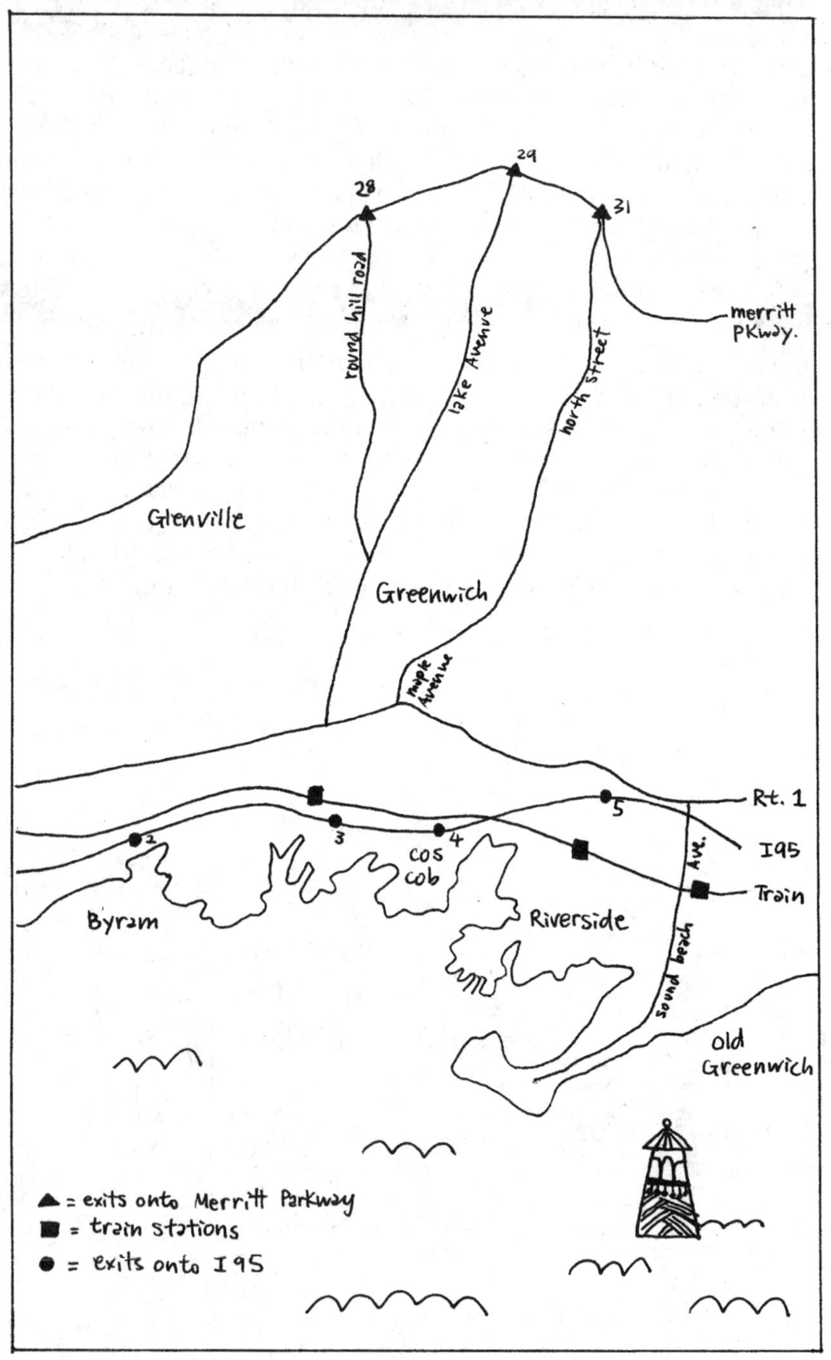

28
29
31
round hill road
lake Avenue
north street
merritt PKway.
Glenville
Greenwich
maple Avenue
Rt. 1
I95
Train
5
2
3
4
cos cob
sound beach Ave.
Byram
Riverside
old Greenwich
= exits onto Merritt Parkway
= train stations
= exits onto I95

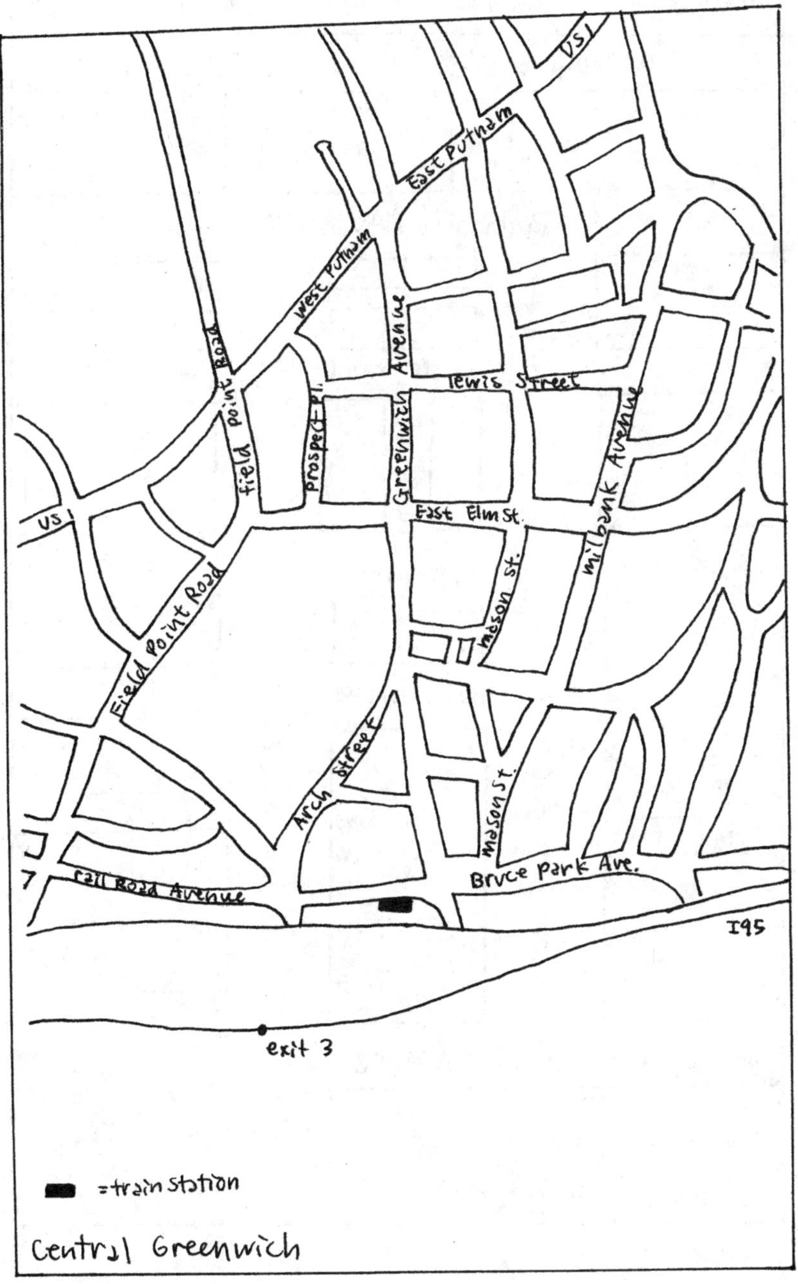
US 1
East Putnam
West Putnam
Field Point Road
Prospect Pl.
Greenwich Avenue
lewis Street
Milbank Avenue
US 1
East Elm St.
Mason St.
Field Point Road
Arch Street
Mason St.
Bruce Park Ave.
railRoad Avenue
I 95
exit 3
= train station
Central Greenwich

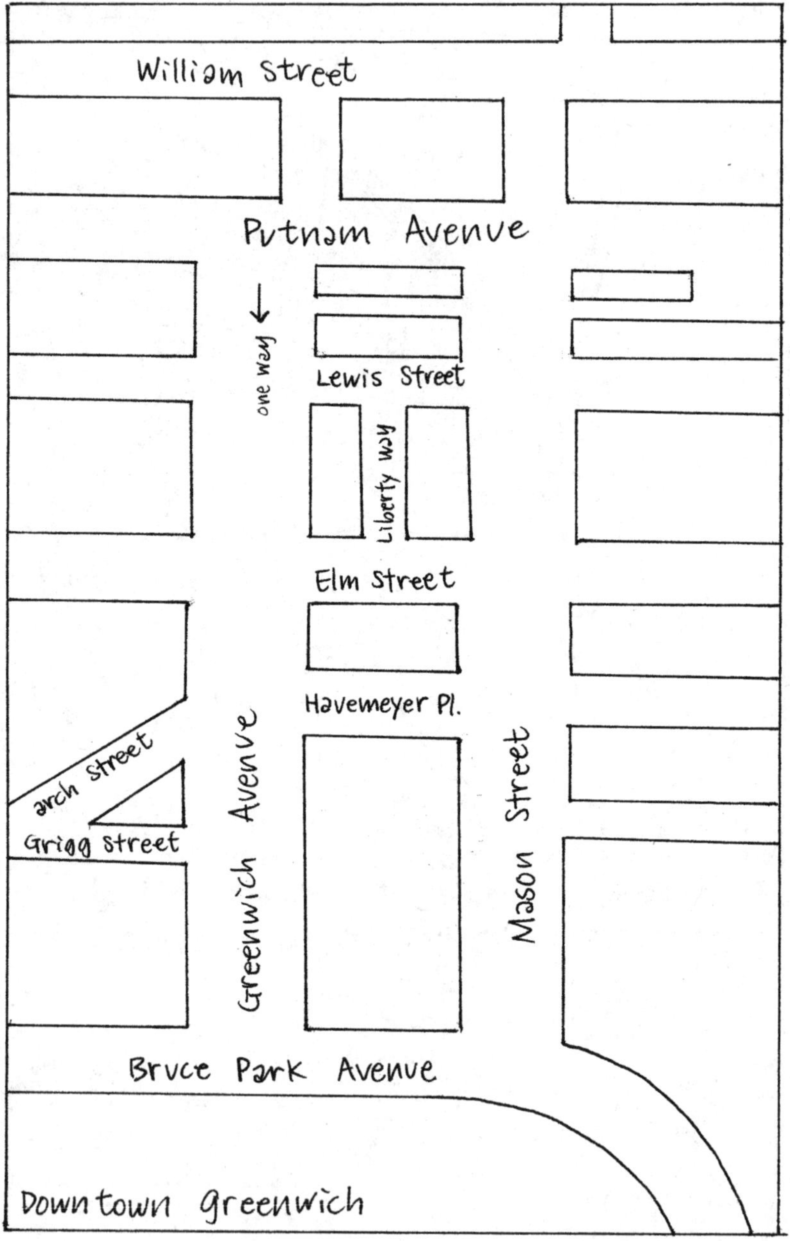
William Street
Putnam Avenue
one way
Lewis Street
Liberty way
Elm Street
Havemeyer Pl.
arch Street
Greenwich Avenue
Grigg Street
Mason Street
Bruce Park Avenue
Downtown Greenwich

ANIMALS

introduction

Pets, popular in Greenwich, bring great cheer to their owners and often assume the role of "Head of the Household." Over 3,000 dogs are masters of homes in Greenwich. If you hear someone calling Maggie, Max, Sabrina, Buddy, Sam, Solan, Molly or Jake, chances are it isn't a child being summoned.

dog license

All resident dog owners are required to license their dogs. All dogs six months or over must be licensed and wear collar and tag at all times. All dogs must be vaccinated against rabies and owners must submit a certificate to the Town Clerk when licensing their dog. Dog licenses expire on June 30th each year. To get a license request and information on licensing go to: http://greenwichct.virtualtownhall.net/Public_Documents/ GreenwichCT_TownClerk/tcDogLicense.pdf or the Town Clerk's office in person.

dog obedience

Dog Training by Ken Berenson
914.699.4982
Held at the Round Hill Community House, 397 Round Hill Road.
They offer very good dog obedience classes, conducted by Ken Berenson's Canine Services. For more information call Ken. *"Ken is a highly qualified educator of humans and, for that reason, an effective educator of dogs."*

TIP: DOG VOLUNTEERS NEEDED

Adopt-a-Dog shelters and places abandoned dogs and cats in loving homes. They need volunteers to help with functions such as fundraising, dog walking, public relations and animal care. If you have a warm place in your heart for these sweet creatures, call 629.9494 for information or www.adoptadog.org.

pets

Pet Stores
The following pet stores are described in the SHOPPING Section:
* Canine Corner
  177 Sound Beach Avenue, Old Greenwich, 637.8819
* House of Fins, 99 Bruce Park Avenue, 661.8131
* Pet Pantry, 290 Railroad Avenue, 869.6444

Animal Shelter
See description under Wildlife and Animal Rescue

AdoptADog
629.9494 or 914.273.1674

www.adoptadog.org

Since 1981, this unique, local, not-for-profit animal agency has helped over 7,000 homeless dogs find loving families. If you have a soft spot in your heart for animals, consider adopting or becoming a foster "parent." You are always welcome to call or visit their kennels. They hold the annual show, "Puttin' on the Dog."

Amanda Jones (Pet Photographer)
North Adams, MA, 877.251.2390

www.amandajones.com

One of our nation's top animal photographers, grew up in Greenwich. Mention Amanda Jones to a dog enthusiast and you will hear how beautiful her work is. Amanda books shooting tours in advance. Check her website for a schedule. Greenwich is on most of her tours.

Bow Wow Barber Mobile Dog Groomers
149 Cedar Heights Rd, Stamford, CT, 968.6214

Calls will be returned in the evening. They are on the road during the day.

Connecticut Canine Law
Dogs over six months of age must have a license issued by the Town Clerk's office (622.7897) in Town Hall (8 am - 4 pm), and the dog must be immunized against rabies. Dogs are not allowed to roam.
The Greenwich Rules can be found at:
http://greenwichct.virtualtownhall.net/Public_Documents/ GreenwichCT_TownClerk/tcDogLicense.pdf

Connecticut Humane Society

455 Post Road East, Westport, CT 203.227.4137
www.cthumane.org
Although the Greenwich Animal Shelter sometimes has pets to adopt, the Humane Society is the major area resource. They have many hopeful dogs, cats and even rabbits and fish waiting to meet you. They maintain a lost and found file and will come to your home to remove injured or sick wild animals or birds.
Hours: Monday - Saturday 10:30am - 5:30pm, Sunday 10am - 4pm.

Dogs in Parks

Dogs are allowed in all town parks with a leash except for Byram Beach and Greenwich Point. From December 1st until March 31st dogs are allowed at Greenwich Point. Call Parks and Recreation 622.7830.

Dog Park

The first (and only) Greenwich Dog Park is located on 3/4 acre at Grass Island. The park is open from sunrise to sunset. For your dog to have a good experience, for the first visit go during a quiet time, usually weekdays between 9 am and 11 am. The rules are posted on the fence. Children under 10 are not permitted and the owners must remain in the fenced area with their dog while the dog is off leash. Aggressive dogs are not allowed and owners are responsible for the behavior of their dog.
For more information email (Liz Horton) vt.gal@sbcglobal.net

Friends of Animals

77 Post Road Suite 205 Darien CT, 203.656.1522
Priscilla Feral, President
www.FriendsOfAnimals.org
An international, non-profit, organization founded in 1957 which is dedicated to increasing awareness of animal rights and to preventing abuse of animals. It provides the names of local veterinarians who do lowcost spaying and neutering.
Hours: weekdays, 9 am - 5 pm.

(The) Good Dog Foundation

718.788.2988

www.TheGoodDogFoundation.org

This foundation, part of a nationwide group, operates training sessions in Greenwich for people willing to bring their animals to visit local patients. The dogs ease depression in the elderly and calm hyperactivity in children.

Greyhound Adoption

• Pups Without Partners, Penny Zwart adoption coordinator, Bridgeport, CT, 203.576.1976. www.pupswithoutpartners.org

• Greyhound Protection League, Melani Nardone, 212.580.0283. Summer, 203.869.8484 www.greyhounds.org

If this listing saves one of these dogs, we will be so grateful.

Greenwich Kennel Club

Cos Cob Community Center, 54 Bible Street, Cos Cob, 203.426.1173 or 426.2881, www.GreenwichKC.org

The GKC is a non-profit organization whose membership is comprised of area dog enthusiasts with interests in conformation, obedience and performance events. The GKC holds an annual allbreed dog show every June. If you are not sure whether you want to bring a beagle or vizsla into your home, attend this show. It is a wonderful way to meet them all, as well as to find a suitable breeder.

Invisible Fencing

• **Canine Fence**

493 Danbury Road, Wilton, CT, 800.628.2264

www.caninefence.com

Hours: Monday - Saturday, 7 am - 8 pm.

• **E-Fence**

329 Longmeadow Road, Orange, CT 203.795.3283

www.efence1.com

If you see small white flags around the perimeter of a Greenwich yard, most likely it is one of the "Invisible Fences." This is a safe way to keep your dog in your yard. Also works to keep your pet out of designated rooms in your home. Moose and Tipsy especially like E-Fence.

pets

North Wind Kennels

Route 22, Bedford, NY, 914.234.3771
If you would like to leave your dog or cat where Glenn Close and Chevy Chase are said to leave theirs, go no further. Jake Feinberg's kennel has four "doggie suites" and can house 225 dogs and 45 cats. Unfortunately, our experience was less than satisfactory.
Hours: Monday - Saturday, 9:30 am - 5:30 pm. On Sunday or off-hours, their machine doesn't take messages.
Directions: North Street to the end, L on Route 22, kennel is on the right in about a mile.

Pet Finders Club of America

661 High Street, Thurman, NY 12810, 800.666.5678
www.petclub.org
This is the oldest non-profit lost and found service in the US.

Poop Patrol

Sally Cimino, 531.6661
www.PoopPatrolCT.com
Got poop? Sally, a graduate of Connecticut College, will scoop! Poop Patrol scoops and removes dog waste from yards, commercial properties and kennels.

Puttin' On The Dog (Annual Dog Show)

Roger Sherman Baldwin Park, Late September
Run by AdoptaDog, 849 Lake Avenue, 629.9494, this show is a great place to show your dog, learn about dogs, or adopt a new friend. Always a hit with children of all ages.

Sherlock Bones

800.942.6637
www.sherlockbones.com
Since 1975 this California pet detective has helped recover missing pets around the USA.

pets

Stray Cats
- Project SaveACat, 661.6855
- PAWS (Pet Animal Welfare Society) Norwalk, CT, 203.854.1798
- SCAT (Southern Connecticut Animal Trust) Stamford, 968.9385
www.adoptatscat.org

If you know of a stray cat that needs to be captured or you would like to adopt a cat, call these volunteer organizations.

pet sitting

Best Friends Pet Resort & Salon
528 Main Avenue, Norwalk, CT, 888.367.7387, 203.849.1010
www.bestfriendspetcare.com

Doggy day camp with 4-legged playmates (assuming your pet can pass the interview process). Longer stays are available. Joya loves their grooming salon.

Hours: weekdays, 8 am - 6 pm; Saturday, 8 am - 5 pm;
Sunday, 3 pm - 6 pm.

Directions: I95 N to exit 15, follow Route 7 expressway N to the end, R on Main (next to the DMV).

Canine Athletic Club
40 Decatur Street, First Floor, Cos Cob, 561.9541

Perhaps your dog would like to belong to the Lunch Bunch. According to one of our pet friends, he is picked up every day, lunches with several of his dog buddies, and then returns home, ready for his afternoon nap. Kristin Leggio and Keith Fernim provide dog walking, exercise, and socialization service as well as in-home pet care services. If you are too busy to take your dog to the vet, they'll do that too.

TIP: TOWN PERMITS AND PASSES
Permits and passes for many Greenwich activities can be applied for on the Town's website, www.Greenwichct.org

Doggie Grandparents

47 Wake Robin Lane, Stamford, 595.0176
www.doggiegrandparents.com
If you hate to put your dog in a kennel while you are away, Francine and Issac Garb have the answer. Their Stamford home was chosen to be the perfect place to make your dog happy in your absence. Dogs can wander around their home and the door to the fenced back yard is always open. They usually board 4-5 dogs at a time. An interview with your dog is required. Our dog, Daisy, has a good time here.
Directions: Merritt Parkway N to exit 34 (Long Ridge) R on Long Ridge, L at stop light onto Wire Mill, bear to Left at the fork, L on Four Brooks, R on Wake Robin.

Pet Care (Pet Sitter)

Liz Horton, 253.0334
This dog sitter / walker makes it possible for your pet to stay happily in their own home while you are at work or on vacation. She adores animals, loves playing with them and comforts them with tummy rubs. Your only risk is that your pet may begin to like Liz better than you. Beside playing with and exercising your pet, as an added bonus, she will pick up your paper, packages and mail while you are away.

Pet Sitters

When in need, try www.petsitters.org or www.petsit.com. These are national organizations that usually have reliable sitters. However, it is wise to ask for references and to make sure they are insured and bonded.

Animal Eye Clinic

at the Veterinarian Referral & Emergency Center
123 West Cedar Street, Norwalk, CT, 203.855.1533
www.AnimalEyeClinic.net
People from all over the area bring their pets here for eye problems.
Hours: Monday 9 am - 11:15 am; 1:00 pm - 4 pm;
Wednesday & Thursday, 1 pm - 7 pm; Friday, 8 am - noon.

Animal Hospital of Greenwich - Stamford

2061 West Main Street, Stamford, CT 967.8008
Our favorite pug, Dart, loves to be boarded here.

Blue Cross Animal Hospital

530 East Putnam Avenue, 869.7755
The ladies behind the desk are very kind and caring. Dr. Wolff provides
holistic pet care, including acupuncture and homeopathy as well as con-
ventional care.
Hours: weekdays, 8 am - 6 pm. Closed Sunday.
Open one Saturday a month 9 am - 1 pm.

Davis Animal Hospital

2053 West Main Street (Post Road), Stamford CT, 327.0300
(On the Greenwich/Stamford border across from the Hyatt Hotel)
The medical and office staffs are very professional and dedicated to the
care and well-being of animals and their owners.
Hours: weekdays, 7:30 am - 7 pm; Saturday, 8 am - 4 pm.

ANIMALS

Greenwich Veterinary Hospital

358 West Putnam Avenue, 661.1437
Many of our knowledgeable friends take their pets to Dr. Sean Bell.
Hours: weekdays, 8am - 6 pm; Saturday, 8 am - 2 pm. Closed Sunday.

Just Cats Hospital

1110 East Main Street, Stamford, 327.7220
Located off of I-95 at exit 9. They provide excellent medical services,
boarding, grooming and TLC, just for cats.
Hours: weekdays, 7:30 am - 8 pm (Friday 6 pm); Saturday, 8 am - 5 pm.
Directions: I95N to Exit 9; L at light; L on East Main.

Veterinarian Referral & Emergency Center

123 West Cedar Street, Norwalk, CT, 203.854.9960
www.vrecnorwalk.com
If your vet is not available, this is a wonderful emergency room for your
pet. During normal hours, appointments must be made for specialists.
Hours: 24 hours a day, 7 days a week.
Directions: I95 N to Exit 13; R on US 1; L on W Taylor; L on W Cedar.

TIP: MAKING YOUR VOICE HEARD

If you feel strongly about an issue in Town which you feel is not
being addressed, gather 20 signatures of Greenwich registered
voters and deliver it with your petition to the Town Clerk's office
in Town Hall. Your petition will be put on the RTM's next call. Be
sure to carefully define in your petition what action you want
and to bring a few articulate, concise speakers to support your
cause. When you deliver the petition, it would be best to tell the
Town Clerk who wants to speak.

ANIMALS

Animal Shelter

Dog Pound, Museum Drive, 622.8299, 622.8081

A Town of Greenwich Police Department service that handles dead or sick animals as well as stray dogs. We have a kind animal control officer, Alison Halm. If your pet is missing, call her first. A few dogs are available here for adoption. Plans are in the works for a move to a $750,000 new 3,400 square foot facility next to the North Street School.

Hours: weekdays, 8 am - 3 pm, weekends, until 2 pm.

All about Bats

323.0468

They carefully remove wildlife from your home and relocate it so you won't have unwanted pets. They can also help prevent furry intrusions.

Wildlife in Crisis

Weston, CT, 203.544.9913

www.WildlifeInCrisis.com

If you happen to have an injured cormorant (as the Greenwich Police Department did recently) and perhaps any other wild animal who needs help, this group is willing to rehabilitate and save the animal or bird.

Wild Wings

637.9822 or 967.2121 Wildlife Hotline: 389.4411

Alison Taintor and Meredith Sampson are state and federally licensed wildlife rehabilitators who operate a wildlife rescue and rehabilitation center in Old Greenwich and Stamford. They will respond to oil spill emergencies that affect wildlife.

Hours: They are on call 24 hours a day, 7 days a week for emergencies.

For general information, call weekdays, 9 am - 5 pm.

travel information

See TRAVEL for airports, trains, taxies, limousines and travel agencies.
For Racing-Auto see FITNESS & SPORTS

Commuting

Local commuters can untangle their morning commutes by consulting the following commuter transportation websites:

MetroPool: www.metropool.com
The site offers news and information on commuting in and around Fairfield and Westchester counties.

Greenwich Traffic Cams: www.ct.gov/dot
(click on traffic cams)

general information

Department of Motor Vehicles Bureau

540 Main Avenue (Route 7), Norwalk, CT, 800.842.8222
860.263.5700
www.ct.gov/dmv
New residents must obtain a Connecticut driver's license within sixty days, even if they hold a valid license from another state. Vehicles must also be registered within sixty days after the owner has established residency. The car must pass an inspection before being registered.
Hours: Tuesday, Wednesday & Friday, 8 am - 4:30 pm (Thursday, until 7 pm, Saturday, until 12:30 pm); Closed Sunday, Monday and holidays.
Directions: I 95 N to exit 15, Rte 7 N; follow Rte 7 expressway to end, R and straight into the DMV.

Driver's License Renewals

Licenses can be renewed at the DMV in Norwalk or at the Connecticut License Bus, which stops in front of Town Hall the first Tuesday of every month from to 10 am - 6 pm.

Parking Meters

Parking meters in Greenwich are not expensive, but parking tickets are. Parking meters are a must Monday - Saturday, 9 am - 5 pm. On Sundays and holidays, parking is free. Old Greenwich is still free of parking meters.

AUTOMOBILES

Parking Permits

•	Call 622.7730, for details about train station parking permits and the location of municipal lots, or go to www.greenwichct.org/Parking/psParkingPermits.asp

•	Call the Senior Center, 622.3990, for parking permits in front of the Center.

Police Directing Traffic

We still have the privilege of having police direct traffic on Greenwich Avenue. They are always helpful and friendly. When you can't find something, they are a great source of information. However, be warned, pedestrians and drivers alike are expected to pay attention. Follow their crossing instructions or face humiliation

TIP: PARKING TICKETS

If by chance you get a parking ticket, you can pay it or request a hearing online by going to the Town's website:
www.greenwichct.org/Parking/psParkingTickets.asp

car dealers

- Acura
  343 West Putnam Avenue, 625.8200
- Aston Martin
  273 West Putnam Ave, 629.4726
- Audi
  181 West Putnam Avenue, 661.1800
- BMW
  355 West Putnam Avenue, 661.1725
- Bugatti
  342 West Putnam Ave, 629.3890
- Cadillac
  144 Railroad Avenue, 869.9100
- Ferrari
  342 West Putnam Ave, 629.3890
- Honda
  289 Mason Street, 622.0600
- Infiniti
  241 West Putnam Avenue, 625.9300 or 869.0255
- Jeep-Chrysler-Dodge
  631 West Putnam Avenue, 531.0505
- Lexus
  19 Railroad Avenue, 800.969.5398 or 869.6700
- Lotus
  249 Railroad Avenue, 914.939.7200
- Maserati
  342 West Putnam Avenue, 629.3890
- Mercedes-Benz
  261 West Putnam Avenue, 869.2850
- Nissan
  273 West Putnam Avenue, 622.7308
- Porsche
  241 West Putnam Avenue, 869.8900
- Rolls Royce-Bentley
  273 West Putnam Avenue, 661.4430
- Saab
  144 Railroad Avenue, 625.6300
- Toyota
  75 East Putnam Avenue, 661.5055
- Volkswagen
  200 West Putnam Avenue, 869.4600

CARS

1380 Post Road, Old Greenwich, 637.5584

If you are envious of your friends' GPS, Satellite Radio, back-up camera and sensors, you don't have to trade in your car. Instead, take it to Ray Garst who has been upgrading cars since 1988.

TIP: COMMUNITY CALENDARS

• Community Events

If you want to know the coming Town events, you will love the Community Answers Planning Ahead Community Calendar. Call Community Answers, 622.7979 and ask to be on their list or check out their calendar on line at:
www.pac.greenwichlibrary.org:82/search/q?+

• Town Committee Meetings

The Town committee and department calendar can be found at:
http://greenwichct.virtualtownhall.net/Public_Documents/GreenwichCT_Calendar/?formid=158

• Social Calendar

Greenwich Magazine publishes a Social Calendar. It can be found on line at: www.FairfieldEvents.com

AUTOMOBILES

car and truck rentals

For renting a bus see tip p86

Budget Truck Rentals

195 Greenwich Avenue at Greenwich Hardware, 661.5548
www.budgettruck.com
Hours: Monday - Saturday, 7:30 - 5:30; Sunday, 9 am - 4 pm.

Enterprise Rent a Car

15 Edgewood Ave (Just off West Putnam Avenue, next to McDonalds)
622.1611
www.Enterprise.com
They often have the lowest rates, but charge for mileage.
Hours: weekdays, 7:30 am - 6 pm; Saturday, 9 am - noon.

Hertz Rent a Car

111 West Putnam Avenue, 800.654.3131 www.Hertz.com
At the Exxon Station next to the Library, 622.4044
Hours: weekdays, 6 am - 5:30 pm; Saturday, 9 am - noon.

City Truck Rentals (Penske)

737 Canal Street, Stamford,359.6818, 800.467.3675
www.pensketruckrental.com
When you need a large, well maintained truck, call them first.
Hours: weekdays, 7 am - 6 pm; Saturday, 7 am - 4 pm;
Sunday, 8 am - noon.

U Haul

Jefferson Street, Stamford, 324.3869
www.uhaul.com
U Haul rents everything from a van to a large truck. They also have a
large stock of boxes and other moving supplies. Their vans are well kept
and are great for local moves. Their best trucks are saved for long dis-
tance runs, so for local runs you might be better using a truck from
Budget. Don't expect customer service to be a high priority.
Directions: I 95 N to Exit 8, R on Canal (second light), L on Jefferson.
Turn down the small side street next to the first building on the Right.
Hours: Monday - Thursday, 7 am - 7 pm; Friday, 7 am - 8 pm,
Saturday, 7 am - 7 pm; Sunday, 9 am - 5 pm.

AUTOMOBILES

car show

Concours of Elegance

To exhibit a concours quality car, call Bruce and Genia Wennerstrom, 618.0460 (Co-chairs)
The Concours takes place in the Roger Sherman Baldwin Park the weekend after Memorial Day is observed. This exciting event for all ages features an exhibit of outstanding motorcars from the last decade of the nineteenth-century through the late 1970s. Car lovers in Greenwich have enjoyed this event for over 10 years. It is one of the most prestigious Concours events in the country, attracting over 10,000 spectators.
Hours: 10 am - 5 pm.

car wash & detailing

Car Wash Express

1429 East Putnam Avenue, Old Greenwich, 698.9531
This is the place to go when you are in a hurry and just want a quick wash, for $5 (at the Mobil station).

Classic Shine Auto Fitness Center

67 Church Street, 629.8077
This car detailing firm does not often advertise, but has been in business for many, many years. They operate primarily on the strength of recommendations.
Hours: Monday - Saturday by appointment.

Splash Car Wash

- 73 Post Road, Cos Cob, 625.0809
- 625 West Putnam Avenue, Byram, 531.4497
www.splashcarwashes.com
Both locations do hand washes and interior cleaning. The Byram location also has an express (machine) lane. Mark Curtis and Chris Fisher, both lifelong Greenwich residents, developed the concept of washing cars in line on conveyor by hand. In 1994, they opened their first hand wash in Greenwich and called it Splash. Now with 15 locations, they wash more than 1,000,000 cars a year. They know that good car care means good business.
Hours: Monday - Saturday, 8 am - 6 pm; Friday, until 7 pm; Sunday, 9 am - 5 pm.

AUTOMOBILES

vehicle inspection

Vehicle Emission Inspections

888 828 8399

www.ctemissions.com

Cars must be inspected every two years. These stations do inspections on a first-come, first-served basis. The following local stations are certified:

Mobile Lube Express

1429 East Putnam Avenue, Old Greenwich, 698.9531

Hours: weekdays, 8 am - 5 pm; Saturday, until 1 pm. Gas is available 24 hours.

Soundview Service Center

35 Arcadia Road, Old Greenwich, 637.2033

Hours: weekdays, 8 am - 5 pm; Saturday until 1 pm.

Shell of Greenwich

83 East Putnam Avenue, 661.8871

Hours: weekdays, 8 am - 5 pm; Saturday until 1 pm. Call 800.842.8222 for directions and times.

TIP: GREENWICH GRAND TOUR

Cheryl Dunson, The League of Women Voters' Land Use Specialist, conducts a very special bus tour of Greenwich every year, usually in early May. Whether you are new to Greenwich or have lived here a while, you are sure to learn something new and to have a good time. Call Greenwich Continuing Education at 203-625-7477 for details.

Book Clubs

The Libraries often sponsor book clubs, such as the Brown Bag Book Club which meets on the third Wednesday of each month at the Cos Cob Library. All are welcome. Bring your own lunch and have a good time. For information on the Brown Bag Book Club, call 622.6883.

Book Exchange

At the Greenwich Recycling Center, Holly Hill Lane, 622.0550
This is fun you cannot miss. Residents drop off unwanted books. A volunteer librarian organizes the books by topic and author. Free books are available on all subjects. Just follow the rules: keep the shelves neat, 10 books per family, enjoy your reading!
Donation hours: weekdays, 7 am - noon.
Exchange open: weekdays, 7:30 am - 3 pm, Saturday, 7 am - noon.

Byram Shubert Book Sale

The Friends of the Byram Schubert Library conduct a not-to-be-missed sale twice a year. Last year over 200 people donated books, CDs, DVDs, and artwork. Proceeds help support the expansion and programs of the library. For more information or to schedule a pickup of your donation, call Lisa Johnson, Sale Chair, 570.8527 or the Library at 531.0426.

Darien Book Aid Plan

1926 Post Road, 203.655.2777
DBA.Darien.org
This worthy group has been sorting and shipping donated books to countries around the world since 1949. They are particularly interested in children's story books, books in braille, grammar texts, teenage literature and books on medicine, agriculture and gardening. They are open for donations 24-hours a day. Check the website for the types of books they are seeking.
Workshop hours: Tuesday, 2 - 4 pm, Wednesday & Thursday 9:30 - noon.

Ferguson Library

Corner of Broad & Bedford StreetsStamford, CT, 964.1000
www.fergusonlibrary.org
We discovered this source for used books over a cup of Starbucks Coffee (Starbucks is next door). The library receives books and book collections from a wide area. They receive so many that there is a whole department devoted to selling used books.

BOOKS and LIBRARIES
book services

Smith College Book Sale
Waveny House, South Avenue, New Canaan, CT, 203.966.0502
For sale or donation information: 203.323.8990, 655.8553, 323.0017
E-Mail smithdonations@yahoo.com
This annual event (now in its 48th year) is sponsored by the Smith College Club of Darien/New Canaan, benefits the Smith College Scholarship Fund and has more than 80,000 well-priced, quality used books including cookbooks, art histories and bound sets to decorate your home. Just a visit to Waveny House is worth the trip. Dealers descend early on the first morning, grabbing books which they later resell at a substantial profit. It's fun to arrive early with them, but be prepared for pushy, overzealous types. The first day there is an admission charge. On the last day books are free. Don't forget to bring a big book bag.
Look for it at the beginning of April.
Directions: Merritt Parkway N to exit 37, L on South Avenue.

Barnes & Noble (Books)
• 360 Connecticut Avenue (Grade A Plaza), Norwalk, CT 203.866.2213
• Stamford Town Center Mall, Stamford, CT (opening Fall 2007)
www.bn.com
These nearby superstores are stocked with a multitude of volumes on all subjects. The Stamford store is 40,000 square feet and stocks 200,000 titles of books, music CDs and DVDs.
Norwalk Hours: Monday - Thursday, 9 am - 10 pm;
Friday and Saturday 9 am - 11 pm; Sunday, 9 am - 9 pm.

Borders Express (Books)
173 Greenwich Avenue, 869.6342
www.bordersstores.com
Greenwich's largest book store, very conveniently located. They carry a good selection of magazines, audio books on CD and books of local interest.
Hours: Monday - Saturday, 9 am - 6:30 pm; Sunday, 11 am - 5 pm.

book stores

Borders Books (Books)

1041 High Ridge Road, Stamford, 968.9700

www.bordersstores.com

Sometimes it just feels good to be surrounded by thousands of books. Even when we stop by for one book, we seem to always leave with several. This mega-bookstore has a nice coffee shop with good treats.

Hours: Monday - Thursday, 9 am - 10 pm;
Friday & Saturday, 9 am - 11 pm; Sunday, 10 am - 9 pm.
Directions: Merritt Pkw N to exit 35, R on High Ridge.

Diane's Books (Books)

8A Grigg Street, 869.1515

www.dianesbooks.com

A family-owned book store which specializes in family books for all ages. You will find a huge selection including a wealth of children's books, an excellent travel book section and, best of all, a knowledgeable, resourceful sales staff. This is a must-visit bookstore.

Hours: Monday - Saturday, 9 am - 5 pm.

Gift Shop at Christ Church

254 East Putnam Avenue, 869.9030

This is the "in" place to go when you need a special gift with meaning. Marijane Marks and her helpful staff have a fine selection of books, gifts, jewelry and greeting cards. During holidays, gifts cascade out of the shop, making the store a joy to visit.

Hours: Tuesday - Saturday 10 am - 5 pm; Sunday 10 am - 1 pm.

Just Books (Books)

28 Arcadia Road, Old Greenwich, 637.0707

www.justbooks.org

Just Books is a haven for the sophisticated reader or someone looking for personal service. Just Books hosts many events to meet important authors, poetry readings, book signings and story hours for children. Check their website for upcoming events and interesting book reviews which will keep you up-to-date with the literary world. Be sure to frequent this charming, locally owned bookstore. They have something for everyone.

Hours: weekdays, 9 am - 5:30 pm; Saturday, 9 m - 5 pm;
Sunday, noon - 4 pm.

Armstrong Court Library

Family Center and Books for Kids Foundation joint venture.

Friends of Greenwich Library

The Library is maintained by the Town but all capital improvements are funded by contributions from the Friends. Joining is inexpensive. If you join at the level of $35 you receive a Friends Book Bag, a very "in" bag to be carrying around Greenwich. In addition you will receive the Keep Posted newsletter with book reviews and program events. A great way to be a part of the Town.

Greenwich Library

www.greenwichlibrary.org

The Greenwich Library is a special treasure used by young and old alike. In a typical year the Library loans 675,000 customers an average of 4.5 books per minute. It is no wonder the library has been rated the best in the country. The library received a $25,000,000 bequest from Clementine Peterson. Based on this bequest and funds raised by the Friends of Greenwich Library, Architect Cesar Pelli designed the 31,000 square-foot addition as well as renovations to the original building. The Byram Shubert branch is also being enlarged, and we have a wonderful new Cos Cob Library. These branches provide convenient neighborhood locations and serve as community centers. The library provides a large number of programs which are noted in other sections of this guide.

Use the website to check a book's availability or phone 622.7910 to reserve items, and ask to have your reserved materials sent to one of the branches. Membership in the Library is free. There is no limit to the number of books you can check out. In addition to books, the library has over 30 data bases which can be used free of charge. If you use your library number, most can be accessed from you home computer.

libraries

- Greenwich Library (Main Library)
  101 West Putnam Avenue, 622.7900
  Hours: weekdays, 9 am - 9 pm (June August, 5 pm);
  Saturday, 9 am - 5 pm; Sunday, 1 pm 5 pm (September - June).
- Byram Shubert Library (Branch)
  21 Mead Avenue, 531.0426
  Hours: Monday, Wednesday & Friday, 9 am - 5 pm;
  Tuesday, 10 am - 6 pm; Thursday, 1 pm - 8 pm.
- Cos Cob Library (Branch)
  5 Sinawoy Road, Cos Cob, 622.6883
  Cos Cob is a new library, perfect for family enjoyment. While the youngest ones enjoy playing or reading in the children's corner, older ones can read favorite books or search the Internet. The dynamic staff organizes events for both children and adults. It is an important part of Cos Cob community life.
  Hours: Tuesday - Saturday, 9 am - 5 pm, Thursday until 6 pm; Closed Sunday & Monday.
  Children's story time: 10:45 am, Thursday.

Perrot Library of Old Greenwich

(Independent Library)
90 Sound Beach Avenue, 637.1066
Children's Library, 637.8802
www.perrotlibrary.org
The Perrot Memorial Library is a non-profit institution independent of the Greenwich Library. It is open to all residents of Greenwich, although it principally serves the residents of Old Greenwich, Riverside and North Mianus. Perrot has a new, beautiful $3.3 million, 7,000 squarefoot Children's Library.
Hours: Monday, Wednesday, Friday, 9 am - 6 pm;
Tuesday & Thursday, 9 am - 8 pm; Saturday, 9 am - 5 pm;
Sunday, 1 pm - 5 pm.

TIP: DOWNLOAD BOOKS FROM THE LIBRARY

The Library provides downloadable audio books to Library card holders. To download a book, go to www.greenwichlibrary.org/downloadablelibrary.htm or http://overdrive.greenwichlibrary.org You will need to install the free media software and have your Library card number handy. The service is not currently iPod compatible.

introduction

Child Safety providers are in SERVICES
See also FITNESS & SPORTS

Greenwich is an ideal place to raise children. We have the top-rated school system in Connecticut, ranked among the best in the country. Children nurtured in Greenwich have unique opportunities to develop their skills and to grow into happy, healthy, mature individuals.

after school programs

For nursery, pre-schools and other public/private schools see SCHOOLS.

Elementary Schools Programs
The following elementary schools have on-site after-school childcare programs for students enrolled in that school.
- Cos Cob School, 869.4670
- Glenville School, 531.9287
- Hamilton Avenue School, 869.1685 (2nd grade scholars)
- International School at Dundee 637.3800
- Julian Curtiss School, 869.1896
- New Lebanon School, 531.9139
- North Mianus School, 637.9730
- North Street School, 869.6756
- Old Greenwich School, 637.0150
- Parkway School, 869.7466
- Riverside School, 637.1440

BANC
Byram Archibald Neighborhood Center
After School Program
289 Delavan Avenue, 531.1522
Ages: 5 -13 yrs. Four days per week. Follows public school calendar.

Children's Center of Cos Cob Inc.
300 East Putnam Avenue, 625.5569

after-school programs

Girls Inc.
PO Box 4040, Greenwich, CT 531.3322, 531.5699
www.girlsinc.org
Girls, ages 6 -18. Hours 9am - 6pm.
An excellent five day-a-week, informal education program for girls.

Greenwich Boys and Girls Club
 4 Horseneck Lane, 869.3224
www.bgcg.org
Co-ed, Ages: 6 and up, Hours: 3pm - 6:30 pm. On school holidays, the
program starts at 8am. Summer hours are 8am - 6 pm.

Kaleidoscope YWCA
259 East Putnam Avenue, 869.6501, x 251
www.ywca.org
Co-ed, Ages: K - grade 5, Hours: 2:30 pm to 6 pm. Follows the public
school schedule, including early release days. Social, educational and
recreational enrichment. Transportation is provided from all Greenwich
schools. Kaleidoscope also provides childcare services during school closings for holidays and vacations.

YMCA After School Program
869.3381
www.gwymca.org
They run after-school childcare programs at Hamilton Avenue, New Lebanon, and North Mianus Schools.

TIP: LUNCH WITH SANTA
Fortunately our Department of Parks and Recreation has a good re-
lationship with Santa. As a result, for the last 18 years Santa has
been coming to the Greenwich Civic Center, Old Greenwich every
November. Mrs. Claus; her friends Frosty, Rudolph; and Santa's elves
are normally on hand to greet children. Tickets are $15 per person.
They must be purchased in advance at the Parks and Recreation
office on the second floor of Town Hall. Call 622.6478 for details.

babysitting

Au Pair & Nannies Club
YWCA, 259 East Putnam Avenue, 869.6501 x 252
Nannies meet to share caregiving ideas and to make new friends.

Babysitting Training
• The Red Cross sponsors a comprehensive all-day babysitting course which is open to 11 - 15 year olds and offered 2 to 3 times a month: 99 Indian Field Road, 869.8444. www.greenwichredcross.org
• Greenwich Hospital "Tender Beginnings" runs a babysitting course for students 11 - 13. Call 863.3655

Child Care and Parenting Services
A wonderful pamphlet compiled by Community Answers and Greenwich Early Childhood Council. Available at the Community Answers desk at the Greenwich Library, 101 Putnam Avenue, 522.7940.

Child Care Infoline
800.505.1000
www.ChildCareInfoLine.org
They provide information on licensed daycare, summer camps and nursery school programs throughout Connecticut.

Kid's Night Out
YMCA, 50 East Putnam Avenue, 869.1630
www.gwymca.org
A few evenings a month, parents of children in grades K -6 can enjoy an evening out, while their children enjoy an inexpensive, fun, safe night of activities, including gym games, swimming, movies, popcorn and board games.

(The) Sitting Service

Suzanne Stillwell, President.
1031 Post Road, Darien, 203.655.9783 or 4123
Office hours are 9am - 1pm, weekdays.
Email: sitserve@aol.com
www.TheSittingService.com
This state-registered babysitting, pet-sitting and house-sitting referral service has been in Fairfield County for over 20 years. Yearly membership is $265 + tax per family plus an hourly rate.

Student Employment Service

Greenwich High School, 625.8008,625.8000
Hours during the school year are weekdays, 11:30 am - 2:00 pm. During the summer, the.service is run through Community Answers, 622.7979.

Utilize Senior Energy (USE)

Senior Center, 299 Greenwich Avenue, 629.8032
Hours: 9:30 am - 12:30 pm, weekdays.
Employment referral service for people 50 years and over.

TIP: KIDS SAFETY TRAINING

The Greenwich Safety Town is sponsored by the Greenwich Red Cross. This full-day program teaches kids (who are ready for kindergarten) about such matters as safety around strangers, household safety and how to cross the street. The program is conducted during the summer, but because it's so popular, register your child before March. Call the Red Cross at 869.8444 for details.

childcare

Children's Day School
139 East Putnam Avenue, 869.5395
8 Riverside Avenue, 637.1122
www.ChildrensDaySchool.net
There may be a third location at the Western Greenwich Civic Center coming soon. All day daycare and pre-school for children ages 6 weeks - 6 years, Hours: 7:30am - 6 pm.
Director: Maryane O'Rourke

Family Centers
Joan Warburg Early Childhood Center
• 20 Bridge Street, 629.2822
• 40 Arch Street, 869.4848
www.familycenters.org
Director Beth Tanner, 203.869.4848
Children ages 6 weeks - 2 years, Hours: 7:30 - 6 pm.

Gateway School
2 Chapel Street, 531.8430
www.familycenters.org
Children ages 3 - 4. Full-day, year-round childcare;
need-based tuition.
Additional information: Beth Tanner, 203.869.4848
Hours: 7:30am - 6 pm.

Little Angels Play Group
Greenwich Catholic School
471 North Street, 869.4000 ext.109
• Children ages 3 - 4; hours: weekdays, 8:30 pm - 11:30 pm;
Tuesday-Thursday, noon - 3 pm.
• Pre K program, ages 4 - 5, hours: 8:30 am - noon; extended day options.

Little Friends
25 Valley Drive, 861.6549
Year-round child care.
Children ages 6 weeks - 5 years; hours: 6:30am - 6:30 pm.
Early drop off, 6:30 am; late pick up, 6:30 pm.
Also 2, 3 and 5 day programs, either half or full day.

CHILDREN

YMCA Child Care

2 Saint Roch Avenue, 869.3381
Children ages 6 weeks to 5 years.
All day, year round childcare. Hours: 7:30am - 5:30 pm.

YWCA Playroom and Playroom Plus

259 East Putnam Avenue, 869.6501 x 221
Children ages 15 months - 3 years. Professional on site childcare services, either for parents attending Y classes or pursuing off site activities. Morning or afternoon sessions available.

TIP: CHILDCARE RESOURCES

Community Answers gathers information about programs and places of interest to children and parents in the Children's Notebook. Community Answers also publishes an excellent leaflet on Child Care and Parenting Services. Our list of childcare resources is not complete, so be sure to ask for these informative pamphlets at their desk in the Greenwich Library.

art

Bruce Museum,
1 Museum Drive, 869.0376 x 325
www.brucemuseum.org
Art classes offered throughout the year, including during school holidays.

Lakeside Pottery
543 Newfield Avenue, Stamford, CT 323.2222
www.lakesidepottery.com
Children's pottery program for ages 8 - 12. They also offer summer and winter camps and birthday parties. Many adult classes offered, too.

Little Rembrant
Rye Ridge Shopping Center
116 South Ridge Street, Rye Brook, NY 914.939.1400
www.littlerembrandt.info
In addition to birthday parties, art classes and art workshops, they have a good selection of unique gift ideas.

Paper Scissors Oranges
551 Post Road, Darien, CT, 203.656 2706
www.paperscissorsoranges.com
Art studio that offers a wide range of art classes, with a variety of themes, for children of all ages, teens and adults.

Signature Art
YWCA, 259 East Putnam Avenue, 869.6501
www.ywcagreenwich.org
Multi-media art projects for young artists ages 5 - 9 who wish to improve.

(The) Greenwich Arts Council
299 Greenwich Avenue, 622.3998
www.greenwicharts.org
Offers after-school art programs.

CHILD ENRICHMENT

art

(The) Greenwich Art Society

299 Greenwich Avenue, 629.1533
www.greenwichartsociety.com
Junior Art Workshop with Elaine Huyer is a lively course for 7 -10 year
old students. They work with pastels, clay, paper collage and sculpture
after school. Adult art classes also available.

chess

National Scholastic Chess Foundation (NSCF)

171 East Post Road, White Plains, NY, 914.683.5322
www.nscfchess.org
If your child enjoys games and problem-solving, chess lessons from these
experts will open up a wonderful world.

cooking

Aux Delices

23 Acosta Street, Stamford, CT, 326.4540 x 108
www.AuxDelicesFoods.com
This wonderful gourmet food shop offers a variety of cooking classes for
children and adults at their Stamford location. Birthday parties are offered at home or in their shop.

Kids Cooking & Table Manners

My Favorite Place, 1 Strickland Road, Cos Cob
Call Jennifer, 869.1500
www.MyFavoritePlaceCT.net
Sessions run on Mondays for 7 - 12 year olds.

Kids 'r' Cookin

Greenwich and Rye Brook
914.937.2012
www.KidsRcookin.com
Restauranteur Bandy Acciavatti offers cooking courses and birthday parties for kids.

computers

Cyber Discoveries
877.376.0048
Greenwich, CT — call for location.
www.Cyberdiscoveries.com
Computer classes for ages 2 -102.

See also computer camps in Summer Camps below.

TIP: GREENWICH PUBLIC DOCUMENTS
http://greenwichct.virtualtownhall.net/public_documents
This is where you find the Call (Agenda) for the Representative Town Meeting and many other fascinating Town documents and calendars.

dance & etiquette

Allegra Dance Studio

37 West Putnam Avenue, 629.9162
www.allegradancestudio.com
Claudia Fletcher has been teaching dance to children in Greenwich for over 25 years. Ages 3 to adult; classes in jazz, ballet, tap, hip-hop and ballroom dancing.

Ballet Des Enfances

Shop Rite Center, 2000 West Main Street, Stamford, CT
973.0144
www.balletdesenfants.net
Ballet studio offering classes for 2 - 6 year olds.

Barclay Ballroom Dancing for Young Children

397 Round Hill Road
Lois Thomson, Director, 908.232.8370
Friday evening classes, starting in September, are held at the Round Hill Community Center. The one-hour classes teach ballroom dancing and social etiquette to children in grades 4, 5, & 6.

(The) Chinese Language School of Connecticut

P.O. Box 515, Riverside, CT
866.301.4906
www.chineselanguageschool.org
Chinese Folk Dance classes. This is the only full-time professional school of Chinese dance in the country. Classes are held at Eastern Middle School. They have an extensive program teaching Mandarin Chinese.

Dance Adventure

230 Mason Street, 625.0930
www.danceadventure.com
Programs for parent and child, 4 months to 2 years;
pre-ballet for ages 3 - 5; ballet, tap & jazz for 1st graders to teens.

dance & etiquette

(The) Etiquette Advantage

914.738.2398

Nancy Stith Williams and Betty Hoover teach after-school programs on manners for children, including birthday parties. Adult classes of 6 or more. Conversation skills: correct use of language, proper introductions, telephone manners, thank you notes, invitational RSVPs. Table Manners: dining dos and don'ts. Total Image: Posture and poise, wardrobe planning, voice appeal. Politeness for Family and Friends and Good Sportsmanship.

Greenwich Ballet Academy

299 Greenwich Avenue, 856.7053

Presently held on the second floor of the Greenwich Arts Center. Their goal is to prepare students for a career in ballet.

Greenwich Ballet Workshop

Felicity Foote, 869.9373

Dedicated children (up to age 18) coached to look their very best on stage. See the Ambassador in Leotard Program under Young Adults.

Greenwich Dance Studio

YWCA, 259 East Putnam Avenue, 869.6501

www.ywcagreenwich.org

Ballet, jazz, hip hop, creative movement classes for children ages 3 years and up.

Mayfair Ballroom Dancing for Young Children

Call the Brunswick School 625.5800

www.brunswickschool.org

Mayfair is sponsored by the Brunswick Parents Association, but is open to all children in Greenwich. Like Barclay, they teach ballroom dancing and etiquette to children in grades 5 and 6. Friday classes start in September, 5th grade 4:30 - 5:30; 6th grade 6:00 - 7:00, and are usually taught at Brunswick. For girls, there may be a waiting list. There's always room for boys.

New Dance

9 Rye Ridge Plaza, Rye Brook, NY, 914.690.9300

www.newdance.net

This studio offers a variety of classes to boys and girls including ballet, tap, hip hop, jazz and cheerleading.

gymnastics

Arena Gymnastics
911 Hope Street, Stamford, CT, 357.8167
www.arenagymnastics ct.com
This one comes highly recommended for more serious gymnasts.

Great Play
Shop Rite Center, 2000 W. Main Street, Stamford, CT, 978.1333
www.greatplay.com
A unique new gym that offers fun classes to help kids develop motor skills, fitness and coordination.

Jack Rabbits Gymnastics
Round Hill Community House
395 Round Hill Road, Greenwich, 203.622.0004
www.jackrabbitsgym.com
Jack Rabbits has classes for kids ages 1- 9 years; a great way to wear your children out!

My Gym
225 Atlantic Street, Stamford, CT, 327.3496
www.my gym.com/locations.asp?page=2#CT
Gymnastics and movement classes for children ages 3 months to 13 years.

US Academy of Gymnastics
6 Riverside Avenue, Riverside, 637.3303
www.TumbleBugsCT.com
Tumble Bugs and Snuggle Bugs for children 18 months to 5 years.
Serious gymnastics training for children from 1st grade through high school.
They also host great birthday parties.

gymnastics

YWCA Programs

259 East Putnam Avenue, 869.6501

www.ywcagreenwich.org

- Jelly Beans ages 16 - 36 months;
  Tumble Tots ages 2 - 3 years.
- Pre-Gymnastics ages 5 - 6 years;
  Gymnastics ages 7 - 8 and 9 - 12.
- Advanced Gymnastics — instructor placement only

YMCA Programs

50 East Putnam Avenue, 869.1630

www.gwymca.org

- Baby Power 12 to 24 months.
- Toddler Gym 24 to 36 months.
- Rockers 3 to 4 years.
- Rollers 4 and 5 years.
- Beginner 6 to 11 years.
- Intermediate 6 to 11years.

TIP: TOUCH A TRUCK

The Junior League of Greenwich holds an annual spring fund raiser, usually in early June, called Touch A Truck. This is lots of fun for children (and adults) who love to climb on interesting equipment such as construction vehicles, public safety equipment, Humvees and other assorted vehicles. For information call the Touch A Truck hotline at 977.0770 or the Junior League office at 869.1979.

Alliance Française

299 Greenwich Avenue, 629.1340
www.afgreenwich.org
Classes for beginners, intermediate and advanced are given in the French Center for children ages 3 - 13 years and teens. "Mommy and Me" lets 2 year olds learn with their mothers. On Tuesdays, French classes are offered for native French-speaking children who are enrolled in English-speaking schools.

(The) Chinese Language School of Connecticut

Eastern Middle School, 51 Hendrie Avenue, Riverside
866.301.4906
www.chineselanguageschool.org
This school operates from September to June. Classes are held on Sundays. This non-profit organization is dedicated to teaching Mandarin Chinese as a second language to children. They also teach dance; see above.

French-American School

Larchmont, Mamaroneck and Scarsdale Campuses
914.834.3002 x 253
www.Fasny.org
Adult and children classes in French, Mandarin Chinese, Russian, Spanish, Arabic and Italian. With a knowledge of basic French, children grades 1 - 3 can enjoy cooking, juggling and circus arts, as well as model airplane making and a variety of sports.

German School

135 School Road, Weston, CT; 203.792.2795
50 Partridge Road, White Plains, NY, 914.948.6513
www.dsny.org, www.germanschoolct.org
Monday and Saturday morning German language and cultural instruction for novice to native speakers. Available for children pre-school through high school. They also have an adult program.
Closed during the summer. Classes begin in September.

(The) Greenwich Japanese School

15 Ridgeway, Greenwich; 629.9039
www.gwjs.org
Grades 1 - 9.

Italian for Toddlers

Greenwich Catholic School, 471 North Street
869.4000 x 165 or 212.501.8524
www.ItalianForToddlers.com
They believe that children should start learning languages at a very young age. Each class is taught totally in Italian using crafts, puppets and instruments.

Linguakids

P.O. Box 2662, Darien, CT; 203.655.6461
www.linguakids.com
Classes in French and Spanish for children ages 2 and up. Several Fairfield county locations.

(The) Language Exchange

Mill Pond Shopping Center, 203 East Putnam Avenue, Cos Cob
422.2024
www.ForeignLanguageExchange.com
Instruction in 18 languages including ESL. Children's classes for ages 3 to 13. They offer total immersion camps for students in Elementary, Middle and High School.

TIP: SEPTEMBERFEST
Be sure this festival, sponsored by the United Way, is marked on your calendar. You and your family will have a wonderful time. You will find rides, kids' activities, food and live entertainment. Call 869.2221 for details.

music and acting

Actor's Garage

Greenwich YWCA, 259 East Putnam Avenue, 869.6501
www.ywcaGreenwich.org
An exciting and entertaining acting program for kids; training for commercials, television and film.

Connecticut School of Music

Kenneth Kuo, 226.0805
www.CTSchoolOfMusic.com
Streaming online instruction.

Greenwich Music & Fraioli School of Music

1200 East Putnam Avenue, 869.3615
www.greenwichmusic.com
This is a music store and a school. They offer instruction in many instruments, voice and even have a class about how to be a rock star.
Hours: Mon - Thursday 10am - 7pm; Friday and Saturday 10am - 6pm.

Greenwich Suzuki Academy

Christ Church, 254 East Putnam Avenue, 203.561.6176
Mailing address: 15 E. Putnam Ave #176 Greenwich, CT 06830
www.greenwichsuzukiacademy.org
The Suzuki method of teaching violin, viola, flute and cello is available for children ages 3 - 18. It is taught in private and group classes. Parent training is available as well as instruction in beginning orchestra, jazz theory, improvisation, and chamber music.

Kinder Musik

Old Greenwich Music Studio
23 Clark Street, Old Greenwich, 637.0461
www.OGMstudio.kindermusik.net
Pre-instrumental programs for infants to 8 years. A delightful way to encourage a child's love of music.
Hours: Monday - Saturday, morning and afternoon sessions.

CHILD ENRICHMENT

Mary Ann Hall's Music For Children
Greenwich YMCA, 50 East Putnam Avenue, 203.854.9797
www.musicforchildren.net
A song, dance, and instrument program for children birth to 10.

MMM Productions, A Theater Arts School
Michelle Marceau, 327.7666, 273.7827
www.mmmProductions.biz
Classes are held at Western Greenwich Civic Center, Greenwich Arts Council, St. Catherine's of Siena and Nathaniel Witherell. Under adult supervision, students can write and perform their own original musicals and standard shows. Classes include acting, tap and creative drama, musical theater, ballet, jazz, improv, on camera classes, voice classes, and private lessons. Classes are $380 - $430.

Music Conservatory of Westchester
Central Avenue, White Plains, NY, 914.761.3900
www.musicconservatory.org
High quality, individual instrumental instruction for children in violin, Suzuki violin, piano, guitar and woodwinds, provided by the Music Conservatory of Westchester. Music theory lessons also available.
Hours: weekdays, 9 am - 8 pm; Saturday, 8 am - 5 pm.

(The) Music Source
1345 East Putnam Avenue, 698.0444
Our favorite source for sheet music is also a place for voice and instrument lessons.

Music Together of Fairfield County
76 Walbin Court, Fairfield, CT, 203.256.1656
www.musictogether.com
Fun, informal family music-making classes for babies to 5 year olds.

Vinny Nobile
914.980.3082
Vinny will come to your home for private lessons in trumpet, trombone or piano.

music and acting

Riverside School of Music

1139 East Putnam Avenue, 637.7413
They sell instruments and give private lessons for violin, viola, cello, piano, guitar & voice for children 2 and up. They are great with kids. Open every day.
Hours: weekdays 10am - 6pm;Saturday 10am - 2pm.

Studio of Victoria Baker

531.7499
Victoria Baker, an opera singer and columnist for the Greenwich Post, gives private voice and piano lessons.

Young Artists Philharmonic

PO Box 3301, Ridgeway Station, Stamford, CT, 532.1278
www.syap.org
For over 40 years, this highly sophisticated regional youth symphony orchestra has inspired youth and entertained adults.

reading

Pre-school Stories

Stories are read to pre-schoolers in the mornings most weekdays. During the summer, stories may be read in a nearby park.
www.greenwichlibrary.org

- **Byram Shubert Library**
    21 Mead Avenue, Byram, 531.0426
- **Cos Cob Library**
    5 Sinoway Road, Cos Cob, 622.6883
- **Weewalkers at Greenwich Library**
    622.7900
    12 - 24 months
    Tuesday, Thursday and Friday mornings 11 am.
- **Perrot Library**
    90 Sound Beach Avenue, Old Greenwich
    637.1066

Tales at Twilight

Greenwich Library, 110 West Putnam Avenue, 622.7900
The Children's Desk, 622.7942
www.greenwichlibrary.org
Story hours are a special time for parents and children. Children, dressed in pajamas, bring their favorite teddy bear and listen to stories. Check the calendar for program times.

Young Critics Club

Perrot Library, 90 Sound Beach Avenue, Old Greenwich
637.8802
www.greenwichlibrary.org
Children in grades 6 - 8 who love to read and talk about books, gather on Friday afternoons with Kate McClelland and Mary Clark for a guided discussion. By application only.

fairs, festivals & carnivals

Many of the town's elementary schools and churches hold fairs as fundraisers:

- **Cos Cob School Fair**
    300 East Putnam Avenue (early May), 869.4670
- **North Mianus School Pow Wow**
    309 Palmer Hill Road (early May), 637.9730
- **Renaissance Festival**
    International School of Dundee, 55 Florence Road, Riverside (early June) Sword fights, horseback jousting and live chess.
- **St. Catherine's Carnival**
    4 Riverside Avenue (middle August), 637.3661
- **St. Paul's Episcopal Church Fair**
    200 Riverside Avenue (late May), 637.2447
- **St. Roch's Bazaar**
    10 Saint Roch Avenue, Byram (early August), 869.4176

United Way September Fest
Roger Sherman Baldwin Park at Arch Street
(middle September), 869.2221
www.UnitedWay-Greenwich.com

Scarecrow Festival
Mill Pond Park. Strickland Road, Cos Cob
Hosted by the Bush-Holly House (869.6899), this fun-filled October day includes live entertainment, lots of food vendors, scarecrow contests, horse-drawn wagon rides, hay maze, art projects, three-legged races and much more.

The Junior League of Greenwich

869.1979

www.jlgreenwich.org

The Junior League hosts several popular fundraising events throughout the year including:

- **Touch a Truck**

    Held at the Greenwich High School field. Children have a chance to climb onto backhoes, dump trucks, and emergency vehicles. Tattoo artists and musicians make it festive, too.

- **Gingerbread House Workshop**

    The Boys and Girls Club is the location for this yummy fundraiser. Each child decorates her own gingerbread house. The big challenge is to keep them from eating all the goodies on the spot!

- **The Enchanted Forest**

    Held at The Hyatt in Old Greenwich each November, The Enchanted Forest is a two-day event which features over 100 decorated trees, wreaths and gingerbread houses and photos with Santa.

TIP: KIDS' TIME

The Performing Arts Center at Purchase College, in addition to their superb adult concert series, has a series of sensational performances designed for children. One series is for ages 4-9 and one is for ages 9 and up. Check it out
www.purchase.edu/Community/ChildrensCenter.aspx
or contact them at 914.251.6200.

Family museums are included here see also, CULTURE, MUSEUMS.

American Museum of Natural History

Central Park West at 79th Street
New York, New York, 212.769.5100
 www.amnh.org
Hours: Sunday - Thursday 10am - 5:45pm;
Fridays and Saturdays 10am - 8:45pm.
This museum is terrific for kids, with lots of special exhibits and programs and workshops.

Audubon Center Greenwich

613 Riversville Road, 869.5272
www.greenwich.center.audubon.org
Founded in 1942, this 686-acre sanctuary has 15 miles of trails and a superb learning and exhibit center, with a terrific nature store. You will want to stay. Open year round except for major holidays.
Hours: Everyday, 9 am - 5 pm.

Bridgeport Bluefish

Harbor Yard, 500 Main Street, Bridgeport, CT, 203.345.4800
www.bridgeportbluefish.com
Professional Minor League Baseball in the Atlantic League.
Hours: May to September, Monday - Saturday, 7 pm; Sunday 1 pm. Verify hours and ticket availability before you go.
Directions: I-95 N to exit 27.

Bridgeport Sound Tigers

600 Main Street, Arena at Harbor Yard, Bridgeport, CT
203.345.2300
www.soundtigers.com
Ice Hockey, New York Islanders "farm" team. They begin playing their 40 home game season in October.
Directions: I-95 N to Exit 27 (Lafayette Blvd.). At the bottom of the ramp continue straight along South Frontage Road past Lafayette Blvd. The next street is Broad Street. Go through the light and the Arena is directly in front of you.

family outings

Bronx Zoo

Fordham Road at Bronx River Parkway, Bronx, NY, 718.367.1010

www.bronxzoo.com

World class zoo with terrific rides and exhibits. Easy to find. Free admission every Wednesday. You can purchase tickets on-line.

Hours: Weekdays, 10 am - 5 pm; Weekends and holidays, 10 am - 5:30 pm; November - March, 10 am - 4:30 pm.

Directions: (30 minutes) I-95 S to Pelham Pkw W; or Merritt Pkw S to Cross County Pkw W, then Bronx River Pkw S.

Bruce Museum

1 Museum Drive, 869.0376

www.brucemuseum.org

Impressive rotating exhibits and many programs for adults and children. They have a terrific gift shop with a large selection of books. The Museum has been accredited by the American Association of Museums as being in the top 10 percent of US museums. The Museum sponsors 2 fairs in Bruce Park every year; the mid-May Craft Fair and the Columbus Day Arts Festival have juried artists from around the country and draw visitors from all over the area.

Hours: Tuesday - Saturday, 10 am - 5 pm; Sunday, 1 pm - 5 pm.

Closed on major holidays.

Bush Holley House Museum

39 Strickland Road, Cos Cob, 869.6899

www.hstg.org

Home of the Historical Society, this is the place to learn about Greenwich history. They also have a good library and a shop with books on Greenwich history, as well as reproductions of 19th-century children's toys and books. While you are there, pick up a list of their informative programs.

Hours: March - December, Tuesday - Sunday, noon - 4 pm;

January - February, weekends, noon - 4 pm.

Dinosaur State Park

400 West Street, Rocky Hill, CT, 860.529.8423

www.dinosaurstatepark.org

Dinosaurs fascinate us all. With over 2,000 tracks, this is one of the best sites in North America. Make your own castings right on the site.

CHILDREN

family outings

Discovery Museum

4450 Park Avenue, Bridgeport, CT, 203.372.3521
www.discoverymuseum.org
Hands-on art and science exhibits for children of all ages and their parents. A special section for pre-schoolers with dozens of attractions based on principles of early childhood development. Families who know about the Discovery Museum go there regularly.
Hours: Tuesday - Saturday, 10 am - 5 pm; Sunday, noon - 5 pm. Open Monday in summer.
Directions: Merritt Parkway N to exit 47, L on Park Avenue
(1 mile S on L).

Donald M. Kendall Sculpture Gardens

PepsiCo World Headquarters
700 Anderson Hill Road, Purchase, NY
Just 15 minutes from Greenwich, these gardens are a nice place to take a leisurely stroll.

Essex Steam Train & Riverboat

One Railroad Avenue, Essex, CT, 860.767.0103, 800.377.3987
www.essexsteamtrain.com
Take a trip back in history through the scenic Connecticut River Valley. Passengers board the 1920 steam train at the Essex station for a one-hour ride. At Deep River Landing the train meets the river boat for a one-hour cruise. The North Cove Express offers brunch, lunch and dinner during a two-hour excursion. Call for reservations on the Dinner Train. Pre-schoolers won't want to miss the Thomas the Tank Engine ride, a 25-minute ride with Thomas held in November.
Hours: Call for seasonal hours.
Directions: I-95 N to exit 69, Rte. 9 N to exit 3, Left (W) 1/4 mile. Across from Sunoco station.
Note: See Connecticut River Valley Inns in the section HOTELS & INNS.

Flanders Nature Center - Maple Sugaring

5 Church Hill (at Flanders Road), Woodbury, CT
203.263.3711
www.flandersnaturecenter.org, www.woodburyct.org
Spend an afternoon at a sugarhouse and learn how to make pure maple syrup and then taste it. During a good season, there is sugaring in Connecticut for six or seven weeks. In an off year, the season could be only a couple of weekends, so be sure to call before you go. The Flanders Nature Center is 1½ to 2 hours from Greenwich. Woodbury is a well-preserved colonial town with a number of antique shops and some top restaurants. The syrup operation is open to the public. Demonstrations are given on weekends from 3 pm to 5 pm from late February through March.
Directions: I-95 N to exit 27A, Rte 8 N to exit 37, Rte 262 /Frost Bridge Rd/Echo Lake Rd towards Watertown, R on Rte 63/Main St, L on Town Hall Rd, L on US 6/Deforest Rd/Woodbury Rd/Main St N, R on Rte 61/ Bethlehem Rd, L on Church Hill Rd.

Franklin Mineral Museum

30 Plant Street, Ogdensburg, NJ, 973.209.7212
www.sterlinghill.org
A world-famous collection of fluorescent rocks, many from the Sterling Mine. For the tour of the mine wear sturdy boots and bring a jacket (it's cool even in the summer). Not appropriate for children under six.
Museum Hours: everyday, April through November
Tour Hours: 1 pm; everyday, July and August, weekends April - June and September - November.
Directions: Cross the George Washington Bridge and take Route 80 to exit for Route 23. Proceed 26 miles, L on Route 517 South, 2.5 miles through Ogdensburg, R on Brooks Flat Road, R on Plant Street.
About 2.5 hours from Greenwich.

IMAX Theater

At the Maritime Aquarium, 10 North Water Street, Norwalk, CT
203.852.0700, www.maritimeaquarium.org
With a screen that is six stories high and eight stories wide and a 24,000 watt sound system, the experience is truly amazing.
Hours: Open daily at 10 am; September - June until 5 pm;
July - Labor Day, until 6 pm.
Directions: I-95 N to exit 14, R at light on West Ave, l at 3rd light on North Main, L at light on Ann.

family outings

Kykuit (The Rockefeller Estate)

Shuttle bus from Philipsburg Manor Visitors Center
Sleepy Hollow, NY, 914.631.9491
www.hudsonvalley.org
Home to four generations of Rockefellers, this is the Hudson Valley's most exceptional house and gardens. Tours include Nelson A. Rockefeller's extraordinary collection of 20th-century sculpture as well as the Coach Barn with its antique carriages and autos. A garden and sculpture tour is offered most weekdays.
Hours: 10 am - 3 pm daily, Weekends 10 - 4
Closed Tuesday's from May13th - November 5th.
Directions: I-95 or the Merritt Parkway (Rt 15) S to the Cross Westchester Expressway (I-287) West. Exit 1, Tarrytown. At the end of the exit ramp L to Route 119 to the end. R at the light onto Route 9 N. Philipsburg Manor is on the L.

Lake Compounce Family Theme Park

822 Lake Avenue, Bristol, CT 860.583.3300
www.lakecompounce.com
The best wooden roller coaster in the world is about 1½ hours north of Greenwich built on the side of a mountain. It is simply "awesome." All rides in the Circus World Children's Area and some rides in Splash Harbor are designed for young children. Children must be under 54" tall to ride, but adults may accompany children on some rides.
In October, the "Haunted Graveyard" can be lots of fun. Check it out at www.hauntedGraveyard.com
Directions: I-95 North to Rt. 8 North (EXIT 27A) to I 84 East to Exit 31 (about 61 miles).

Lyndhurst

635 South Broadway, Tarrytown, NY, 914.631.4481
www.lyndhurst.org or www.hudsonvalley.org
 America's finest Gothic Revival mansion. A visit to the house and its 67-acre park is a must for all who are interested in 19th century architecture, decorative arts, and landscape design.
Hours: Mid-April through October, Tuesday - Sunday and holiday Mondays, 10 am - 5 pm. Entrance gate closes at 4:15 November - Mid-April; Weekends only and holiday Mondays, 10 am - 4 pm.
Directions: I-95 or the Merritt Parkway (Rt 15) S to the Cross Westchester Expressway (I-287) West. Exit 1, Tarrytown. At the end of the exit ramp L to Route 119. Then L onto Broadway (Route 9). Lyndhurst is 1/4 mile on R.

Maritime Aquarium

10 North Water Street, Norwalk, CT, 203.852.0700
www.MaritimeAquarium.org
Interactive exhibits often including a Shark Touch Pool. Cited as one of the 10 Great Aquariums to visit.
Hours: Open daily; September - June, 10 am - 5 pm;
July Labor Day, 10 am - 6 pm.
Directions: I-95 N to exit 14. See directions for IMAX Theater above.

Mystic Seaport and Museum

Mystic, CT, Visitor Information: 888.973.2767
www.mysticseaport.org
Mystic is a two-hour drive. The Mystic Seaport Museum has a world-renowned waterfront collection of ships and crafts that tells the story of America and the sea. Mystic also has a good aquarium, with exciting special exhibits.
While in the Mystic area, stop by Stonington, which is about five miles east on US-1. Stonington is a nineteenth century fishing village which has kept its charm and has become a center for antique shops.
Don't forget Mystic Pizza, which inspired the movie. There is one in Mystic, 860.536.3700 and one in North Stonington, 860.599.5126.
Hours: Open every day except December 25th;
Ships & exhibits, 9 am - 5 pm; Museum grounds, 9 am - 6 pm.
Directions: I-95 N to exit 90. Rte 27 S.

family outings

NY Botanical Gardens

Bronx River Parkway at Fordham Road, Bronx, NY, 718.817.8700
www.nybg.org
They have recently undergone a $25 million renovation and are considered the best in the country.
Hours: Open year round, Tuesday - Sunday, 10 am - 6 pm.
Free admissions on Wednesdays. November -March, open until 4 pm.
Directions: (30 minutes) Merritt/Hutchinson Pkw S to exit 15; Cross County Pkw W to exit 6; Bronx River Pkw S to exit 8W (Mosholu Pkw), at second light, L into Garden.

Philipsburg Manor

Sleepy Hollow, NY, 914.631.8200, 914.631.3992
www.HudsonValley.org
An 18th-century working farm, with water-powered grist mill and livestock. Tours are conducted by interpreters in period costumes.
Hours: April - December, open every day except Tuesday, 10 am - 5 pm.
Open on weekends in March; closed January & February.
Directions: I-287/87 W to exit 9; follow signs for Rte. 9.

Pick Your Own Fruits & Vegetables

Picking your own fruit and vegetables has become a popular pastime in Connecticut. There are nine farms in Fairfield County offering urbanites the opportunity to pick their own produce.
For more detailed information call 860.713.2569 or 1 800.861.9939
www.state.ct.us/doag
Some you might consider are:

• Bishop's Orchards

1355 Boston Post Road (I-95, exit 57), Guilford, CT
203.458.7425, 203.453.2338
www.bishopsorchards.com
They have a great many varieties of fruit to pick, including over twenty varieties of apples, nine kinds of blueberries, twelve of peaches, three of pears, eight of strawberries and two varieties of raspberries. This orchard is definitely worth the trip.
Market hours: From June through October, Monday - Saturday, 8 am to 6 pm; Sunday, 9 am to 6 pm.

family outings

- **Eden Farms**

947 Stillwater Road, Stamford, 203.325.3445
www.edenfarmsllc.com
Open 7 days a week. Just minutes from Greenwich, Eden Farms has special seasonal celebrations: Easter Bunnies, Halloween Hayrides, Pumpkin Patch, Haunted House and Santa visits.

- **Jones Family Farm**

606 Walnut Tree Hill Road & Route 110, Shelton, CT
203.929.8425
www.jonesfamilyfarms.com
This pick-your-own farm began in the 1940s. They have strawberries in June, followed by blueberries in July and August, and pumpkins in the autumn. Hayrides are offered in October, and in December, come and cut your own Christmas tree.
Hours: Best to call, hours change seasonally. Closed Sunday & Monday.

- **Silverman's Farm**

451 Sport Hill Road (exit 46 off the Merritt Parkway)
Easton, CT, 203.268 0321
www.silvermansfarm.com
Peaches in July, apples in August. Three-acre animal farm for youngsters.
Hours: Weekdays, 9 am - 5 pm. Closed on major holidays. Call for hours in January or in case of bad weather.

- **White Silo Farm**

32 Route 37 East, Sherman, CT, 860.355.0271
www.whitesilowinery.com
Strawberries, asparagus, raspberries, blackberries and rhubarb.

CHILDREN

Playland Park

Playland Parkway, Rye, NY, 914.813.7010

www.ryeplayland.org

Recently renovated amusement park, just 15 minutes away. A wide variety of rides for older kids from Go Karts to Zombie Castle and Old Mill. Kiddyland has 20 of Playland's 50 rides. Playland also has a beach, swimming pool, lake cruises, ice casino, miniature golf and sightseeing cruises on Long Island Sound.

Hours: Open May to mid-September. The ice rink is open from October to April. Call for hours.

Directions: I-95 S exit 19.

Putnam Cottage

243 East Putnam Avenue, 869.9697

www.PutnamCottage.org

Originally a tavern serving travelers along the Post Road, it is now a museum owned by the Daughters of the American Revolution. Each year on the last Sunday in February (1 pm 3 pm), the Putnam Hill Revolutionary War battle is recreated. A definite must-see for adults and children alike.

Hours: Wednesday, Friday, Sunday, 1 pm - 4 pm.

Renaissance Fair

Route 17A, Sterling Forest, Tuxedo, NY, 845.351.5174

www.renfair.com

Over 300 actors, in costume, mingle with the visitors (who can also don costumes) in a mock sixteenth century village. A wonderful way to enjoy a day of improvisation and learning.

Hours: August to mid-September weekends only; 10 am - 7 pm.

Directions: I-287/187 West to exit 15A. Route 17N to 17A, Left to Faire.

TIP: RENTING A BUS

Have you ever wanted to take a large group on a trip, but wondered how? Our own local Fjord has the answer. They have luxury motor coaches for charter at competitive rates. Call 800.925.2622 for prices. Another choice is J&R Tours in Mount Vernon, NY, 800.444.5786, www.Buses.com

family outings

Six Flags Great Adventure

Route 537, Jackson, NJ, 732.928.1821
www.sixflags.com/parks/greatadventure
The park is a 2½ hour drive from Greenwich. But if you like roller coasters, it is worth a trip. Their large amusement park has rides for every age, although the Nitro and Medusa roller coasters (2 of their 13) are well known by coaster aficionados. Six Flags Wild Safari is the world's largest drive thru Safari outside Africa. Hurricane Harbor has water rides. Be sure to call for hours of operation before you go.
Directions: Take the George Washington Bridge to NJ Turnpike south to exit 7A. Proceed on I-195 east to exit 16A, then one mile west on Rte. 537 to Six Flags.

Stamford Museum & Nature Center

39 Scofieldtown Road (corner of High Ridge Rd), Stamford
322.1646
www.stamfordmuseum.org
118-acres, with a 10-acre working farm, pond life exhibit, boardwalks, natural history exhibits, planetarium and observatory. If your child hasn't grown up on a farm, this is the perfect place to learn about farming and farm animals.
Hours: Open year round except for major holidays,
Monday - Saturday, 9 am - 5 pm; Sunday, 11 am - 5 pm;
Planetarium shows Sunday at 3 pm;
Observatory, Friday, 8:30 pm - 10:30 pm.
Directions: Merritt Parkway N, exit 35 (Rte 15).

Stepping Stones Museum for Children

303 West Avenue (Mathews Park), Norwalk, CT, 203.899.0606
www.steppingstonesMuseum.org
Excellent interactive museum for kids under 10.
Hours: Tuesday - Saturday, 10 am - 5 pm, Sunday noon - 5 pm, open Mondays in the summer.
Directions: I-95 north to exit 14N.

Sterling Hill Mine & Museum

(Thomas Warren Museum of Fluorescence)
30 Plant Street, Ogdensburg, NJ, 973.209.7212
www.sterlinghillminingmuseum.org
The Sterling Hill mine operated from about 1761 to 1986. The museum opened on August 4, 1990. Tours take about 3 hours. Be sure to bring light jackets or sweaters. It is 56° year round in the mine.
Hours: Museum is open every day from April 1 to November 30.

United States Military Academy

West Point, NY, 845.938.2638
www.usma.edu
Visitors now need a military ID to enter the grounds of the academy, except for the visitor's center and military museum. One-hour guided tours are available but photo IDs are required.
Hours: Guided tours: Daily 9am - 4:45pm. Closed Thanksgiving, Christmas and New Years Day.
Directions: I-95 to I-287/I 87 (NYS Thruway). Over bridge, take exit 13N onto the Palisades Interstate Parkway heading north. Take the PIP north to its end (Bear Mountain traffic circle). Follow signs for Route 9W north (3rd exit off traffic circle). Exit 9W via West Point exit, Stony Lonesome exit, or Route 293 exit.

parties at home

Open Greenwich photo albums and you'll see pictures of fabulous parties. Many of the best parties are hosted by imaginative parents at home. However, if you want help, read on.

See ENTERTAINING for tents, caterers, party supply shops and other useful party information. Another resource for party information is www.KidsEvents.com, developed by local residents covering a wide area of children's events. A good place to get party ideas.

Aux Delices

23 Acosta Street, Stamford, CT 203.326.4540 x 108
www.AuxDelicesFoods.com
Fun, hands-on cooking parties can be held in their Stamford location or at your home.

Awesome Science Parties

203.227.8112, 800.311.9993
www.hightouch hightech.com/franchises/connecticut/index.html
Hands-on interactive parties where each child is involved with every experiment. Children have lots of science fun making edible gummy drops or volcanoes and launching rockets. Parties are age appropriate. They also do after-school programs in our elementary schools. Ages: 5 - 11.

Dave's Cast of Characters

914.235.7100
www.davescast.com
They specialize in professional entertainment, from full-costumed characters to carnival rides and inflatables.

Fire Trucks

Check with your local firehouse. Many will bring a truck over to your house in exchange for a donation. The fire department's non-emergency phone is 622.3950. The non-emergency numbers for all of the local fire companies are in NUMBERS YOU SHOULD KNOW.

Graham Clarke

914.669.5843
www.grahamclarke.com
Graham is well known by many a Greenwich child. He sings silly songs with his guitars and the kids go crazy!

Little Cooks

888.695.2665 Gina

They have a variety of upscale parties for different groups and themes, including holidays and international cuisine (youngsters cook recipes from and learn about a country). Parties include invitations, party favors, chef hats, aprons and all ingredients. Ages: 4 to 12.

Mad Science of Fairfield County

888.381.9754

www.madscience.org/connecticut

Interactive experiments for children, combining science with entertainment. Party programs are tailored to the age group and can include chemical magic, vortex generators, indoor fireworks, or model rocket launchings. Ages: 5 to 12.

Pied Piper Pony Rides

203.431.8322

www.piedpiperponyrides.com

You may want to invite one of their gentle ponies and friendly staff members to your party. The children will have a good time and the pony droppings will be removed. Closes for the winter.

Princess Tea Parties by Eileen

203.532.0547

Dress-up parties with tea sandwiches and entertainment to charm little girls in your home.

parties away from home

AMF Rip Van Winkle Lanes

701 Connecticut Avenue, Norwalk, 203.838.7501
47 Tarrytown Road, White Plains, NY 914.948.2677
www.amfcenters.com
Bowling parties have been a hit for generations.

Audubon Center

613 Riversville Road, Greenwich, 869.5272
www.greenwich.center.audobon.org
Holding a party at the Audubon is a wonderful way to foster a love of nature. Highly trained guides will lead nature walks. You can rent space in the gorgeous center for a party.

Boys and Girls Club of Greenwich

4 Horseneck Lane, 869.3224
www.bcgc.org
This newly renovated building has a large gym for multi-sport activities led by friendly staff and a party room nearby for the kids to do arts/crafts, bouncy castle, etc. Another option is to have an ice skating party. Charlie really enjoyed his party here.

Chocopologie Birthday Parties

12 South Main Street, Norwalk, CT 203.838.3131
www.Kinpschildt.com
What could be better than wearing a chef's hat, watching chocolate being made and then eating super sundaes and chocolate treats?

Clearview Cinemas

356 Greenwich Avenue, 323.3456 or 908.918.2001
www.clearviewcinemas.com
You can watch the current movie or bring in your own DVD. They will put your child's name on the marquee. Theater rental $250-$300 Friday or Sunday, $150 - $200 Monday - Thursday.

Dance Adventure

230 Mason Street, 625.0930
www.danceadventure.com
They offer sweet theme parties for young girls.

parties away from home

Dorothy Hamill Skating Rink
Sherman Avenue, Greenwich, 531.8560
Call about renting the facility for a fun party.

Dynamic Martial Arts
202 Field Point Road, 629.4666
A party where children can learn karate. Ages: 4 and above.
Hours: Saturday parties, noon - 1:30 pm.

Fun For Kids
370 West Main Street, Stamford,203.326.5656
www.fun4kidsarcade.com
Though the location seems a bit seedy, once inside this arcade makes for
a super party. Either choose soft play theme for young kids under 8 or go
for the laser tag for the older ones.

Great Play
2000 W. Main Street (Shop Rite Shopping Center), Stamford
203.978.1333
www.greatplay.com
Customized 90-minute parties right on the border of Greenwich. Choose
from Field Day (age 3 -10), Fun and Games (ages 1 - 6) and Multi Sport
(ages 4 -10).

**Greenwich and Western Greenwich Civic Center
Gymnasiums**
Call Frank Gabriele at Parks & Recreation for details 622.7821

Greenwich Skatepark
100 Arch Street, Roger Sherman Baldwin Park, 622.7830
www.greenwichct.org
The Greenwich Skate Park offers birthday parties on Saturday and Sunday mornings 10 am - noon. The fee is $125 which includes 10 children.
Lessons are available for $25 per instructor. Bring a cake and pizza and
have fun!

Kids U

633 Hope Street, Stamford, 203.358.9500
www.kidsu.com
The gym parties include an hour of soft free play then the kids march into the gym for supervised activities and pizza.

My Gym

225 Atlantic Street, Stamford, 203.327.3494
www.my gym.com
2 hours of non-stop fun. Games, gymnastics, puppets, rides, songs you can customize to your child's liking.

Nimble Thimble

21 Putnam Avenue, Port Chester, NY, 914.934.2934
Choose a project for your age group; for instance, make a fabric covered bulletin board or a vest. Parents can bring cake and ice cream. Ages: 5 and up.
Hours: Call to schedule a party.

Norwalk Aquarium

10 North Water Street, Norwalk, 203.852.0700 x 2206
www.maritimeaquarium.org
Everyone loves this aquarium and having a party here combines fun and education.

Route 22 Restaurant

1980 West Main Street, Stamford, 203.323.2229
www.rt22restaurant.com/rt22stamford/about.htm
Contact: Lance Root
Donut Machines, Video Games, Movies, Kid friendly food.

Sharkey's Cuts For Kids

220 East Putnam Avenue, Cos Cob, 629.kids
www.sharkeyscutsforkids.com
Glamour Girl parties are bound to make young girls smile. They make-up, dress-up and put on a fashion show.

CHILDREN

Slot Car Raceways
- 17 Raceway Lane, Elmsford, NY, 914.592.5375
- 7 Hyde Street, Stamford, CT, 316.8630

www.flatoutfun.com
For 38 years the del Rosario family has entertained children and their parents with 62" slot car racing. Ages: 4 to 99.
Hours: weekdays, noon to 9:30 pm; Saturday, 11 am to 9:30 pm; Sunday, noon to 7 pm.

Stepping Stones Museum
Matthews Park, 303 West Avenue, Norwalk, 203.899.0606 x 228
www.steppingstonesmuseum.org
Parties for up to 20 children ages 4 and up. After the guided tour, they have a special party room with cake and crafts.

T Party Birthday Teas
2 Squab Lane, Darien, CT 203.662.9689
www.TPartyAntiques.com
For children age 6 and up. Besides tea, scones, and birthday cakes, children dress up and are treated to Victorian parlor games and etiquette lessons.

Tumblebugs
6 Riverside Avenue, 637.3303
www.TumbleBugsNY.com
Great party for the 3 to 4 year old set. Friendly staff leads the kids in games around the gym and then they go into a party room for pizza and cake.

Whimsies Dollhouse & Miniature Shoe Party
18 Lewis Street, Greenwich, 629.8024
Young kids can have a dress-up and make-believe party with arts and crafts. Older girls can choose between a Tea Party, a Miniature Creations Parties (build a doll house, stuff a bear) and many other themes.

YWCA

259 East Putnam Avenue, 869.6501 x 235

www.ywcagreenwich.org

Rent a party room and/or hire one of their special instructors to teach the children activities such as soccer, swimming, gymnastics or climbing their rock wall. Parents provide the refreshments. All ages.

Hours: Parties are held during regular Y hours: weekdays, 6:30 am - 10 pm; Saturday, 7:30 am to 5 pm (summer Saturday hours are shorter).

YMCA

50 East Putnam Avenue, 869.1630

www.gwymca.org

Rent the gym or pool for your party with cake and presents in the Rendezvous room. The Y can even provide a clown or magician. All ages.

Hours: weekdays, 5 am to 10 pm; Saturday, 6:30 am to 7 pm; Sunday, 8 am to 5 pm (summer hours may be shorter).

CHILDREN

playgrounds

Town playgrounds are open from 9 am to 4 pm. From late June through early August, the Greenwich Department of Parks and Recreation conducts supervised activities at the playgrounds for children ages 7 to 15. There are a number of small playgrounds scattered throughout the town (Binney Park, Bible Street Park, Christiano Park, Eastern and Western Greenwich Civic Centers, Island Beach and Loughlin Avenue Park), however, only a few are worth a trip if you don't live in that area. Here are our favorites.

Bruce Park

60 acres, across from the Bruce Museum on Museum Drive. One of Greenwich's prettiest parks, with excellent play equipment.

Byram Park

30 acres, located on Ritch Avenue and Byram Shore Road in Byram. The park has an attractive beach area and the town's only public fresh water pool. (The playground is tucked behind the Byram Shore Boat Club.) How can you go wrong?

Greenwich Common

16 acres, located adjacent to Greenwich Avenue, with an entrance on Greenwich Avenue next to the Havemeyer Building (Board of Education). This is a wonderful place to rest during a busy shopping day and let your children play. The Common has a small but attractive playground area.

Island Beach

See PARKS & BEACHES for information on ferry operation and beach passes.

Public Elementary Schools

These playgrounds are well kept and extensive. They are available to residents during the weekends and summer when school is not in session. For more information on the location of the elementary schools, see the Public Elementary School section under SCHOOLS.

Western Greenwich Civic Center

10 acres, located on the corner of Glenville Road and Pemberwick Road. This playground is a favorite with kids.

scouting

Adventure Guides

YMCA, 50 East Putnam Avenue, 869.1630

www.gwymca.org

Outings and camp-outs for fathers and their five to ten year old children.

Boy Scouts of America

Greenwich Council #67, 63 Mason Street, 869.8424

www.scouting.org or www.GreenwichBSA.com

This is the headquarters of the local chapter of the non-profit organization dedicated to instilling ethical values in young people. The Scouts are fortunate to own the Seton Reservation, a large preserve located at 363 Riversville Road. It serves as the site for the Cub Scout day camp as well as many other scouting outdoor programs. Call to check on a troop near you. The chapter sponsors the following programs.

Programs open to boys: Tiger Cubs, age 6; Cub Scouts, ages 7 - 10; Boy Scouts, ages 11 - 18.

Programs open to boys and girls: Explorers, ages 14 - 20 (specialties: aviation, scuba, emergency rescue.)

The Greenwich office has a small store for uniforms. A larger selection is available at the Darien Sports Shop (1127 Post Road, Darien, CT, 203.655.2575), and the Connecticut Yankee Council #72, Boy Scouts of America (in Norwalk, CT, exit 40A on the Merritt Parkway, 362 Main Avenue, 203.847.2445).

Hours: Greenwich Scouts office: weekdays, 8:30 am - 4:30 pm.

Girl Scout Council of Southwestern Connecticut

529 Danbury Road, Wilton, CT, 800.882.5561, 203.762.5557

www.gscswct.org

This is the headquarters of the local chapter of the non-profit organization dedicated to addressing girls' interests and their future contemporary roles as women. The current Executive Director is Betsy Keefer; the Greenwich Unit Manager is Joan Karasick.

Programs: Daisies, kindergarten; Brownies, grades 1 - 3; Junior Girl Scouts, grades 4 - 6; Cadettes, grades 7 - 9; Seniors, grades 9 - 12.

Uniforms are available from Best & Co. in Greenwich and from the Darien Sports Shop, 1127 Post Road, Darien, CT, 203.655.2575.

Hours: weekdays, 9 am - 5:30 pm, Thursday until 8:30 pm.

summer camp information

No need to travel to New Hampshire or Maine, the Greenwich area has all sorts of camps. For a more complete list:

- **American Camping Association**

New England Section, 800.446.4494

www.acacamps.org

A national non-profit educational organization that accredits children's summer camps. Call to get a copy of their directory.

- **Community Answers**

Call 622.7979 for a copy of their Summer Resource Guide.

- **www.KidsEvents.com**

A Greenwich based website which includes a guide to summer camps.

- **www.MySummerCamps.com**

A site run by Toronto-based Target Directories (416.544.9925) and used by many Greenwich Residents.

It lists over 15,000 camps.

- **Summer Camp Fair**

Greenwich High School, 625.8000

www.greenwich.k12.ct.us/ghs/ghs.htm

Known as "Summerfare," this event is sponsored by the Greenwich High School PTA and draws hundreds of camps from around the USA. The fair is usually held in February.

- **Summer Camp Expo**

Greenwich Academy, 625.8990

www.greenwichacademy.org

Their Summer Opportunity Fair is usually held at the end of January.

Packages Plus-N-More

215 East Putnam Avenue (Mill Pond Shopping Center), Cos Cob

625.8130

They will pack and ship your child's camping gear.

CHILDREN

Allegra Summer Stock Performing Arts Camps

37 West Putnam Avenue, 629.9162
www.AllegraDanceStudio.com
Drama, theater, jazz, tap and other fantastic art programs.

Arch Street Teen Center

100 Arch Street, Greenwich, 629.5744
www.archstreet.org
Hands-on arts and crafts, graphic design, film and radio production for kids entering grades 7 to 9.

Art Scampers

www.fpcg.org
First Presbyterian Church, 37 Lafayette Place, 869.7782
Focus on art, music, drama, ages 3 to 6 years.

Audubon Summer Children's Programs

Audubon Center, 613 Riversville Road, 869.5272
www.greenwich.center.audubon.org
The Audubon Summer Nature Day Camp offers three themes for children entering K to 5 and for older children. Outstanding Teens Training in Ecological Research for grades 6 to 8.

Banksville Community House Summer Camp

12 Banksville Road, 622.9597
A perfect camp for those living in the Banksville area, featuring summer fun activities such as archery and swimming.

Bible Camps

- St. Paul Evangelical Lutheran Church, 531.8466
- Greenwich Baptist Church, 869.2437
- Stanwich Congregational Church, 661.4420

Boy Scouts of America

Greenwich Council, 63 Mason Street, 869.8424

www.GreenwichBSA.com

The Seton Reservation at 363 Riversville Road is a great treasure. Day camp is available for boys in grades 1 to 4 with no prior Scouting experience. The camp does a good job of teaching outdoor sports such as swimming, archery, canoeing and fishing.

Bruce Museum

869.0376

www.brucemuseum.org

Weeklong summer workshops held at Tod's Point. Co ed ages 6 - 9 years. For older children Palette, Brushes and Paint At the Bruce Museum; Co-ed, ages 7 - 13. Explores the basics of painting.

Brunswick School Baseball Camp

100 Maher Avenue, 625.5822

www.brunswickschool.org

Six one-week summer baseball camps for boys ages 7 - 13, as well as co-ed summer play camps for ages 3 - 5.

Bush Holley Camps

39 Strickland Road, Cos Cob, 552.5329

www.Hstg.org

• Summer History Camp: 2-week sessions focusing on history and art. Co-ed, grades 2 - 4.
• Young Artists Camp, grades 5 - 7.

Camp Pelican

471 North Street, Greenwich, 869.4000 or 869.4243

www.pelicandaycamp.com

Established in 1965, this day camp provides instruction in a variety of outdoor and indoor activities. The camp begins in June and ends in August. Sessions are four to seven weeks. Co-ed ages 3 - 13. Capacity 500. The camp is located on the campus of Greenwich Catholic School.

summer camps

Camp Simmons

744 Lake Avenue, 869.0176
Run by the Boys and Girls Club of Greenwich, 869.3224
www.BGCG.org
Two-month session includes canoeing, swimming, field sports, archery, and nature hikes. Camp for ages 6 - 12.

Camp Sunbeam

254 East Putnam Avenue, 869.6600 x 11
www.christchurchgreenwich.com
Run by Christ Episcopal Church and Temple Sholom. Two 3-week sessions.
Daily from 9 - 3 with about 55 children in each.
Focus on crafts, sports, games and music for ages 5 - 8 years.

Cardinal Baseball Camp

Directed by Greenwich High Varsity Coach, Mike Mora, 869.3736
www.cardinalbaseballcamp.com
For players ages 7 - 13; held at GHS from 9 am - noon.

Children's Day School

139 East Putnam Avenue, 869.5395
Ages 3 - 7. Art, cooking, creative movement and music.

Computer Camps

• emaginationComputer Camps

877.248.0206
www.computercamps.com
Email: camp@computercamps.com
For the kid who can think of nothing but computers. Like-minded children come from all over the world to learn programming, computer graphics and rocketry. The closest camp is just outside Boston.

• iD tech Camps

888.709.8324
www.internalDrive.com
Princeton, Columbia, Vassar and Sacred Heart all have programs for children ages 7 - 17 from beginner to advanced.

summer camps

Connecticut All Star Lacrosse Clinic
Held at Greenwich Country Day School, Old Church Road, 863.5675
www.GCDS.net
Lacrosse clinic is co-ed for all levels grades 2 to 8.

Connecticut Children's Musical Theater
at Arch Street Teen Center, Arch Street, 852 9275
www.ArchStreet.org
Co-ed day camp for ages 8 to 13. Children create a musical which they perform for their parents.

Creative Summer at The Mead School
1095 Riverbank Road, Stamford 595.9500 x 63
For boys and girls ages 6½ to 16 interested in dance, painting, design, drawing and more.

Department of Parks and Recreation
622.7830
www.greenwichct.virtualtownhall.net/Public_Documents/
GreenwichCT_ParkRec/GreenwichCT_Recreation/programs/summer
There is a great variety of town-sponsored co-ed camps, such as Kamp Kairphree (ages 5 to 12), the Music and Art Program (children ages 8 - 15 who have had at least one year of study with an instrument) and Future Stars Tennis Camp (ages 6 - 14). Don't forget to ask for their program bulletin.
- Baseball programs:
- Co-ed T Ball for 5 & 6 year olds.
- Small Fry Baseball 7 to 9 year olds.

ESF Sports Camp
869.4444
www.esfcamps.com
Held at the Greenwich Academy, 200 North Maple Avenue.
Open to boys and girls.
- Day Camp (Crafts, Sports, Music) ages 4 - 8
- Sports Camp (8 sports), ages 7 - 14
- Senior Camp (Sports, Arts & Adventures), ages 9 - 15
- Tennis Camp (full or half-day), ages 6 to 15. Full or 2-day for beginner, intermediate and advanced players.

summer camps

Field Club Squash Camp

276 Lake Avenue, 869.1309
A private club that offers a weekly Junior Summer Squash Camp, sometimes open to the public. The camp instructors are some of the best players in the world.

First Church Day Camp

First Congregational Church, 108 Sound Beach Avenue
637.1791
www.fccog.org
Co-ed day camp for ages 3 to 9. Beach activities, games, music and sports.

Future Stars Sports Camps

546 Bedford Rd, Armonk, NY, 914.273.8500
www.fscamps.com
In its 27th year, this camp allows boys and girls, ages 6-16, to focus on a sport of their choice: tennis, soccer, lacrosse, basketball, baseball, softball, even sports and computer, circus arts and magic. Programs run 9 am - 4 pm at SUNY Purchase College and some Greenwich locations.

Gan Israel Camp

180 Lake Avenue 629.9059
www.campgan.com
Run by Chabad Lubavitch of Greenwich, provides traditional camp activities for ages 20 months - 3 years, and 4 to 11 years. Co-ed. July.

Gilman Lacrosse Camps

877.536.2267
Greenwich camp taught at Greenwich Middle
www.gilmanlacrosse.com
Summer day camps for boys and girls, grades 1 to 11.

Girls Inc. Summer Camp

PO Box 4040, Greenwich, CT 531.3322, 531.5699
www.girlsinc.org
Camp for 6 to 8th grade girls. Girls can sign up for individual weeks or longer sessions. The camp presents science and math in a fun atmosphere. Several campers have won science awards.

summer camps

Greenwich Academy Squash Training Camp
200 North Maple Avenue, 625.8900
During the summer, the Academy uses their five international squash courts to provide training for children in grades 5 and above.

Greenwich Country Day School
Old Church Road, 863.5601
www.GCDS.net
Summer day camps for ages 4 - 12. Now in its 48th year, they have many programs for each age group, including swimming, tennis, arts, crafts, computers, woodworking and sailing.

Greenwich Flame Basketball Camp
203.613.2262
www.flamecamp.com
Summer co-ed day camp for ages 7 - 15 and co-ed specialized skills clinic for ages 8 - 12.

Greenwich Public Schools Summer Program
Western Middle School, 531.7977
www.greenwichschools.org
Enrichment and review courses for all students from pre-K to grade 12.

Greenwich Racquet Club Tennis and Sports Camp
1 River Road, Cos Cob, 661.0606, Contact: Ricardo Leon
www.GreenwichRacquetClub.com
Tennis and sports camp for children ages 4 - 7 and 8-16.

Greenwich Crew
49 River Road, Cos Cob, 661.4033
www.GreenwichWaterClub.com
ages 12 to 18.

Greenwich Skate Park Summer Ramp Camp
100 South Arch Street, 496.9876 or 622 7821
www.greenwichct.org
Director: Harry Lefflebine
Ages 6 - 12.

CHILDREN

Greenwich Youth Stage Summer Workshop
Temple Sholom, 300 East Putnam Avenue, 914.484.2605
Chandra Lee Mann, Artistic Director
Ages 9 - 18.

Intro Sports, Junior 5 Star Basketball
203.938.9996
www.introsportsusa.com
Sponsored by the Greenwich Parks and Recreation Department, it provides high quality instruction for boys and girls, pre-K through the 5th grade. Camps begin in June.

Mad Science Summer Camp
888.381.9754
www.madscience.org/connecticut
Sponsored by Mad Science and the Greenwich Department of Parks and Recreation. Programs for children ages 6 to 12.

Manhattanville College
2900 Purchase Street, Purchase, NY, 914.323.5214
www.mville.edu
The college (914.694.2200) provides a summer writing workshop for young people in grades 4 - 11, and hosts a number of sports camps, including soccer, basketball and tennis.

Nike Swim Camps
800.645.3226
www.us sportscamps.com
Nike runs a number of swim camps around the country for boys and girls ages 10 to 18. The Peddie School program (June and July) in Hightstown, NJ is the closest.

Nike Volleyball Camps
800.645.322
www.us sportscamps.com
Nike sponsors a number of volleyball camps around the country for ages 13 to 18. The closest camp is at Cornell University, Ithaca, NY.

Nike Golf Schools and Junior Camps

800.645.3226

www.us sportscamps.com

Nike sponsors a great number of adult and junior golf camps. The closest are Williams College, Williamstown, MA; Stowe, VT and Loomis Chaffee, Windsor, CT.

Nike Tennis Camps

800.645.3226

www.us sportscamps.com

Nike sponsors a great number of adult and junior tennis camps. The closest are: Amherst College, Amherst, MA; Loomis Chaffee, Windsor, CT; Peddie School, Hightstown, NJ; Lawrenceville School, Lawrenceville, NJ.

Project Fitness Camp

PO Box 1072, Greenwich, CT, 861.6835

www.projectfitnessonline.com

Held at North Street Elementary, this camp is designed to improve your child's performance at any sport. They emphasize strength, speed and fitness.

Purchase College

735 Anderson Hill Road, Purchase, NY, 914.251.6500

www.Purchase.edu

The State University of New York (SUNY) at Purchase offers a number of Summer Youth Programs in the Arts (art, music, and acting) for ages 6 - 17. They have early drop-off and extended-day options.

Robin Hood Camp

Herrick Road, Brooksville, ME, 831.659.9143 (winter)

207.359.8313 (summer)

www.robinhoodcamp.com

One of the best all around camps in the US. It has a strong Greenwich connection. Proud to count myself as an alumnus.

summer camps

Saint Paul's Summer Camp
200 Riverside Avenue, Riverside, 637.3503
Camp for children 3-6; art, dance, sports, music, water play & nature.

Sandpiper's Beach Camp
637.3659
www.ogrcc.com
Sponsored by the Old Greenwich Riverside Community Center for children ages 3 -10.

Silvermine School of Art
New Canaan, CT, 203.966.6668
www.silvermineart.org
Creative summer camp for the artistically inclined, ages 5 - 17. Learn painting, drawing, photography and sculpture on an attractive 4-acre campus.

U.S. Academy of Gymnastics
6 Riverside Avenue, 637.3303
Tumble Bugs Day Camp.

Whitby School Summer Camp
www.whitbyschool.org
969 Lake Avenue, 869.8464
• Co-ed, ages 4 - 6. Montessori staff teaches gardening, cooking, arts, crafts and nature study; as well as math and science enrichment.
• Co-ed, ages 7-14, multi-sports camp.

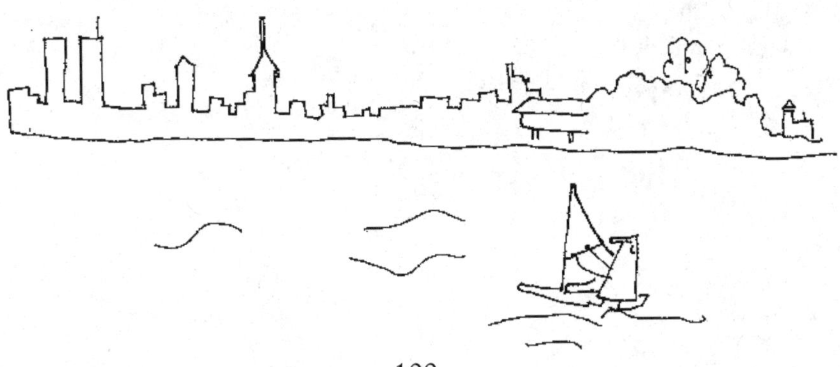

CHILDREN

Windswept Farm

107 June Road, Stamford, CT, 322.4984
Co-ed ages 5 - 17
Weekly horseback riding, horse care, grooming, show prep and games.
No previous riding experience necessary.

YMCA

50 East Putnam Avenue, 869.1630
www.gwymca.org
Summer Fun Clubs four 2-week co-ed sessions begin at the end of June.
They include field trips, sports, and environmental education.

YWCA

259 East Putnam Avenue, 869.6501, ext. 225
www.ywcagreenwich.org
• Camp Ta Yi To is a co-ed camp for grades K to 5; includes swimming
and tennis.
• Pre-school Camp, ages 15 months - 2 years; songs, stories, play.
• Pre-school Camp, ages 3 - 5; gymnastics, swimming, cooking.
• Dance Camp, ages 10 - 16; Ballet, jazz, choreography, hip hop.

TIP: LYME DISEASE
Ticks, unfortunately, also live in Greenwich, even some carrying Lyme
Disease. If you remove a tick you might want to take it (dead or
alive) to the Department of Health in Town Hall. They will test it for
the Lyme Disease bacteria. For information on Lyme disease, call the
Greenwich Lyme Disease Task Force at 203.969.1333
www.timeforlyme.org or
www.cdc.gov/ncidod/diseases/submenus/sub_lyme.htm

support services

ARC Greenwich
50 Glenville Street, 531.1880
www.arcgreenwich.org
Family support services and after-school programs for families of children with special needs.

Child Guidance Center of Southern Connecticut
23 Benedict Place, 983.5294; 24/hour crisis line, 203.323.9797
www.childguidancect.org
Professionally staffed mental health center for children and adolescents. Individual, group and family therapy, parent guidance, 24-hour crisis services, and community education programs.

Community Answers
622.7979
www.communityanswers.org
Information on parent education programs, support groups, crisis programs, counseling services, nannies, au pair and babysitting services.

Family Centers
40 Arch Street, 869.4848
20 Bridge Street, 629.2822
www.familycenters.org
This United Way human service agency offers a multitude of helpful programs such as the Den for Grieving Kids and individual or family counseling.

Family Health
Greenwich Department of Health, 622.6488 or 622.7836
Prenatal and postpartum home visits, well child clinics (birth to age 5), immunization and hypertension screening clinic (5 years to adult); school health services; early childhood/daycare licenses.

Kids in Crisis
1 Salem Street, Cos Cob, 203.327.5437
www.kidsincrisis.org
Crisis intervention counseling and short term shelter.
Ages: Newborn to 17 years.

support services

Le Leche League

869.5344

www.lalecheleague.org

Support groups and information on breastfeeding.

Parents' Exchange

25 Valley Drive, Greenwich Health at Greenwich Hospital

863.3780, 863.4444

Weekly discussion groups led by child development specialists. A good environment to stimulate and provide parents with opportunities to exchange ideas. Parents are grouped by their children's age from infants to adolescents. Babysitting is available.

Parents Together

PO Box 4843, Greenwich, CT, 06831-0417

869.1789 or 203.329.2234

An independent, non-profit organization working in cooperation with the PTA Council and public and independent schools in Greenwich. They publish two good newsletters, one for parents of children from birth - fifth grade and another for grades 6 - 12. For an annual subscription, send a check for $10 and indicate the newsletter you want to receive.

Parent to Parent Network

50 Glenville Street, 629.1880, x 300

Information network for families with children who have special needs.

Tender Beginnings

At Greenwich Hospital, 863.3655

www.greenhosp.org/programs_tb.asp

Expectant parent classes, Lamaze classes, baby care and breastfeeding classes, nutrition, prenatal exercise, newborn parenting groups, grandparenting, baby food preparation, babysitting, sibling classes.

CLUBS/ORGANIZATIONS

community

This partial list of Community Clubs and Organizations will give you an idea of the multitude of interests in Greenwich. The energy, enthusiasm and brilliance of individuals in these organizations is remarkable, as is the abundance of good works they accomplish.
* *Garden Clubs are listed in the section FLOWERS & GARDENS*
* *Volunteer Organizations are described in more detail on our website www.GreenwichVolunteerGuide.com*
* *Information about clubs and organizations is also* available from Community Answers www.greenwichlibrary.org

AARP

Greenwich Chapter 1210
www.aarp.org
www.benefitscheckup.org
Louise Burns President, 531.4572

Alliance Francaise of Greenwich

299 Greenwich Avenue (Greenwich Arts Center 2nd Floor)
www.AFGreenwich.org
629.1340

AmeriCares

88 Hamilton Avenue, Stamford, CT
www.americares.org
658.9500

American Association of University Women

Greenwich/Stamford/Darien Branch
www.aauw.org
800.326.2289 ext 160

American Legion

Greenwich Post 29
248 Glenville Road, 531.0109
Emile Smeriglio, Commander

American Pen Women

Greenwich Branch
www.penwomen.org
Ann Caron, President, 869.8313

American Pen Women
Connecticut Pioneer Branch
www.penwomen.org
Constance Walton, Membership Chairman, 637.0213

American Red Cross
Greenwich Chapter
99 Indian Field Road, 869.8444
www.greenwichredcross.org

Archaeological Associates of Greenwich
33 Byram Drive, 661.4654
www.people.brandeis.edu/~jbernard/brucemuseum/lectures.html
Archaeology Briefs Blog www.archaeologybriefs.blogspot.com
Nancy Stone Bernard, Director

Art Society of Old Greenwich
PO Box 103, Old Greenwich
www.sidewalkartshow.com
Gretchen Tatge, President, 637.9949

Astronomical Society of Greenwich
Bowman Observatory at Julian Curtiss Elementary, 869.6786 x 338

Audubon Society of Greenwich
613 Riversville Road, 869.5272
www.greenwich.center.audubon.org
Tom Baptist, Executive Director

Boys & Girls Club of Greenwich
4 Horseneck Lane, 869.3224
www.bgcg.org
Robert DeAngelo, Executive Director

Breast Cancer Alliance
48 Maple Avenue
www.breastcanceralliance.org
Mary Ann Henry, Executive Director, 861.0014
Polly Hyman, President

community

Button and Bows
(Bob Button Orchestra)
Bob Button, Director
Peggy de la Cruz, 977.8627

Children of the American Revolution
Mary Bush Society, Putnam Cottage
243 East Putnam Avenue
Contact: Katie Bacon, Senior Registrar, 637.6789

Common Threads Quilters
Greenwich Arts Center, Barbara Hicks, 322.0221

Council of Churches and Synagogues
(Interfaith Council of Southwestern Connecticut)
461 Glenbrook Road, Stamford, CT, 322.9417
www.interfaithcouncil.org
Rev. Dale Pauls, Executive Director

Daughters of the American Revolution
Putnam Hill Chapter
243 East Putnam Avenue, 869.9697
www.dar.org/chapters/putnam.htm

Friends of Binney Park
Nancy Standard, 637.9894

Friends of the Byram Shubert Library
www.greenwichlibrary.org/byram2.htm
Lise Jameson, 531.0426

Friends of the Cos Cob Library
Cos Cob Library, 5 Sinawoy
Mary Jane (MJ) Brogan, President, 622.6883

Friends of Greenwich Point
PO Box 711, Old Greenwich, 06870
www.friendsofgreenwichpoint.org
Anne Orum, 869.7410

Friends of the Greenwich Library
www.greenwichlibrary.org
Susan Ferris, 625.6550, 622.7938

Friends of Grass Island
Sylvester Pecora, Sr., Chairman
Jo Conboy, Secretary, 661.6343

Friendship Ambassadors Foundation
299 Greenwich Avenue, 622.7420 or 542.0652
www.faf.org
Patrick Scuiarratta, Executive Director

German Club of Greenwich
Freunde Deutscher Sprache
PO Box 7733, Greenwich
Heilwig Barker, President, 322.6840

Glenville Senior Citizens
Western Greenwich Civic Center
Bernice Carroll, President, 637.0134

Greenwich Art Society
Greenwich Arts Center, 299 Greenwich Avenue, 629.1533
www.greenwichartsociety.com
Liana Moonie & Douglas More, Co-Presidents

Greenwich Chamber of Commerce
45 East Putnam Avenue, 869.3500
www.greenwichchamber.com
Mary Ann Morrison, President & CEO

Greenwich Democratic Town Committee
PO Box 126, Greenwich 06836
www.greenwichdemocrats.org
Jim Himes, Chairman, cell: 917.443.7255

community

Greenwich Hospital Auxiliary
Greenwich Hospital, 5 Perryridge Road
Auxiliary office: 863.3220
Medicare Assistance: 863.3222
Barbara Khouri, President,

Greenwich Jaycees
PO Box 232, Greenwich 06836
www.greenwichjaycees.org
Maria Larrea, President, 358.3134

Greenwich Kiwanis Club
PO Box 183, Greenwich 06836
www.greenwichkiwanis.org
Nick Edwards, President, 869.4250

Greenwich Land Trust
132 East Putnam Avenue (Food Mart Building)
2 East, Suite D Cos Cob
PO Box 1152, Greenwich 06836-1152
www.gltrust.org
Van Parker, Executive Director, 629.2151

Greenwich Old Timers Athletic Association
PO Box 558, Greenwich 06836
Dr. Jeff Ranta, President, 637.8119

Greenwich Point Conservancy
www.greenwichpoint.org
Chris Franco, President, 637.6806
Sue Baker, Treasurer, 637.4610

Greenwich Recycling Advisory Board (GRAB)
Greenwich Town Hall, department of Public Works
Sally Davies, Chair, 531.0006

Greenwich Republican Roundtable
Scott Franz, Chairman, 629.9889

community

Greenwich Republican Town Committee
P.O. Box 4030 Greenwich CT 06831
www.greenwichgop.com
John Raben, Chair

Greenwich Riding and Trails Association
PO Box 1403 Greenwich CT 06836-1403
661.3062

Greenwich Seniors Club
John Titsworth, President 531.6618
Jean Connaughton, Membership, 637.1251

Greenwich Women's Civic Club
PO Box 26, Greenwich 06836
Jackie Cannon, President, 353.9100

Greenwich Women's Exchange
28 Sherwood Place, 869.0229
Veronica Schmitz, President

Greenwich World Hunger
PO Box 7444
Sarah Boyle, President, 661.9771

Hadassah, Greenwich Chapter
Temple Sholom, 300 East Putnam Avenue
Fran Blaustein, Co-President, 622.0225
Felice Robinou, Co-President, 625.9666

Historical Society of the Town of Greenwich
39 Strickland Road, Cos Cob
www.hstg.org
Debra Mecky, Executive Director, 869.6899

Japan Education Center
15 Ridgeway, 629.5922
Ryuichiro Shima, Director

Junior League of Greenwich
231 East Putnam Ave, 869.1979
www.jlgreenwich.org
Eileen Bartels, President

League of Women Voters of Greenwich
PO Box 604, 352.4700
www.lwvct.org/greenwich
Donna Nicktis, President
Jara Burnett, Co-President
Rosemarie Skoglund, Co President

Lions Club of Greenwich
PO Box 1044 Greenwich CT 06836-1044
www.lionsclubs.org
Rick Brooks, President, 598.1727 x9101

Lions Club of Old Greenwich
PO Box 215, Old Greenwich CT 06870
www.lionsclubs.org
Jim Stafford, President, 637.9292

Lions Club of Western Greenwich
www.lionsclubs.org
Jack Nearing, President, 922.4123

Missionaries on Call
(Volunteers on Call)
29 Sachem Lane, Greenwich CT 06830
www.volunteersoncall.com
Roxana Bowgen, President, 550.2222

NOW, Greenwich Chapter
PO Box 245, Cos Cob
www.now.org
Irene Senter, President, 661.4453

Organization of Chinese Americans
Fairfield County Chapter
P.O. Box 16492 Stamford CT 06905
www.oca-fc.org
Miriam Yeung President, 860.677.9442
Fang Zhou VP-Membership
Tak Eng, Treasurer, 637.5512

P.E.O. Sisterhood, Greenwich Chapter
www.peointernational.org
Dottie Angel, President,661.4579

Pegasus Therapeutic Riding
Office: 356.9504
www.pegasustr.org
Betty Foulk, Chapter Chair, 661.8738

Philoptochos
www.philoptochos.org
Despina Fassuliotis, 661.5991

Planned Parenthood
1039 East Main Street, Stamford, CT 327.2722,
Emergency 900.820.2488
www.ppct.org

Retired Men's Association
50 East Putnam Avenue (YMCA)
James Fahy, 531.6075

Rotary Club of Byram-Cos Cob
PO Box 4632, Valley Drive Station
www.rotary.org
Tomas Menten, President, 622.0458

Rotary Club of Greenwich
PO Box 1375 Greenwich CT 06836
www.greenwichrotary.org
Vince Glenn, President, 356.8633

community

Round Hill Country Dances
Round Hill Community House
www.roundhill.net
Bernie Koser, President, 914.244.7248
For information call 215.4299

Trout Unlimited (Mianus Chapter)
PO Box 663, Riverside CT 06878
www.mianustu.org www.tu.org
703.522.0200 National Headquarters (Arlington VA)

UJA Federation of Greenwich
One Holly Hill Lane, 622.1434
www.ujafedgreenwich.org
Pamela Ehrenkranz, Executive Director

United Way of Greenwich
1 Lafayette Court, 869.2221
www.unitedway-greenwich.com
Stuart Adelberg, President

Veterans of Foreign Wars
Cos Cob Post 10112
PO Box 8, Cos Cob 06807
www.vfw.org
Mike Benvenuto, Commander, 637.4044

Veterans of Foreign Wars
Greenwich Post 1792
PO Box 128, Greenwich
www.vfw.org
James Clifford, Quartermaster, 326.0773

Woman's Club of Greenwich
89 Maple Avenue, 869.2046
Marie C. Krumeich, President

community

YMCA

50 East Putnam Avenue, 869.1630
www.gwymca.org
John P. Eikrem, President and C.E.O.
Contact: Pamela Hearn, Director of Development and Marketing

YWCA

259 East Putnam Avenue, 869.6501
www.ywcagreenwich.org
Adrianne Singer, Director

TIP: HOW TO GET ON A TOWN BOARD
OR COMMISSION

There are a number of independent boards and commissions that are completely volunteer and yet have great power in how the Town runs. The Board of Selectmen interviews candidates and recommends their appointment to the Representative Town Meeting (RTM). The Appointments Committee of the RTM and one or more of the other RTM standing committees will interview the candidate. The nomination is then brought to the RTM for a vote. If you are interested in serving on one of these boards you can nominate yourself or talk to the Selectman's nomination committee by going to:
http://greenwichct.virtualtownhall.net/Public_Documents/
GreenwichCT_FirstSelect/committees/nominations/index

country clubs

Greenwich has a number of country clubs. Costs to join a country club vary from about $5,000 to $40,000 for the initiation fee with annual dues ranging from approximately $2,000 to more than $4,000. Country clubs with golf courses are typically the most expensive. Clubs with dining rooms usually require a quarterly food minimum. In addition, country clubs may have assessments for capital improvements. Membership in most private clubs requires a proposer and one or more seconders who are members. Therefore, the more members you know, the easier it is to join. Clubs which serve a particular area, such as Belle Haven or Milbrook, often give preference to area residents. The waiting period to join a club can be several years.

Bailiwick Club of Greenwich
(Swimming and tennis)
Duncan Drive, 531.7591 (summer)
Tennis Shop: 531.8480
Mark Hatten, Manager

Burning Tree Country Club
(Dining, golf, swimming, tennis, paddle tennis)
120 Perkins Road, 869.9004
John Schoelner, Manager

Fairview Country Club
(Dining, golf, tennis, paddle tennis, swimming)
1241 King Street, 531.6200
www.fairviewcountryclub.org
Timothy Clinton, Manager

Field Club
(Dining, tennis (grass & indoor), squash, paddle tennis, swimming)
276 Lake Avenue, 869.1300
Martina Halsey, Manager

Greenwich Country Club
(Dining, golf, tennis, squash, paddle tennis, swimming, skeet)
19 Doubling Road, 869.1000
Jim Cirillo, Manager

country clubs

Innis Arden Golf Club
(Dining, golf, tennis, paddle tennis, swimming)
120 Tomac Avenue, Old Greenwich, 637.6900

Milbrook Club
(Dining, golf, swimming, paddle tennis, tennis)
61 Woodside Drive, 869.4540
Scott Kloster, Manager

Round Hill Club
(Dining, golf, swimming, tennis, skeet)
33 Round Hill Club Road, 869.2350
Dennis Meermans, Manager

Stanwich Club
(Dining, golf, swimming, tennis, paddle tennis)
888 North Street, 869.0555
Peter Tunley, Manager

Tamarack Country Club
(Dining, golf, swimming, tennis)
55 Locust Road, 531.7300
Brian Gillespie, Manager

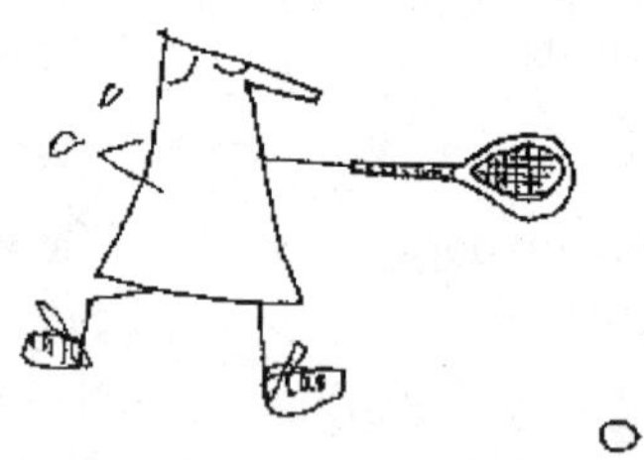

newcomers clubs

Several organizations are designed to help new residents make friends and feel welcome.

Greenwich Newcomers' & Neighbors' Club

YWCA, 259 East Putnam Avenue, 869.6501
www.greenwichnewcomers.com
Kathy Ferraro, President, 625.4899
Robin Pastore, Events Co Chairman, 249.7871
The club has a comprehensive program of coffees, luncheons, dinners and special interest groups. Be sure to ask for their excellent newsletter. The Y playroom is available for baby-sitting during daytime events. A good resource whether you have lived in Greenwich for two weeks or twenty years.

International Club of the YWCA

YWCA, 259 East Putnam Avenue
www.ywcagreenwich.org
Bessie del Castillo, President, 968.9111
For luncheon reservations contact Rashida Ahmed, 869.3032
Founded in 1975, the club holds monthly functions to help women of all nationalities who are new to Greenwich make friends in the community. New members, including Americans, are welcome.

OGRNC (Old Greenwich-Riverside) Newcomers' Club

PO Box 256, Old Greenwich, CT 06870
www.greenwichnewcomers.com
Mairead Finn, President, 698.2382
Elaine Krikorian, Membership Chairman, 340.9148
The Club is 44 years old and hosts a great variety of functions, from wine tastings to museum trips. There are events for everyone, and they welcome new and established residents of Greenwich and surrounding areas. Be sure to ask for their excellent newsletter.

CLUBS/ORGANIZATIONS

skating club

Greenwich Skating Club
Cardinal Road, Greenwich, 863.5602
www.greenwichskatingclub.org
An always popular club, apply early. You must be proposed by a member.
Your children must be interested in actively participating in their hockey
or figure skating programs.

yacht clubs

As one might expect for a town on the water, Greenwich has a number of
excellent yacht and boating clubs. Many yacht clubs have long waiting
lists (some as long as 12 years).

Belle Haven Club
(Dining, boating, tennis, swimming)
100 Harbor Drive, 861.5353
Neil P. MacKenzie, Manager

Byram Shore Boat Club
PO Box 4335
Byram Park, 531.9858 (clubhouse)
Jeffrey Stempien, Commodore, 531.6141
Mooring/docking adjacent to town park and beach.

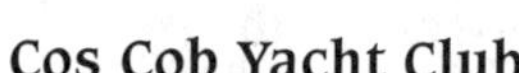

Cos Cob Yacht Club
PO Box 155, Riverside CT 06878
Walter X. Burns, Jr, Commodore, 661.5946

Greenwich Boat & Yacht Club
(Club House, Mooring/docking and picnic areas)
Grass Island, PO Box 40 Greenwich, CT 06830
www.gbyc.org
Dick Grabarz, Commodore, 637.1151

Indian Harbor Yacht Club
(Dining and boating facilities including mooring/docking)
710 Steamboat Road, 869.2484
www.indianharboryc.com
Peter J. Commiskey, Commodore
David Foster, Manager

yacht clubs

Mianus River Boat & Yacht Club
98 Strickland Road, Cos Cob, 869.4689
www.mrbyc.com
Frank Mazza, Commodore, 869.0145
Boat and yacht club open to any Greenwich resident. Meets the first Monday of the month at 7:30 pm at the clubhouse.

Old Greenwich Yacht Club
PO Box 162, Old Greenwich, 637.3074
www.ogyc.org
Gene Fignar, Commodore
Membership is open to all Greenwich residents
Clubhouse, launch and moorings are handled through the town hall.

Riverside Yacht Club
(Dining, swimming, beach, tennis and boating)
102 Club Road, Riverside, 637.1706
www.riversideyc.org
Bob Goodchild, Commodore
Gary Ashley, Manager

Rocky Point Club
(Clubhouse, mooring, salt water pool)
Rocky Point Road, Old Greenwich, 637.2397 (summer only)
PO Box 359
Alex Fraser, Commodore

Water Club
(Dining, swimming, aquatics, fitness, boating, rowing)
49 River Road, Cos Cob, 661.4033
www.GreenwichWaterClub.com
Carla Catanzaro, General Manager
Applications for membership are available at the front desk.

CONSIGNMENT & THRIFT SHOPS

Thrift Shops and Consignment Shops are "win-win" for everyone! Donating your unwanted possessions to thrift shops is a practical way to help our neighbors in need. Proceeds from these shops, which are often run by volunteers, go to helping others.

Consigning your unwanted possessions is a good way to dispose of items without holding a tag sale or selling on e-bay. Without doubt, your unwanted item is bound to be another person's treasure. With our wish to help others and recycling our mission, donate, consign and explore the shops for fabulous buys!

See BOOKS for Book donations

See SERVICES for Computer and Cell Phone donations

consignment shops

Consign It (Clothing, Furniture)
115 Mason Street, 869.9836

This shop is a good place to consign and a good place to buy. Not a lot of display room, as a result they are often light on furniture. During the summer months, they are able to display a wider variety by using an outdoor tent. A good source for pre-owned jewelry, silver and china. Fairly priced. They do high-level tag sales.

Hours: Monday - Saturday, 10 am - 5 pm.

Consigned Couture (Clothing)
134 East Putnam Avenue

(entrance from Milbank Avenue), 869.7795

Consigned designer clothing for women.

Hours: Monday - Saturday, 10 am - 5 pm.

Consigned Designs by Ellen (Clothing)
115 Mason Street (Village Square off Mason Street), 869.2165

Designer consignments for women and children.

Hours: Monday - Saturday, 10 am - 5 pm.

Drapery Exchange (Drapery)
1064 Boston Post Road, Darien, CT, 203.655.3844

What a great idea! A consignment shop for beautiful draperies. Some almost new. None over 3 years old.

Hours: weekdays, 10 am - 5 pm; Saturday, 10 am - 1 pm.

consignment shops

Estate Treasures of Greenwich (Furniture)

1162 East Putnam Avenue, Riverside, 637.4200

www.EstateTreasures.com

An antique consignment shop which has a wide selection of jewelry and china. A good source for silver services and serving pieces. A large number of tables and desks, although some are high-quality reproductions (always marked as reproductions).

Hours: Monday - Saturday, 10 am - 5:30 pm; Sunday, noon - 5:30 pm.

Roundabout (Clothing)

48 West Putnam Avenue, 552.0787

Clothes must be from a wellknown designer, in perfect condition, and less than two years old to be consigned. The store also buys show and end-of-season stock from designers.

Hours: every day except Sunday, 10 am - 5 pm.

Silk Purse (Furniture)

118 Main Street, New Canaan, CT, 203.972.0898

www.thesilkpurse.com

Nice quality consignment shop for furniture, silver and jewelry.

Hours: Monday - Saturday, 10 am - 5 pm; Sunday, noon - 5 pm.

Directions: Merritt Parkway N to exit 37, L on Rte 124/South Street, R on Elm, L on Main.

e-bay consignment

i-SOLD-it (Consignment, eBay)

• 607 Main Ave (Rt. 7 across from the DMV), Norwalk
203.845.0290

• 1299 North Ave (Quaker Ridge Shopping Cntr), New Rochelle
NY 914.636.1981

www.isoldit.com

A chain of 180 stores, helping people sell their items on eBay. They photograph, write copy, ship and collect payment for you. The item must sell for at least $75. Their commission is 33% - 25% of the money received, depending upon the value of the item.

Hours: Norwalk, Monday- Saturday, 10 am - 7 pm.

Hours: New Rochelle, Tuesday - Friday, 10 am - 6 pm; Saturday to 5 pm.

thrift shops

Act II Consignment Shop (Clothing)

48 Maple Avenue, 869.6359

In a lovely old stone house behind the Second Congregational Church there are five rooms of gently worn women's, men's and children's clothing. Also bricabrac and small household items.

Store Hours: Wednesday, 10 am - 5 pm; Thursday and Saturday 10 am - 1:30 pm.

Consignment Hours: Wednesday noon - 3 pm; Thursday, 10 am - 1 pm. Closed June through September.

Goodwill Industries of Western CT (Clothing, Home)

Greenwich Recycling Center, Holly Hill Lane, 576.0000, 800.423.9787 www.goodwillwct.com

A large trailer with a friendly person ready to receive your donations is conveniently parked just inside our town "dump." Goodwill needs clothing, shoes, toys, tools, kitchenware, linens and small appliances in "saleable" condition. This is recycling in the true sense of the word.

Hours: weekdays, 7 am - 3 pm; Saturday, 7 am - noon.

Greenwich Hospital Thrift Shop (Clothing, Furniture)

29 B Sherwood Place, 869.6124

Large furniture items plus clothing and books are welcome here. Our finds: an old steamer trunk and a lovely white Laura Ashley graduation dress for $45! One of our friends found a chesterfield coat! A holiday sale had so many people, the customers were waiting in line to get inside for embroidered sweaters and evening gowns.

Hours: weekdays, 9 am - 5:30 pm; Saturday, 10 am - 4 pm.

MerryGoRound (Clothing)

38 Arch Street, 869.3155

Clothing and small objects are all neatly displayed.

Our finds: two pretty framed watercolors and a tennis skirt for $3.

Hours: Tuesday - Saturday, 10 am - 3 pm; Closed July and August.

CONSIGNMENT & THRIFT SHOPS

thrift shops

Laurel House Thrift Shop (Clothing, Furniture)
501 Summer Street, Stamford, CT, 327.7334
www.laurelhouse.net
They will pick up items or you can drop them off.
Proceeds from their sales helps educate, house and clothe people with mental illness.
Hours: Monday - Saturday, 9 am - 4 pm.

Rummage Room (Clothing)
191 Sound Beach Avenue, Old Greenwich, 637.1875
Notice the artistic window displays of this gem of a shop manned by cheerful volunteers. The shop is filled with clothing for young and old and interesting bricabrac.
Shop Hours: weekdays 10 am - 5 pm; Saturdays, 10 am - 1 pm.
Donation Hours: Monday - Thursday, 9 am - 5 pm;
Fridays, until 1 pm; Saturdays, 10 am - 1 pm. Closed in August.

TIP: HAVING A TAG SALE
No Town permit is required. The best days for sales are Saturday and Sunday 9 am - 4 pm. The best seasons are Fall and Spring. Avoid sales on or near a holiday. Advertise one week before and the weekend of the sale in The Greenwich Time (629.2204) in Friday Tag Sale section.
If you are planning a large sale, off-duty Greenwich Police can help you manage crowds. Call the traffic division (622.8016). Professional Tag Sale managers typically charge from 20% to 30% commission, depending on the services rendered.

donations only

Salvation Army (Clothing, Furniture)

Truck pickup: 800.958.7825

Stamford Thrift Shop, 896 Washington Blvd, 975.7630

www.salvationarmy.com

A marvelous service is available for picking up furniture for donation. Every time we have called, a courteous, strong man has arrived promptly to take items destined to help people serviced by this most worthy organization. 2 to 4 days' notice is appreciated for pickups. A bin for donations (clothing only) is located inside our Recycling Center on Holly Hill Lane.

Dispatcher Hours: Monday - Saturday, 7 am - 3 pm.

Green Demolitions (Kitchen & Bathroom Equipment)

15 East Putnam Avenue, Greenwich, 969.4354

www.GreenDemolitions.org

Before you consider a dumpster, call Steve Feldman. Donate your kitchen and bathroom equipment and appliances that are in good condition to this non-profit charity. They sell the items to the general public. Profits are given to the Answer to Addiction program.

Neighbor to Neighbor (Clothing, Food)

Christ Church Annex, 248 East Putnam Avenue, 622.9208

This volunteer organization is greatly respected and appreciated in our Greenwich community. They have helped many people in a sensitive way. Donations of food, warm coats and clothing (in good condition) are always needed. The shop is restricted to people identified by our social service agencies as "in need" and the selections made in the nicely organized shop are free.

Hours: weekdays, 8:30 am - 12:30 pm. Open two Saturdays every month.

CONTINUING ED for ADULTS

There are many language schools and other continuing education resources in and around the town. The following are some of our favorites. For additional information on art, dance or music instruction, see the appropriate section under CULTURE.

For Sports Instruction, see FITNESS & SPORTS.

art

Greenwich Arts Council (GAC)

299 Greenwich Avenue, 622.3998

www.greenwicharts.org

The GAC maintains a talent bank of all types of music, theater, dance and art teachers and publishes an informative newsletter three times a year. It is a good resource for classes as disparate as O-Tatsu Taiko Japanese drumming, classical ballet or acting.

Greenwich Art Society Art Classes

299 Greenwich Avenue, 629.1533

www.GreenwichArtSociety.org

A delightful place to study painting, drawing, botanical illustration, sculpture or monotype.

Silvermine Guild Art Center

New Canaan, CT, 203.966.6668 x 2

www.silvermineart.org

Excellent art instruction for adults and youngsters alike in famed art site.

Directions: Merritt Pkw N, exit 38; R onto Rte 123 N; straight until Rte 106 junction; R onto 106 N; at stop sign, R onto Silvermine Rd; 1 mile on R.

Westchester Art Workshop

196 Central Avenue (Westchester County Center),
White Plains, NY, 914.606.7500

www.Sunywcc.edu

They offer a wide variety of classes in fine arts, photography, commuter arts and crafts.

computer training

Diane McKeever, CPP

www.dianemckeever.com

If you want to learn a Microsoft program, you should enroll in one of Diane's Continuing Education classes at the Greenwich High School. But if you don't have the time, she gives private lessons for students of all levels. She is a CPP (Certified Patient Person).

Greenwich Continuing Education and Norwalk Community College have a large variety of computer education courses.

Find computer courses designed for seniors in the Seniors section.

cooking

Aux Delices Cooking School

23 Acosta Street, Stamford, 326.4540 x 108

Debra Ponzek, well known for her delicious Aux Delices foods, chef-instructor Lynn Manheim, and pastry chef Cyril Chaminade, have a series of hard to resist cooking classes, such as: Easy Asian Cooking, Tapas, Cooking with Kids, Cooking for the Jewish Holidays, Spa Cooking and For Chocolate Lovers Only. Usually, classes are for up to 20 people and cost $75 per person.

Chocopologie Cooking School

12 south Main Street, Norwalk, CT, 203.854.4754

Fritz Knipschildt, named one of the best chocolatiers in the world by *Gourmet Magazine*, shares his secrets for making chocolate truffles.

Cucina Casalinga

Wilton, CT, 203.762.0768

www.cucinacasalinga.com

Sally Maraventano has been teaching homestyle Italian cooking for over 15 years. She has daytime and evening classes and can accommodate groups as large as 15 students. Classes cost about $85 per person (which includes dinner).

cooking

Custom Culinary Classes

622.4040

Small group classes, run by Greenwich residents Mary May and Tracey Utton, graduates of the Institute of Culinary Education. Classes are held in Mary's own beautifully designed Greenwich kitchen or in your own kitchen. They teach the latest cuisine techniques, with easy-to-follow recipes which will make your next dinner party a raving success. She especially enjoys teaching people just learning to cook. A good shower or wedding gift. Classes are hands on, usually for about 6 people and are $100 per person.

Greenwich Continuing Education

Greenwich High School, 625.7474, 7475

www.greenwichschools.org/gce

Well-priced, well-taught classes. Besides their specialized courses, they often have classes in basic cookery for beginners. Check the Culinary Arts section of their catalog.

Institute of Culinary Education

50 West 23rd Street, NY, NY, 800.522.4610, 212.847.0700

www.iceculinary.com

Although this school is in New York City, it has from time to time conducted courses in the Greenwich area. Founded by Peter Kump, it has been in business since 1975 and has established a large Greenwich following. The school provides hands-on courses and workshops from 5 to 25 hours. The emphasis is on techniques of fine cooking. The average class size is 12 for hands-on instruction and 30 for demonstrations. The school has a staff of 45 who operate from a large facility with 9 kitchens. Hands-on classes range from $85 $525. For additional cooking schools in New York City try www.ShawGuides.com.

Lauren Groveman's Kitchen

55 Prospect Avenue, Larchmont, NY, 914.834.1372

www.laurengroveman.com

Established in 1990, the school provides 5-session participation courses as well as individual classes for adults and young people. The emphasis is on techniques and the preparation of comfort foods, breads and appetizers. The average class size is 6. Cost is $450 for a five-session course and $100 for a specialty course.

cooking

Ronnie Fein School of Creative Cooking

32 Heming Way, Stamford, 322.7114

Year-round cooking workshops with an emphasis on ingredients, techniques and menus. She also has children's classes or will tailor a course to fit your needs. Workshops are usually 4 people and cost $250 per session. She has been teaching cooking and writing food stories for the *Greenwich Time* for over 20 years.

Thali Indian Cooking School

87 Main Street, New Canaan, 203.972.8332
www.thali.com
What better place to learn Indian cookery than in our favorite Indian restaurant?

Time To Eat

Christopher Peacock, 2 Dearfield Drive, Greenwich
Contact: Nicole Straight, 203.221.8306
www.Time-to-Eat.com
Ninety-minute classes designed to teach busy moms to prepare healthy meals in 15 minutes. $85 to $95 per person.

Williams-Sonoma Cooking Classes

Stamford Town Center, Stamford, CT, 961.0977
125 Westchester Avenue, White Plains, NY 914.644.8360
www.WilliamsSonoma.com
Classes in this popular store are held on Wednesday evenings from 6 pm to 9 pm. Be sure to call for a reservation. Classes are demonstration only, for 12 - 15 people and cost $50 per person. They teach courses such as: Elegant Holiday Dinners Made Easy, The Antipasto Table, Hors d'oeuvres and First Courses.

dancing

Arthur Murray

6 Lewis Street, 983.5546
www.TryDancing.com
Learn the latest dances with experienced instructors.

Dick Conseur's Ballroom Dancing

596 Stillwater Road, Stamford, 325.1332
www.dickconseursdancestudio.com
For confidence on the dance floor, give Dick Conseur a call. Discreet private lessons for ballroom or country and western dancing. He also teaches social and Latin dance at Greenwich Adult and Continuing Education.

gardening

Garden Education Center

Montgomery Pinetum, Bible Street, Cos Cob, 869.9242
www.gecgreenwich.org
The Center's new horticulture buildings provide classrooms and workrooms for a variety of excellent programs and lectures. Founded in 1957, the center is not only a strong educational facility, but also provides a good framework for new residents to make friends. They are closed during the summer.

Loretta Stagen Floral Designs

30 Commerce Street, Stamford, 323.3544
www.lorettastagen.com
She provides innovative flower arrangements and party decorations for corporate events and weddings. She also offers classes and workshops in flower arranging. For five or more students, she will create a special class in their area of interest. Her website has interesting links to wedding sites.

Fairfield University

Fairfield, CT, 203.254.4220, 4000

www.fairfield.edu

Fairfield is a major university with a 200-acre campus and great offerings in almost every conceivable subject. Definitely worth a call to get their catalog. They have over 1,000 continuing education students.
Directions: I-95N to exit 22; L at 2nd stop sign; R onto Barlow; at light, L onto N. Benson.

Greenwich Adult and Continuing Education

625.7474,

http://greenwichschools.org/gce

This amazing program offers a wide range of courses taught at the high school by interesting teachers. It is always priced right. Registration is in January and August/September. Be sure to call for a catalog; you are bound to see several courses you can't resist.

Lifetime Learners Institute

Norwalk Community College, 188 Richards Avenue, 203.857.3330
office: Room W013, West Campus, Lower Level
www.LifeTimeLearners.org

A fabulous organization, affiliated with the Elderhostel Institute Network. It is an independent continuing education program within NCC. To join you must be over 50 and want to continue learning. Members can choose from over 40 courses.

Manhattanville College

Purchase, NY, 914.694.2200, 800.328.4553
www.mville.edu

A local college with an attractive campus and good course offerings.
Directions: King St. N to Anderson Hill Rd., L onto Rte 120 (Purchase St.).

CONTINUING ED for ADULTS

general

Norwalk Community College
Norwalk, CT, 203.857.7080
www.ncc.commnet.edu
A surprisingly large selection (more than 300 courses) of adult education courses on a variety of subjects. Nice, modern facilities. They also offer courses at satellite locations in Stamford, Greenwich and Darien.
Directions: Exit 13 off I-95 N.

Stamford Adult Education
Adult Learning Center, 369 Washington Blvd., 977.4209
www.stamfordadulted.com
Check their website for their large number of enrichment classes.

SUNY Purchase
735 Anderson Hill Road, Purchase, NY, 914.251.6500
www.purchase.edu
Purchase College is a part of the State University of New York. It has beautiful grounds and striking modern buildings. Check out their adult education offerings.
Directions: King St. N to Anderson Hill Rd., R into SUNY.

UCONN Stamford
Connecticut Information Technology Institute
One University Place, Stamford, 251.8400
www.stamford.uconn.edu
Close by in Stamford is an exciting new facility where the University of Connecticut offers undergraduate programs plus professional and technical continuing education courses.
Directions: I-95 N to exit 7, L on Washington, L on Broad.

Alliance Française

299 Greenwich Avenue, 629.1340

www.afgreenwich.org

An ideal way to learn or refresh your French.

French-American School

Larchmont, Mamaroneck and Scarsdale Campuses

914.834.3002 x 253

www.Fasny.org

Adult and children classes in French, Mandarin Chinese, Russian, Spanish, Arabic and Italian. They also teach adult classes in creative writing, Shakespeare, sculpture and watercolors. They do tours of Manhattan museums to help practice skills in conversation.

(The) Language Exchange

Mill Pond Shopping Center, 203 East Putnam Avenue, Cos Cob

422.2024

www.foreignlanguageexchange.com

Instruction in 18 languages including ESL. Adult courses as well as children's classes for ages 3 to 13. They offer total immersion camps for students in elementary, middle and high school.

TIP: SoNo ARTS CELEBRATION

In early August South Norwalk has an exciting art festival with over 150 juried artists as well as an interesting mix of performances on five stages. The festival runs from 10 am to midnight and is appropriate for children as well as adults. Visit www.sonoarts.org

music

Greenwich Arts Council (GAC)

299 Greenwich Avenue, 622.3998
www.greenwicharts.org
The GAC maintains a talent bank of all types of music, theater, dance and art teachers and publishes an informative newsletter three times a year. It is a good resource for classes as disparate as O-Tatsu Taiko Japanese drumming, classical ballet or acting.

Fraioli School of Music @ Greenwich Music

1200 East Putnam Avenue, Riverside, 869.3615
www.greenwichmusic.com
Their store is filled with sheet music and instruments. They have a large selection of guitars & drums and a helpful staff. A full line of instruments are available for rent; a great way to discover if that instrument is right for you or your child. They have a music school (Fraioli School of Music) next door where they give lessons for the instruments they carry. Hours: Monday - Thursday, 10 am - 7 pm; Friday & Saturday, 10 am - 6 pm; Sunday, noon - 4 pm.

Robert Marullo

869.4943
This popular, talented piano teacher at Greenwich Academy, also gives private lessons. We strongly recommend him for lessons as wells as piano repairs and tuning.

CONTINUING ED for ADULTS

woodworking

Woodworkers Club

215 Westport Avenue, Norwalk, 847.9663
www.woodworkersclubnorwalk.com
Classes are in their 5,000 square foot shop, next to their store. They teach beginner and intermediate levels. Learn to build bookshelves, build a mortise and tenon bench or turn a spindle.

Wooden Boat Workshop

11 Day Street, South Norwalk, CT, 203.831.0426
www.woodenboatworkshop.com
Have you ever wondered how to build a boat? Students range from novices to seasoned professionals.

TIP: GREENWICH LIBRARY DATABASES

The Greenwich Library subscribes to over 60 databases which can be accessed free of charge to Library card holders. Almost all of these databases can be accessed from your computer. To find a database of interest, like the Antiques Reference Database, call the Greenwich Library Reference Desk at 622.7910
or go to www.greenwichlibrary.org/Business.htm

Greenwich has a rare and full appreciation of the arts. Note the peaceful expressions on the faces in the audience of the Greenwich Symphony, or the joyful chatter of a family in the Bruce Museum, or the smiles surrounding the Grace Notes, and you may discover how many of our high-powered, busiest residents relax and refresh themselves.

Art galleries are listed under SHOPPING
For art education see CONTINUING EDUCATION or CHILDREN
Libraries are described under BOOKS & LIBRARIES

art organizations

Art Society of Old Greenwich
PO Box 103, Greenwich
Gretchen Tatge, President, 637.9949
www.sidewalkshow.com
An organization of amateur and professional artists with membership open to everyone. We always enjoy their Sound Beach Avenue sidewalk art show in September.

Greenwich Arts Council (GAC)
299 Greenwich Avenue, 622.3998
www.greenwicharts.org
Frank Juliano, Executive Director in combination with a tiny staff and an outstanding board, is keeping this non-profit organization dynamic. Established in 1973, the GAC provides year-round, high-quality arts programs, educational outreach programs and gallery exhibits. Housed in the lovely landmark Greenwich Arts Center building in downtown Greenwich's shopping district, the GAC is home to The Bendheim Gallery, and offers affordable performance, meeting, exhibition and office space, art studios and a large dance studio. It is also home to the Choral Society, Symphony and the Art Society, as well as the Alliance Francaise and Friendship Ambassadors Foundation (a United Nations-affiliated cultural organization). The GAC maintains a talent bank of all types of music, theater, dance and art teachers and publishes an informative newsletter three times a year. It is a good resource for classes as disparate as O-Tatsu Taiko Japanese drumming, classical ballet or acting. The Bendheim Gallery is available to rent for private functions.

Greenwich Art Society
299 Greenwich Avenue, 629.1533
Liana Moonie & Douglas More, Co-Presidents
The Art Society has been stimulating interest in the arts since 1912. Greenwich has many talented artists. While walking along Greenwich Avenue, stop in the Greenwich Art Center to see the latest show.
Hours: Monday, Wednesday, Friday and Saturday 10 am - 5 pm.

area theaters

See Theater Tickets below for an easy way to buy your movie and performance tickets.
See Movie Rentals for Video and DVD rentals.

The Greenwich Time on Thursdays has a Week End supplement with a calendar of events, shows and reviews.

All out of town theaters are mapped on the Greenwich Guide Website www.greenwichguide.com/theaters.htm

film - greenwich

Not many towns still have movie theaters left in their downtown area. Enjoy the luxury of strolling from a nice restaurant to one of these theaters.

Bow Tie Cinema Plaza 3

2 Railroad Avenue, 869.4030

www.fandango.com

Clearview Twin Cinema

356 Greenwich Avenue, 869.6030

www.clearviewcinemas.com

Focus on French Cinema

203.698.2742 or Renee Ketcham, 531.9101

www.FocusOnFrenchCinema.org

Held at Pepsico Theater, Performing Arts Center, Purchase College, this annual 3-day event is organized by Alliance Francaise of Greenwich. Last year over 2,000 people attended. All films are in French with English subtitles. This exciting film festival, held at the end of March, includes films not usually available in the US and gives a unique insight into the French film industry. Not only do you get to see great films, but the audience has the opportunity to meet actors and directors.

Greenwich Classic Film Series

914.725.0999

http://members.aol.com/gcfs10am

Now in its 33th season and with over 500 members, it has two 6-film series. Movies from the 30s through the 70s with lectures by guest film critics are shown at the Crown Plaza theater, Saturday mornings at 10 am and Monday evenings at 7 pm. Membership is $120 for each 6-film series.

Greenwich Library Friday Films

101 West Putnam Avenue, 622.7910

www.greenwichlibrary.org/currfilm.htm

At 8 pm (doors open at 7:40) in the Cole Auditorium, the library presents award-winning US and foreign films. Admission is free. Call to get a schedule and verify that a film is being shown.

AMC Loews 14
40 Westchester Avenue, (Waterfront Place) Port Chester, 914.510.1000
Lots of free parking and 14 screens in the new Waterfront complex.

Avon Art Films
272 Bedford Street, Stamford, 967.3660
The Avon Theater is a fully restored classic movie theater. Built in 1939, the Avon was run by Crown Theaters until it closed in 1998. In 2001 it was purchased by a private investor from Greenwich. The theater was fully restored and reopened January, 2004 and shows independent, art and foreign films as well as Hollywood classics.

Bow Tie Cinemas Landmark Nine
5 Landmark Square, Stamford, 324.3100

Bow Tie Cinemas Majestic
118 Summer Street, Stamford, 323.1690
The newest theater in Stamford.

Garden Cinemas
9 Isaac Street, Norwalk, CT, 203.838.4504
Great movie theater for foreign movies you won't find in local multiplexes. The theater has lots of leg room.
Directions: I-95 N to exit 16, L on East Ave, L on Wall, L on Isaac.

IMAX Theater
At the Norwalk Aquarium, 10 North Water Street, SoNo
203.852.0700
The screen is six stories high and eight stories wide and the visual effects are stunning. See full description under CHILDREN, FAMILY OUTINGS.
Hours: Open daily, 10 am - 5 pm.

Rye Ridge Twin Cinema
1 Rye Ridge Plaza, Rye Brook, NY, 914.939.8177

State Cinema
990 Hope Street, Stamford, 325.0250
One of the least expensive theaters in the area. A good place to take a group of children and your best bet for avoiding long lines.

film - rentals video & dvd

Greenwich residents campaigned against the establishment of a chain video store in town.

Academy Video

132 East Putnam Avenue, 629.3260
1998 W. Main St, Stamford/Greenwich border
A good selection in a convenient location with average service.
Hours: every day, 10 am - 10 pm.

Glenville Video

1 Glenville Street, 531.6030
A popular store conveniently located in south western Greenwich
Hours: weekdays, 9 am - 9 pm; weekends, 10 am - 9 pm.

Greenwich Library

www.greenwichlibrary.org
The Library has an extensive collection of Video Tapes and DVDs. Use the website to reserve availability or phone 622.7910 to reserve items. Ask to have your reserved materials sent to one of the branches.

TIP: SALUTE TO VETERANS

Every year on the Fourth of July weekend, a dramatic, moving event honoring our veterans is held at the Havemeyer Field behind Town Hall. The events include demonstrations by Navy SEALs. The event is organized by the Veterans Appreciation Council, founded by Jim Carrier and Scott Frantz. This is a wonderful way for our young people to have more appreciation of our veterans. For more information contact Jim Carrier at 981.4340 or visit www.salutetovets.com

Caramoor Center for Music and Arts

Girdle Ridge Road, Katonah, NY, 914.232.1252
www.caramoor.com
Caramoor has wonderful music programs in a very intriguing setting. It should be on everyone's "must do" list. For evening performances, it is fashionable to bring a fancy picnic supper and eat on one of the lawns before the show. Caramoor has 100 acres of parklands and formal gardens. Most performances are open air, unless it rains. Mosquitoes are sparse but bringing some bug spray in the summer can't hurt. The main season is June through August although Caramoor provides fall, winter and spring indoor programs on a more limited schedule.
Directions: About 20 minutes from Greenwich. Take North Street N to the end (Bedford Village), R at the end, L on Route 22 N, R on Girdle Ridge Road; or I684 N to exit 6, E on Rte 35, R on Rte 22 S.

Chamber Players

Jim Daniel, President, 637.0849
For more information call; 869.2664 or 869.6468
Musicians selected from the Greenwich Symphony Orchestra present 4 dual concerts each year; 4 pm on Sunday afternoons at Round Hill Community Church and 8 pm Monday evenings at the Bruce Museum. A wine and cheese reception at each concert is a wonderful way for the audience to become acquainted with the musicians.

Connecticut Grand Opera

307 Atlantic Street, box office 327.2867
www.ctgrandopera.org
A not-for-profit, professional opera company founded in 1993, it performs at the Palace Theater in Stamford.

Fairfield County Chorale

61 Unquowa Road, Fairfield, CT, 203.254.1333
www.fairfieldcountychorale.org
Founded in 1963, the Chorale's repertoire consists of more than 100 classic works by composers from the 16th through the 20th century. Most performances are held at the Norwalk Concert Hall.

music

Grace Notes
Anne Marcus, President, 869.8428
www.TheGraceNotes.com
A women's "a cappella" singing group that has been entertaining Greenwich audiences for over thirty years. Singing with this group is a rewarding experience.

Greenwich Choral Society
For information call 622.5136
Founded in 1925, the Society performs throughout the area during the winter months. Their annual Christmas concert held at Christ Church is a very popular event.

Greenwich POPS Concert
For information call 622.3998
www.greenwicharts.org/popsconcert.asp
The POPS concert is presented during the Summer by the Greenwich Arts council. It is held at Roger Sherman Baldwin Park. For a lovely evening, pack a picnic to enjoy before the 7:30 concert.

Greenwich Symphony Orchestra
869.2664
www.greenwichsym.org
This 90-member professional orchestra is in its 50th season. They play consistently excellent music at low ticket prices. Ask for a CD of their music highlights. Concerts are Saturday evenings and Sunday afternoons at Greenwich High School. Be sure to attend pre-concert lectures. Patricia Handy's 30-minute free informative explanation of the music is terrific.

Palladium Musicum
For information contact Marie Williams, President, 661.6856
www.PalladiumMusicum.org
They offer two events each season which combine musical performances and lectures.

music

Stamford Symphony Orchestra
Palace Theatre, 61 Atlantic Street, Stamford.
Check the box office schedule at 325.4466.
To order by phone call 325.1407 x305.
www.stamfordsymphony.org

Town Concerts and other summer events
622.7830
During July and August the Department of Parks and Recreation arranges free Tuesday afternoon and Wednesday evening concerts. Call for locations.

Acting Company of Greenwich

Call 629.2094 for information & 863.1919 for reservations
www.tacog.org www.actgreenwich.org
This local amateur theater group, with good acting and good fun, welcomes actors and audiences for its annual series of plays held in the auditorium of the First Congregational Church in Old Greenwich.

Cameo Theater

Pat Brandt, 637.4870
Caroline Wilkins McDonough, is director and the president of the Cameo Theater in Old Greenwich. The theater company in its 22th season, performs at the First Congregational Church in Old Greenwich. A friendly group, open to anyone who is interested in acting or helping put on a show.

Connecticut Playmakers

325.8543
Live theater open to adult participants from age 16. In addition to their major productions, the monthly meetings include dramatic presentations. The Playmakers Young People's Theater puts on a musical each summer. This is an enjoyable way for young people to meet each other and learn about the theater.

Curtain Call Theaters

1249 Newfield Ave, Stamford, 329.8207
www.curtaincallinc.com
Curtain Call has two theaters at this location. Recently updated, "The Kweskin Theater" presents fullrun productions such as "The Odd Couple" and "Arsenic and Old Lace." "The Dressing Room" has cabaret-style seating. Bring your own food and enjoy charming dramas and musicals, such as the Fantastics. Evening performances start at 8pm, Matinees at 2 pm. For the aspiring actor, Curtain Call offers a full line of educational workshops in the performing arts, ages 5 through adult.

Emelin Theater

153 Library Lane, Mamaroneck, NY, 914.698.0098
www.emelin.org
Speakers, cabaret, jazz, classical music, musical theater, children's theater and more. Wonderful programs. Call for a catalog.

Fairfield Theater Company

70 Sanford Street (directly in front of the Metro-North train station). Box office: 203.259.1036
www.FairfieldTheatre.org
The Fairfield Theatre Company was founded in 2000. Their mission is "to bring the best of New York's Off and Off-Off Broadway directly to Fairfield." This is professional theater from NYC, brought intact, and delivered to our backyard.

Festival Theater

1850 Elm Street, Stratford, CT
www.stratfordfestival.com
This Connecticut Shakespeare theater is reopening.
For information contact the Town of Stratford's Mayors office at 385-4001 or Catherine Gallagher at 203.260.3050

Long Wharf Theater

222 Sargent Drive, New Haven, CT,
Box office: 203.787.4282, 800.782.8497
www.longwharf.org
Professional theater which produces traditional plays as well as plays by new playwrights. Over the last 40 years, Long Wharf has presented numerous world premieres, dozens of American premieres and transfers to Broadway.
Directions: I-95 N to exit 46.

Palace Theater

61 Atlantic Street, Stamford, 358.2305, Box Office 325.4466
www.onlyatsca.com
The Palace, along with the Rich Forum, is part of the Stamford Center for the Arts. The Palace is a 1,584-seat vaudeville theater that was acclaimed as "Connecticut's most magnificent" when it opened in 1927.
Box office hours: weekdays, 10 am - 5 pm.
Directions: I-95 N to exit 8, L on Atlantic.

Play with Your Food

299 Greenwich Avenue (Greenwich Arts Council)
www.PlayWithYourFood.org
A winter series of noon-time theater. All shows are noon to 1:30 and include lunch and professional readings of one-act plays for $35. Can there be a better way to spend your lunch time? Call well in advance to reserve.

Rich Forum

307 Atlantic Street, Stamford, CT, 358.2305,
Box Office: 325.4466
www.onlyatsca.com
This theater has excellent facilities and an eclectic program of high quality events. Rich Forum, like the Palace, is committed to presenting the best of live theater, concerts, comedy and dance entertainment.
Box office hours: weekdays, 10 am - 5 pm.
Directions: I-95 N to exit 8, L on Atlantic.

Shubert Theater

247 College Street, New Haven, CT, Box Office: 888.736.2663
www.capa.com/newhaven
For tickets contact: www.tickets.com at 800.228.6622
This not-for-profit theater is considered the crown jewel of downtown New Haven. Some shows come directly from Broadway.
Box office hours: weekdays, 9 am - 9 pm, Saturday 9 am - 7 pm, Sundays Noon - 6 pm

Stamford Theater Works

200 Strawberry Hill Avenue (on the Campus of
Sacred Heart Academy)
Box office: 359.4412
www.stamfordtheatreworks.org
If you love going to the theater and haven't discovered this (New York quality) group, you are in for a treat. The Purple Cow Children's Theater has shows geared to children 3 to 8 years old throughout the Summer and during the holiday season.

theater

Summer Theater of New Canaan

Box office, 203.966.4634

www.stonc.org

What fun to have this regional theater so near by! It produces professionally staged family musicals and Shakespearian productions during the summer. Shakespeare is performed in the outdoor walled garden at Waveny Park in New Canaan, CT. Musicals and other performances are held in the Saxe Middle School Theater, South Avenue, New Canaan.

SUNY Performing Arts Center

745 Anderson Hill Road, Purchase, NY, 914.251.6200

www.artscenter.org

The Performing Arts Center at the State University of New York at Purchase, just a few minutes from Greenwich, has wonderful music and dance performances, as well as plays. They have a number of summer offerings although the main season is September to May.

Westport Country Playhouse

25 Powers Court, Westport, CT, 203.227.4177

www.westportplayhouse.com

A 6-play summer season starting in June. Very professional. The theater recently underwent $17 million renovation. Only a 20-minute trip. While there, try dinner at the Splash Restaurant (See the restaurant section) or Paul Newman's restaurant, *The Dressing Room*, at 27 Powers Court (adjacent to the Westport Country Playhouse). Phone: 203.226.1114; Lunch: weekdays, 11:00 am to 3:00 pm; Dinner: Seven days a week, 5:00 to 10:00 pm.

Yale University Repertory Theater

1120 Chapel St., PO Box 1257, New Haven, CT, 203.432.1234

www.yale.edu/yalerep/

It is a drive (about an hour) but it's well worth it. Often as good as Broadway, but with much less hassle, better seats and lower prices. You can park right next to the theater for free. Subscribers can get front row seats.

More Museums are listed in CHILDREN under Family Outings worth a trip.

Bruce Museum
1 Museum Drive, 869.0376, 8696786
www.BruceMuseum.org
This year the Bruce attracted over 100,000 visitors to their exciting exhibitions making the Bruce one of the most popular museums in Connecticut. In addition, the Bruce sponsored over 50 lectures and gave educational programs to over 18,000 children. Under the leadership of Peter Sutton, the Museum has been able to attract major art exhibits. No wonder the Bruce is placed in the top 10% of US museums. The Museum sponsors two fairs in Bruce Park every year. The mid-May Craft Fair and the Columbus Day Arts Festival have juried artists from around the country and draw visitors from all over the area. When you become a member (which you should), you will be informed about their wonderful events. There are a number of organizations affiliated with the Bruce.
  • Astronomical Society of Greenwich, 869.6786 x 338
  • Connecticut Ceramics Study Circle, 869.9478
  • Greenwich Antiques Society, 869.9531 or 661.7988
  • Forum for World Affairs, 356.0340
Hours: Tuesday Saturday, 10 am - 5 pm; Sunday, 1 am - 5 pm.

Bush-Holley House Museum
39 Strickland Road, Cos Cob, 869.6899
www.hstg.org
Home of the Historical Society, this is the place to learn about Greenwich history. They have a good library and a shop with books on Greenwich history, as well as reproductions of 19th century children's toys and books. The museum showcases eight period rooms from the late 1890's when it was a boarding house for the Cos Cob art colony. Be sure to take the guided tour. While you are there, pick up a list of the wonderful programs and events sponsored by the Greenwich Historical Society.
Hours: Tuesday - Sunday, noon - 4 pm.

museums

Donald M. Kendall Sculpture Gardens

At Pepsico, 700 Anderson Hill Road, Purchase, NY, 914.253.2000
www.sirpepsi.com/pepsi1.htm
One of the world's finest sculpture gardens is located right next to Greenwich. The collection includes forty pieces by such 20th century artists as Noguchi, Moore, Nevelson, and Calder. The sculptures are set on 168 carefully landscaped acres. Pick up a map at the visitors' parking lot. There are some picnic tables.
Hours: every day from dawn to dusk, except for Saturdays in August.
Directions: From Glenville, R on King, L at light on Anderson, L at light into Pepsico.

Historical Society of the Town of Greenwich

39 Strickland Road, Cos Cob, 869.6899; Archives ext.23
www.hstg.org
Their mission is to collect, preserve and disseminate the history of Greenwich. The society conducts a wide variety of adult and children's educational programs, exhibitions and workshops. Their extensive archives are open to anyone wanting to research town history. We sincerely appreciate this organization's dedication to preserving our community's historical roots.
Hours: weekdays, 9 am - 5 pm.

Katonah Museum of Art

Route 22 at Jay Street, Katonah, NY, 914.232.9555
www.katonahmuseum.org
The Museum offers an extensive range of activities to engage visitors of all ages. Exhibitions present art from the past to the present. The Museum's Learning Center is an interactive exhibition space in which children can experience the fun of artistic exploration.
Hours: Tuesday, Thursday, Friday & Saturday, 10 am - 5 pm (Wednesday until 8pm); Sunday, noon - 5 pm.
Directions: I-684 to exit 6, East on Route 35 to Route 22, then South 1/4 mile on Route 22 to the Museum on L.

museums

Neuberger Museum

735 Anderson Hill Road, Purchase, NY, 914.251.6100
www.neuberger.org
The museum is located on the 500-acre campus of the State University of New York (SUNY) at Purchase. It has 25,000 sq. ft. of gallery space, a café, a store and an interactive learning center. It houses a notable collection of modern art.
Hours: Closed Monday; Tuesday - Friday, 10 am - 4 pm; Saturday & Sunday, 11 am - 5 pm.

Putnam Cottage

243 East Putnam Avenue, 869.9697
www.putnamcottage.org
Originally a tavern serving travelers along the Post Road, it is now a museum owned by the DAR. Each year on the last Sunday in February (1-3 pm) the Putnam Hill Revolutionary War battle is recreated. A definite must-see for adults and children alike.
Hours: April December; Wednesday, Friday, Sunday, 1 pm - 4 pm. Special tours anytime.

Storm King Art Center

Old Pleasant Hill Road, Mountainville, NY, 845.534.3115
www.stormking.org
Take a walk or picnic in this leading outdoor sculpture museum with 120 masterworks set in a stunning 400-acre landscaped park. Great place to take the kids for a picnic. Open April 1 - November 15th.
Hours: Wednesday - Sunday, 11 am - 5:30 pm. Open Saturdays until 8 pm Memorial Day Labor Day. (Closed Monday & Tuesday)
Directions: New York State Thruway, I-87 North to exit 16, Harriman; N on Route 32 for 10 miles; in Cornwall follow signs for the center.

Union Church of Pocantico Hills

555 Bedford Road, North Tarrytown, NY, 914.631.8200, 2069
www.hudsonvalley.org/unionchurch/index.htm
Stained glass windows created by Henri Matisse (1869-1954) and Marc Chagall (1887-1985).
Hours: April - October, open daily except Tuesday, 11 am - 5 pm; Saturdays, 10 am - 5 pm; Sundays, 2 pm -5 pm.
Directions: I -95 to I-287 W, Exit 1; R on Rte 119 W, R on Rte 9 N; R on Rte 448.

tickets

Concert Connection

165 West Putnam Avenue, Greenwich, 869.0060

www.tkt.com

Ticket broker to major sports, music, theater and family entertainment events. They can get you those high demand tickets you want, but the price is often four to six times the cost. If you can wait to the last minute you will often get a deal, sometimes even below cost. A good place to sell tickets you can't use.

Hours: weekdays, 9 am - 7 pm; Saturday, usually 10 am - 4 pm.

Golden Ticket Events

261 East Putnam Avenue ,Cos Cob, 629.1300

www.GoldenTicketEvents.com

Sporting events, concerts, Broadway plays. Tickets sold at face value + a mark-up depending on scarcity.

Hours: weekdays, 10 am - 6 pm; Saturday, 10 am - 4 pm.

Movie Phone

323FILM (3456)

On Friday and Saturday nights, the demand for tickets is high and the lines can be very long. They often run out of tickets before you can get in. Call to hear previews and to buy your tickets in advance with your credit card. You should still arrive early for the best seating, but when you arrive you don't have to wait in the line. Just show your credit card and get your tickets.

When calling Movie Phone, their advertisements can sometimes be a nuisance. To get around this: press "*" to repeat or change your previous selection; "***" to start over; if you already know the theater you want, "#" plus the Theater Express Code will get you there immediately.

Movie Tickets & Theater Showtimes

www.fandango.com

Another online resource to purchase movie tickets.

(The) Ticket Exchange

Tickets up front

15 E Putnam Ave, Greenwich, 661.7111

Hours: weekdays, 8:30 am - 5 pm.

ENTERTAINING

Party information specific to Children is listed in CHILDREN
For wine, see FOOD AND BEVERAGES
To practice your dancing, see Adult Continuing Education in SCHOOLS
Cakes are listed under Bakeries in FOOD AND BEVERAGES
Florists and Nurseries are listed in FLOWERS AND GARDENS.
Landscapers and Tree services are listed in SERVICES

caterers

These caterers have delicious food, they arrive on time and are depend-
able. As a result, they are often in high demand. Reserve early.

Abigail Kirsch Culinary Productions

914.631.3030
www.AbigailKirsch.com
Caterer of choice for many Greenwich residents when they are having a
large party. Dear friends used Abigail for both daughters' weddings.

Aux Delices Gourmet Food Shop & Catering

1075 East Putnam Avenue, Riverside
shop, 698.1066 xt 3; catering, 326.4540 xt 2
www.AuxDelicesFoods.com
Debra Ponzek and Aux Delices are well known for excellent food. They
will cater or plan events of all types and sizes. In our Tasting Contest,
Aux Delices received the highest overall score.

Fjord Fisheries

137 River Road, Cos Cob, 661.5006
www.FjordCatering.com
If you are invited to a clambake or lobster party, chances are Fjord is the
provider. They are a full-service caterer. You must try their salmon. From
May through September, Fjord can cater a party of 40 to 120 on one of
their four ships. Breakfast, lunch and dinner cruises lasting two to three
hours are available.

Garelick and Herbs

4448 West Putnam Avenue, 661.7373
This gourmet delicatessen caters everything from a light lunch to fancy
dinners. They will also provide staff for your events.

Great Performances

287 Spring Street, New York City, 212.727.2424
www.greatperformances.com
Michael Way Director
We recently went to a Greenwich party where they were serving fabulous hors d'oeuvres, entrees and desserts.

LexZee Gourmet

187 Sound Beach Avenue, Old Greenwich, 698.9277
www.LexZeeGourmet.com
LexZee scored at the top during our Catering Contest. To taste their delicious food, try one of their daily take-out specials. We have found them to be a pleasure to work with.

Libby Coverly Cooke Catering

49 Brownhouse Road (Sportsplex Health Club), Stamford
406.9664
www.LibbyCookeCatering.com
Known for her fabulous presentations, she is equally competent with an intimate dinner party or a grand affair. If you want to try her food, order a take-out (48-hours in advance).

Marybeth's Catering

136 Hamilton Avenue, 661.8833
www.MarybethsCaterers.com
Marybeth Boller, called one of the top ten rising star chefs by Food and Wine magazine has purchased the Susan Morton Catering company. This chef with great credentials is making party goers happy.

Patricia Blake Catering

7 Tokeneke Road, Darien, CT, 203.655.1221
www.PatriciaBlake.com
Many choices on her catering menu from comfort foods to exotic delicacies. She has an impressive repertoire of hors d'oeuvres. She especially enjoys customizing the menu to meet your needs. Whether your party is for 25 or 500, she can do it.

caterers

Plum Pure Foods

236 East Putnam Avenue, Cos Cob, 869.7586

www.PlumPureFoods.com

Plum provides delicious takeout foods made primarily from natural products grown locally. They are exceptional caterers. Plum scored at the top during our 2005 Catering Contest.

Le Potager Catering

116 Woodbury Ave, Stamford, CT, 975.2546

www.LePotagerCatering.com

Joseph Jenkins, one of New York City's upscale caterers, has moved to our area. He is receiving rave reviews for his tasteful, elegant parties. He was one of the winners in our Catering Contest.

Royal Tea Company

Trumbull, CT, 203.452.1006

www.RoyalTeaCompany.net

Listed in Connecticut Magazine's Best of Connecticut 2005, their teas are perfect for bridal and baby showers, birthdays and Christmas parties. Every one loves their tea sandwiches and scones.

Victorian Teas

Victorian tea parties by Eileen Grossman, 203.406.9820

www.VictorianTeasCuisine.com

For an elegant event, with a creative presentation, a Victorian tea party will make your party memorable. Eileen caters weddings, corporate functions and home events, including tea parties for children.

Watson's on Pemberwick

63 Pemberwick Road, 532.0132

www.WatsonsCatering.com

You will want to have a cocktail or dinner party just to have Sue Scully's delicious food. Although large parties are her forte, she handles intimate parties equally well.

party invitations

Kate's Paperie

125 Greenwich Avenue, 861.0025

www.KatesPaperie.com

Whether you're looking to design an invitation for a baby shower, birthday party or wedding, you will be impressed with the variety of creative and custom options.

Hours: weekdays, 9:30 am - 6 pm; Saturday, 10am - 6pm; Sunday, 12 pm - 5 pm.

Papyrus

268 Greenwich Avenue, 869.1888

www.papyrusonline.com

The Papyrus sells fine custom social stationery and invitations from a great variety of sources. If you want a traditional or an out-of-the ordinary invitation, you will have fun here. The staff is extraordinarily talented at helping you choose and design invitations.

Hours: weekdays, 9:30 am - 6 pm; Saturday, 10 am - 6 pm; Sunday, noon - 5 pm.

Saint Clair (Stationery)

23 Lewis Street, 661.2927

www.theresesaintclair.com

Going to Cartier's for fine stationery is not necessary if you live in Greenwich. For many years Greenwich residents have shopped here for their invitations and elegant stationery. Stop in and see the range of things they can do.

Hours: Monday Saturday, 9:30 am - 5:30 pm.

party planners

Hollywood Pop Gallery

372 Greenwich Avenue, 622.4057

www.hollywoodpop.com

A global event production company. They will create and coordinate every element of your event from amazing decorations to cutting edge entertainment. If you want your party to be remembered decades later, just give them a call. They put together about 200 adult and 1,000 children's parties a year.

Hours: weekdays, 10 am - 5 pm.

TIP: TENT PERMITS

Yes, Greenwich requires a permit for tents. If you have lights or a sound system, you will need additional inspections. For your basic permit and the latest regulations, contact the Building Department on the second floor of Town Hall, 622.7754. Unfortunately, the permit forms and rules are not yet on line, but should be soon at www.greenwichct.org. If you have over 200 people attending, you will also need an additional permit from the Fire Department.

PM Amusements

36 Bush Avenue, Port Chester, NY, 914.937.1188
www.PMAmusements.com
This is the ultimate party rental source. If you want to turn your backyard into an amusement park or just rent a cotton candy machine, they have it all. Ask about sumo wrestling, a velcro wall, miniature golf, karaoke, clowns, inflatable rides, or perhaps an Abe Lincoln or Mick Jagger look-a-like/impersonator. They have a great catalog.
Hours: weekdays, 8 am - 5 pm; sometimes on Saturday. Call before going.

Northeast Tent Productions

55 Poplar Street, Stamford, 961.8100
www.NorthEastTent.com
You will be impressed with the variety of tent styles and lighting possibilities.

Party Fixins

1 Havemeyer Lane, Old Greenwich, 359.3922
www.PartyFixins.com
Ice cream carts to pretzel machines, they have everything you may wish to rent for a party.

party rentals

Prestige Party Rental

Prospect Park, NJ, 973.942.5300

www.PrestigePartyRental.com

For a large tented affair, they have nice service, great tents and usually the best prices. Because they aren't in Greenwich, you will need to go to Town Hall for the tent permit. Of course, they rent all the equipment, plates, table cloths, podiums, etc.

Smith Party Rentals

133 Mason Street, 869.9315

www.SmithPartyRentals.com

For years this has been the leading party rental source in town. They are still the source for just about everything possible for adult and children's parties. If they don't have it, you probably don't need it.

Stamford Tent and Party Rental

84 Lenox Avenue, Stamford, 324.6222

www.StamfordTent.com

A good local resource for almost any type of tented party. Check the website for helpful tent sizing advice.

TIP: HORS D'OEUVRES CONTEST

Carolyn & Jerry Anderson hosted a "blind" tasting party to evaluate hot and cold hors d'oeuvres from 10 local Greenwich caterers. Over 200 present and former Anderson Associates' clients evaluated the hors d'oeuvres. Details of the hors d'oeuvres that won are on www.GreenwichGuide.com.

The winners were:

- Aux Delices, 203.326.4540 x 101
- Gourmet Galley, 203.629.8889
- Le Potager Catering, 203.975.2546
- LexZee Gourmet, 203.698.9277
- Libby Cook, 203.406.9664
- Plum Pure Foods, 203.869.7586

party services

Advanced Parking Concepts (APC)

Verona, NJ, 973.857.2008

www.AdvancedParkingConcepts.com

They are totally professional, impeccably groomed and knowledgeable about Greenwich.

East Coast Ice

Byram, 531.9385

Tom will deliver the ice you need just before your party. If you need a refrigerated box, he has those to rent as well.

Greenwich Town Traffic Division

622.8015

If you are having a large party, consider hiring an off-duty policeman to help your guests know where to park safely. Be sure to call well in advance and to confirm back that someone has signed up to help you.

Parking Productions

Clark, NJ, 629.0003

www.ParkingProductions.com

We are impressed by their ability to effortlessly take care of a large number of cars in a short period of time. Valet parking at its best.

Round Hill Tree Service

1 Armonk Street, Greenwich, 531.5759

Rick Masi will make sure your limbs are trimmed back and your yard sprayed for mosquitos just before your party.

TIP: MAKING FRIENDS

Whether you are new to Town or a long term resident and want to have an easy, fun way to meet others, join one of the two newcomers' clubs.

For details see www.greenwichnewcomers.com.

party supplies

East Putnam Variety
Whole Foods shopping Center,
88 East Putnam Avenue, 869.8789
This conveniently located shop has a myriad of party goods, including a fabulous balloon selection. Great customer service.
Hours: Monday - Saturday, 7 am to 10 pm.

Fiesta Place
985 East Main Street, Stamford, 961.0034
They sell party favors including piñatas of all kinds.
Hours: Monday - Saturday, 9 am - 8 pm.

Party City
535 Boston Post Road, Port Chester, NY, 914.939.6900
www.partycity.com
A giant store with an impressive inventory of party supplies. Like the Strauss Warehouse Outlet, they have a very large assortment of Halloween costumes during the season.
Hours: Monday - Saturday, 9 am - 9 pm; Sunday, 10 am - 6 pm.

Party Paper and Things
410 East Putnam Avenue,   661.1355
An excellent selection of high quality party paper goods, wrapping paper, disposable serving dishes and lots of balloons. They will deliver for a very modest fee.
Hours: weekdays, 10 am - 5:30 pm; Saturday, 10am - 5pm.

Party Warehouse
24 Harbor View Avenue, Stamford, CT, 203.967.3313
They say they are the largest discount party Super Store, and we believe it. Besides a large selection, they have very good customer service. When we needed some special order items they went out of their way to make sure we received them on time.
Hours: weekdays, 10 am - 6 pm (Thursday until 7 pm);
Saturday, 9:30 am - 5 pm; Sunday, 11 am - 4 pm.

Strauss Warehouse Outlet

140 Horton Avenue, Port Chester, NY, 914.939.3544, 7132
www.straussoutlet.com

Gift wrapping, party favors, balloons, paper goods, just about anything you might want for a party at great prices. They carry a huge selection of Halloween costumes during October.

TIP: WHERE TO FIND THE BEST PIZZA IN TOWN

Anderson Associates had a blind tasting of regular pizzas from twelve of our local pizza places. The winners of the best pizza in town were:

1: Express Pizza, 160 Hamilton Avenue, 622.1693
(they deliver): Score 57.

2: Glenville Pizza, 243 Glenville Road, 531.9852
(no delivery): Score 56.

3: Pizza Post, 522 East Putnam Avenue, 661.0909
(no delivery): Score 54.

4: Pizza Factory, 380 Greenwich Avenue, 661.5188
(no delivery): Score 52.

The lowest score for a pizza was 31. All of the others had scores in the 40s.

FITNESS & SPORTS

introduction

Fans and players of almost every imaginable sport live in Greenwich. Paddle tennis was even invented in Greenwich. Best of all, whether you are a professional or an amateur, finding a place to fish, skate, golf, sail or play ball is easy in our town.
Uniforms and Equipment listed in SHOPPING
Children's Summer Camps are listed in CHILDREN

archery

Cos Cob Archers

205 Bible Street, 625.9421 Ron Mangilit, President
www.CosCobArchers.com
Twenty-four regular targets. Members must have their own equipment and be over 18. Members have a key to the range and can practice any time. To join, visit the range Saturday or Sunday or attend the meeting on the second Wednesday of each month at 7 pm.

badminton

Greenwich Hawks

Contact: Judy Tanaka, 661.0019
www.usabadminton.org
An affiliate of the USA Badminton Association, they play at the Boys & Girls Club, www.bgcg.org.

YWCA

259 East Putnam Avenue, 869.6501
www.YWCAGreenwich.org
The Y provides supervised round robin youth badminton for all skill levels 7:30 - 9:30 pm, Tuesday, Thursday and Friday evenings March through November. The Y hosts tournaments sanctioned by the USA Badminton Association.

baseball

All Pro Sport Academy

www.allprosportsacademy.com
Sponsored by the Department of Parks and Recreation and located at North Street School. Intensive co-ed summer program for 7 to 12 year-olds. Instruction by current high school coaches, college and minor league players.

Blue Fish Professional Baseball

Harbor Yard 203.345.4800
www.bridgeportbluefish.com

Bobby Valentine Sports Academy

72 Camp Avenue, Stamford, CT, 968.2872
www.BobbyVAcademy.com
Just finishing construction. This facility in the Springdale section of Stamford is planned to be a state of the art baseball and softball training center.

Cos Cob Athletic Club

Contact: Teresa Burhans, 698.2817
This community organization sponsors spring coed T-Ball for beginners in grades K-2. T-Ball uses a batting tee. Held at the Cos Cob Community center on Bible Street.

Doyle Baseball Academy

www.doylebaseball.com/siebert
Hosted by Greenwich Department of Parks and Recreation in April at the Eastern Greenwich Civic Center. Groups are divided by age: 6-8, 9-10, 11 & 12.

Greenwich Babe Ruth League
Hotline: 618.7659
Contact: Bill Boutelle, President, 629.1633
www.greenwichbaberuth.org
Non-profit organization sponsoring baseball. The Bambino division is for children 10 - 12; Junior division is for ages 13 - 15; Senior division is for ages 16 - 18. Teams play from late May through mid-July at the Greenwich High School and Julian Curtiss Elementary School. Registration starts in February at Town Hall.

Greenwich Department of Parks and Recreation Programs
Town Hall, 101 Field Point Road, 622.7830
www./greenwichct.org/ParksAndRec/ParksandRec.asp
Indoor baseball clinics January through March, at Dundee School for children ages 7 to 13. Co-ed spring outdoor clinics for Small Fry age 7; Midget for age 8. Doyle Baseball School for ages 7 - 12, during school vacation in April; July & August co-ed baseball league for ages 9 - 12. Indoor softball clinics for girls ages 10 to 15.

Old Greenwich Riverside Community Center Programs
Eastern Greenwich Civic Center, 90 Harding Road, 637.3659
They sponsor a variety of baseball and softball teams and instruction programs for girls and boys from kindergarten through 8th grade. Evaluations are usually in March.

YMCA Baseball Programs
50 East Putnam Avenue, 869.1630
www.gwymca.org
The Y provides sessions for boys & girls, ages 4 - 8 to learn the fundamentals of baseball, as well as clinics for children in grades 1 - 5.

TIP: SCARECROW FESTIVAL
Every year in October, the Mill Pond Park on Strickland Road is taken over by scarecrows waiting to be judged. Activities include pumpkin painting, scarecrow making, games, crafts and lots of fun for everyone. For information on the event contact the Greenwich Chamber of Commerce, 869.3500.

Greenwich Basketball Association

Dr. Scott Fisher, 869.2929

Bob Haugen, 698.0273

Now in its 16th season, the Association was founded by a group of Greenwich fathers. It provides a townwide instructional and competitive co-ed basketball program for 5th - 10th graders, designed to encourage and stimulate each child to build basketball skills. All skill levels are welcome and everyone is guaranteed to play at least a half of each game. Registration and evaluation start in October.

Intro Sports, Junior 5-Star Basketball

203.938.9996

www.introsportsusa.com

Sponsored by the Greenwich Parks and Recreation Department, it provides high quality instruction for boys and girls, Pre-K to 5th grade. Camps begin in June.

Men's Basketball League

Call 622.7821 for information.

A recreation program from January through March at the Eastern Greenwich Civic Center, Central and Eastern Middle Schools and Greenwich High School. Programs for Town resident teams, B and C corporate teams. Start times: weekdays, 6:30, 7:30 and 8:30 pm.

basketball

OGRCC Athletic Programs

Eastern Greenwich Civic Center, 90 Harding Road, 637.3659
www.ogrcc.com
Starting in October, OGRCC sponsors a number of basketball programs
for young children through adults: Youth Basketball for boys and girls in
the 3rd and 4th grades; Boys' Basketball and Girls' Basketball for 5th to
8th graders; Adult PickUp Basketball for 18 and over.

Parks and Recreation Basketball Clinics

Greenwich Parks and Recreation Department, 622.7830
Register in October
Co-ed Clinics, K to 6th grade at the Glenville and Dundee Schools.
Girls' Clinics, K to 6th grade at the Dundee School.
Girls' Middle School Clinics, 6th through 8th grade at Dundee School.

YMCA Programs

50 East Putnam Avenue, 869.1630
The Y provides clinics in basketball for children in grades 1 - 5. They also
sponsor A and B levels and an Adult Summer Outdoor Basketball League
for ages 19 and up.

bicycling

'(The) Bicycle Tour Company
9 Bridge Street, Kent, CT, 888.711.5368
www.BicycleTours.com
Bicycle explorations give you a whole new perspective. Tour Greenwich and many other interesting sites on the Eastern Seaboard. Bicycle Tour Company routes are generally 25 - 30 miles per day. They rent bicycles & construct routes for all ability levels. Owner, Sal Lilienthal grew up in Greenwich.

Connecticut Department of Transportation
Information: 860.594.2000
2800 Berlin Turnpike, PO Box 317564, Newington, CT 06131-7564
The Connecticut Bicycle Map is published by the State. Write for a copy.

East Coast Greenway
The East Coast Greenway Alliance has created a bicycle route between Greenwich and New Haven. A map of this route, championed by local resident Franklin Bloomer, is available by calling 401.789.4625 or check out www.greenway.org.

Greenwich Department of Parks & Recreation
622.7830
A tour map/guide of the Town's Bicycle Master Plan is available at the Recreation Division Office. It is available on-line at
www./greenwichct.virtualtownhall.net/Public_Documents/
GreenwichCT_FirstSelect/committees/Transportation/
fsTransportationBikePlan.pdf
All Greenwich bikers should read this.

Greenwich Safe Cycling
Franklin Bloomer, Chairman, 637.0031
Vince DiMarco, Vice Chairman
The mission of this organization of Town residents, both serious cyclists and recreational riders, is to make Greenwich a bicycle and pedestrian friendly community. They helped develop the Town's Master Bicycle Plan. They are responsible for the 7.5-mile bicycle trail from Grass Island to Greenwich Point.

bicycling

Sound Cyclists

203.840.1757
PO Box 3323, Westport, CT
www.SoundCyclists.com
This social cycling club offers, at no cost, rides for all levels of ability led by experienced cyclists. Routes are along scenic coast lines and country roads and vary from 12 miles to 60+ miles.

Road Hogs

17 East Putnam Avenue, 661.0142
www.roadhogs.org, www.justhogs.org,
A Greenwich-based club for running, cycling and swimming enthusiasts.

TIP: ONLY GEESE HONK IN GREENWICH

Residents know that Greenwich is a place to relax, unwind and enjoy life. Yes, we still need to get places on time, but we drive with consideration. Honking (except in dangerous situations) is taboo. If someone is honking inappropriately, it is probably a car with an out-of-town license plate. We like to say "in Greenwich only the geese honk."

boating / sailing

Greenwich Community Sailing

PO Box 195, Old Greenwich, 698.0599
www.GreenwichSailing.com
CT approved safe boating certificate courses. They have a variety of junior and adult programs open only to Greenwich residents. The Junior programs are for ages 9 - 16. Learn to sail, keelboat or kayak in group or private lessons.

Greenwich Marine Facilities

Superintendent: Fred Walters 622.7818
Location: Town Hall, Second Floor
Office Hours: 8:00 am - 4:00 pm
Customer Service Desk: Open from 8:15 a.m. to 3:45 p.m.
www.greenwichct.org/ParksAndRec/prBoating.asp
Assigns boat moorings for the town. To apply for a slip (as always, bring in a utility bill as proof of residency and a photo ID) you must own a boat and know the vessel's length, draft and beam. Boats are categorized as sail or power and over or under 20 feet; 20 feet and over receive deepwater moorings. After registering, you are put on a waiting list. The list is never short, but the amount of time varies with the vessel's type and size, as well as the location you request. The town has moorings at Greenwich Point, Cos Cob, Grass Island and Byram.

Greenwich Power Squadron

Contact: Rich Malloy 862.9411
www.captainharbor.org
The Power Squadron is an all-volunteer civic organization with 200 Greenwich members. The Squadron's primary goal is education and boating safety—both sailing and power boating. The Squadron teaches two courses at the Greenwich High School through the Continuing Education program (830.8144) and depending upon demand, runs additional courses throughout the year. All boaters (even jet skiers) must have a Connecticut Boating License. The Power Squadron course qualifies you for your Connecticut license. This course is the first step for anyone who wants to enjoy the miles of coastline available to Greenwich residents.

Greenwich Water Club

67 River Road, Cos Cob, 601.4033

www.GreenwichWaterClub.com

The Club has a full working marina with a 250-slip capacity, onsite repair service, fueling dock, visiting slip privileges, winter storage facilities, and a ship's store. They teach safe boating as well as other boating classes.

Indian Harbor Yacht Club

710 Steamboat Road, 869.2484

Ask for the Sailing Office

One of the few private clubs with a sailing program open to the public. The program has such a good reputation that it is usually filled by February.

Longshore Sailing School

260 Compo Road South, Westport, CT, 203.226.4646

www.longshoresailingschool.com

If you or your children (ages 9-16) want to learn to sail and can't get into one of the Greenwich programs, try this school in Westport. It provides instruction from basic sailing to racing techniques. Register in February for two-week sessions blending fun and substance.

Old Greenwich Yacht Club

Greenwich Point, Old Greenwich, 637.3074

www.ogyc.org

Open to all residents with beach cards. It has deep water moorings as well as Mercury sailboats for member use. The club provides sailing lessons on weekends and trophy races during the summer. See the section on CLUBS & ORGANIZATIONS for details on other yacht clubs.

Safe Boating and PWC Jet Ski Courses

Sound Environmental Associates, 800.510.9995

www.seadolphin.com

One day courses to meet Connecticut requirements.

FITNESS & SPORTS

boating / sailing

Sound Sailing Center
South Norwalk, CT, 203.838.1110
After hours, call 203.454.4394
www.SoundSailing.com
Selected to manage the Old Greenwich Yacht Club sailing program, SSC focuses on adult education at its Norwalk Harbor facility.

Yachting Magazine
299.5900
www.yachtingnet.com/yachting
Published in Norwalk, this is the magazine for sailors.

bridge

Lest you wonder why bridge is in this section, we regard it as fitness for the brain.

YWCA
259 East Putnam Avenue, 869.6501
www.YWCAGreenwich.org
The Y provides a variety of bridge lessons from beginner to advanced. Each Monday at 12:30 pm - 4:30 pm and Friday at 9:30 am - noon, up to 100 serious players gather at the Y to participate in 3 hours of duplicate or tournament bridge, played under the oversight of Steve Becker, who writes a syndicated bridge column. The game is franchised by the American Contract Bridge League and players can earn master points toward becoming life masters. Bridge lessons are available.

canoeing/kayaking/rowing

The Mianus River in Greenwich is a good place to practice canoeing. There is no need to worry if you fall in because the water is very clean. For the more adventurous, the Housatonic River has class I and II rapids, and is a center for trips and instruction. Outfitters come and go, but check out the following:

Clarke Outdoors

West Cornwall, CT, 860.672.6365

www.clarkeoutdoors.com

Rentals, lessons, and white water rafting on the Housatonic River.

Greenwich Rowing Club

on the Mianus River at the Greenwich Water Club,

67 River Road, Cos Cob, 661.4033

www.GreenwichWaterClub.com

The Club staff is ready to help you learn, train, and push the limits to meet your every goal, whether you are a competitive crew team or a new trainee. The club has 35 rowing machines and a training staff available to accommodate your needs, whether you are a novice, intermediate, or highly advanced rower. Membership is open to men and women of all ages and juniors 12- 18. Stop by the Club to see their facilities and meet the coaches. You don't have to join the club to participate in crewing.

Kittatinny Canoes

Dingmans Ferry, PA, 800.356.2852, 570.828.2338

www.kittatinny.com

Canoeing, kayaking or rafting the Delaware. Calm water for families or beginners, white water for experts.

Kayak/Canoe Guide

SWRPA (South Western Regional Planning Agency) publishes a fullcolor laminated guide to help you find your way around Norwalk's 23-island archipelago. SWRPA is located at 888 Washington Blvd in Stamford. Call 316.5190 for a copy.

North American Whitewater Outdoor Adventure

Kent, CT, 800.727.4379

www.nawhitewater.com

See CHILDREN for summer camps.

camping

Camping on Greenwich Islands

www.greenwichct.org/ParksAndRec/prOverNightCamping.asp
You can camp on Island Beach & Great Captain's Island between June 10th and Sept 16th. Families find this lots of fun. Reservations must be made in person at the Department of Parks and Recreation, 2nd floor, at least 2 weeks prior to date. We suggest reserving much earlier. Many people make their reservation requests in January. Proof of residency is required. Camping reservations are limited to one night per family per season.

Camping with RVs

www.campConn.com

State Forest Camping Areas

Campsites are usually available May - September.
www.dep.state.ct.us/stateparks/camping
There are 11 Connecticut State Park camping areas and 2 State Forest camping areas. The State Forests also have equestrian camp grounds.

cheerleading

Youth Football Cheerleaders

Banc Raiders, Cos Cob Crushers, Glenville Mavericks, North Mianus Bull-dogs, Putnam Generals.
www.greenwichfootball.com
Each team has a cheerleading squad for grades 3-8.

Greenwich Tumble and Cheer

222 Mill Street, 532.1223
www.greenwichtumbleandcheer.com
Gigi Lombardi runs a year-round cheerleading and tumbling training center located at the Sokol Gymnastic Club in Byram. The school is for children in kindergarten through grade 12, all interest levels and abilities.

FITNESS & SPORTS

croquet

Greenwich Croquet Club

661.6066 or 661.9122

Founded by Greenwich residents Bill and Marjorie Campbell in 1986, this private club is open to everyone. It plays on the Bruce Park Green. Besides providing instruction, the Club holds the Greenwich Invitational Tournament every July 4th, and in August, hosts the Connecticut State Championship.

exercise

Yoga and Tai Chi are listed in their own category below.

Bodd

181 Greenwich Avenue (upstairs), 983.5470

www.Boddfitness.com

The Bodd technique class is an intense 60-minute workout. The movements are rigorous but gentle and are designed to help you improve your posture, strength, stamina and flexibility. Babysitting is available. They also sell exercise clothing.

Curves for Women

37 West Putnam Avenue, 661.2700

www.curvesinternational.com

Curves for Women presents a new concept of 30-minute fitness, strength training and weight loss guidance for women. The system is built around a variety of hydraulic resistance machines that are easy to learn. This is a different approach to fitness that seems to be catching on.

Fitness Edge

1333 East Putnam Avenue, 637.3906

www.FitnessEdge.net

A popular place to work out. Lots of machines and classes, including one-on-one personal training. The Kidz care program is a plus, children exercise while you are working out.

Hours: Monday - Thursday, 5 am - 10 pm; Friday, 5 am - 9 pm; Saturday, 8 am - 6 pm; Sunday, 8 am - 5 pm.

exercise

Go Figure Exercise Studio

141 West Putnam Avenue, 625.7616
www.gofigurestudio.com
This method combines the principles of ballet, yoga, Pilates and orthopedic exercises to give you great posture, flexibility and lean muscles. This studio believes in using a holistic approach to exercise to create a method that is gentle, yet challenging. In addition to the Figure Method classes, which are held for different levels, they also offer a half hour abdominal class and a 75-minute cycling class. Their website is very informative.

Greenwich Fitness Center

5 Oak Street, 869.6189
Well-equipped fitness center with weight rooms. They have a staff of 10 personal trainers, but they also allow members to bring in their own personal trainer. Summer members welcome. Initiation fee approximately $200.
Hours: Monday Thursday, 6 am - 8 pm; Friday, 6 am - 6:30 pm; Saturday, 8 am - 2 pm.

Greenwich Pilates Center

309 Greenwich Avenue (second floor), 204, 869-3900
With over ten years teaching experience, Edvins Puris personalizes every client's workout, ranging from elite athletes to post-physical therapy rehabilitation. It is an exclusive one-on-one studio experience. Edvins offers Pilates combined with Gyrotonics for $95 a session; $65 each for duets. We like Edvins!

MeJo Wiggin Pilates Center

52 Lewis Street, 629.3743
www.mejowiggin.com
Certified and trained by master teacher Romana Kryzanowska. They are recognized by the Pilates Studio of New York and Romana's Pilates, LLC. Pilates is a methodology of movement based on carefully developed principles that teach you to use your buttocks, abdominal and lower back muscles. Fully equipped with all 16 pieces of equipment, they give private lessons only. Lessons range from $100 to $130 per hour.

exercise

NY Sports Club

6 Liberty Way, 869.1253
www.nysportsclubs.com
In addition to a 6,000 sq. ft. state-of-the-art fitness center, the aerobics and spinning' studios offer classes seven days-a-week. Medically based health and wellness programs include nutrition, massage, personal training and a Medicare certified physical therapy department. Childcare available. Initiation fee approximately $150.
Hours: weekdays, 5:30 am - 9:30 pm; Saturday, 7 am - 5 pm; Sunday, 8 am - 5 pm.

Kneaded Touch

83 Harvard Avenue, Stamford, 967.1121
www.KneadedTouch.com
For 9 years Anthony Mirabel and William Asher have, as the name implies, encouraged optimal fitness for many Greenwich residents. The very helpful, friendly staff will help you evaluate your needs. They are well-known for their sports massage therapies.

Peak Physique

50 Holly Hill Lane, 625.9595
www.peakphysique.biz
If you are not down to the weight you want for your beach vacation, sign up for their bikini boot camp. In one month (5-day a week program of diet and exercise) they promise to have you ready for the beach. Dom Novak, the owner of Peak Physique, is a well regarded trainer keeping many Greenwich residents fit year round.

Pumping Iron

209 Bruce Park Avenue, 661.5017
A lot of independent personal trainers use this gym.
Hours: weekdays, 5:30 am - 9 pm; Saturday, 7 am - 3 pm; Sunday, 8 am - 1 pm.

exercise

Sportsplex

49 Brownhouse Road, Stamford, 358.0066
www.Sportsplex-CT.com
On the border of Stamford and Old Greenwich is a complete training facility for adults and children. Morning programs for pre-schoolers and after school programs for ages 6 - 8. Supervised nursery for children. In addition to machines and spinning, they have an Olympic-length pool, four squash courts and one racquetball court. Swimming and squash lessons are available. The aerobics center has a specially designed exercise floor. Call for an enthusiastic tour.
Hours: Monday - Thursday, 5:30 am - 10 pm; Friday, 5:30 am - 9 pm; Saturday 7 am - 8 pm, Sunday 7 am - 8 pm. (Different summer hours.)

Thompson Exercise

203.274.6890, cell: 203-496.9944
www.thompson-exercise.com
Thompson Method classes work on stretching, strength and stamina (including combinations). Associates who attend the school love it. Classes are held at the Boys & Girls Club and at the Ivan Lendl Grand Slam Tennis Club. Bill believes that anyone, no matter what age or ability has the potential to achieve a high level of fitness and well being.

YMCA (Greenwich Family Y)

50 East Putnam Avenue, 869.1630
www.gwymca.org
Renovated facility with an impressive weight room. The Y also provides aerobics, swimming, studio cycling, tennis, basketball, yoga, etc. Nice indoor track. The Y is open to men and women. You should consider joining, but you don't have to be a member to use their facilities. Experienced babysitters are available to watch children while you work out.
Hours: weekdays, 5 am - 10 pm; Saturday, 6 am - 7 pm;
Sunday, 8 am - 5 pm.

YWCA

259 East Putnam Avenue, 869.6501
www.ywcagreenwich.org
Gymnasium, climbing wall, badminton, tennis, racquet ball, weight room, classes, etc. Good indoor pool and swimming programs. Experienced babysitters are available to watch children while you work out. They have instructors trained in the Boutelle Method.
Hours: weekdays, 6 am - 10 pm; Saturday, 9 am - 5 pm.

FITNESS & SPORTS
fishing

Greenwich is ideally located on the Long Island Sound for excellent salt water fishing from May to December. Going east or west at different times of the year provides a multispecies catch including Striped Bass, Bluefish, Fluke, Porgies and Blackfish. Light spin, fly or bait tackle is the most fun. Freshwater fishing for Trout and Bass is good in the Mianus River. Fishing in reservoirs is prohibited. Blue ribbon trout streams in CT and NY are within a 90-minute drive. The resources below can help you. Also see Fishing Stores, such as Orvis or the Sportsman's Den, under SHOPS for more than just equipment.

Connecticut Angler's Guide

Connecticut Department of Environmental Protection
860.424.FISH
www.dep.state.ct.us/burnatr/fishing/fishinfo/angler.htm
This guide should come with your license. It provides a summary of the rules and regulations governing sport fishing in Connecticut, descriptions of places to fish, the kinds of fish found there, and license information.

Fishing Charters
- **Bill Fish Charters**
914.967.8246; sails from Cos Cob
- **Greenwich Guide Service**
203.650.7696; sails from the Greenwich Water Club
www.GreenwichGuideService.com
- **Salty Flies Charters**
203.561.9683; sails from Rowayton
www.SaltyFlies.com
- **Snow Goose Fishing Charters**
203.255.4522; sails from Byram
www.SnowGoose2.com
- **Sparky Charters**
914.747.5825; sails from Cos Cob

Fishing Licenses

Licenses can be obtained from the Town Clerk's office, 622.7897
www.greenwichct.virtualtownhall.net/Public_Documents/
GreenwichCT_TownClerk/tcHuntingFishingApp.pdf Fishing licenses are $20 for residents and $40 for non-residents. They are good for the calendar year.

fishing

Mianus River Park

Merrybrook Road (Cognewaugh Road), 622.7814
Good trout fishing. Be sure you have your license, they do check.
See section on PARKS & BEACHES for directions.

Noreast Saltwater Fishing

www.noreast.com
A publication devoted to Northeast Sportfishing.

Shell Fishing

Due to the efforts of our wonderful Shellfish Commission (which is working to restore the oysters beds in Greenwich waters), residents can have the fun of digging for shellfish (clams and oysters) in the sand at Greenwich Point. A season permit is required and can be obtained from the Town Clerk's office. The season starts about mid-October, but call 622.7777 first to learn which beds are open.

Trout Unlimited, Mianus Chapter

Jim Glowienka, President, 203.857.4325
Mike Law, Vice President, 203.966.3364
PO Box 663, Riverside, CT
www.mianustu.org
Non-profit organization dedicated to preserving water quality. Classes in flyfishing and fly tying.

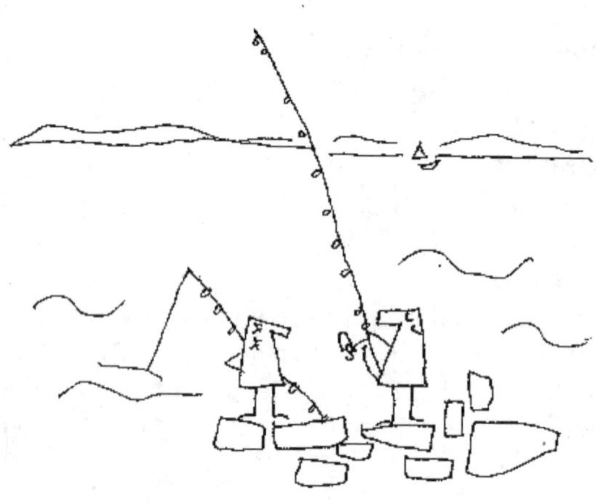

flying

See also soaring, skydiving & ballooning below.

Fighter Pilot for a Day

800.522.7590
www.aircombat.com
Since 1988 they have been giving civilians the experience of being a fighter pilot. Guest pilots fly real military fighters with licensed fighter pilots in the cockpit with them. Aircraft are outfitted with high end digital multi-camera systems to capture your fighter pilot experience. No pilot's license is required. Course begins with pilot training, then real dogfight experience, then a briefing on your performance (or lack thereof). They travel around the country, but fly out of Montgomery, New York in April & October.

Flight Safety

Vero Beach Florida, 772.564.7600 or 800.800.1411
www.flightsafetyacademy.com
The premier flight training school. It is directed toward teaching people who want to be professional pilots, but there is no better place for a private pilot to begin their training. The weather is great so you will be able to fly every day.

Panorama Flight School

Westchester County Airport, 914.328.9800
www.flypfs.com/Flight_School.htm
Flight lessons for all levels of pilots. A good place to get experience in the NY air traffic area.

Westchester Flying Club

Westchester Count Airport
Vice President, Tom Fleischman, 845.358.0799
www.wfchpn.org

football

Cos Cob Athletic Club

Contact: Teresa Burhans, 698.2817
A community organization sponsoring elementary and middle school football teams for ages 8 -13. The Cos Cob Crushers, (ages 8 - 13 or in 8th grade) with cheerleaders in the fall.

Greenwich Youth Football League

Gateway Youth Football League
Contact Will Dunster, 625.0842, 637.0766
www.gyfl.net, www.greenwichfootball.com
Townwide instructional/competitive tackle football league for children ages 8 - 13. Registration takes place in August. The season runs from September to November.
Practices are held 2 - 3 time a week. Games are on Sunday.
The teams are: Glenville Mavericks, Banc Raiders, Cos Cob Crushers, North Mianus Bulldogs and Putnam Generals. Each team has three levels: Bantam, 3rd & 4th graders; Junior, 5th & 6th graders; Senior, 7th & 8th graders.

YMCA Flag Football League

50 East Putnam Avenue
contact: Ron Monroe at 869.1630 or rmonroe@gwymca.org
www.gwymca.org
One-hour games played at North Street School.
League runs September 9 - October 28 for children 7 to 12 years-old.

Public Golf Courses

There are a number of nearby courses open to non-residents. Some of these have limited times for non-residents Many facilities have discounts for seniors, juniors, early morning or late afternoon play, or for 9-hole rounds. If you like the course, check out their policy on season passes. Be sure to book before you go.
www.ctgolfer.com or www.co.westchester.ny.us/parks

Doral Golf Club

Anderson Hill Road, Rye Brook, 914.939.5500
Nine holes, par 35. 5,689 yards, pro shop, driving range, putting green and restaurant.
Hours: Monday - Thursday: 7:00am - 6:00pm

Gaynor Brennan Municipal Golf Course

451 Stillwater Road, Stamford, 324.4185
www.ci.stamford.ct.us, search "Golf"
Par 71. You can reserve seven days in advance.

Griffith Harris Memorial Golf Course

13231 King Street, 531.7200, 6944, 7261, 8253, 1138
www.greenwichct.org/ParksAndRec/prGolfCourse.asp
Open only to Greenwich residents (including tenants). This par 71, 18-hole golf course designed by Robert Trent Jones has a club house, pro shop, putting green and driving range. Call about obtaining a membership card. You will need to bring proof of Greenwich residency (such as a current phone bill) and a photo ID such as a driver's license. Membership is $75 for an adult permanent resident or $135 for a summer resident.

Lake of Ilses Golf Course

North Stonington, CT (Near Foxwoods Casino),
888.475.3746
www.lakeofisles.com
36-hole top rated golf course and golf academy.

Maple Moor

1128 North Street, White Plains, NY, 914.995.9200
automated reservations: 914.995.4653
www.maplemoorgolf.com
Par 71, You can reserve seven days in advance.

golf

Oak Hills Golf Course

165 Fillow Street, Norwalk, CT, 203.838.0303

www.oakhillsgc.com

Par 71; You can reserve seven days ahead for weekdays only. They have an automated tee time reservation system.

Richter Park Golf Course

100 Aunt Hack Road, Danbury, CT

203.792.2552 x 12, 748.5743, 792.2550, x 11.

www.richterpark.com

Considered to be the top public course in Connecticut. 18 holes, weekday starting times can be reserved 3 days in advance; slots start at 9 am.

Ridgefield Golf Course

545 Ridgebury Road, Ridgefield, CT, 203.748.7008

www.RidgefieldCT.org

Par 71; You can reserve up to 3 days ahead for weekends.

Saxon Woods

Mamaroneck Road, Scarsdale, NY, 914.231.3461

Automated reservations: 914.995.4653

www.westchesterny.com/parks/golf/SaxonWoods.htm

Par 71

Sterling Farms

1349 Newfield Avenue, Stamford, 461.9090

www.sterlingfarmsgc.com

Par 72; On weekends, non-residents can play after 2:30 pm. You can reserve up to seven days in advance.

Vails Grove Golf Course

PO Box 417, Peach Lake, North Salem, NY, 845.669.5721

Par 66 (9-hole, doubletee).

On weekends, non-members can play after 1 pm.

golf practice

If you need a little practice before playing, use the golf range at Griffith Harris Memorial Golf Course or one of these.

Golf Training Center in Norwalk

145 Main Street, Norwalk, CT, 203.847.8008
www.golftraining.com
They provide indoor practice for your pitching and putting techniques, including driving bays with computer replay, virtual reality golf and exercise areas.
Hours: Monday - Thursday, 10 am - 9 pm;
Friday - Sunday, 10 am - 6 pm.

Nike Golf Schools and Junior Camps

800.645.3226
www.ussportscamps.com
Nike sponsors a great number of adult and junior golf camps. The closest are Williams College, Williamstown, MA; Stowe, VT; and Loomis Chaffee, Windsor, CT.

Putting Edge Minature Golf

Le Count Place, New Rochelle, NY, 914.632.3346
www.puttingedge.com
Glow-in-the-dark course at the New Rochelle City entertainment complex. Indoor course with 350 props and obstacles.

Westchester Golf Range

701 Dobbs Ferry Road, White Plains, NY, 914.592.6553.
Seventy-five lighted tees. PGA teaching professionals conduct individual lessons and instruction programs.
Hours: Summer hours: open every day, 8:30 am - 9 pm.
Directions: I-287 W to exit 3, Sprain Brook Pkw S to Rte 100B.

hockey

Boys and Girls Club of Greenwich
4 Horseneck Lane, 869.3224
Melissa Hawkins Program Coordinator/Hockey Coach ext 111
www.BGCG.org
They have an extensive hockey program, including co-ed Broomball, girls ice hockey clinics and Mite Development Hockey League.

Department of Parks and Recreation Field Hockey Programs
Pemberwick Park, Moshier Street & Pemberwick Road
www.greenwichct.org/ParksAndRec/prRecPrograms.asp
Co-ed field hockey clinics for grades 2 - 8 on Saturday mornings from late September through October. August registration.

Department of Parks and Recreation Ice Hockey Programs
At Dorothy Hamill Skating Rink, 622.7830
www.greenwichct.org/ParksAndRec/ParksAndRec.asp
Prep League for boys and girls ages 13 - 14. Junior Hockey League for ages 15 - 17. Sunday evening games, weekly practices. High school varsity participants are not allowed.

Dorothy Hamill Skating Rink
Sherman Avenue, 531.8560
September March; 622.7830, offseason.
www.greenwichct.org/ParksAndRec/prSkating.asp
An excellent municipal skating facility for Greenwich residents and their guests. You will need proof of residency such as a beach card. The Rink offers a full schedule of skating lessons and ice hockey programs for children, teens, and adults.
Hours: September - March, weekends, 2 pm - 4 pm. Daily schedules are available.
Directions: US-1 W, L on Western Junior Highway, R on Henry, R on Sherman Avenue.

hockey

Greenwich Blues Youth Ice Hockey Association

PO Box 1107, Greenwich, CT 06836
Contact: Joe Bastone, President, 203.252.1080, joebast@optonline.net
www.greenwichblues.com
Non-profit organization sponsoring competitive travel teams for boys and girls: Mites, under age 9; Squirts, 9 - 11; Peewees, 11 - 13; Bantam, 13 - 15. Dorothy Hamill Rink is their home rink. Season is from September through March, tryouts are in early September.

In-Line Roller Hockey

Old GreenwichRiverside Community Center
90 Harding Road, Old Greenwich, 637.3659
Adult pickup roller hockey as well as spring and summer instruction and games for boys and girls ages 6 - 14. Call for times and details.

Stamford Twin Rinks

1063 Hope Street, Stamford 968.9000
www.icecenter.com
They have a wide variety of programs for all level and interests.

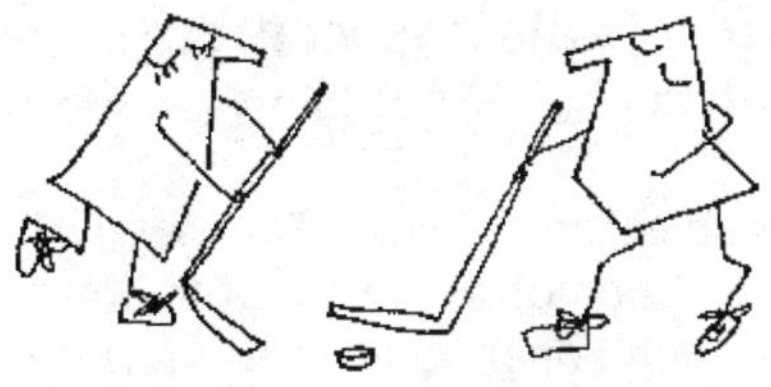

horseback riding

Picture fall leaves, stone walls and a rider on a handsome horse on a scenic woodland trail. Yes, this is Greenwich. Where we have over 150 miles of riding trails which connect to the 100 miles of trails in Stamford. For insurance reasons, most stables will not rent horses for unaccompanied trail rides unless you have been taking a series of lessons and they have determined your skill level.

Coker Farm

69 Stone Hill Road, Bedford, (North Salem) NY
914.234.3954, 6706
Set on 100 acres with indoor and outdoor riding areas, they give lessons from beginner to advanced.
Directions: North St. to the end, R onto Rte 22. Go thru Bedford Village, the road will bear L. R onto Rte 121. Go 2 miles, R onto Rte 137. The farm is 1/4 mile on the R. Sign says Coker Farm.

Getner Farm

40 Oak Hill Avenue, Norwalk, CT, 203.838.6245
Barn is located at 22 Richards Avenue
www.getnerfarm.com
English riding in a relaxed atmosphere. Blue jeans are the norm.

Greenwich Polo Club

80 Field Point Road
Conyers (White Birch) Farm, North Street, 863.1213
www.GreenwichPolo.com
People interested in playing polo should call the club for information about membership and events.

Greenwich Riding and Trails Association

PO Box 1403, Greenwich 06836, 661.3062
www.thegrta.org
Greenwich has an extensive trail network. This nearly 100 year-old organization maintains 150 miles of horse trails in town and devotes its resources to conservation and open space. For information and help, call them. A great organization to join.

horseback riding

Greenwich Polo Club

80 Field Point Road, 661.5420
www.GreenwichPolo.com
Kirsten Lewis, 863-1202
Greenwich has a world class polo facility. Most summer Sundays you can watch a good polo match in a beautiful setting. Matches begin at 3 pm, the gates open at 1 pm. General admission is $30 per car.

Lionshare Farm

404 Taconic Road, 869.4649
www.lionsharefarm.com
An excellent riding academy with programs for children and adults. The farm, owned by Peter Leone, an Olympic silver medalist, has two indoor rings and an outdoor ring, as well as access to the Greenwich trails. It is the premier show jumping stable in the Greenwich area. This is the first place to go if you want to buy a jumper.

New England Farm

203 Greenwich Road, Bedford, NY, 914.234.6692
Boarding and lessons both indoor and outdoor.

On The Go Farms

1145 King Street, 532.4727
A friendly stable, focused on safety, with horses that are well cared for. Participants like the camaraderie.

Ox Ridge Hunt Club

512 Middlesex Road, Darien, CT, 203.655.2559
www.oxridge.com
There are many places to learn to ride, but serious riders will like Ox Ridge. This private hunt club offers riding lessons to the public. Ten half-hour private lessons are $800. You will find good horses, indoor and outdoor facilities and top instructors.

Pegasus Therapeutic Riding Inc

45 Church Street, Stamford, CT, 356.9504
www.pegasustr.org
Non-profit organization provides riding as therapy for disabled children and adults.

horseback riding

Red Barn Stables

43 Den Road, Stamford, CT, 223.3358
Indoor riding stables, boarding, horses for sale.

Stratford Stables

120 Cottage Avenue, Purchase NY, 914.686.3691
Lessons for beginners through advanced, with a specialty in training for show.

Windswept Farms

107 June Road, Stamford, 322.4984
Windswept, is a stable with a warm family atmosphere. Both Western and English saddles are available. They give outdoor riding lessons for boys and girls 6 - 17. No previous riding experience is required. Located at the Greenwich/Stamford border, the stable has access to the Greenwich trail system. Their June through August pony summer camp is extremely popular. Sign up early. Campers have fun riding, learning horse etiquette and how to tack and clean their horses. The day often finishes with a dip in the swimming hole.

hunting

Hunting Licenses are issued by the Connecticut Department of Environmental Protection, (DEP License and Revenue Unit,79 Elm Street, Hartford, CT 06106-5127). License applications can be obtained from the Town Clerk's office, 622.7894 or on line at:

* http://dep.state.ct.us/burnatr/wildlife/wdhome.htm
* http://greenwichct.virtualtownhall.net/public_documents/ FOV10000DE97/

A special landowner permit to hunt deer on their own property is available on line at:
http://greenwichct.virtualtownhall.net/Public_Documents/ GreenwichCT_TownClerk/tcDeerLandowner.pdf

The Hunting and Trapping Guide and Wildlife area maps can be obtained from the Town Clerk's office, 622.7894 or on-line at:
http://dep.state.ct.us/burnatr/wildlife/fguide/fgindex.htm

TIP: OX RIDGE HORSE SHOW

Enjoy the nationally acclaimed hunter-jumper competition in June at the Ox Ridge Hunt Club in Darien, CT. Olympic as well as local riders compete in this Grand Prix event.
Call 203.655.2559 for details.

ice skating

Binney Pond
Sound Beach Avenue, Old Greenwich
This is the prettiest pond for skating and it is town-tested for safety.

Boys and Girls Club of Greenwich
4 Horseneck Lane
Melissa Hawkins Program Coordinator, 869.3224 x 111
www.BGCG.org
Private lessons, learn to skate, figure skating and hockey clinics on their indoor ice rink.

Dorothy Hamill Skating Rink
Sherman Avenue,www.greenwichct.org/ParksAndRec/prSkating.asp
531.8560 Mid-Sept through Mid-March
622.7830 during the off season
We expect more Dorothy Hamills to graduate from this rink!
Ask about figure skating lessons.

Greenwich Skating Club
Cardinal Road, 622.9583
www.GreenwichSkatingClub.org
The Skating Club, set inconspicuously off Fairfield Road, has an outdoor rink and offers a strong skating program for children. Because of its small membership, it is one of the more difficult clubs to join.

Mianus River
Park off of Valley Road, bring your skates and hockey sticks (a snow shovel, too.)

Stamford Twin Rinks
1063 Hope Street, Stamford 968.9000
www.icecenter.com
They have a wide variety of programs for all levels and interests.

Windy Hill Figure Skating Club
Linda Myder, Membership Chair, 531.7774
Non-profit skating club affiliated with the US Figure Skating Association. Membership is open to all figure skaters who have progressed beyond "Basic 6". Home ice is the Dorothy Hamill Rink.

karate / kendo

Almost every school has a variety of children and adult classes.

Devita Karate

37 West Putnam Avenue, 629 2467
www.devitakarate.com
Tang-soo-do Karate and kickboxing. Joseph Devita is a 6th degree Black Belt and has been teaching in Greenwich since 1981.

Dynamic Martial Arts Family Center

202 Field Point Road, 629.4666
www.GreenwichKarate.com
They have fitness programs, many children's classes and Kempo karate and Tai Chi classes for adults.

Calasanz Physical Arts

• 47 West Main Street, Stamford, CT, 977.7791
• 507 Westport Ave (Rt. 1) in Norwalk, CT, 203.847.6528
www.Calasanz.com
Self defense using a number of techniques. The original school is in Norwalk.

Kang Tae-kwon-do & Hapkido

263 Sound Beach Ave, Old Greenwich, 637.7867 or 8253
One of several locations run by Grand Master Ik Jo Kang.

Old Greenwich School of Karate (Action Arts)

242 Sound Beach Avenue, 698.1057, 637.2685
www.greenwichkidskarate.com
Japanese Isshinryu Karate and Filipino Jitsu taught by 6th dan Sensei Rick Zimmerman

Shidogakuin

38 Mary Lane, Riverside, CT 637.5475
www.kendoka.org
Kendo and Iaido
Contact: Shozo Kato, 212.431.1322 or skato@kendoka.org
Shidogakuni Dojo, Stamford CT Learning Center, 65 Research Drive

karate / kendo

Tiger Schulmann's

2333 Summer Street, Stamford, 969.0352
www.tsk.com
A franchise teaching self-defense skills combining karate, kickboxing and
submission grappling.

White Tiger Tae Kwon Do

181 Greenwich Avenue (second Floor), 661.6054
Master Kwan Ji, 5th Degree Black Belt.

TIP: SIDEWALK SALES

Greenwich residents eagerly await summer sidewalk sales. Expect a
good time with bargains galore. Don't forget to go inside the stores;
they are also full of incredible buys during these sales. Mid- July (on
a Thursday, Friday and Saturday) in Central Greenwich and Old Greenwich. Call the Chamber of Commerce, 869.3500.

FITNESS & SPORTS

lacrosse

NOTE: Bridgeport Barrage major League Lacrosse is listed in CHILDREN, FAMILY OUTINGS.

Greenwich Youth Lacrosse

www.GreenwichYouthLacrosse.org
PO Box 4627, Greenwich, CT 068310412, 352.3933
A non-profit organization sponsoring lacrosse teams. House League for boys and girls in grades 1 - 6; Travel teams for boys and girls in grades 3 - 4 and 5 - 6. Boys travel teams for grades 7 - 8. Registration is usually in March.

Greenwich Department of Recreation

Indoor Lacrosse Clinic, Claudia Collins, 622.6485
Co-ed introductory, non-contact clinic (ages 7 & 8, 9 & 10) teaching fundamentals at the Greenwich Civic Center in Old Greenwich.

The Academy of Sports

55 Crescent Street, Stamford, CT, 353.1199
Www.theacademyofsports.com
Lacrosse clinics for boys and girls, 4th through 12th grades.

lawn bowling

Greenwich Lawn Bowls Club

869.0087 or 323.7451
www.geocities.com/greenwichbowls
This 25-member club, welcomes men and women of all ages. The group has fun bowling on the course, built in 1940 in Bruce Park. The club is affiliated with the Northeast Division of the U.S. Lawn Bowl Association.

paddle tennis

paddle tennis courts

Loughlin Avenue, Cos Cob

This 6-acre park has the only paddle tennis courts in Greenwich. The courts are lighted and open year-round. A small playground adjoins the tennis and paddle tennis courts. Call the Department of Parks & Recreation (622.7830) for a card to use the courts and for information on using the lights.

paintball

Liberty Paintball

Thunder Ridge Ski Area, 845.878.6300

www.libertypaintballny.com

350 acres of varied terrain just North and West of Danbury, CT. Friends tell us they rate it 5 stars. They suggest the beginner bring their own group of about 20-participants and rent equipment there. Don't forget to wear protective clothing.

Paintball Madness

737 Canal Street, Building 19 (Stamford Industrial Park)
 975.2973

www.stamfordpaintball.com

A 14,000 square foot facility where locals go when they can't go outside. A great place to rent for a birthday party.

polo

Greenwich Polo Club

80 Field Point Road, 661.5420

www.GreenwichPolo.com

Kirsten Lewis, 863-1202

Greenwich has a worldclass polo facility. Most summer Sundays you can watch a good polo match in a beautiful setting. Matches begin at 3 pm, the gates open at 1 pm. General admission is $30 per car.

racing - auto

Alpine Motor Sports Club

Eldred Township, Monroe County, Pennsylvania
Contact; Kim Bowers, 610.670.7657 or Deb Smith, 800.795.2638.
www.AlpineSignature.com
Located on 350 acres, you can put the (pedal to the metal) on their 4 mile straightaways and high speed turns.

Greenwich Road Rally

www.greenwichroadrally.com
A sports car rally put on annually by the Greenwich Jaycees. www.GreenwichJaycees.org. The route runs through scenic areas in Westchester and Fairfield Counties.

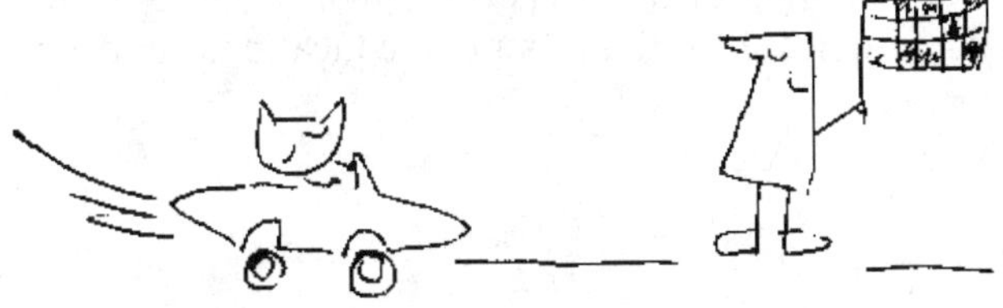

Lime Rock Park

Lakeville, CT, 800.Race.LRP
www.limerock.com
About two hours north of Greenwich is the Lime Rock Race Track. The track is closed on Sundays, but most Saturdays (from early April to November) there are formula and sports car races. Lime Rock has no grandstands. You can get tickets online or at the gate. Call to find out about the race schedule or to get a copy of their free newspaper, Track Record. The biggest race days are usually Memorial Day and Labor Day.

Overland Experts

East Haddam, CT (near Essex and Old Lyme), 877.931.3343
www.overlandexperts.com
4WD on and off-road driving instruction as well as international expeditions.

racing - auto

Skip Barber Racing School

Lime Rock Park, Lakeville, CT, 860.435.1300, 800.221.1131
www.skipbarber.com
Skip Barber is the largest racing school in the country. If you have always wanted to learn to race, this is the place to go. Two basic driving courses are offered, with a lot of variations for each course: Advanced Driving School (one and two-day courses driving three different cars supplied by the school); Racing School (three hours to eight days) The school supplies the formula cars.

Sports Car Driving Association

23 Belmont Avenue, Deep River, CT, 860.526.4423
www.scda1.com
SCDA provides drivers of all skills the opportunity to experience high performance driving. Events are strictly educational and non-competitive.

TIP: VOTER REGISTRATION

622.7889, 7890 , vote@greenwichct.org
www.greenwichct.org/VoterRegistration/VoterRegistration.asp
You must be registered at least 14 days before a regular election and by noon of the last business day before a party primary. You must be registered by the day before a special election or referendum. Register in person at the Town Clerk's Office or Registrar of Voter's Office at Town Hall, at any office of the State Motor Vehicles, or at libraries throughout the state. Proof of residency and age 18 or over on election day are required.

See also FITNESS & SPORTS, walking/hiking.

Appalachian Mountain Club

Fairfield County Group, 7 Vera Drive Bethel CT, 203.762.0216

www.ctamc.org

The Fairfield County group sponsors or participates in a variety of outdoor activities, such as hiking, mountain and road biking, rock climbing, canoeing and kayaking, and crosscountry skiing.

Go Vertical

727 Canal Street, Stamford CT 358.8767

www.govertical.com

8,000 square feet of safe, challenging, indoor climbing surfaces, with onsite equipment. Lessons for beginners aged 13 and over. All necessary equipment can be rented. Be sure to call in advance if you are a beginner.
Hours: weekdays, 10 am - 10 pm; weekends, 10 am - 8 pm.
Directions: I-95 N to exit 8. R on Canal (2nd Light).

Outward Bound

100 Mystery Point Road Garrison NY
845.424.4000 general inquiries
866.467.7651 Admissions Advisor

www.obusa.com

It was founded in Greenwich in 1961 and offers adventure-based learning to develop personal growth through experience and challenge. One of its five core programs is climbing.

YWCA

259 East Putnam Avenue, 869.6501

www.ywcagreenwich.org

The Y provides training for beginning climbers on their gym climbing wall.

roller skating / skate boarding

See also FITNESS & SPORTS, HOCKEY.
For skate boards and inline skates, try Chili Bears or Rink & Racquet.

Eastern Civic Center

90 Harding Road, Old Greenwich, 637.4583
www.ogrcc.com
The Greenwich Civic Center offers roller skating from October - April.
Call for details.

Greenwich Skateboard Park

Roger Sherman Baldwin Park, Arch Street, 496.9876
www.greenwichct.org
The 7,754 sq. ft. skate park was a gift of the Junior League of Greenwich.
The maximum number of skaters is 40. Membership is $10 for a day
pass. Greenwich residents may apply for a $60 ten-time pass or an an-
nual membership. The Department of Parks and Recreation conducts clinics in basic techniques, safety and etiquette. Call 622.7830 for information.
Hours vary depending upon when schools are in session.

running

Babcock Preserve

North Street, 622.7700
Two miles north of the Merritt Parkway, 297 acres of well-marked running trails.

Greenwich Kids Triathlon

www.greenwichkidstri.com
The triathlon consists of a swim, bike and run, at the Greenwich High School campus. It is for 7-10 and 11-12 year olds. Founded in 2003 by Fionnuala Mackey, it is run by Bill Bogardus, a physical education teacher at North Street School and head of Project Fitness, a personal training company for kids. www.projectfitnessonline.com

Greenwich Point (Tod's Point)

Entrance at the south end of Shore Road in Old Greenwich.
This 147-acre beach has lots of jogging and biking trails.
A beach card is required, see PARKS AND BEACHES.

Jim Fixx Memorial Day Race

Greenwich Recreation Office, 622.7830
Threads and Treads, 661.0142
This five-mile race, which starts and ends on Greenwich Avenue, begins the running season. If you run in no other event, you should consider it. It is always well attended and attracts a great variety of talented and not-so-talented runners.

Threads and Treads

17 East Putnam Avenue, 661.0142
www.ThreadsAndTreads.com
www.RoadHogs.org
This fine outfitting store has sponsored and created all kinds of running events for our town. Stop in to find out about running events all over Fairfield County.

Measured Running and Walking Routes

Department of Parks and Recreation, 618.7649.
www.greenwichct.org/ParksAndRec/ParksandRec.asp
Patrick Carino created this useful map as an Eagle Scout project.

soccer

Department of Parks and Recreation
Town Hall, 622.7830
www.greenwichct.virtualtownhall.net/Public_Documents/
GreenwichCT_ParkRec/GreenwichCT_Recreation/programs/youth
The Department sponsors summer, spring and fall co-ed programs.

Greenwich Soccer Association
PO Box 1535, Greenwich, CT 06830, 203.292-6208
www.greenwichtravelsoccer.com
Will Fay, Boys' Coordinator; John Massad, Girls' Coordinator
Girls' and boys' travel soccer teams for ages 9 to 14. They play travel teams from other Fairfield County towns on Sunday afternoons. Tryouts are required and usually begin in November for the spring season.

Greenwich Soccer Club
PO Box 383, Cos Cob, CT 06807, 661.2620
www.greenwichsoccer.com
The Greenwich Soccer Club is a volunteer based, all-inclusive, recreational and instructional program with a firm commitment to safety, fun and fairness. The GSC is a townwide recreational program open to every boy and girl, ages 6 - 14, who either resides in or attends school in town. In the fall, over 1,700 boys and girls participate on Saturdays (coached by some 350 parent volunteers) with mid-week clinics taught by professional instructors. There are separate leagues for the boys and girls. The GSC is a privately funded, non-profit community service organization founded in 1976. Peter Clauson is the President.

Indoor Soccer
Greenwich Parks and Recreation, 622.7830
Winter co-ed training for children K - 6th grade. Limited to twenty-five children, so apply early. Registration by mail only: Greenwich Parks & Recreation, Recreation Division, 101 Field Point Road, Greenwich, CT 06836-2540.

soccer

Old Greenwich-Riverside Soccer Association

637.6776

www.Ogrcc.com

Part of the Old Greenwich-Riverside Community Center and the Connecticut Junior Soccer Association, the club provides a comprehensive soccer program for over 700 youngsters who just wish to play for fun, as well as for those who wish to compete.

YMCA

50 East Putnam Avenue, 869.1630

www.gwymca.org

The Y provides spring training in the basics for youngsters ages 4 - 5 and 6 - 8. The emphasis is on sportsmanship and having fun.

shooting

Cos Cob Revolver & Rifle Club

451 Steamboat Road, 622.9508

www.ccrrc.com

For those looking for a safe way to practice target shooting, this Greenwich club (despite its Cos Cob name), just across from the train station, has terrific facilities and a very helpful membership (including the Greenwich Police, many of whom practice here). To join, call and listen to the recorded announcement. Usually, all you have to do is attend a meeting (the second Wednesday of each month at 8 pm). To transport a gun to and from the club you need a Connecticut handgun license, which they can help you obtain.

Smith & Wesson Academy

299 Page Boulevard, Springfield, MA, 800.331.0852

www.smithwesson.com

20 shooting lanes open to the public. Private lessons and a number of handgun courses such as defensive shooting and handgun techniques.

Old Greenwich-Riverside Community Center

90 Harding Road, 637.3659

www.ogrcc.com

Day ski trips for members in grades 5-8.

LOCAL FAMILY SKI AREAS

There are a great variety of ski areas in the Northeast. For fun on the slopes try some of the following areas:

Hunter Mountain

Hunter, NY, 800.486.8376

www.huntermtn.com

Difficulty: Beginner, Intermediate, Advanced.

Size: 12 lifts, 53 trails, snowmaking, snowtubing.

Distance: 2.5 hrs, I-87 N exit 20, Rte 32 N, Rte 23A W.

Mohawk Mountain

46 Great Hollow Road, Cornwall, CT, 860.672.6100, 800.895.5222

www.mohawkmtn.com

Difficulty: Beginner & Intermediate.

Size: 5 lifts, 24 trails, snowmaking, night skiing.

Distance: 1.5 hrs, I-95 N to Rte 8 N to exit 44.

At the second light, left onto Rte 4 W (about 20 minutes).

Mount Southington

396 Mount Vernon Road, Plainsville, CT

860.628.0954, 800.982.6828

www.mountsouthington.com

Difficulty: Beginner & Intermediate.

Size: 7 lifts, 14 trails, snowmaking, night skiing.

Distance: 2 hrs, I-84 N exit 30.

skiing

Powder Ridge

99 Powder Hill Road, Middlefield, CT
877.754.7434, 860.349.3454
www.powderridgect.com
Difficulty: Beginner & Intermediate, snowtubing.
Size: 7 lifts (2 for tubing), 5 wide runs, 14 trails, night skiing.
Distance: 45 minutes, Merritt Pkw N exit 67.

Windham Mountain

Windham, NY, 518.734.4300, 800.754.9463
The snow report hotline, 800.729.4766
www.skiwindham.com
Difficulty: Beginner, Intermediate & Expert.
Size: 33 trails, 7 lifts, snowmaking.
Distance: 2.5 hrs, I-87 N exit 21, Rte 23 W.

Winding Trails Cross Country Ski Center

50 Winding Trails Drive, Farmington, CT, 860.674.4227
www.windingtrails.com
Difficulty: Beginner, Intermediate.
Size: 20 Kilometers of trails in 350 acres of woodland, lakes and wildlife.
Distance: 2.5 hrs, I-84 N exit 39, Rte 4 W.

LARGE REGIONAL SKI AREAS

These areas also have extensive summer family activities.
Check the websites for details.

Killington Resort

4763 Killington Road, Killington, VT
800.621.6867, 802.422.6200
www.killington.com

Mount Snow Resort

12 Pisgah Road, West Dover, VT
800.451.4211, 800.245.7669
www.mountsnow.com

Stowe Mountain Resort

5781 Mountain Road, Stowe, VT
802.253.3000, 800.253.4754
www.stowe.com

Stratton Mountain Resort

Stratton Mountain (South Londonderry), VT
802.297.4000, 800.787.2886
www.stratton.com

Whiteface Mountain

Route 86, Wilmington, NY , 518.946.2223
www.Whiteface.com

FITNESS & SPORTS

soaring, skydiving & balloooning

See also Flying above.

Schweizer Soaring School

Elmira, NY, 607.739.3821 x 4202
www.sacusa.com
The oldest glider school in the world is about four hours away. Courses
are available for beginners.

Hot Air Balloons, Soaring and Skydiving

Soaring Adventures of America, Wilton, CT
800.762.7464
www.800soaring.com
Call them to arrange for a fun adventure for you or your family.

TIP: THE JOB SEARCH

If you are looking for a job or an employee, check out the Job Board.
This free public bulletin board is run by Community Answers for
people from the age of 22 and up. It can be viewed in the window of
Community Answers during Library hours. Postings can be phoned
in at 622.7979 or posted in person weekdays, 9 am to 5 pm at the
central Greenwich Library. For other job needs, check out USE (Utilizing Senior Energy) at the Greenwich Senior Center, (629.8032) or
The Student Employment Service at the Greenwich High School
(625.8008) until June and at Community Answers during the summer.

squash / racquetball

Doral Arrowwood

975 Anderson Hill RD. Rye Brook, NY, 914.935.6687
www.doralarrowwood.com/health_racquetballandsquash.asp
Two racquetball courts and one squash court located in their fitness center.

Field Club

276 Lake Avenue, 869.1309
A private club which offers a weekly Junior Summer Squash Camp often open to the public. They have international singles and doubles courts.

Greenwich Academy Squash Training Camp

200 North Maple Avenue, 625.8900 x 7287
During the summer, the Academy uses their five international squash courts to provide training for children in grades 5 and above.

Sportsplex

49 Brownhouse Road, Stamford, CT, 358.0066, 536.4308
www.sportsplex.com
Right on the border of Old Greenwich and Stamford, the Sportsplex has a complete training center, including four hardball squash courts, one racquetball court and squash instruction.

Westchester Squash

628 Fayette Avenue, Mamaroneck, NY 914.698.0095
www.westchestersquash.com
They have four international squash courts with programs for adults and juniors.

YMCA

50 East Putnam Avenue, 869.1630
www.gwymca.org
The Y is spending $4,000,000 for a new gymnasium, racquetball & squash courts.

For Greenwich Beaches see PARKS & BEACHES.

Department of Parks and Recreation

622.7830
www.greenwichct.org/ParksAndRec/ParksandRec.asp
They organize Family Swims at Greenwich High School.

Greenwich Youth Water Polo League (GYWP)

P.O. Box 38 Cos Cob, 352.3405 (recording)
Bill Smith, President
Contact: Walter Lorenz, Girls Division 698.0133
Founded by the coaches of the Greenwich High School water polo team, the GHS has one of the strongest programs on the Eastern seaboard. This league is for boys and girls ages 9 to 15 who want to learn to play water polo.

Town Swim Team: The Dolphins

In addition to the high school swim team, the town has a superior competition swim team, the Dolphins (YWCA 869.6501). The Dolphins are for serious swimmers. Kids start early: swim practice is every day, with meets held on most Sundays. All that is required to join is parental consent and the ability not to sink. Some children start as early as four.

swimming

Town Swim Team: The Marlins

Contact Kristina Lewis, 203.869.1630 x 206

Run at the YMCA, this swim team competes with the Dolphins. The Marlins is a year-round swim club that starts at age 6. They compete in USA sanction swim meets and the Connecticut Summer Swim League. A prerequisite to joining the team is to be able to swim two lengths of the Y pool using two different strokes.

YMCA Programs

50 East Putnam Avenue, 869.1630

www.gwymca.org

The Y is spending $6,000,000 to build an Olympic size pool.

Skippers for parents and babies 6 months to 2 years;

Perch for ages 2 - 3. Children, with help of a parent, propel themselves using flotation aids.

Progressive youth lessons: Polliwog, Guppy, Minnow, Fish, Flying Fish, Shark, for ages 5-12.

Private swimming lessons are available.

Marlins Swim Team, ages 6-18, September to March.

YWCA Programs

259 East Putnam Avenue, 869.6501

www.ywcaGreenwich.org

Aqua Babies for parents and babies 6 months to 3 years;

Aqua Tots/Kids for ages 2 to 4 years who are ready to participate without the parent. Both are ideal introductions to swimming and safety in and around the water.

Junior Aquatics K to 12 years. Progressive learn to swim lessons.

Dolphins Swim Team K to high school. Competitive technique instruction. Private swimming lessons are available.

tennis

Doral Arrowwood
975 Anderson Hill RD. Rye Brook, NY, 914.935.6687
www.doralarrowwood.com/proform_tennis.asp
www.doralarrowwood.com/health_tennis.asp
4 hard courts (2 indoor and 2 outdoor), with ATP professionals to provide junior and adult programs.

Greenwich Racquet Club
1 River Road, Cos Cob, 661.0606
www.leontennis.net
4 indoor DecoTurf hard-surface courts. They have an excellent junior development program, as well as adult clinics taught by USPTA certified pros to all levels. You can play in round robins for men and women or rent a court for the season.

Greenwich Tennis Headquarters
54 Bible Street, Cos Cob, 661.0182
There are 38 all-weather courts available throughout Greenwich, as well as a paddle tennis court location. The town runs junior and adult clinics for all levels and provides private lessons. It also sponsors a junior and adult town tennis tournament which attracts some very good players. Call for information, a map of the courts and a tennis permit.
For more information call Contact Frank Gabriele at 203.622.7821.
- Directions to Town Tennis Courts
  www.greenwichct.org/ParksAndRec/prDirectionsTennis.asp
- Tennis Passes
  www.greenwichct.org/ParksAndRec/prTennis.asp

Grand Slam at Banksville
1 BedfordBanksville Road, Bedford, NY, 914.234.9206
www.grandslamtennisclub.com
Five HarTru courts, five DecoTurf II (hard surface) courts. During the winter, eight are indoor, during the summer, five are outside. Excellent junior and adult programs including USTA League Play.

tennis

Nike Adult and Junior Tennis Camps
800.645.3226
www.ussportscamps.com
Nike sponsors a great number of adult and junior tennis camps. The closest are: Amherst College, Amherst, MA; LoomisChaffee, Windsor, CT; Peddie School, Hightstown, NJ; Lawrenceville School, Lawrenceville, NJ.

Old Greenwich Tennis Academy
151 Sound Beach Avenue, 637.3398
5 indoor HarTru courts. Mainly used by groups who contract for court time. Open September to May. They are also the home for Park Tennis.

Park Tennis USA
Cos Cob, 422.0249, support@ParkTennisUSA.com
www.ParkTennisUSA.com
Rita and Scott Staniar have a terrific idea. Bring high quality tennis instruction to the 70% of players who don't belong to private clubs. Park Tennis has assembled a group of professional instructors which any club would be proud to have. These professionals teach on public courts during the summer and at the Old Greenwich Tennis Academy (151 Sound Beach Avenue) during the winter. Now players of all ages and all skill levels can get superior instruction at modest prices. What are you waiting for?

Personal Pro Services
May - October, Greenwich, 962.2673;
November - April, Scottsdale, Arizona, 480.575.9702.
email: personalpro@earthlink.net
Tim Richardson is a USPTA Pro 1 tennis instructor. During the playing season, Tim will help you perfect your tennis game in the privacy of your own court and on your own schedule. Tim has been teaching on private Greenwich courts for almost 20 years.

Platform Tennis
The town has two Platform Tennis courts, located at Loughlin Avenue in Cos Cob. The courts can be used by Greenwich residents and their guests. Courts are open October to April. Contact the Greenwich Tennis headquarters (above) for a permit. For reservations and cancellations call 622.6478, Monday - Thursday, 9 am - 3 pm.

tennis

Shippan Racquet Club
Harbor Drive, Stamford, 323.3129
www.shippanracquet.com
Junior, adult clinics & ATP program on their 6 hard courts.

Sound Shore Tennis
303 Post Road, Port Chester, NY, 914.939.1300
Twelve indoor hard surface courts. Open September to May and rain-only weekends after May.

Stamford Indoor Tennis Club
23 Radio Place, Stamford, CT 359.0601

Sterling Farms Tennis Center
1349 Newfield Avenue, Stamford, CT 461.8329
www.sterlingfarmsgc.com (look under Facility Information)
Located on the grounds of Sterling Farms Golf Course, the tennis facility has 6 recently resurfaced outdoor courts.
Spring Session Begins May 1st; Summer Session Begins June 26th; Junior Camp Begins June 12th.

Wire Mill Racquet Club
578 Wire Mill Road, Stamford, 329.9221
www.leontennis.net
Just off exit 35 of the Merritt Parkway, Wire Mill (four outdoor red clay courts) is owned by the pros who teach in the winter at the Greenwich Racquet Club. Excellent junior and adult programs. Season is May to September. There is no membership fee.

YWCA Programs
www.YWCAGreenwich.org
259 East Putnam Avenue, 869.6501
Beginner and intermediate lessons for adults and children as young as six.

volleyball

Department of Parks and Recreation Volleyball Programs

Contact: Frank Gabriele, 622.7821

www.greenwichct.org/ParksAndRec/ParksandRec.asp

The town sponsors adult co-ed volleyball games and the Greenwich Volleyball League, an adult, winter co-ed volleyball league for A and B flight teams. They play at Glenville Elementary School on Tuesday & Thursday nights. Greenwich residents 16 years and older may participate. Registration normally starts in September at Town Hall.

YMCA Volleyball Programs

50 East Putnam Avenue, 869.1630

www.gwymca.org

The Y sponsors informal, co-ed volleyball games for adults.

walking / hiking

See also FITNESS & SPORTS, rock climbing.

Audubon Guidebook to Walking Trails

A 63-page guide to 26 area walking trails is available from the Greenwich Audubon Society, PO Box 7487, Greenwich, CT 06831.

Audubon Center

613 Riversville Road, 869.5272

www.greenwich.center.audubon.org

280 acres of well-kept trails, a delightful place to walk. The entrance is on the corner of Riversville Road and John Street.

Babcock Preserve

North Street, Greenwich, 622-7700

297 acres stretching between North Street and Lake Avenue. The entrance is on North Street about 2 miles north of the Merritt Parkway. An extensive network of trails which range in length from 1 to 3.5 miles.

Connecticut Walk Book

The books (Eastern and Western Connecticut) are published by the Connecticut Forest and Park Association. They are available on their website. The Association is a non-profit group of hikers and conservationists. The Walk Books are complete guides to day trips, with fold out maps. For information call 860.346.2372 or go to www.ctwoodlands.org

Greenwich Point

Shore Road, Old Greenwich

Craig Whitcomb (Operations Manager) 622.7814

147 acres at the end of Sound Beach Avenue. at the end of Shore Road. Greenwich Point is a popular spot for water sports, as well as walking, bicycle riding, roller blading and running. A network of trails leads along the changing coastline and through the woods. A trail guide is available at the Seaside Center of the Bruce Museum. During the summer a beach pass is required. See PARKS & BEACHES.

walking / hiking

Mianus River Park

Cognewaugh Road, Cos Cob, 622.7814

220 acres stretching from Greenwich into Stamford. The entrance is ½ mile east of Stanwich Road on Cognewaugh Road. The two trails of most interest are the Pond Trail and the Oak Trail.

Montgomery Pinetum Park

Bible Street, Cos Cob, 622.7814

91 acres, just off of Bible Street in Cos Cob. The entrance is on the west side directly opposite Clover Place. Obtain a map and tree guide from the Garden Center office, then enjoy the extraordinary diversity of trees and plantings. One path leads to the 22-acre Greenwich Audubon Society's Mildred Bedard Caldwell Wildlife Sanctuary.

TIP: TOUR THE CONNECTICUT STATE CAPITOL

The Connecticut League of Women Voters conducts tours of our State Capitol. When the House and Senate are in session, it is especially interesting to watch their proceedings. To find out details call 860.240.0222 or visit
www.cga.ct.gov/capitoltours

Glow Yoga

1075 East Putnam Avenue, 2nd Floor, Riverside, 637.5065
www.GlowYourway.com
Vinyasa yoga and yoga form with low heat. Classes 60 or 75 minutes.
Hours: Classes & workshops scheduled Monday - Sunday, beginning at
7:30 or 8:15 am. Thursday 7 pm session.

Greenwich Continuing Education

At Greenwich High School, 625.7474, 625.0141
www.greenwichschools.org/gce
Beginning and advanced yoga courses as well as tai chi ch'uan classes.

Greenwich Health at Greenwich Hospital

25 Valley Drive 863.4277, 888.305.9253
www.greenhosp.org/programs.asp
They offer a number of wellness programs including yoga and t'ai chi
ch'uan classes.
Hours: weekdays, 9 am - 4 pm.

Old Greenwich-Riverside Community Center

www.ogrcc.com
90 Harding Road, Old Greenwich, 637.3659
They offer a beginning yoga program.

YMCA

50 East Putnam Avenue, 869.1630
Barbara Taylor, Fitness Center Manager x 519
www.gwymca.org
The Y offers a beginning course in yoga and tai chi.

yoga

YWCA

259 East Putnam Avenue, 869.6501

www.ywcagreenwich.org

The Y offers yoga programs for all levels.

Yoga Center

125 Greenwich Avenue, 661.0092

www.yogacentergreenwich.com

In the heart of Greenwich, this popular studio for yoga, is run by a mother and daughter team, Toni Goodrich and Heather Trzuskowski. You will find a variety of classes at this center, including hot yoga. Call for more information.

Yoga Samadhi

328 Pemberwick Road @ The Mill, 532.0660

www.greenwichyoga.com

The key to a happy and healthy life is balance, and this yoga studio is a wonderful place to start. With views of the Byram River, this studio offers a wide variety of classes designed for all levels. Classes range from "Foundations" and "Restorative," which are gentle and great for beginners, to "Vinyasa" and "Astanga" classes, which are more vigorous and powerful. They also hold invigorating classes such as "Contempo Yoga," set to modern music. This studio has a variety of specialty classes (held regularly) for pregnant women, women with newborns, teens and seniors. The studio is committed to enriching the yoga practice of their students, so you will often find well-known national and international teachers who have been recruited for workshops. Their website is very informative.

FLOWERS & GARDENS

The Greenwich Department of Parks has a green thumb and together with the talents of garden club volunteers (who you will see gardening on many of the town's intersections) make Greenwich so beautiful.

education

Garden Education Center

Montgomery Pinetum, Bible Street, Cos Cob, 869.9242
www.gecgreenwich.org
The Center's horticulture buildings provide classrooms and workrooms for a variety of programs and lectures. Founded in 1957, the center is not only a strong educational facility, but also provides a good framework for new residents to make friends. The quality of their programs is amazing. Each month they have speakers who have written books and are experts in their fields. If you are interested in gardening, these programs should not be missed. Call and get on the list for their newsletter.
Hours: Closed during the summer.
Open September 1 to Memorial Day; weekdays, 9 am - 3:30 pm;
In October and December, also Saturday, 10 am - 3 pm.

New York Botanical Gardens

Bronx, NY, 718.817.8700
www.nybg.org
Greenwich garden enthusiasts know their way to the NY Botanical Gardens. The gardens have recently undergone a $25 million renovation and are considered the best in the country.
Hours: Tuesday - Sunday, 10 am - 6 pm. Wednesdays are free.
Directions: (30 minutes) Merritt/Hutchinson Pkw S to exit 15; Cross County Pkw W to exit 6; Bronx River Pkw S to exit 8W (Mosholu Pkw); at second light, L into Garden.

Loretta Stagen Floral Designs

30 Commerce Road, Stamford, 323.3544
www.lorettastagen.com
Innovative flower arrangements and party decorations for corporate events and weddings. She created a glorious party for us. She also offers classes and workshops in flower arranging. For five or more students, she will create a special class in their area of interest. Her website has links to wedding sites.

FLOWERS & GARDENS

florists

The following florists and nurseries are described in the SHOPPING Section:

- **Cherry Blossoms**
  2 Lewis Court, 869.2733

- **Colony Florist**
  315 Greenwich Avenue, 227.7836

- **Cos Cob Farms**
  61 East Putnam Avenue, Cos Cob, 629.2267

- **Flowers By George**
  7 Strickland Road, Cos Cob, 661.0850

- **Greenwich Orchids**
  106 Mason Street, 661.5544

- **McArdleMacMillen**
  48 Arch Street, 661.5600

- **Tulips Greenwich**
  91 Lake Avenue, 661.3154

- **Sam Bridge Nursery**
  437 North Street, 869.3418

- **Shanti Bithi Nursery**
  3047 High Ridge Road, Stamford, 329.0768

garden clubs

Byram Garden Club

Byram Shubert Library
21 Mead Avenue, Byram
Lynn Elise Friend, President, 531.7978
This friendly group is dedicated to preservation and beautifiction. Membership is open to anyone in Western Greenwich.

Garden Club of Old Greenwich

PO Box 448 Old Greenwich CT 06870
Louise Weber, President, 637.0430
They care about keeping the Old Greenwich area beautiful and work on many civic projects. They share their talents and knowledge through horticulture programs designed for the young and the elderly. Membership is by invitation.

Garden Education Center

130 Bible Street, Cos Cob, 869.9242
www.gecGreenwich.org
Barbara Collier, President
This is a gardener's heaven. Started in 1957, this volunteer organization is dedicated to the appreciation of horticulture and nature through educational programs and special events. All kinds of classes in gardening, flower arranging, landscape design are happening all the time. Volunteers are needed to work in the greenhouse, gift shop, and also to help with workshops, trips and special events.

Green Fingers Garden Club

PO Box 4655, Greenwich 06830
Gaby Hall, President, 661.4056
An active club, responsible for the biennial "Preview of Spring", a major flower show usually held at Christ Church in early March. Membership is by invitation.

Greenwich Daffodil Society

38 Perkins Road
Nancy B. Mott, President, 661.6142
In the Spring, daffodils burst into bloom all over town. If you love daffodils you will love membership in this group. The group sponsors the annual Connecticut Daffodil Show at Christ Church.

garden clubs

Greenwich Garden Club
PO Box 4896, Greenwich 06831
Nina King, President, 869.8244
Founded in 1914, they promote interest in horticulture, flower arranging, and conservation. Membership is by invitation.

Greenwich Green & Clean
Yantoro Community Center, 113 Pemberwick Road, 531.0006
Mary G. Hull, Executive Director
When someone says, "Wow, Greenwich is so beautiful!" tell them about this dedicated group of volunteers, working hard to keep it that way. Founded in 1986, when the town was going through some drastic budget cutting, this group formed and took action. Now working in partnership with the town, they are the inspiration for the pretty flowering baskets along the Avenue and the flowers on many of the traffic islands. Join this group and take part in the fall and spring Town Clean Up. Take a bag, join your neighbors and have fun in this well organized effort to clean our streets and parks.

Greenwich Woman's Club Gardeners
89 Maple Avenue, 661.2228
Joy Noble, President
The Woman's Club, a greatly enjoyed, highly respected philanthropic service organization in our town has a special branch of women devoted to gardening, horticultural education and projects to enhance the beauty of our town. New members to the Woman's Club and to this special branch of Gardeners are welcomed.

Hortulus
PO Box 4666
Diane Jennings, President,622.4572
This garden club, founded in 1930, is dedicated to furthering a knowledge and love of gardening. Membership is by invitation.

garden clubs

Knollwood Garden Club

PO Box 1666, Greenwich 06836
Bobbie Laing, Co-President, 869.6665
Raghnild Dewey, Co-President, 661.3487
This garden club, founded in 1955, maintains and supports the Seaside Garden at Greenwich Point and they provide garden therapy at Nathaniel Witherell. Membership is by invitation.

Riverside Garden Club

PO Box 108, Old Greenwich
Ann Isaacson, President, 637.8884
Jane Cumming, Membership, 637.1394
This local club is a member of the National Council of State Garden Clubs and is a charter member of the Federated Garden Clubs of America. Members have a wonderful time together as they work on horticultural education programs and on projects to enhance the beauty of Greenwich. New members are heartily welcomed.

TIP: MAKING FRIENDS

Whether you are new to Town or a long-term resident and want to have an easy, fun way to meet others, join one of the two newcomers' clubs.
For details see www.greenwichnewcomers.com.

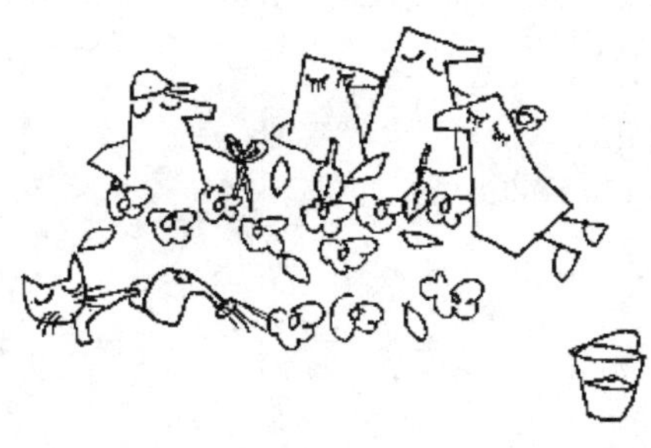

Bakeries
Black Forest
Beyond Bread
Di Mare Pastry Shop
Dunkin Donuts
Kneaded Bread
Neri Bakery
Sal's Pastry Shop
St. Moritz
Sweet Lisa's Exquisite Cakes
Upper Crust Bagel Co.
Versailles
Whole Foods
Weston Bakery Outlet

Caterers
Reviewed in ENTERTAINING

Cheese & Milk
Balducci's
Marcus Dairy
Plum Cheese Shop
Whole Foods

Chocolates & Candy
Ada's Candy Store
Bridgewater Chocolates
Darlene's Heavenly Desires
Deborah Ann's Homemade
         Chocolates
Godiva Chocolates @ The Papyrus
Knipschildt Chocolatier
Lindt Chocolates
Munson's Chocolates
Schakolad Chocolate Factory

Coffee Shops
Reviewed in RESTAURANTS
Arcadia Coffee Co.
Dunkin' Donuts
(The) Drawing Room
Starbucks
T Party Antiques and Tea Room
Waterfront Roasters Café

Ethnic Groceries
Bella Cucina (Italian)
Fuji Mart (Japanese)
Scandia Food and Gift
  (Scandanavian)

Fish
Bon Ton
Fjord Fisheries Market
Lobster Bin
Whole Foods

Fruit & Vegetables
Augustine's Farm
Balducci's
Bishop's Orchards
Cos Cob Farms
Greenwich Farmer's Market
Jones Family Farm
Port Chester Farm Market
White Silo Farm
Whole Foods

Caterers are reviewed in ENTERTAINING
Delicatessens are reviewed in RESTAURANTS
Coffee Shops are reviewed in RESTAURANTS
Ice Cream Shops are reviewed in RESTAURANTS

Ada's Variety Shop (Candy)
112 Riverside Avenue (Corner of Chapel Lane & Riverside Ave), 637.0305
An old-fashioned candy store loved by children and their children.
Hours: weekdays, 7:30 am - 5 pm; weekends, 7:30 am - 2 pm.

Augustine's Farm (Fruit & Vegetables)
1332 King Street, 532.9611
For more than 50 years Kathy and John Augustin have been providing Greenwich residents with fresh corn, tomatoes, apples, pumpkins, honey and cider. In the Fall, many youngsters have enjoyed hay rides. The town proclaimed August 15th as Farmer John Day in Greenwich. Great fun to stop here, load up on fresh vegetables and buy one of Grandma Ann's homemade pies. This is the perfect place to buy your Christmas tree or holiday wreath.
Hours: Open every day, 9 am - 5 pm during the season.
Call farm for hours during the winter.

Balducci's (Gourmet Grocery)
1050 East Putnam Avenue, Riverside, 637.7600
www.balduccis.com
A sophisticated, gourmet country shop for fruits, vegetables and treats. This delightful place carries a large selection of imported and American cheeses. A wonderful deli and take-out section. Don't go in hungry!
Hours: Monday - Saturday, 8 am - 8 pm; Sunday, 8 am - 7 pm.

Bella Cucina (Italian Grocery)
160 Hamilton Avenue, Byram, CT 422.0492
The owners of Express Pizza, who won the best Pizza contest, operate an Italian grocery next to their pizza shop.
Hours: Monday - Saturday, 10 am - 10 pm; Sunday, 11 am - 10 pm.

Beyond Bread (Bakery)

214 Sound Beach Avenue, Old Greenwich, 637.2543

Who would ever dream that croissants as divine as the ones in Paris are being made on Sound Beach Avenue? Harvey, the baker, often begins his day at midnight so you can have fresh croissants, *pain au chocolat*, Danish pastries and many other breads right out of the oven by 6 am. Insiders also know that this tiny shop, with its few tables, is a good place for soup and sandwich at lunch. Be sure to order ahead for their quiche and pie.

Hours: Closed Mondays; Tuesday-Saturday, 6 am - 4 pm; Sunday, 6 am - 1 pm.

Bishop's Orchards

1355 Boston Post Road (I-95, exit 57), Guilford, CT

203.458.7425, 203.453.2338

www.bishopsorchards.com

They have many fruits to pick, including over twenty varieties of apples, nine kinds of blueberries, twelve of peaches, three of pears, eight of strawberries and two varieties of raspberries. This orchard is definitely worth a family trip.

Market hours: From June through October, Monday - Saturday, 8 am to 6 pm; Sunday, 9 am to 6 pm.

Black Forest (Bakery)

52 Lewis Street, 629.9330

www.blackforestpastryshop.com

German-style bakery. Don't miss the black forest cake and chocolate mousse bombe, summer fruit tarts, delicious wedding cakes. We love their melt-away pastry. They have chocolate-cherry bread on the weekend.

Hours: Monday - Saturday, 7:30 am -6 pm; Sunday, 8 am - 1 pm.

Bon Ton (Fish)

343 Greenwich Avenue, 869.0462

www.lobsterscanfly.com

This is a reliable fish store. They have high quality fish as well as prepared seafood specialties, including poached and smoked salmon platters, and a full line of Russian caviar. No need to park; they have curbside service.

Hours: weekdays, 7 am - 6 pm; Saturday, 8 am - 6 pm; Sunday, 9 am - 1pm.

Connecticut Wines and Liquors (Wine)
1071 King Street, 531.8135
A selection of over 500 wines from around the world.
Hours: Monday - Saturday, 9 am - 8 pm.

Cos Cob Farms (Fruit & Vegetables)
6163 East Putnam Avenue, Cos Cob, 629.2267
Fresh fruit, vegetables and flowers at reasonable prices.
Hours: Monday - Saturday, 8 am - 7 pm; Sunday 9 am - 6 pm.

Costco (Grocery & Department Store)
1 Westchester Avenue, Port Chester, NY, 914.935.3103
www.costco.com
You have to buy a membership to shop at this international chain, but that hasn't kept this megastore, a.k.a. warehouse, from being a Greenwich hit. From pesto in their grocery section to a refrigerator, this huge store tries to give good value. Don't miss their flower section. If you want to run in quickly to get something, forget it.
Hours: weekdays, 10 am - 8:30 pm; Saturday, 9:30 am - 6 pm, Sunday, 10 am - 6 pm.

Darlene's Heavenly Desires (Chocolate & Ice Cream)
185 Sound Beach Avenue, Old Greenwich 622.7077
www.darlenesHeavenlyDesires.com
The chocolates are delicious and Darlene always makes you feel glad you shopped there. Ask her about special chocolate deliveries. Plus they have a wonderful variety of ice cream cones and cups and other treats. In the summertime, Darlene's is open till 10 pm every night so it's great for a late evening ice cream stop! (Just remember: chocolate solves everything!) Sedutto's ice cream 25 flavors, Coney Island custard and Weight Watcher's Smart Ones saucers.
Hours: Monday - Saturday, 10 am - 8 pm (Friday and Saturday until 10 pm); Sunday noon - 6 pm. Expanded holiday hours.
Hours vary in summer and winter. Call store for hours.

Di Mare Pastry Shop (Bakery)
Riverside Commons Shopping Center (1263 East Putnam), 637.4781
www.DimarePastryShop.com
The hot spot to order your child's birthday cake with a large selection of themes & characters for decoration (computerized and handmade).
Hours: Monday - Saturday, 8 am - 6:30 pm; Sunday, 8 am - 3 pm.

Dunkin' Donuts (Bakery)
- 375 East Putnam, Cos Cob, 869.7454
  This location also sells Baskin-Robbins, ice cream.
- 271 West Putnam Avenue, Greenwich, 869.5791

www.DunkinDonuts.com
We are addicted to their coffee. But who can resist their donuts?
Hours: Open every day, 5 am - 11 pm.

Farmer's Markets (Fruits & Vegetables)
From mid-May to mid-October, farmers come to the local area, set up stands and sell their produce. It is usually picked the day it is sold and couldn't be fresher. At some of the stalls you can also find homemade items such as breads, jellies and cheese. Farmer's markets have become so popular that Greenwich residents dash to nearby towns on days the Greenwich Market is closed. Each market has its own character.
- Saturday: Greenwich, Horseneck Parking Lot (across from the Boys & Girls Club), 9:30 am - 1:30 pm.
- Monday & Thursday: Stamford, Columbus Park, 10 am - 3 pm.
- Wednesday: Darien, CVS Parking Lot, noon - 6 pm.

Fjord Fisheries Market (Fish)
137 River Road, Cos Cob, 661.5006
www.fjordcatering.com
Fresh fish and friendly service. Imported smoked salmon and herring from Norway. On one of your busy days, stop by for one of their soups or some fresh sushi. Parking is easy.
Hours: weekdays, 8 am - 7 pm; Saturday, 8 am - 7 pm; Sunday 8 am - 6 pm.

Food Emporium (Grocery)
160 West Putnam Avenue, 622.0374
www.thefoodemporium.com
A good general purpose grocery, structuring itself to compete with Whole Foods.
Hours: Monday - Saturday, 7 am - 10 pm; Sunday, 7 am - 9 pm.

Porricelli's Food Mart (Grocery)
- 120 Post Road (East Putnam Road), Cos Cob, 629.2100
- 26 Arcadia Rd, Old Greenwich, 637.4412

www.porricellis.com

Both stores are full-service supermarkets which have been family-owned and operated for the past 56 years. They are neighborhood meeting spots where regulars highly praise their family service and excellent meat, fish and produce departments. Their deli makes some of the best sandwiches in town.

Hours: Monday - Thursday, 7 am - 7 pm; Friday, 7am - 8pm; Saturday 7 am - 7 pm; Sunday 8 am - 6 pm. Closed most holidays.

Fuji Mart (Japanese Grocery)
1212 East Putnam Avenue, Riverside, 698.2107
An authentic Japanese grocery. Buy a bag of frozen gyoza.
Hours: Tuesday - Friday, 10:30 am - 7 pm;
Saturday & Sunday, 10am - 6:30pm.

Greenwich Prime Meats (Meat)
100 Bruce Park Avenue, 861.6328
A shop run by former members of famed Manero's butcher shop. Same terrific meats (even Kobe steaks) and friendly advice along with Manero's special take-out treats: Gorgonzola salad, garlic bread, fried onions, steak fries and steak sandwiches. Easy parking behind the store. Free delivery in the local area.
Hours: Every day, 9 am - 6 pm.

Harrington's of Vermont (Gourmet Grocery)
83 Railroad Avenue, 661.4479
www.HarringtonHam.com
They sell their line of smoked meats, imported cheeses and a variety of jams, relishes, maple syrup and other gourmet products. They are a great resource for a food basket gift. If you need a ham for a party, this is the place. Try one of their ham sandwiches and you will know what we mean.
Hours: Monday - Saturday, 9:30 am - 5:30 pm; Sunday, 11 am - 4 pm; Sundays from 4th of July through Labor Day, 11am - 3pm.

Horseneck Liquors (Wine)

25 East Putnam Avenue, 869.8944

www.horseneck.com

Established in 1934, it was purchased by Terry Rogers in 1989. Always known as the premier wine store in Greenwich, Terry has continued to make it the favorite destination for wine lovers. Horseneck has the largest inventory of Bordeaux, Burgundy and Italian wines in Connecticut, plus an excellent selection of wines from California and all over the world. You can count on their friendly, good advice. They will deliver and, if needed, giftwrap for you.

Hours: Monday - Saturday, 9 am - 7 pm.

Horse Ridge Cellars

11 South Road, Somers, CT, 860.763.5380

www.HorseRidgeCellars.com

Where serious collectors store their wine. (About a 2 hour drive from Greenwich.)

Jones Family Farm

266 Israel Hill Road & Route 110, Shelton, CT,
203.929.8425

www.jonesfamilyfarms.com

This pick-your-own farm began in the 1940s. They have strawberries in June, followed by blueberries in July and August, and pumpkins in the autumn. In December, come and cut your own Christmas tree. They even have hay rides in October.

Hours: Best to call, hours change seasonally. Closed Sunday & Monday.

(The) Kneaded Bread (Bakery)

181 North Main Street, Port Chester, NY, 914.937.9489

www.kneadedbread.com

A first rate bread bakery. Every day they bake over 17 varieties of crusty, Europeanstyle breads. They also have croissants, Danish, and sandwiches. Make their fresh donuts a Sunday morning treat or take home their Cinnamon Swirl. It makes great French toast. There are a few seats, so stop in for a good coffee and sandwich. Be sure to order holiday breads in advance. They only accept cash or local checks.

Hours: Tuesday - Friday, 7am - 5pm; Saturday, 8 am - 4 pm;
Sunday, 8am - 1pm.

Knipschildt Chocolatier (Chocolates)

Chocopologie Factory, 4 New Canaan Avenue, Norwalk, CT, 203.838.3131

www.knipschildt.com

One of the world's best chocolates are made nearby. These chocolates can often be found at Whole Foods and Aux Delices. You can order them online from www.echocolates.com or by phone from Fritz Knipschildt. Hours: Wednesday, 11 am - 9 pm; Thursday, 11 am - 10 pm; Friday & Saturday, 11 am - midnight; Sunday, 10 am - 5 pm.

Lobster Bin (Fish)

204 Field Point Road, 661.6559

Just off Railroad Avenue. Plenty of fresh fish as well as parking. We like their helpful advice when we not sure which fish to select. Hours: Monday - Saturday, 8 am - 6 pm; Sunday, 9 am - 1 pm.

Marcus Dairy

Danbury, CT, 800.243.2511

www.MarcusDairy.com

Get milk delivered? Apparently 6,000 customers do. Isn't it wonderful that we still have milk boxes and milk delivery? In addition they deliver products such as juices, eggs, yogurt, cottage cheese, sour cream and butter.

Neri Bakery (Bakery)

Pearl Street, Port Chester, NY 914.939.3311

At a beautiful wedding, we discovered this resource for delicious wedding cakes at reasonable prices. Ask for Daniel Champsaur, 914.937.3235 x 24. Be sure to check out their delicious frosted donuts. Hours: Monday - Saturday, 7am - 7:30 pm; Sunday, 7am - 4:30 pm.

The Papyrus (Godiva Chocolates)

268 Greenwich Avenue, 869.1888

www.papyrus.com

Papyrus sells fine custom social stationery and invitations for formal and casual parties. Its quite natural the gift most people love to receive, Godiva Chocolates, is available here. Hours: weekdays, 9:30 am - 6 pm; Saturday, 10 am - 6 pm; Sunday, noon - 5 pm.

Penzey's Spices (Spices)

197 Westport Avenue, Norwalk, CT, 203.849.9085

www.penzeys.com

Fresh spices make all the difference. Penzey's has a large selection of spices, spice blends and even extracts. Pretty wooden boxed sets of spices make appreciated hostess gifts.

Hours: weekdays, 9:30 am - 5:30 pm; Saturday, 9:30 am - 5 pm.

Directions: I-95 N to exit 16, L on East, R on US1 (Westport Avenue), on L just past Stew Leonards.

Palmer Hill Market & Deli

322 Palmer Hill Road, Riverside, 637.2835

Havameyer Park and Palmer Hill Road residences are delighted to have this local deli and grocery.

Hours: weekdays, 6 am - 8 pm; Saturday, 7 am - 8 pm; Sunday, 7 am - 2 pm.

Plum Cheese Shop

238 East Putnam Avenue, Cos Cob, 869.7586

Good news for cheese connoisseurs. This sophisticated, European-style shop's goal is to have the best of the best, featuring artisan cheeses. At any one time they have between 80 and 120 choices.

Hours: Wednesday - Saturday, 11 am - 7 pm.

Port Chester Farm Market (Fruits & Vegetables)

604 North Main Street, Port Chester, NY, 914.935.1075

When you are looking for fresh fruit and vegetables at off hours, this store, located next to Carvel in the circle between Greenwich and Port Chester, is a good bet. In addition, their prices are very reasonable.

Hours: every day, 8 am - 9pm.

(The) Round Hill Store (Grocery)

Corner of Old Mill and Round Hill Road, 869.5144

This small country store, which opened in 1801, still provides milk, eggs and staples for the surrounding area. Try one of their delicious turkey sandwiches. About half of their customers are people who work in the backcountry and half live nearby. The owners are working hard to restore it, while keeping its old-fashioned appeal.

Hours: weekdays, 7 am - 7 pm; Saturday, 7 am - 5 pm.

St. Moritz (Bakery)

383 Greenwich Avenue, 869.2818
Luscious, rich pastries and cakes. Be sure to try the Sarah Bernhardt cookies.
Hours: Monday - Saturday, 7 am - 6 pm; Sunday, 8 am - 1 pm.

Sal's Pastry Shop (Italian Bakery)

91 High Ridge Road (Bull's Head Shopping Center), Stamford 323.0789
A family-owned and run Italian pastry shop. The owners take great pride in their fresh cannolis. As an added bonus their prices are reasonable.
Hours: Tuesday - Saturday, 8:30 am - 6:30 pm; Sunday 8 am - 2 pm.
Directions: Merritt Pkw N to High Ridge Exit, R on High Ridge.

Scandia Food and Gifts (Scandinavian foods)

30 High Street (off US1), Norwalk, CT, 203.838.2087
www.scandiafood.com
The area source for Scandinavian food and gifts.
Hours: weekdays, 9 am - 5 pm; Saturday, 10 am - 5 pm.
Directions: I-95 N to exit 16, L on East, L on US1, L on High.

Stop & Shop Home Shopping (Grocery)

Peapod
Local Stores located at:
• 161 West Putnam Avenue, 625.0622
• 11 Glenville Road, Glenville, 531.0541
Place orders through www.StopAndShop.com or www.PeaPod.com
Call 800.573.2763 for information.
For orders over $75.00 the delivery fee is $4.95, for orders less than $75.00 the delivery fee is $9.95. The minimum order is $50.00.

Stew Leonard's (Grocery)

100 Westport Avenue, Norwalk, 203.847.7214
www.stewleonards.com
Famous throughout the metropolitan area. Worth the trip. This huge food store has been called the Disneyland of grocery stores by the New York Times. Bring your children.
Hours: every day, 7 am - 11 pm.
Directions: I-95 N to exit 16; L on East; R on Westport (6th light).

Super Stop and Shop (Grocery)
15 Waterfront Place, Port Chester, NY 914.937.7318
Hours: Every day, 7 am - midnight.

Sweet Lisa's Exquisite Cakes (Bakery)
3 Field Road, Cos Cob, 869.9545
www.sweetlisas.com
Wonderful cakes, party pastries and designer cookies by special order only. They usually require seven days' notice.
Hours: Tuesday - Saturday, 9 am - 5 pm.

Trader Joe's (Grocery)
436 Boston Post Road (US 1), Darien, CT 203.656.1414
www.TraderJoes.com
Trader Joe fans will be glad to know there is a store not far from Greenwich. A grocery store selling healthy food at good prices. Try one of their soups or frozen dinners.
Hours: every day, 9 am - 9 pm.
Directions: I-95 N to exit 13, Left to US 1, L on US 1.

Upper Crust Bagel Company (Bakery)
197 Sound Beach Avenue, Old Greenwich, 698.0079
Our favorite bagels! They have tasty old-fashioned kettle-boiled and hearth-baked bagels, as well as gourmet spreads and coffees. They accept checks but no credit cards.
Hours: weekdays, 6 am - 4pm; Saturday, 7 am - 4 pm;
Sunday, 7 am - 3pm.

Var Max Liquor Pantry (Wine)
16 Putnam Avenue, Port Chester, NY, 914.937.4930
www.varmax.com
They have a very large selection of well-priced wine. Nice descriptions on their wine specials.
Hours: Monday - Thursday, 8:30am - 9pm;
Friday - Saturday, 8:30am - 10pm.

Versailles (Bakery)

315 Greenwich Avenue, 661.6634

A small, very French bistro with a front counter full of pastries and croissants that will make your day worth living. Try their operas and éclairs. Just the right place to order a take-out quiche. The good food and atmosphere are reminiscent of our Paris favorites.

Hours: Weekdays, 7:30 am - 9:30 pm; Saturday, 8 am - 10 pm; Sunday Brunch 11 am - 4 pm Dinner 5:30 pm - 8 pm.

Village Prime Meats (Meat)

475 Main Street, Armonk NY, 914.273.5222

An old-fashioned butcher shop. It is worth the trip when you want something special. Where else can you get rabbit, game birds, Peking or Muscovy duck or just that special cut of meat you need? They also have a number of unique food products, such as white or black truffle oil and a large number of fresh pates.

Hours: weekdays, 8 am - 6 pm; Saturday, 8 am - 5:30 pm.

Directions: I-95 S to I-287 W to I684 N to exit 3S. Continue R to 22 South, R at 2nd light onto Rt 128 (Main Street). It is in a shopping center on your left just past the main part of town.

Weston Bakeries Outlet (Bakery)

10 Hamilton Avenue, Byram (between I-95 exits 2 and 3)
531.4770
www.arnold.gwbakeries.com/history.cfm

That good smell wafting onto I-95 just before Greenwich comes from this commercial bakery. Their bread is available at local grocery stores, but for a wide selection of bread (including Thomas and Entenmanns) at bargain prices visit the factory outlet shop.

Hours: Monday - Wednesday, 8 am - 6 pm; Thursday - Friday, 8 am - 6 pm; Saturday, 8 am - 5 pm; Sunday, 10 am - 4 pm.

White Silo Farm

Sherman, CT, 860.355.0271
www.whitesilowinery.com

Pick your own strawberries, asparagus, raspberries, blackberries and rhubarb.

Whole Foods (Grocery, Cheese, Bakery, Fish, Vitamins)
661.0631
www.wholefoods.com
Our favorite natural and organic food store. When you shop here you are bound to meet your friends buying their Sunday bagels, fresh fish, vitamins, deli foods, cheese, beautiful flowers, fruits and vegetables. It is great to have an expert available in each food area to happily give you advice about selections. In addition to its amazing assortment of natural foods, the store has many strong departments including seafood, produce, nutrition, meat and cheese. We love their first-class deli. The vitamin and herbal section of the store is complete. They have over 300 cheeses from all over the world.
Hours: Monday - Sunday, 8 am - 10 pm.

Wine Wise (Wine)
122 East Putnam Avenue, 340.2440
This unusual wine store stocks wines from many smaller vineyards. If you don't know the wine, you can taste almost any wine in the shop, free of charge.
Hours: Monday - Saturday, 10 am - 8 pm.

TIP: FLOATING CONFERENCE ROOMS
Fjord Charters and the Delamar Hotel have partnered to create a floating conference center. The 117-foot Cayah Michelle and the 74-foot Cayah Sarita are often tied up at the Delamar Hotel dock. Lunches are served by Fjord. They can accommodate up to 100 people. Call 800.925.2622

Gambling has come to Connecticut and our two casinos are closer and more attractive than those in Atlantic City, NJ. The casinos are very close to each other. For bus transportation call Dattco, 888.770.0140. For more information on the area see HOTELS & INNS.

Foxwoods Resort Casino

800.369.9663

www.foxwoods.com

Just seven miles from Mystic, CT, this resort is owned by the Mashantucket Pequot Tribal Nations. It is the largest hotel complex in the Northeast. The 312-room Grand Pequot Tower is very comfortable, and—in addition to an array of restaurants, entertainment and, of course, gaming tables—there is a 36-hole golf course, www.lakeofisles.com.

Directions: I-95 N to exit 92, West on Rte 2.

About 2½ hours from Greenwich.

Mohegan Sun

General Info: 888.226.7711; Hotel Reservations: 888.777.7922

www.mohegansun.com

www.sunint.com

Somewhat smaller than Foxwoods, this casino still has over 192 gaming tables and 3,000 slot machines. The casino is owned by the Mohegan Nation and Sun International. The Mohegan Sun complex reflects the culture and history of the Mohegan Nation. Many people prefer its Native American theme decoration.

Directions: I-95 N to exit 76, 395 N to exit 79 A, Rte. 2A less than 2 miles to Mohegan Sun Boulevard. About 2 hours from Greenwich.

Benford Barber Shop at The Palm

20 Church Street, 661.7383

This out-of-the way barber tucked in the back of the Palm Barber Shop is used by many of Greenwich's prominent residents. Haircuts are by appointment.

Hours: Wednesday - Saturday, 8 am - 5 pm.

Graham's Kids Cuts of Greenwich

60 Greenwich Avenue, 983.6800

Unique children's hair salon and toy store.

Hours: Monday & Saturday, 10 am - 5 pm;
Tuesday - Friday, 10 am - 6 pm.

(The) Hair Cut Place

259 Sound Beach Avenue, Old Greenwich, 637.1313

An Old Greenwich institution formerly called Off Center Barber Shop. Kids love haircuts in the Jeep. Appointments are available, walk-ins welcomed.

Hours: Monday - Saturday, 8 am - 5 pm (Thursdays until 7).

Palm Barber Shop

20 Church Street, 869.0292

Tony gives good cuts and relates well to both youth and adults.

Hours: 7:30 am - 5:30 pm.

Sharkey's Cuts for Kids

220 East Putnam Avenue, Cos Cob, 629.5437

www.sharkeyscutsforkids.com

This is all about kids having fun while their hair is being cut.

Hours: weekdays, 10 am - 6 pm; Saturday, 9 am - 5 pm;
Sunday, 10 am - 4 pm.

Subway Barber Shop

315 Greenwich Avenue, 869.3263

The children and grandchildren of many Greenwich residents had their first cut here and have continued to call this their favorite.

Hours: Monday - Saturday (closed Wednesday), 8 am - 5 pm.

day spas

Celia B. Skin Care
11 Maple Avenue, 861.6850
Celia offers a wonderful menu of facials and waxes carefully and gently.
A very nice experience. Easy parking behind the building.
Hours: By appointment.

Empy's Day Spa
138 Hamilton Avenue, 661.6625
Excellent facials and waxing in a low key atmosphere - not a chi-chi
place. The prices are better than most.
Hours: Walk-in Monday & Tuesday, 9 am - 6 pm;
By appointment, Wednesday, Thursday & Friday, 9 am - 6 pm;
Saturday, 9 am - 4 pm.

Noelle Spa for Beauty and Wellness
1100 High Ridge Road, Stamford, 322.3445
www.Noelle.com
Complete day spa with a great variety of services from hair color, make-
up, bridal, hand & foot, massages, body treatment, esthetic, teeth whit-
ening, healing therapies & yoga. Spa for men.
Hours: Monday & Wednesday, 9 am - 5:30 pm;
Tuesday & Thursday, 8 am - 9 pm; Friday, 8 am - 8 pm;
Saturday, 8 am - 6 pm.

Serenity Spa
116 East Putnam Avenue, 629.9000
www.SerenitySpa.com
Experience the essential indulgence of nurturing skin care services and
all natural facial products in a serene environment.
Hours: Monday, Wednesday & Friday, 9 am - 6 pm;
Tuesday, 9 am - 7 pm; Thursday, 9 am - 8 pm;
Saturday, 9 am - 5 pm; Sunday, 10 am - 3 pm.

Stonewater Spa & Boutique
151 Greenwich Avenue (above Talbots), 622.0300
www.PremierSpaCollection.com
Professional treatments and products for your specific needs. Services
include: facials, massage therapies, body treatments, pedicure, mani-
cure, waxing, make-up, eyebrow and lash tinting. Spa for men.
Hours: Monday - Saturday, 9 am - 6 pm
(Wednesday & Thursday to 8 pm); Sunday, 10 am - 5 pm.

GROOMING

hair salons

Carlo and Company

70 East Putnam Avenue (Whole Foods shopping center)
869.2300
Long established in Greenwich, you will enjoy the friendly, attentive atmosphere as well as their expert haircuts, coloring and styling. Thank you, Alison!
Hours: Monday - Saturday, 9 am - 5 pm.

Enzo Ricco Bene Salon

1800 East Putnam Avenue(at the Hyatt), Old Greenwich
698.4141
This attractive salon located off the lobby of the Hyatt Regency Hotel offers a pleasant and talented staff of colorists and stylists. For the easiest access use the free valet parking.
Hours: Monday, 9 am - 5 pm;
Tuesday, Wednesday & Friday, 8 am - 5:30 pm;
Thursday, 8 am - 7 pm; Saturday, 8 am - 4 pm.

Greenwich Salon and Day Spa

120 Post Road, Cos Cob (above Food Mart), 661.4093
Popular full service salon - styling, cuts, manicures, pedicures, facials and waxing. Free parking.
Hours: Monday - Saturday, 8:30 am - 4:30 pm.

Hopscotch

10 Railroad Ave, 661.0107
A cutting-edge high-tech salon with very nice owners catering to a fashionable clientele. People come from New York City to go here.
Hours: Monday - Saturday, 9 am - 5 pm (Tuesday & Thursday to 8 pm);
Sunday, 10 am - 5 pm.

Partners Salon and Spa

1200 East Putnam Avenue, Riverside, 637.0478
Full salon and spa services with excellent staff. Valet Parking.
Hours: Tuesday & Thursday, 10 am - 7 pm; Wednesday & Friday, 9 am - 5 pm; Saturday, 8 am - 4 pm.

Salon 221

221 East Putnam Avenue (2nd floor Mill Pond
Shopping Center), Cos Cob, 661.8838
Full service salon with custom hair color and precision cuts. Lynn, a
client for a decade, would follow Joe anywhere.
Hours: Tuesday, Wednesday, Friday, 9:30 am - 5 pm;
Thursday, 9:30 am - 7 pm; Saturday, 9 am - 5 pm.

Visible Changes

204 Sound Beach Avenue, Old Greenwich, 637.9154
If you've seen a great haircut, it's likely to have been cut here.
Hours: Tuesday - Saturday, 8:30 am - 7 pm, (Saturday to 5:30).

Warren Tricomi Salon

1 East Putnam Avenue, 863.9300
www.WarrenTricomi.com
Popular, NYC-style salon - but friendlier. Some excellent talent, particularly the colorist. Tamara is one of the best make-up artists and eyebrow
shapers in the area. Great stop for bridal parties. Free parking.
Hours: Monday, Wednesday, Friday, 8 am - 6 pm; Tuesday, 8 am - 5 pm;
Thursday & Saturday, 8 am - 8 pm.

TIP: GREENWICH DOLLARS
This is the perfect gift when you are not sure what to give. Gift Cer-
tificates, sponsored by the Greenwich Chamber of Commerce, are accepted at 140 local businesses. Purchase them online
www.GreenwichChamber.com.

nail salons

Cozy Nails

237 Sound Beach Avenue, Old Greenwich, 637.0711
Serving Greenwich residents for 10 years.
Hours: weekdays, 9:30 am - 6:30 pm; Saturday, 9 am - 6 pm.

Greenwich Nails

38 West Putnam Avenue, 422.5553
Strongly recommended by a good friend with high standards. This salon
goes the extra mile and they also give a really good back massage.
Hours: weekdays, 9:30 am - 7 pm; Saturday, 9:30 am - 6 pm;
Sunday, 10:30 am - 5 pm.

Hilltop Nails

235 Old Mill Road, Glenville, 532.8000
Several of our associates treat themselves to the services here, including
the manicure/pedicure combination package. Walk-ins are accepted.
Hours: weekdays, 9:30 am - 7 pm; Saturday, 9 am - 6:30 pm;
Sunday, 10 am - 5:30 pm.

Tiffany Nails

349 Greenwich Avenue, 661.3838
Walk-ins only.
Hours: Monday Saturday, 9:30 am - 7 pm; Sunday 10 am - 5:30 pm.

Tip Top Nails

1 Havemeyer Lane, Old Greenwich, 698.3320
By appointment or walkin.
Hours: weekdays, 9:30 am - 7 pm; Saturday, 9 am - 7 pm;
Sunday, 10 am - 5 pm.

See FITNESS & SPORTS for:
Yoga, Trainers and Exercise Classes

Drugstores (Pharmacies)
CVS 24-Hr Pharmacy
Finch Pharmancy
Grannick's Pharmancy
North Street Pharmacy
Walgreens 24-Hr Pharmacy

Emergencies
Dial 911
Access Ambulance
Greenwich Emergency
   Medical Service (GEMS)
Greenwich Hospital
   Emergency Room

Exercise Equipment
Dave's Cycle and Fitness
Omni Fitness

Glasses and Contact Lens
20/20 Optical (20/20 Kids)
Copeland Optometrists

Hair Replacement
Mega HairSystems

Health Information
211 Infoline
Connecticut Magazine Survey of
   Top Doctors and Hospitals
Greenwich Hospital Consumer
Health Reference Center
Greenwich Library Health
   Information Center
Health Extensions
Info Tapes
Physician Referral Service

Hearing Aids
SolomonShotland Audiology

Hospitals
Burke Rehabilitation Hospital
Convenient Medical Care Walk-in
Clinic
Greenwich Hospital
Physician Referral Service
Silver Hill Hospital
Westchester Medical Center
Yale New Haven Hospital

Medical Insurance Assistance
National Medical Claims

Medical Supplies & Equipment
Care Center
Relax the Back

Physical Therapy & Chiropractors
Burke Rehabilitation Hospital
Greenwich Physical Therapy
Greenwich Sports Medicine
Performance Physical Therapy
Physical Therapy & Sports
   Rehabilitation
Sam Schwartz
Tully Health Center

Senior Housing
See SENIORS

Shoes and Orthotics
Foot Solutions
Stride Custom Orthotics

Vitamins
GNC
Greenwich Health Mart
Vitamin Shoppe
Whole Foods

20/20 Optical
20/20 Kids
15 Arcadia Road, Old Greenwich, 698.2255
The optician has a specialty working with children. Youngsters love to go there to pick out glasses.
Hours: weekdays, 9:30 am - 5:30 pm, Saturday, 9 am - 5 pm.

211 Infoline
Dial 211 or www.infoline.org
Free, confidential 24 hours a day information on a variety of subjects such as pre-natal care, legal assistance, AIDS testing, crisis intervention and emergency assistance, from trained call specialists.

Access Ambulance
1111 East Putnam Avenue, Riverside, 637.2351 for dispatch
Private, for-profit, non-emergency ambulance service operated by GEMS. It provides transportation between patients' homes and medical facilities such as hospitals, nursing homes, and cancer centers.

Burke Rehabilitation Hospital
785 Mamaroneck Avenue, White Plains, NY, 914.597.2500
www.burke.org
A nearby 60-acre private, not-for-profit, facility specializing in inpatient and outpatient multi-disciplinary physical rehabilitation and research. They have a national reputation for their programs tailored to lessen disability and dependence resulting from disease or injury.

The Care Center (Equipment)
29 Arcadia Road, Old Greenwich, 637.3599
www.TheCareCenter.com
A home medical equipment company with just about everything you need to recover from a short illness or long term care. They specialize in scooters, power wheelchairs, seat lift chairs and courteous service.
Hours: weekdays, 8:30 am - 5:30 pm; Saturday, 9 am - 1 pm.

Connecticut Magazine Survey of Top Doctors and Hospitals
www.connecticutmag.com

Convenient Medical Care Clinic

1200 East Putnam Avenue, Old Greenwich, 698.1419
Walk-in clinic. Quick and efficient for minor injuries and ailments.

Copeland Optometrists

203 South Ridge Street, Rye Brook, NY, 914.939.0830
For years, they were just over the border in Port Chester, but recently they moved another 5 minutes away to Rye Brook. We followed them because of their reliable, caring service. Owned and operated by the Copeland Family, you can count on a good eye examination, the correct prescription and a set of fashionable glasses or contact lens at a reasonable price.
Hours: weekdays, 9 am - 6 pm (Wednesday until 1 pm, Thursday until 9 pm); Saturday, 9 am - 5 pm.
Directions: Rte 1 S through Main St, R on Westchester, L on Bowman, L on South Ridge.

CVS (Pharmacy)

www.cvs.com
• 1239 East Putnam Ave (Thru Way Shopping Center), Riverside 698.4006
This location is open 24-hours.
• 99 Greenwich Avenue, 862.9341, pharmacy 862.9320
 Pharmacy Hours: weekdays, 8 am - 9pm; Saturday, 8 am - 6 pm; Sunday, 9 am - 6 pm.
• 225 Sound Beach Avenue, Old Greenwich, 698.2428,
 Pharmacy 698.1457. Pharmacy Hours: weekdays, 8 am - 9 pm;
 Saturday & Sunday, 8 am - 6 pm.

Finch Pharmacy (Pharmacy)

3 Riversville Road, Glenville, 531.8494
Friendly pharmacy in the heart of Glenville, where people know you and care about your needs.
Hours: weekdays, 8 am - 6 pm; Saturday, 9 am - 6 pm.

Foot Solutions (Shoes and Orthotics)

168 South Ridge Street, Rye Brook, NY, 914.939.6565
www.footsolutions.com/ryebrook
One of a large chain of stores solely devoted to making sure you have shoes that fit properly. They make orthotics and they sell seam free socks ideal for diabetes and edema.
Hours: weekdays, 10 am - 6 pm; Saturday, 10 am - 4 pm.

GNC (Vitamins)
1237 East Putnam Avenue, Riverside, 637.4262
www.GNC.com
General Nutrition Center is the largest retailer of nutritional supplements designed to help improve quality of life.
Hours: Monday - Saturday, 9 am - 8 pm (Saturday to 7 pm); Sunday, 11 am - 5 pm.

Grannick's Pharmacy (Pharmacy)
277 Greenwich Avenue, 869.3492
They know and care about their customers. They sell and rent some medical equipment. Call for their delivery policy.
Hours: Monday Saturday, 9 am -6 pm.

Greenwich Emergency Medical Service (GEMS)
111 East Putnam Avenue, 637.7505 (general information)
GEMS has six ambulances, 11 paramedics and 12 full-time EMTs. GEMS also provides programs in CPR and basic first aid. GEMS ambulances have the latest equipment and well-trained Emergency Medical Technicians and paramedics. Once you call 911, their computer-aided dispatch system allows them to reach 75% of patients within 5 minutes and 95% with 8 minutes. Greenwich is lucky to have such a coordinated ambulance organization. GEMS also operates a for-profit non-emergency ambulance service called Access Ambulance, listed separately.

Greenwich Health Mart (Vitamins)
30 Greenwich Avenue, 869.9658
A well-stocked health product store, including some foods and a great variety of vitamins and homeopathic remedies. Their cheerful service makes everyone feel well. Be sure to ask for their excellent newsletter.
Hours: Monday - Wednesday 8:30 am - 5:30 pm; Thursday 8:30 am - 7:30 pm; Friday 8:30 am - 5:30 pm; Saturday 8 am - 5 pm; Sunday, 11 am - 3 pm.

Greenwich Hospital

5 Perryridge Road, 863.3000

www.greenhosp.org

Greenwich Hospital is a 160-bed, non-profit, community teaching hospital, affiliated with Yale-New Haven Hospital. Since 1996, the Hospital has been completely rebuilt and it is a model for health care. The cost of the entire project (including the Helmsley Building and the Watson Pavilion) was $220,000,000, of which $138,000,000 came from private community donations. The rooms have been carefully designed to make the patient feel comfortable. As a result, many feel it's more like staying at a fine hotel than a hospital. Even the intensive care unit has woodland views and amazing amenities. Word is spreading fast that this is the most comfortable place to have your baby. Greenwich Hospital is ranked first in Connecticut in patient satisfaction and was named in the "Top 100 Most Wired Hospitals."

Greenwich Hospital has a wonderful emergency room: 863.3637

The entry is on Lake Avenue and is clearly indicated.

Greenwich Hospital Consumer Health Reference Center

863.3285

Hours: weekdays, 8:30 am - 4:45 pm.

Greenwich Library Health Information Center (Health Information)

www.greenwichlibrary.org/health.htm

Now everyone in Greenwich can be a well-informed healthcare consumer. The main branch of the Greenwich Library has established an extensive health information center. 18 subscription databases are part of this Center. Most of these databases are available through the library's website by merely entering your library card number. In addition the Center has over 100 authoritative reference materials, 40 journals, 5,000 circulating books, more than 300 videos and a large collection of audiobooks. A specially trained librarian is on duty to assist with healthcare research. The library also has speakers on current health topics. If you give them your email address, they will keep you posted.

Greenwich Physical Therapy Center (Physical Therapy)

1171 East Putnam Avenue, Riverside, 637.1700
An independent (non-physician owned) physical therapy center specializing in orthopedic and sports-related injuries. Everyone raves about Scott Gelbs and his team.
Hours: Monday, Wednesday, Friday, 7 am - 4 pm;
Tuesday & Thursday 9 am - 7 pm.

Greenwich Sports Medicine (Physical Therapy)

7 Riversville Road, 531.3131
www.GreenwichSportsMedicine.com
www.FitAndFunctional.com
Dr. Gil Chimes is a sports chiropractor who specializes in Active Release Techniques (ART) to help athletes recover from injuries. ART breaks up scar tissue, eliminates pain and increases range of motion. Their treatments can incorporate acupuncture, chiropractic, exercise therapy, weight loss and nutritional counseling.
Hours: Monday & Wednesday, 8 am - 7 pm (break 1:45 to 3);
Tuesday, 8 am - 7 pm; Thursday, 2 pm - 7 pm;
Friday, 8 am - 5:45 pm (break 1:45 - 3).

Health Extensions (Health Information)

Community Wellness Programs @ Greenwich Hospital
863.3126
www.greenhosp.org
The Greenwich Hospital publishes an extensive schedule and description of the community's many wellness programs. The extent of the programs is amazing.
To get your copy contact the Public Relations office at 863.3126.

Info Tapes (Health Information)

Rocky Hill, CT, 800.635.4592
www.CtParentsPlus.org/resources/infotapes.asp
Sponsored by the United Way and CT Parents Plus, you can listen in English or Spanish to educational messages 24 hours a day, on 350 topics such as aging, reasons to say no, alcohol abuse, family planing, sexual abuse, substance abuse and prenatal care. The website has a list of topics and their selection number.

Mega Hair Systems (Hair Replacement)

280 Railroad Avenue, Suite 203, 861.4134

Susan Parent is the person to contact when you are facing the prospect of hair loss. She is absolutely wonderful in helping you look completely natural. Her hair extensions and wigs are so natural and well fitted, no one will know.

Hours: By Appointment.

National Medical Claims Service (Insurance Assistance)

3 Thorndal Circle, Darien, CT 06820, 203.655.1800

If you or someone you know is overwhelmed with the task of understanding and obtaining insurance benefits, call this Greenwich family business. They are caring, reliable and greatly helpful.

Hours: weekdays, 9 am - 5 pm.

North Street Pharmacy (Pharmacy)

1061 North Street, 869.2130

In a world where change is the norm, it is wonderful to be greeted by Paul Fiscella and his wife who have been running this neighborhood pharmacy for more than 20 years.

Hours: weekdays, 9 am - 6 pm; Saturday, 9 am - 5 pm.

Omni Fitness (Exercise Equipment)

20 Railroad Avenue, 422.2277

www.omnifitness.com

A wide selection of high-end fitness equipment at reasonable prices and very nice people to work with.

Hours: weekdays, 10 am - 7 pm, Thursday until 8 pm; Saturday 10 am - 6 pm; Sunday, 11 am - 5 pm.

Performance Physical Therapy (Physical Therapy)

35 River Road, Cos Cob, 422.0679

www.CtPerformancePT.com

Todd Wilkowski has been the rehabilitation consultant for the New York Rangers. His specialty is working with adolescent sports injuries.

Physical Therapy and Sports Rehabilitation (Physical Therapy)

6 Greenwich Office Park, 869.3470

Owned and supervised by the Orthopaedic & Neurological Surgery Specialists. Many doctors are ranked as Top Docs by Connecticut Magazine. The therapists in this group are always positive, encouraging and friendly. Their enthusiasm is contagious. They are determined to make you feel better and they do.

Physician Referral Service (Health Information)

863.3627 or 888.357.2409

Sponsored by Greenwich Hospital, this service is available weekdays between 8:30 am and 4:30 pm. They will find the doctor with the qualifications you are looking for and will even make your first appointment.

Relax the Back (Equipment, Furniture)

367 Greenwich Avenue, 629.2225

www.relaxtheback.com

For people seeking relief and prevention of back and neck pain, they offer attractive posture and back support products and self-care solutions.

Hours: Monday - Wednesday, 10am - 5:30pm;
Thursday - Saturday, 10am - 6pm.

Dr. Sam Schwartz (Chiropractor)

492 Northridge, Rye Brook, 914.939.0558

Dr. Sam has boundless energy and great comprehension of each individual's needs. In addition to his years in Chiropractic, he has a 14 year background as a Registered Respiratory Therapist. He spends every minute of each visit personally with each patient. We will be forever grateful for his rehabilitation of my father, which saved him from surgery.

Silver Hill Hospital

208 Valley Road, New Canaan, CT 800.899.4455, 203.966.3561
www.silverhillhospital.com

A private, not-for-profit, full-service psychiatric and substance abuse hospital, providing inpatient, outpatient, partial hospital programs and transitional care. Their DBT program provides treatment for people with a history of impulsive behaviors, including suicide attempts. Anonymity is important. Many celebrities have quietly restored their health here.

Solomon-Shotland Audiology (Hearing aids)

Julie O'Shea, Au.D, FAAA

Debra Skorney, MS, FAA, Patricia Martucci, MS, FAA

at the Burke Rehabilitation Hospital

785 Mamaroneck Avenue, White Plains, NY, 914.949.0034

www.sandsaudiology.com

If you or someone you know is having some difficulty with their hearing, head straight to this audiologist. They are very competent and caring. They provide comprehensive diagnostic hearing testing for all ages. They work with the latest technologies from a number of the best hearing aid companies.

Stride Custom Orthotics (Orthotics)

80 Turnpike Drive, Middlebury, CT 203.758.8307, 671.549.3735

www.StrideOrthotics.com

Their only business is orthotics. You can make an appointment at the factory (Middlebury is about 1 hr.) or arrange a local fitting with one of their certified representatives.

Tully Health Center (Physical Therapy)

32 Strawberry Hill Court, Stamford, 355.4567, 353.2000

www.stamhealth.org

A modern 250,000 sq. ft. healing facility for those who have suffered from illness or injury. The Tully Center is part of the Stamford Health System. They offer, among many other programs, a number of sophisticated massage therapies and water therapies.

The Vitamin Shoppe (Health)

- 535 Post Road, Port Chester, NY, 914.939.5189
- 1003 High Ridge Road, Stamford, 609.0147

www.vitaminshoppe.com

A national chain with a good website and large selection of products.
Hours: Monday - Saturday, 9 am - 9 pm; Sunday, 11 am - 6 pm.

Walgreen's (Pharmacy)
1333 East Putnam Avenue, Riverside, 637.1496
Pharmacy: 637.1029
www.walgreens.com
In addition to normal drugstore items, they carry a large variety of general grocery foods, staples and snacks.
Hours: Even their pharmacy is open 24-hours, every day.

Westchester Medical Center
Valhalla, NY, 914.493.7000
www.wcmc.com
Connected with the New York Medical College, their Trauma Center and Children's Hospital are renowned.

Whole Foods (Grocery, Vitamins)
90 East Putnam Ave, 661.0631
www.wholefoods.com
Our favorite natural and organic food store has an excellent vitamin and herbal section. It is great to have an expert available to happily give you advice about selections.
Hours: everyday, 8 am - 10 pm.

Yale-New Haven Hospital
20 York Street, New Haven, CT, 203.688.2000, 4242
www.ynhh.org
This private, not-for-profit hospital, is the teaching hospital for Yale University School of Medicine. It is considered one of the premier hospitals in the area. Greenwich Hospital is affiliated with this hospital.

TIP: PAMPER YOURSELF WITH PREMIER SERVICES WHILE AT THE HOSPITAL

Greenwich Hospital has been equated with staying in a Hyatt Hotel. All patients have their meals served on china and have access to the Get Well Network, an interactive system that allows them to watch television, check e-mail and order movies from their beds. Now patients can be pampered even more if they wish to spend an extra $125 per night. Premier Services include secretarial services as well as many other amenities and perks.

Cos Cob Inn

50 River Road, Cos Cob, 661.5845

www.coscobinn.com

Charmingly redecorated, 1870 Federal bed-and-breakfast. Many of the fourteen rooms have scenic views of the Mianus River; each has its own bath. There are data ports in every room. Continental breakfast, no restaurant.

Rate: $99 - $199 per night, Suites $139 - $199 per night.

Delamar Greenwich Harbor

500 Steamboat Road, 661.9800, 866.335.2627

www.thedelamar.com

Greenwich's newest hotel. An 83-room Mediterranean-style luxury hotel with wonderful harbor views, just minutes from the Greenwich train station and Greenwich Avenue. Tiger Woods reportedly stays here. Yachts can safely dock at their 600-foot private dock. This is a pet-friendly hotel. High-speed internet is available.

Rates: $249 to $1,550.

Doral Arrowwood

975 Anderson Hill Road, Rye Brook, NY, 914.939.5500

www.doralarrowwood.com

Just on the border of Greenwich is a 373-room resort hotel, with golf, tennis, squash and swimming. A great place for a conference. Rates: $149 -$229. Weekend packages with golf are $299 per night.

Harbor House Inn

165 Shore Road, Old Greenwich, 637.0145

www.hhinn.com

This 100-year-old Victorian mansion has always served as an inn. Guests are corporate clients, people relocating and out-of-town visitors. The twenty-three room bed-and-breakfast is within walking distance of the beach. No restaurant. The atmosphere is very informal. If you need the latest amenities, this may not be your place.

Rates: $169 - $279

Homestead Inn

420 Field Point Road, 869.7500

www.homesteadinn.com

Exceptionally attractive country inn, with 22 lovely rooms/suites and superb food. Some rooms have wireless internet connections. A great choice.

Rates: $250 - $495

Hyatt Regency
1800 East Putnam Avenue, Old Greenwich, 637.1234
www.greenwich.hyatt.com
This 374 room luxury hotel has an elegant interior with excellent food. Greenwich residents often check into this hotel for a weekend of pampering. The hotel also has a very nice health club. High speed internet access.
Rates: $149 - $1,000

Rye Town Hilton
699 Westchester Avenue, Rye Brook, NY, 914.939.6300
www.hilton.com
Situated on 45 acres just next to Greenwich this large hotel with a pleasant restaurant hosts many conventions.
Directions: I-95 S to exit 21, 287 W to exit 10, at second light, R on Westchester Ave.
Rates: $149 - $650

Stanton House Inn
76 North Maple Avenue, 869.2110
www.shinngreenwich.com
Located in Central Greenwich, within walking distance of the shops and restaurants, this turn-of-the-century home, converted into a 24-room bed-and-breakfast, is a welcoming first stop for many new residents. Internet access in some rooms. No restaurant.
Rates: $129 - $239

Stamford Suites
720 Bedford Street, Stamford, 359.7300, 866.394.4365
www.stamfordsuites.com
An extended-stay hotel with 45 furnished suites for nightly or longer term residence. Each unit contains a bedroom, living room, bathroom and a full-size kitchen. Dialup internet access. Renovated in 1998.
Directions: I-95 N, exit 8, L on Atlantic (becomes Bedford).
Rates: Daily $169 - $229, Seven-day rate: $139, 30-day rate: $119

Connecticut River Valley

The Connecticut River Valley (Middlesex County), has outstanding inns in interesting, quaint New England towns, particularly: Chester, Clinton, Deep River, Essex, Old Lyme and Hadden. They are loaded with antique shops, art galleries and interesting activities such as the **Essex Steam Train** (described under Family Outings), the beach in Old Lyme and the Camelot dinner, Long Island or **Murder Mystery dinner cruises**, Rte.9, exit 7 in Hadden, 860.345.8591 or the **Goodspeed Opera House** in East Hadden, 860-873-8668, www.Goodspeed.org. Excellent restaurants also abound in the area. **The Restaurant Du Village** is located in Chester at 59 Main Street, 860.526.5301. This restaurant is one of the fine French restaurants in the state. You should also try what many consider the best pizza in Connecticut, served at **Alforno,** 1654 Boston Post Road, Brian Alden Shopping Plaza, Old Saybrook, open daily from 4:30 pm to 10 pm, 860.399.4166. Another great place for lunch or Sunday brunch is the **Water's Edge** at 1525 Post Road (I-95 exit 65) in Westbrook, 860.399.5901. Ask for a table on the water. You will also want to try these two Old Lyme Inns for a meal: the **Old Lyme Inn**, 85 Lyme Street, Old Lyme, 800.434.5352, and the **Bee and Thistle Inn**, 100 Lyme Street, (Rte.1, I-95 exit 70), Old Lyme, 860.434.1667. Both inns, particularly the Bee and Thistle, have received many awards for excellent dining. In the area, there is a large shopping mall (**Clinton Crossing** - see description under Outlets) at I-95 exit 63 and another large mall in Westbrook at exit 65. The state's two casinos, **Foxwoods** (I-95 exit 92) and **Mohegan Sun** (I-95 exit 76) are within easy driving distance (see directions under GAMBLING). See also Essex Steam Trains and Riverboat under CHILDREN, FAMILY OUTINGS.

Bee and Thistle Inn (New London County)

100 Lyme Street, Old Lyme, CT, 800.622.4946
www.beeandthistleInn.com

About 1½ hours from Greenwich (close to the Clinton Crossing clothing outlets and the Connecticut casinos) is one of the great old inns in Connecticut. Often written up as the most romantic. As an added plus, it has good, artfully simple American food. At a recent party, one of our guests arrived very late. The staff cheerfully allowed us to enjoy the evening with no hint of the inconvenience of the late hour. Room rates: $140 - $260.

Directions: I-95N to exit 70 CT-156, L on Ferry, L on Lyme.

Copper Beach Inn (Middlesex County)

46 Main Street, Ivoryton, CT
www.copperbeechinn.com
860.767.0330, 888.809.2056
Gracious inn with 13 guest rooms and excellent food in a charming New England town, about 1½ hours from Greenwich. High on our list, this inn fits the perfect image of what a New England inn should be. The inn is best suited for adults unless the children have very nice manners. Rooms range from $165- $375 per night. January through March, the dining room is closed Tuesday as well as Monday evenings.
Directions: I-95 N to Exit 69, Rte 9 N to exit 3, L (west) 1.75 miles.

Inn at Chester (Middlesex County)

318 West Main Street (Rte. 148), Chester, CT, 860.526.9541
www.innatchester.com
The Inn is relatively large with 44 rooms and suites. It is about 1½ hours from Greenwich. It is open every day for lunch and dinner and serves very good food in attractive surroundings. Wireless internet access is available throughout the grounds and direct connections in the rooms.
Room rates: $133 to $450.
Directions: I-95 N to exit 69, Rt. 9 North to exit 6 (Chester), L off ramp. The Inn is 3.2 miles on the right.

Mayflower Inn & Spa (Litchfield County)

118 Woodbury Road, Route 47, Washington, CT 860.868.9466
www.mayflowerinn.com
Set on 58 acres of lovely grounds, this 30-room Inn is a perfect place to rest and refresh. Enjoy fine dining, walks in the garden, and antiquing in nearby shops and, of course, the spa. The Inn is about 1½ hours from Greenwich.
Room rates: $400 to $1,300.

(The) Water's Edge (Middlesex County)

1525 Boston Post Road, Westbrook, CT, 860.399.5901
www.WatersEdgeResortAndSpa.com
Not a charming old inn, but a highly rated resort hotel with excellent food. It is often used for upscale meetings. 169 rooms, rates are $140 - $240.

magazines

atHome Magazine
203.869.0009
www.athomefc.com
Published semi-annually in April and October. This magazine is filled with inspiration, information and decorating trends in Fairfield County.

Connecticut Cottages & Gardens
203.227.1400
www.CTCandG.com
A free, very high quality magazine with pretty photos and good articles. Even if you just use it for a coffee table book, you will love it.

Connecticut Magazine
800.974.2001
www.connecticutmag.com
This comprehensive, attractive magazine always has well-researched articles on the best of Connecticut. Subscribe! You will love this magazine. They do a great job of rating everything from golf courses to towns to the top doctors.

Fairfield County Weddings Magazine
203.222.0600
www.fairfieldweddings.com
Published semi-annually in June and December. Plan your wedding with this magazine. Available at local newsstands.

Greenwich Magazine
869.0009
www.greenwichmag.com
Sophisticated articles on topics of interest for everyone. A valuable source of information about Greenwich and Greenwich residents. A subscripton to Greenwich Magazine is essential. The Mofflys also publish the leading magazines for Westport and New Caanan/Darien.

Westchester Magazine
800.254.2213
www.westchestermagazine.com
This magazine focuses on Westchester and Fairfield counties. It often has articles on Greenwich. It is an excellent resource for discovering events and resources you will want to take advantage of in our neighboring towns.

newspapers

See SERVICES for newspaper delivery information.

Fairfield County Business Journal

914.694.3600

www.fairfieldcountybusinessjournal.com

This weekly newspaper tracks trends and developments that impact local businesses. If you are thinking of opening a business or simply want to know the commercial news, this paper is just the ticket.

Greenwich Citizen

41 West Putnam Avenue, 750.5313

www.greenwichcitizen.com

This free weekly newspaper, conveniently sized for commuters, is focused on local news. It is a must read for anyone living in Greenwich. If you miss any of the Town events, this paper with its articles and many pictures will keep you in the know. Every month you will enjoy reading their supplement - Inside Fairfield County.

Greenwich Post

22 West Putnam Avenue, 861.9191

www.acornonline.com/news/publish/greenwich.shtml

The Greenwich Post is a lively weekly newspaper covering the Town. Each week they publish a comprehensive Real Estate section, with real estate news you won't want to miss. Each paper is filled with good articles, updates, editorials and summaries of what is happening in Greenwich. They have extensive calendars of local and regional activities, and many special publications, including Home Magazine and 100 Things to Do. This is a free newspaper, so be sure to give them a call if you are not on their list. Check their website for "Things to Do."

Greenwich Time

20 East Elm Street, 625.4400

www.greenwichtime.com

If we were judging a national competition for the best daily local newspaper, Greenwich Time would win the top award. Joseph Pisani's editorials stimulate thought about important Town topics. The Letters from Readers section is a good barometer of Town concerns. To understand what is happening in Greenwich, you must read this paper.

Voices (formerly TeenSpeak)

www.voicesoftomorrow.org

This internet newspaper by and for tomorrow's leaders was founded by Greenwich resident Debra Mamorsky. It is a weekly international publication written solely by 17 to 25-year-olds for their peers around the world. The publication tackles important domestic, international and youth-related issues.

TIP: PUTNAM'S RIDE RE-ENACTED

In February, the Putnam Hill Chapter of the DAR re-enacts General Putnam's 1779 ride. Men are in official revolutionary attire, with muskets and conduct Revolutionary War drills and skirmishes. General Putnam's ride is featured on the seal of the Town. What better way to learn history. The location is Putnam Cottage, 243 East Putnam Avenue. For details contact Jenny Larkin 869.4735 or visit www.PutnamCottage.org

radio & television

Bloomberg News AM 1130

www.Bloomberg.com
Good national and international news. Best for financial news.

Cablevision Channel Lineup

http://www.optimum.com/lineup.jsp?regionId=30

Connecticut Television

www.cpbi.org
Connecticut Public Television has Connecticut-based documentaries as well as sports coverage of Connecticut teams.
• Channel 79 is our local community access station. It broadcasts "Greenwich Weekly Video Magazine" Wednesdays at 10:30 pm and Fridays at 9:30 am. RTM meetings are shown live. The meeting calendar is shown between broadcasts.
• Channel 78 is the Greenwich Educational Access Channel.
• Channel 79 - Connecticut Government Access.

Channel 12 - Connecticut News

www.news12.com/CT
Continuous news, weather and traffic reports.
• CBS AM 880, www.NewsRadio88.com
• WINS AM 1010, www.1010wins.com

Greenwich Radio

1490 Dayton Avenue, 869.1490
AM 1490
www.wgch.com
Tune in between 6 am and 10 am for an update on Greenwich happenings. Their interviews with Greenwich people making the news are essential to understanding town issues. "Ask the First Selectman" airs Fridays at 9 am. A fun Greenwich program, "A Fashionable Life" with Jayne Chase and Jennifer Goodkind, airs Wednesdays at 9:30.

Public Radio

Great indepth coverage of national and international events without commerical interruption.
• Connecticut Public Radio FM 88.5, www.cpbi.org/radio
• National Public Radio AM 820 & FM 93.9, www.npr.org

For a complete list of useful Greenwich numbers, see:
www.GreenwichLiving.com/contacts_relocation.htm

Greenwich Telephone System

Greenwich is on the border between Verizon (formerly Bell Atlantic, formerly Nynex) and AT&T (formerly SNET, formerly SBC) coverage areas. Old Greenwich exchanges (637 & 698) are covered by AT&T. From there you can dial many Connecticut 203 numbers directly. The rest of Greenwich is controlled by Verizon. This means that many numbers outside of Greenwich require you to dial 1.203 first.

Most Stamford numbers do not require the 203 prefix, but information for Stamford requires you to dial 203.555.1212. Greenwich information can be accessed by dialing 411. We have tried to organize the numbers in this guide to make it clear when you have to dial 203 (if you are in the Verizon coverage area) or when you can simply dial the local number.

Anderson Associates

Greenwich real estate specialists.
Main number: 629.4519
www.greenwichliving.com
If you don't know where to turn, call us.

Ambulance - Greenwich Police

911 Emergency
622.8000 (non-emergency)
see GEMS below.

Aquarion (formerly The ConnecticutAmerican Water Company)

www.aquarion.com
869.5200 (office)
203.445.7310, 800.732.9678 (emergency)
800.292.2928, 800.732.9678 (customer service)

AT&T/SNET/SBC: Old Greenwich exchanges 637 & 698

From AT&T coverage area, dial 811 for repairs; from out-of-state, 800.453.7638 (Customer Service); 203.420.3131 (repairs) or 611 from cell phone
www.snet.com
www.sbc.com

Cablevision of Connecticut
348.9211, 203.846.4700, 203.750.5600
www.cablevision.com
www.optimum.com

Community Answers
101 West Putnam Avenue, 622.7979
www.greenwichlibrary.org/commanswers.htm
• Funded by the United Way and private donations, this volunteer group is located in the Greenwich Library. Ask them anything about Greenwich (all calls are confidential). Their website is a storehouse of valuable information.
• Community Calendar
Community Answers provides a Community Calendar of all Greenwich events. It comes out every three months. Be sure to call and ask for it.
• Useful Article Reprints
Stop by and pick up articles which might be helpful, such as: Childcare and Parenting Services, Summer Camp and Programs in Greenwich.
Hours: weekdays, 9 am - 5 pm.

Connecticut Natural Gas
869.6900 (customer service)
869.6913 (repair & emergency)
www.cng.com

Connecticut Vacation Planning Guide
800.282.6863
www.CTVisit.com
You might also try Coastal Fairfield County Tourist Information at 800.866.7925 or 203.853.7770

Federal Express
800.238.5355, 800.GO.FEDEX
www.fedex.com

FedEx/Kinkos
48 West Putnam Avenue, 863.0099

GEMS (Greenwich Emergency Medical Service)
911 for emergency ambulance
203.637.7505 (office)

Greenwich Fire Department
911 Emergency
622.3950 (non-emergency)
- Amogerone Fire Company(Havemeyer Place), 249.2421 or 622.3959
  www.amogerone.com
- Byram Fire Company, 532.9752 or 622.3973
- Cos Cob Fire Company, 622.3972 or 622.1506
- Glenville Fire Company, 532.9606 or 622.3974, www.911fire.org
- Old Greenwich Fire Company, 637.1806 or 622.3975, www.sbvfd.com
- Round Hill Vol. Fire Company, 869.7185
- Banksville Independent Fire Company, 234.7104
- Back Country Fire Company, 661.2452

Greenwich Hospital
863.3000
www.GreenwichHosp.org
See complete description in HEALTH.

Greenwich Police
911 Emergency
622.8000 (complaints and information)
www.greenwichpolice.com

Greenwich Public Schools
625.7400
www.greenwich.k12.ct.us
See complete description and other numbers in SCHOOLS.

Northeast Utilities/Connecticut Light & Power
800.286.2000, 800.286.5000
www.nu.com

Post Offices

Post Offices and Zip Codes are listed under their own heading.
www.GreenwichPost.com

Poison Control Center

800.343.2722 (Connecticut)
800.222.1222 (national)

Telemarketing (NO CALL(List

CT Department of Consumer Protection
800.842.2649
www.state.ct.us/dcp/nocall.htm

Connecticut State and Federal Representatives

* US Senator, Chris Dodd (Democrat), 202.224.2823
  www.dodd.senate.gov
* US Senator, Joseph Lieberman (Independent), 202.224.4041
  www.lieberman.senate.gov
* US Congressman Chris Shays (Republican), 202.225.5541
  www.house.gov/shays
* Governor Jodi Rell (Republican), 800.406.1527
  www.ct.gov/governorrell/site/default.asp
* State Senator Bill Nickerson (Republican), 860.240.8787
  www.senaterepublicans.ct.gov/senainfo/Nickerson.htm
* State Representative Livvy Floren (Republican), 800.842.1423
  www.housegop.state.ct.us/members/floren.htm
* State Representative Lile Gibbons (Republican), 860.240.8700
  www.housegop.state.ct.us/members/gibbons.htm
* State Representative Claudia (Dolly) Powers (Republican)
  860.240.8778
  www.housegop.ct.gov/members/powers.asp

NUMBERS YOU SHOULD KNOW

Town Hall

622.7700 (all departments)

www.greenwichct.org

- Meeting Rooms:
  1st Floor: Town Hall Meeting Room, Mazza & Gisborne
  2nd Floor: Cone Meeting Room
  3rd Floor: Hayton & Evaristo Meeting Rooms
- Assessors's Office, 622.7885
  1st floor, 8:30 am - 3:30 pm.
- Beach Card Office, 622.7817

1st floor, 9 am - 3 pm, April through November 15th .

See section PARKS & RECREATION, Beaches for information on obtaining a beach card.

- Building Department, 622.7754

2nd floor, 8 am - 2:30 pm. Summer hours from June through October: Monday, Tuesday & Thursday, 7:30 am - 3 pm, Wednesday & Friday, 7:30 am - noon.

- Conservation Department, 622.3736

2nd floor, 8 am - 3:30 pm. Call ahead to make an appointment to meet with a staff member.

- Geographic Information Department (GIS), 622.7771

Basement, 9 am - 4 pm; print out on site or pick up large map on Friday.

- Health (Septic) Department, 622.7838

3rd floor, 8 am 2:30 pm, after 2:30 by appointment.

- Highway Department, 622.7766

2nd floor, 8 am - 4 pm.

- Parks & Recreation Department, 622.7814
  2nd floor, 8 am - 4 pm.
- Planning & Zoning Department, 622.7894

2nd floor, 8 am - 4 pm.

  To meet with a planner, 1 pm 3:30 pm.

- Probate Court, 622.7879

1st floor, 8 am - 4 pm.

- Public Works (Sewer) Department, 622.7760

2nd floor, 8:30 am - 4 pm.

- Selectman's Office, 622.7710
  1st floor, 8 am - 4 pm, Call for appointment.
- Social Services Department, 622.3800
3rd floor, 9 am - 5 pm.
- Tax Collector, 622.7891
  1st floor, 8:30 am - 3:30 pm.
- Town Clerk, 622.7897
  1st floor, 8 am - 4 pm.
- Wetlands, 622.7736
2nd floor, 8 am - 3:30 pm.
  To meet with a compliance officer, 1 pm - 3:30 pm.
  Call ahead for an appointment.

USE (Senior Center Job Placement Service)
629.8031
Utilize Senior Energy, run by volunteers, is a good resource for everything from office help to painters to babysitters.
Hours: weekdays, 9:30 am - 12:30 pm

Verizon
869.5222 (new service)
661.5444 (repairs), 611 from Cell phone.
625.9800 (customer service)
www22.verizon.com
Verizon is offering, FIOS, a fiberoptic service competing with Cablevision.
www.verizonfios.com

TIP: CBYD

Never dig around your home without first calling "Call Before You Dig (CBYD)." 800.922.4455. This clearing house will arrange free-of-charge to locate and mark the underground utilities on your property.

PARKS & RECREATION

Greenwich extends over 47 square miles with rolling hills, woodlands, meadows and 32 miles of gorgeous shoreline bordering the Long Island Sound. Greenwich's main beaches are at Greenwich Point (147 acres), Byram Beach and the 2 city-owned islands (Captain's Island & Island Beach). Greenwich has 8,000 acres of protected land, over 1,500 acres of town parks, 35 town tennis courts (not including the YWCA Courts), an indoor ice rink (open only to residents), 14 public marinas and a 158-acre, 18-hole golf course (open only to residents).

beaches

Greenwich beaches are open to residents and non-residents. You must have a beach pass before entering the beach. Passes are strictly enforced. Apply early and be sure to have it when you enter. Passes are required from May 26 to September 17. Dogs are allowed on a leash from December 1st to March 31st. No charge is required from the middle of November to the middle of April.

Beach Cards and Passes

The Beach Card Office (622.7817) is located on First Floor of Town Hall. It is open weekdays, 9 am to 3 pm from March through December. Proof of residency is required for a Beach Card. The Town will accept: moving documents, lease papers, a drivers license, phone or electric bills. Beach cards cost $25 for adults, $5 for children ages 5 to 13, and are free for seniors and toddlers. Daily admission passes for non-residents cost $10 per person and $20 per vehicle per day. Passes can be purchased at Eastern Civic Center or Town Hall. The Town also requires residents to obtain a seasonal parking sticker for each car or pay $20 for daily parking. Parking stickers can be obtained free with a copy of a current vehicle registration indicating that the car is on the Greenwich tax rolls. If the car is not on the tax rolls, the sticker costs Greenwich Residents $100 per season.

beaches

Byram Beach
531.8938
This beach on Byram Shore Road has a swimming pool, 3 tennis courts, a picnic area and playground.

Cruise to Nowhere
The Cruise is popular and had 11 of its 12 cruises sold out for the last two years in a row. For $7 a person you can cruise around the Islands of Greenwich. For information on the cruise dates, call the Department of Parks and Recreation at 622.7814.

Ferry Information
Ticket office, 661.5957; Ferry schedule, 618.7672
The ferry service from the Arch Street dock to Great Captain's Island or Island Beach varies according to the tides. Service begins in the middle of June and lasts until the middle of September.

Great Captain's Island
622.7814
Captain's Island is rustic with no concession stand, so bring a picnic lunch. Camp sites available with permits. For camping reservations, call 622.7824. Take a ferry from the Arch Street dock to this 17-acre island with beach and picnic area. Several morning and afternoon ferries are available depending upon the day and date. Consult the the ferry schedule information 618.7672 or www.greenwichct.org/ParksAndRec/prFerryService.asp for details.

Greenwich Point (Tod's Point)
Entrance at the south end of Shore Road in Old Greenwich. This 147-acre beach, with concession stand, has jogging, hiking and biking trails, lots of picnic facilities and wind surfing.

Island Beach (Little Captain's Island)
661.5957
Take a ferry from the Arch Street dock to this 4-acre island with beaches, picnic area and concession stand.
Hours: weekdays, every hour 10 am - 7 pm through mid-August; 10 am - 6 pm through mid-September, weekends every half-hour.

PARKS & RECREATION

The Civic centers are the sites for many sporting events and public events such as antique shows. Call for their latest catalog of events.

Eastern Greenwich Civic Center

(Also called: Greenwich Civic Center or Old GreenwichRiverside Civic Center)

90 Harding Road, Old Greenwich, 637.4583

The center is 14 acres and operates weekdays from 8 am - 10 pm, weekends as scheduled. The center has a basketball court, 2-tennis courts with lights, a baseball diamond and playground. The center is used extensively for a wide variety of activities such as roller skating, men's basketball, soccer, tennis for tots, Old Greenwich Art society painters and Halloween Happenings.

Western Greenwich Civic Center

449 Pemberwick Road, Glenville, 622.7830

The newly renovated center on 9.97 acres, is the pride of the Town. From 1997 the Glenville Community led by the 9th district RTM and other concerned citizens started a fundraising campaign to reburbish the Civic Center. After the group raised approximately 3.5 million dollars, the Town of Greenwich matched the gift and work began in June of 2005. The new building features a state of the art Daycare Center, a new gym/auditorium, a dance, exercise studio, weight room and meeting rooms.
Call for a program guide.

TIP: TOWN PERMITS AND PASSES

Permits and passes for many Greenwich activities can be applied for on the Town's website, www.Greenwichct.org

parks & nature preserves

Greenwich, in addition to its beaches and 32 miles of coastline, has 8,000 acres of protected land, with over 1,000 acres of Town parks. The parks and nature preserves listed below are some of the more popular of the twenty parks in Greenwich. Call Greenwich Department of Parks & Recreation (622.7830) for a complete list and directions. www.greenwichct.org and click on the sidebar for Parks and Recreation

Audubon Center
613 Riversville Road, 869.5272
www.greenwich.center.audibon.org
686 acres with well-kept trails, a great place to walk.

Babcock Preserve
North Street, 622.7700
297 acres located two miles north of the Merritt Parkway. Well-marked running, hiking, and crosscountry ski trails.

Binney Park
Sound Beach Avenue, Old Greenwich, 622.7824
4 tennis courts, a playground, fields and pond skating. A favorite place for wedding photos.

Bruce Park
Bruce Park Drive and Indian Field Road, 622.7824
Athletic fields, bowling green, fitness trail, picnic area, tennis courts and playground.

Mianus River Park
Cognewaugh Road, 622.7824
215 acres owned by Greenwich and Stamford. Trout fishing, wooded hills and steep cliffs with miles of hiking trails. Take Valley Road to Cognewaugh; the entrance is on Cognewaugh Road about three miles on the right. (There is no sign.)

parks & nature preserves

Montgomery Pinetum

Bible Street, Cos Cob

Armed with a map and tree guide from the Garden Center, you will have fun exploring this beautiful 91-acre wilderness.

To reach Montgomery Park and Pinetum, go north on Orchard Street from the Post Road in Cos Cob. Bear right onto Bible Street and continue .7 mile. The entrance is on the west side directly opposite Clover Place.

Greenwich Land Trust

629.2151

Greenwich and its residents are committed to expanding the Town's large amount of green space. Funding comes from a variety of sources, including the Town, the State, the Federal Government (www.tpl.org), the Greenwich Land Trust (www.gltrust.org) and private donations. Some of the most recent acquisitions include the following

- **Treetops**

In 2002 the Town of Greenwich and 3 land trusts raised $11.5 million dollars to purchase 110 acres bordering the Mianus River. This tract forms the southern boundary of the 220 acre Mianus River Park. Inspired by David Ogilvy, residents from Town officials to school children united to make this possible.

- **Sabine Farm Field**

A field along Round Hill Road was purchased in 2001 for $2.9 million by the Greenwich Land Trust. However, all of the money came from private donations, raised primarily through the efforts of a local resident, Edward Bragg.

Calves Island

This 28-acre island off Byram Shore was purchased from the YMCA for $6 million by the Stewart B. McKinney National Wildlife Refuge.

Pomerance-Tuchman Preserve

This 118-acre tract adjacent to the Montgomery Pinetum lies between Orchard and Bible Streets in Cos Cob. The Town has undertaken to purchase the property for $35 million. Along with the Pinetum and Bible Street playing fields, this tract gives the Town a corridor of 227 acres of pristine woodlands.

specialized parks & facilities

Dog Park

The Greenwich Dog Park is located on 3/4 acre at Grass Island. The park is open from sunrise to sunset. For your dog to have a good experience, for the first visit go during a quiet time, usually weekdays between 9 am and 11 am. The rules are posted on the fence. Children under 10 are not permitted and the owners must remain in the fenced area with their dog while the dog is off leash. Aggressive dogs are not allowed and owners are responsible for the behavior of their dog.

Dorthy Hamill Skating Rink

Skating Rink Road off Sherman Avenue in Byram, 531.8560

Set on 18 acres, this large skating facility has brought joy to Greenwich skaters for 34 years. All kinds of programs are available, such as: hockey clinics, Town-wide figure skating competition and general skating. Its normal hours of operation are 6 am - 12 am, from September to Mid-March. Sessions are open to Greenwich residents. Guests are admitted when accompanied by a Greenwich resident and proof of residency is required. During the off season the rink is covered with indoor turf for lacrosse and soccer.

TIP: DOG VOLUNTEERS NEEDED

Adopt-a-Dog shelters and places abandoned dogs and cats in loving homes. They need volunteers to help with functions such as fundraising, dog walking, public relations and animal care. If you have a warm place in your heart for these sweet creatures, call 629.9494 for information or www.adoptadog.org.

specialized parks & facilities

Griffith E Harris Golf Course

1300 King Street, General Information: 531.7200
Reservations: 531.8253,
Pro Shop: 531.7261 (Head Pro Joseph Felder)
This 18-hole, Robert Trent Jones-designed course, is the Town's only municipal golf course and the only non-private golf course in the Town. Use of the course is open to all Town of Greenwich residents who become members. Members are permitted to bring guests with them to play at the course as well. All guests are required to be accompanied by a member to play.

Skate Park

Located at Roger Sherman Baldwin Park, Arch Street
622.7830
The Greenwich Skate Park is a supervised facility for youths 6 years of age and over to skateboard and inline skate. The area is supervised whenever the park is open. Full protective gear is required. Children 6 to 9 years of age must be accompanied by an adult (18 years or older) during the time they are in the park. The facility provides a friendly and supportive environment for beginners to experts. Private and semi-private lessons are offered during regular skate park hours. They offer beginning techniques as well as tricks. The park is open 3 pm to 7 pm on weekdays from April 2th to October 28th. Weekends and holidays noon to 7 pm. Off- peak hours are between October 29th and March 31st, check the schedule. It is closed December and January.

Tennis and Paddle Courts

For information, call Frank Gabriele at 622.7821.
Tennis courts are located all over Town. There are also two Paddle Courts. Tennis passes are required from May through August. Applications for tennis passes are available at Town Hall or on line at www.greenwichct.org/ParksAndRec/prTennis.asp. Proof of Greenwich residency required. The Town offers instruction and holds an annual Town-wide tournament.

PHOTOGRAPHY

Framers are described in SHOPS
Passport photos are described in TRAVEL

Photography Stores:

The following stores are described in SHOPPING

- Camera Wholesalers, 1034 High Ridge Road, Stamford 357.0467
- Images, 202 Sound Beach Avenue, Old Greenwich, 637.4193
- Ritz Camera, 82 Greenwich Avenue, Greenwich, 869.0673

photographers

Action Arts

242 Sound Beach Avenue, Old Greenwich, 637.2685
www.ActionArtsPhotography.com
Action Arts has been doing portrait photography of children and families since 1972.

Amanda Jones

North Adams, MA, 877.251.2390
www.AmandaJones.com
One of our nation's top animal photographers, grew up in Greenwich. Mention Amanda Jones to a dog enthusiast and you will hear how beautiful her work is. Amanda books shooting tours in advance. Check her website for a schedule. Greenwich is on most of her tours.

Annie Watson

125 Spencer Place, Mamaroneck, NY 914.777.7505
www.AnnieWatson.com
A photographer with an artist's eye.

Ben Larrabee

26 Fairview Avenue, Darien, CT 203.656.3807
www.BenLarrabee.com
Ben is a graduate of RISD and Yale University. His pictures are in museums in New York and Boston.

PHOTOGRAPHY

Classic Kids

54 Greenwich Avenue, 622.2358
www.ClassicKidsPhotography.com
Charlie and Stephanie had a wonderful time having Kathleen Miller take their photographs here.

Bob Capazzo

358.3402
Bob is the senior photographer for Greenwich Magazine. He likes to photograph people and events and he has a wonderful way of helping people relax and look their best. It is easy to see his work, just pick up an issue of Greenwich Magazine.

Kathleen DiGiovanna

661 Steamboat Road, 869.5432
A freelance photographer specializing in weddings and special events. You can depend on her to capture the spirit of the occasion.

Jeffery Shaw Portrait Photography

39 Lewis Street, 622.4838
www.JefferyShaw.com
You will treasure his photographs of your family.
Hours: Tuesday- Friday, 10 am - 5 pm.

TIP: TOUR GREENWICH HOMES

www.hstg.org/index.cgi/634
Each year in December, Antiquarius (The Greenwich Historical Society) organizes a fabulous tour of some of Greenwich's most beautiful homes. The annual fundraiser costs about $100. You can also buy a ticket for lunch, held at one of the Country Clubs. Call Pam at 869.6899 for details.

www.GreenwichPost.com

There are six post offices and five zip codes in Town. The window service hours are different for each office. Mail for Greenwich zip codes is usually sent to Stamford to be sorted. The only post office with bins for all Greenwich zip codes is in Old Greenwich.

Greenwich Avenue Post Office [Zip: 06830]

310 Greenwich Avenue, 869.3737
Hours: weekdays, 8:30 am - 5 pm;
   Saturday, 8 am - 2 pm.

Greenwich Post Office [Zip: 06831]

29 Valley Drive, 625.3168
Hours: weekdays, 8:30 am - 6 pm;
   Saturday, 8:30 am - 2 pm.

Glenville Post Office [Zip: 06831]

25 Glen Ridge Plaza, 531.8744
Hours: weekdays, 8:30 am - 4 pm;
   Saturday, 8:30 am - noon.

Cos Cob Post Office [Zip: 06807]

152 East Putnam Avenue, 869.0128
Hours: weekdays, 8:30 am - 4:30 pm;
   Saturday, 8:30 am - 12:30 pm.

Riverside Post Office [Zip: 06878]

1273 East Putnam Avenue, 637.9332
Hours: weekdays, 7:30 am - 5 pm;
   Saturday, 8 am - 1 pm.

Old Greenwich Post Office [Zip: 06870]

36 Arcadia Road, 637.1405
Hours: weekdays, 8 am - 5 pm;
   Saturday, 9 am - 1 pm.

Buyer Agency

On June 1, 1997, Connecticut mandated that Realtors represent either the buyer or the seller, but not both (unless dual or designated agency is disclosed and agreed to by both parties) in the same transaction.

Buyers like being represented by their own Realtor because their Realtor can now tell them what they think a house is worth and provide excellent guidance through the real estate process. This extra protection costs the buyer nothing because the buyer's Realtor is still paid by the seller. In the first meeting, the buyer signs a representation agreement with their Realtor much the way a seller signs a listing agreement with their Realtor.

For more information on Buyer Agency see:
 www.GreenwichLiving.com/buyeragency.htm

Greenwich Multiple Listing Service

Greenwich has an outstanding organization devoted to local real estate. This service is funded by the Realtors in town and is extremely helpful to homeowners, buyers and Realtors. Member Realtors follow a strict code of ethics. Greenwich properties are valuable and unique. It is important to understand how Greenwich real estate works. For more information on the home buying process in Greenwich, see www.GreenwichLiving.com/salesprocess.htm

When many other towns gave up their local boards, Greenwich did not. In Greenwich all properties, with rare exceptions, are multiple-listed with the Greenwich MLS. To buy property in Greenwich, you need to select a Realtor you like and trust and you will have access through your Realtor to the entire market.

Anderson Associates

164 Mason Street, 629.4519, 800.223.4519
www.greenwichliving.com
Anderson Associates are Greenwich real estate specialists.
We all live, as well as work, in Greenwich. We spend our full time on Greenwich real estate. You can depend on us to represent your best interests. Our knowledge of Greenwich and our real estate expertise will make your real estate transaction rewarding and stress-free. As we mentioned in the introduction, we wrote the book you are reading to help our buyers feel at home in this wonderful community.

"With special thanks for all you do;
for knowing what we wanted better than we did;
for giving us that extra push when we needed it, but never pushing us hard;
for your expertise;
for much more, but especially for just being you."
- Naomi & Steve Myers

"Whether you are buying or selling, you will love working with Anderson Associates. Their website is filled with information—just what you'd expect from a company as customer-driven as they are. I found information on renovating my house, my children found statistics for school projects, and there are pictures of lots of Greenwich houses for sale. Highly recommended."
- Melanie Kuperberg

For more comments by Anderson Associates' clients, see:
 www.GreenwichLiving.com/recommend.htm

For more information and comments about Carolyn Anderson, see:
 www.GreenwichLiving.com/meetcarolyn.htm

Strategy Mortgage Corporation

222 Railroad Avenue, 618.4444

www.strategymortgage.com

Call Lucy Krasnor, Vice President Loan Origination.

Strategy is located in Greenwich. They started in 1994 and originated over $42 million in their first year. Strategy now represents fifty-eight of the most aggressive national and regional lenders and generates over $400 million a year in mortgage loans. They work hard to find the best loans for their clients, and best of all, they are available from 8 am - 10 pm every day.

TIP: HOW TO PRICE YOUR GREENWICH HOME

How much your home is worth is determined not by Realtors, but by supply and demand at the time you list. Buyers are comparison shoppers. They look at what has sold and what is for sale. Then they decide value. It is the job of your Realtor to educate you about the local real estate market and how your home fits into it. It is your job to set an informed price for your home.

When you list your home it will be competing with similar homes on the market, as well as those that have recently sold. Your Realtor should provide you with a complete analysis of the real estate market, the sales in your neighborhood and comparable homes presently for sale. You should consider driving by these homes and let your Realtor explain how they compare, and why they sold or were priced the way they were. Don't confuse pricing your property with choosing your Realtor. Choose a Realtor you like and trust first. Then work with them to price your home.

Each week the Greenwich Time publishes Sabbath services in the Thursday issue and church services in the Saturday issue. This is the best place to find updated information and times of services.

houses of worship

Albertson Memorial Church of Spiritualism
293 Sound Beach Avenue, Old Greenwich, 637.4615
www.AlbertsonChurch.org

Anglican Church of the Advent
(Anglican-Episcopal)
Meeting at North Congregational Church
606 Riversville Road, 861.2432
www.ChurchOfTheAdvent.org

Annunciation Greek Orthodox Church
1230 Newfield Avenue, Stamford, 322.2093

Bethel African Methodist Episcopal Church
42 Lake Avenue, 661.3099

Chabad Lubavitch of Greenwich
75 Mason Street, 629.9059
www.ChabadGreenwich.org

Chavurat Deevray Torah
(Reform/Conservative Jewish Study Group)
49 Arcadia Road, 637.9478

Christ Church of Greenwich
254 East Putnam Avenue, 869.6600
www.christchurchgreenwich.com

Church of Jesus Christ of LatterDay Saints
800 Stillwater Road, Stamford, 662.0867

Church of the New Covenant
128 Knapp Street, Stamford, 324.5797

houses of worship

Diamond Hill United Methodist Church
521 East Putnam Avenue, 869.2395
www.diamondhillumc.org

Dingletown Community Church
(Nondenominational Protestant)
Stanwich Road and Barnstable Lane, 629.5923
www.Dingletown.org

First Baptist Church
10 Northfield Street, 869.7988

First Church of Christ, Scientist
Church: 11 Park Place, 869.2503
Reading Room: 333 Greenwich Avenue
www.ChristianScienceCT.org/greenwich

First Church of Round Hill
(interdenominational)
464 Round Hill Road, 629.3876

First Congregational Church
108 Sound Beach Avenue, Old Greenwich, 637.1791
www.fccog.org

First Lutheran Church
38 Field Point Road, 869.0032

First Presbyterian Church
One West Putnam Avenue, 869.8686
www.fpcg.org

First United Methodist Church
59 East Putnam Avenue, 629.9584
www.fumcgreenwich.org

Grace Church of Greenwich
(Presbyterian Church in America)
Meets at Woman's Club of Greenwich
89 Maple Avenue, 861.7555
www.GraceChurchGreenwich.com

Greek Orthodox Church of the Archangels
1527 Bedford Street, Stamford, 348.4216
www.archangels.ct.goarch.org

Greenwich Baptist Church
10 Indian Rock Lane, 869.2437
www.GreenwichBaptist.org

Greenwich Congregation of Jehovah's Witnesses
471 Stanwich Road, 661.1244

Greenwich Reform Synagogue
257 Stanwich Road, 629.0018
www.grs.org

Harvest Time Assembly of God
1338 Kings Street
www.HTChurch.com

Japanese Gospel Church
(Protestant Evangelical Christian Church for Japanese speakers)
Meeting at St. Paul Evangelical Lutheran Church
286 Delavan Avenue, 531.6450

North Greenwich Congregational Church
606 Riversville Road, 869.7763

Presbyterian Church of Old Greenwich
38 West End Avenue, Old Greenwich 637.3669
www.pcogonline.org

Round Hill Community Church
(independent & nondenominational Christian)
395 Round Hill Road, 869.1091
www.roundhillcommunitychurch.org

Sacred Heart Roman Catholic Church
95 Henry Street, Byram, 531.8730 (Rectory)

St. Agnes Roman Catholic Church
247 Stanwich Road, 869.5396 (Rectory)
www.Stagnesrc.org

St. Barnabas Episcopal Church
954 Lake Avenue, 661.5526
www.stbarnabasgreenwich.org

St. Catherine of Siena Roman Catholic Church
4 Riverside Avenue, 637.3661
www.stcath.org

St Mary's Holy Assumption
(Russian Orthodox)
141 Den Road, Stamford, 329.9933

St. Mary Roman Catholic Church
178 Greenwich Avenue, 869.9393 (Rectory)
www.StMaryParishGreenwich.org

St. Michael the Archangel Roman Catholic Church
469 North Street, 869.5421 (Rectory)
www.stmichaelgreenwich.org

St. Paul Evangelical Lutheran Church
286 Delavan Avenue, 531.8466

St. Paul Roman Catholic Church
84 Sherwood Avenue, 531.8741
www.StPaulGreenwich.org

houses of worship

St. Paul's Episcopal Church
200 Riverside Avenue, 637.2447
www.stpaulsriverside.org

St. Roch Roman Catholic Church
10 St. Roch Avenue, 869.4176

St. Saviour's Episcopal Church
350 Sound Beach Avenue, Old Greenwich, 637.2262
www.SaintSaviours.org

St. Timothy Church
1034 North Street, Banksville, NY, 869.5421

Second Congregational Church
139 East Putnam Avenue, 869.9311
www.2cc.org

Stanwich Congregational Church
202 Taconic Road, 661.4420
www.stanwichchurch.org

StamfordGreenwich Religious Society of Friends
572 Roxbury Road, Stamford, 869.0445

Temple Sholom
300 East Putnam Avenue, 869.7191
www.TempleSholom.com

Trinity Church
15 Sherwood Place, 618.0808
www.trinitychurchonline.org

Unitarian Universalist Society
20 Forest Street, Stamford, 348.0708
www.uusis.org

organizations

Hadassah, Greenwich Chapter

Temple Sholom, 300 East Putnam avenue, 869.7191
www.scarsdalenet.com/hadassah/chapters.html

Interfaith Council of Southwestern Connecticut

(formerly the Council of Churches and Synagogues)
1 Canterbury Green, Stamford, 348.2800
www.InterFaithCouncil.org

UJA Federation of Greenwich

1 Holly Hill Lane, 622.1434
Pamela Ehrenkranz, Executive Director
www.UJAFedGreenwich.org

Young Life of Greenwich

(nondenominational Christian organization for teenagers)
340.2123
www.greenwich.younglife.org

TIP: BEACH SERVICES

www.fccog.org
The First Congregational Church in Greenwich conducts Sunday services on the beach at Tod's Point during the summer months at 8:00 am. Visitors are welcome. A beach pass is not required for these services. The Saturday Greenwich Time lists all of the religious services in the area.

** Stars indicate the ones we like the best in a category. This does not mean that you shouldn't go to the others. If we don't like a restaurant we don't include it.*

American
Winfield's at the Hyatt*

American, Casual
Augie's
Beach House
Beehive
Brew House *
Buffalo Wings
Cafeteria at
   Greenwich Hospital
Chocopologie *
Cobble Stone
Dressing Room
Favorite Place*
Gates
Garden Café at
Greenwich Hospital
Ginger Man
Horseneck Tavern
I-HOP
Jordan's Hilltop
Landmark Diner *
Long Ridge Tavern
MacDuffs *
MacKenzie's Grill *
Putnam Restaurant
Q *
Rotisserie
Skylight Café
Smokey Joe's *
Sundown Saloon
Thataway Café
Upper Crust Bagel Co.
Waterfront Grill

American, New
American Bounty
  (Culinary Institute) **
Blue Hill at Stone
Barns **
Gaia
Match *
Mirage Café *
Rebecca's **
River Cat Grill
Saavy *
Xaviar's **

Asian
(Indian, Chinese & Japanese are listed separately)
Asiana Café *
Penang Grill
Plateau
Tengda Asian Bistro

Asian Fusion
Baang *
Ching's Table
Nuage **
Wasabi Chi *
Wild Ginger *

Bakeries
(Bakeries are listed under Food)

Catering
(Caterers are listed under Entertaining)

Chinese
Hunan Café *
Hunan Gourmet
Oriental Gourmet *
Panda Pavilion 3

Coffee and Tea Shops
Arcadia Coffee Co. *
Dunkin' Donuts
(The) Drawing Room *
Starbucks
T Party Antiques and
Tea Room *
Waterfront Roasters
  Café

Delicatessens / Take-Out
(Bakeries listed separately under Food)
Alpen Pantry
Arcuri's
Aux Délices *
Balducci's
Chicken Joe's
Garden Caterers
Garelick and Herbs
Paesano's Deli
Plum Pure Foods *
Upper Crust Bagel Co.
Villarina's
Whole Foods

by cuisine

** Our favorite in category*

Fast Food
Bruckner's *
Cosi
Beyond Bread
Boston Market *
Katzenberg Express
Jimmy's Grill
Kneaded Bread
McDonald's
Panera *
Rodney's Roadhouse
Rotisserie
SoNo Baking Company & Café
Subway Sandwich
Taco Bell
Top Dog *
Wendy's

Diners
City Limits *
Glory Days
Landmark Diner *

French
Aux Délices *
Bistro Bonne Nuit *
(Le) Château
Chez Jean-Pierre
(La) Crémaillère *
Escoffiêr at the
  Culinary Institute **
(Le) Figaro
Jean-Louis **
L'Escalê *
Meli-Melo *
(La) Panetière **
Thomas Henkelmann **
Versailles *

German
Brew House *

Ice Cream
Baskin Robbins
Capriccio
Carvel
Cold Stone Creamery *
Darlene's *
Gofer Ice Cream
Häagen-Dazs
Longford's *
Meli-Melo *

Indian
Bengal Tiger *
Chola
Dakshin *
Tandoori
Thali **
Utsav

Inns Worth a Trip
(see Hotels & Inns for Description)
Bee and Thistle Inn
Copper Beach
Mayflower

Italian
(Pizza restaurants are listed separately)
Albas
Applausi Osteria *
Bella Nonna
Caterina de' Medici
at the Culinary
  Institute **
Cava Wine Bar and
Restaurant
Centro *
Frank's
Frankie & Louie's
Giorgio's
Hostaria Mazzei
Mediteraneo *
Pasquale
Pasta Nostra **
Pasta Vera *
Pellicci's
Per Voi
Pierangelo **
Piero's
Polpo **
Pomodoro
Quatro Pazzi
Quatro Regali *
Solaia *
Terra
That Little Italian
Restaurant
Valbella**
Vuli

by cuisine

** Our favorite in category*

Japanese
Abis *
Edo
Kazu
Kira Sushi *
KU
Ramen Stand
Tingda

Latin American
Brasitas *
Habana
Pantanal
Sonora *

Mexican
Fonda La Paloma
Olé Mole *

Pizza
Arcuri's
Bella Nonna
Match
Mediterraneo *
Pizza Express *
Pizza Factory
Pizza Glenville *
Pizza Hut
Pizza Post
Planet Pizza

Pubs
Brewhouse *
Ginger Man
Mac Duffs *
MacKenzie's Grill Room *

Seafood
Crabshell
Ebb Tide
Elm Street Oyster * *
F.I.S.H. *
Mediterraneo
Ocean 211 **
Pacifico *
Paradise Bar & Grill
Rowayton Seafood *
SoNo Seaport Seafood
Splash *
Streets of London

Southwestern
Boxcar Cantina *
Q *
Smokey Joe's Bar-B-Q *
Sundown Saloon
Telluride *

Spanish
Barcelona *
Meigas **

Steak
Abis *
Edo
Morton's of Chicago *
Pantanal
Q *
Porterhouse
Smokey Joe's Bar-B-Q *

Swiss
Melting Pot
Roger Sherman Inn *

Thai
Kit's Thai Kitchen *
Little Thai Kitchen *

Vegetarian
Bruckner's
Chola
Greenwich Healthmart

Afternoon Tea
T Party Antiques and
Tea Room
The Drawing Room

Best in Greenwich
Jean-Louis
Nuage
Polpo
Rebecca's
Thomas Henkelmann
Valbella

Breakfast
Aux Délices
City Limits Diner
Glory Days
I-HOP
L'Escale
Landmark Diner
Versailles

Brunch on Sunday
Abis (buffet)
Doral Arrowwood
 Atrium (buffet)
Fjord Sunday Brunch
Cruise
Hunan Café (Dim
 Sum) *
L'Escale (buffet)
Roger Sherman Inn
Silvermine Tavern
(buffet)
Splash (buffet)
Versailles
Winfield's at the
 Hyatt (buffet) *

Dinner, Less Expensive
*(Fast Food and Pizza
restaurants are listed
separately)*
Asiana Café
Augie's
Bella Nonna
Brew House
Cafeteria at
 Greenwich Hospital
Centro
Cobble Stone
Ebb Tide
Favorite Place
Frank's
Frankie & Louie's
Garden Café at
 Greenwich Hospital
Gates
Glory Days
Horseneck Tavern
Hunan Café
I-HOP
Kit's Thai Kitchen
Landmark Diner
MacDuffs Public
House
MacKenzie's Grill
Meli-Melo
Olé Mole
Oriental Gourmet
Panda Pavilion
Pellicci's
Penang
Pomodoro
Putnam Restaurant
Q

Smokey Joe's Bar-B-Q
SoNo Seaport Seafood
Streets of London
Sundown Saloon

Dinner, Late Night
Barcelona
Beach House
City Limits
Cobble Stone
Crabshell
Glory Days
McDonald's
Mirage Café
Planet Pizza
Smokey Joe's Bar-B-Q
Sundown Saloon
Taco Bell
Tengda Asian Bistro
Thataway Café
Wendy's

Family Restaurants
(Fast Food and Pizza restaurants are listed separately)
Abis
Beach House
Bella Nonna
Boxcar Cantina
Centro
Chocopologie
City Limits
Cobble Stone
Ebb Tide Seafood
Edo
Favorite Place *
Frank's
Frankie & Louie's
Gates
Glory Days
Hostaria Mazzei
Hunan Gourmet
I-HOP
Jordan's Hilltop
Landmark Diner
Long Ridge Tavern
Melting Pot
Oriental Gourmet
Panda Pavilion 3
Paradise Bar & Grill
Pasquale
Pellicci's
Pomodoro
Putnam Restaurant
Q
Quattro Regali
Rotisserie
Rowayton Seafood
Silvermine Tavern
Skylight Cafe
Smokey Joe's Bar-B-Q
SoNo Seaport Seafood
Streets of London
Sundown Saloon
That Little Italian Restaurant
Thataway Café
Upper Crust Bagel Company

Hot Spots
Baang
Barcelona
Beach House
Crabshell
L'Escalle
Gingerman
MacDuffs
MacKenzie's Grill
Sundown Saloon
Splash

Lunch, For Ladies Who...
Jean-Louis
L'Escale
Figaro
Gaia
Mediterraneo
Rebecca's
T Party Antiques and Tea Room
Terra
The Drawing Room
Thomas Hinkelmann
Versailles
Wild Ginger
Winfield's at the Hyatt

Lunch, Late
Asiana
Augie's
Aux Délices Café
Beach House
City Limits
Cobble Stone
Elm Street Oyster
Horseneck Tavern
Hunan Gourmet
Hunan Café
I-Hop
Landmark Diner
MacKenzie's Grill
Meli-Melo
Panda Pavillion 3
Panera
Pasta Vera
Penang
Polpo
Versailles

Romantic
(Le) Château
(La) Crémaillère
Jean-Louis
L'Escale
(La) Panetière
Polpo
Roger Sherman Inn
Thomas Henkelman
Valbella
Xavier's

Armonk, NY
Beehive

Banksville, NY
(La) Crémaillère

Byram
Garden Caterers
Little Thai Kitchen
That Little Italian
Restaurant

Cos Cob
Arcuri's
Augie's
Bella Nonna
Chicken Joe's
Drawing Room
Dunkin' Donuts
Favorite Place
Fjord Sunday Brunch
Fonda La Paloma
Gofer's Ice Cream
KU
Landmark Diner
Nuage
Pizza Post
Plum Pure Foods
Ramen Stand
Top Dog
Villarina's

Darien
Melting Pot
T Party Antiques and
Tea Room

Glenville
Centro Ristorante
Pizza, Glenville
Pizza Hut
Rebecca's
Rodney's Roadhouse
Wild Ginger

Greenwich (Central)
Abis
Asiana Café
Aux Délices
Barcelona
Boxcar Cantina
Bruckner's
Cafeteria at Green-
wich Hospital
Chola
Cold Stone Creamery
Cosi
Dunkin' Donuts
Elm Street Oyster
House
Figaro
Gaia
Garden Café at
Greenwich Hospital
Garelick & Herbs
Ginger Man
Glory Days
Gofer Ice Cream
Häagen-Dazs
Horseneck Tavern
Hunan Gourmet

Jean-Louis
Jimmy's Grill
Katzenberg's Express
Kira Sushi
L'Escale
MacDuffs Public House
McDonald's
Mediterraneo
Meli-Melo
Paesano's Deli
Panda Pavilion 3
Pasta Vera
Penang Grill
Pierangelo
Pizza Express
Pizza Factory
Planet Pizza
Polpo
Rotisserie
Putnam Restaurant
Skylight Café
Solaia
Starbucks
Subway Sandwich
Sundown Saloon
Tengda Asian Bistro
Terra
Thataway Café
Thomas Henkelmann
Versailles
Wendy's
Whole Foods

Hyde Park, NY
Culinary Institute,
  American Bounty
  Caterina de'
    Medici
  Escoffier

New Canaan, CT
Bistro Bonne Nuit
Cava
Ching's Table
Gates
Roger Sherman Inn
Savvy
Thali

Norwalk, CT
Barcelona
Brewhouse
Chocopologie
Habana
Kazu
Match
Meigas
Pasta Nostra
Porter House
Quattro Pazzi
Silvermine Tavern
SoNo Baking Company & Cafe
SoNo Seaport Seafood
Streets of London
Wasabi Chi

Old Greenwich
Alpen Pantry
Applausi Osteria
Arcadia Coffee Co
Arcuris
Beach House Café
Beyond Bread
Boston Market
Garden Caterers
Hunan Café
MacKenzie's Grill
Oriental Gourmet
Upper Crust Bagel Co
Winfields at the Hyatt

Piermont, NY
Xaviar's

Port Chester, NY
Albas
Buffalo Wild Wings
Carvel
Ebb Tide
Edo
F.I.S.H
Frank's
Frankie & Louie's
Garden Caterers
Giorgio's
Hostaria Mazzei
Kneaded Bread
Mirage Café
Pacifico
Panera
Pantanal
Pasquale
Piero's
Q
Sonora
Tandoori
Waterfront Grill
Waterfront Roasters
Café

Purchase, NY
Cobble Stone
Jordan's Hilltop

RESTAURANTS

Riverside
Aux Délices
Baang
Balducci's
McDonald's
Pomodoro
Valbella

Rowayton, CT
River Cat Grill
Rowayton Seafood

Rye, NY
Longford's Ice Cream
(La) Panetiere

Rye Brook, NY
Doral Arrowwood
Atrium

South Salem, NY
Le Châeau

Stamford, CT
Brasitas
Capriccio
Chez Jean Pierre
City Limits
Crab Shell
Dakshin
I-Hop
Kit's Thai Kitchen
Long Ridge Tavern
Morton's of Chicago
Ocean 211
Olé Mole
Paradise Bar & Grill
Pellicci's
Plateau
Quattro Regali
Smokey Joe's Bar-B-Q
Telluride
Utsav
Vuli

Tarrytown, NY
Blue Hill at Stone
Barns

White Plains, NY
Bengal Tiger

Westport, CT
Dressing Room
Splash

TIP: CHOWDER COOKOFF

Want to find the best bowl of New England clam chowder? Every year, in early June, chefs in Norwalk, CT compete in the annual "Splash! Clam Chowder Cook-Off." Check their website www.norwalk.ws/splashfestival/chowder1.htm for the annual winner and their recipe. Better yet, for a $5 donation you can attend the festival, taste the soups and place a vote for the best. Call 203.838.9444 for details.

Abis (Japanese) *

381 Greenwich Avenue, 862.9100

www.abis4u.com

A restaurant with two personalities—one side traditional Japanese cuisine, the other an Hibachi steakhouse. In the steakhouse, youngsters have a wonderful time watching their hibachi meals being prepared. The other side offers more relaxed dining with a menu full of familiar choices, including a sushi bar, with a large selection. We are fans of their Japanese noodle dishes such as udon or soba. For lunch be sure to try their box lunch. If you like to indulge yourself with sushi and other Japanese delicacies you will love their, all-you-can-eat, Sunday Brunch buffet.

Hours: Lunch, weekdays, 11:30 am - 2:30 pm, Saturday, noon - 2:30 pm; Sunday, 11:30 am - 2:30 pm; Dinner, weekdays, 5:30 pm - 9:30 pm (Friday until 10:30 pm); Saturday, 5 pm - 10:30 pm; Sunday, Brunch 11:30 am - 2:30 pm, Dinner 5 pm - 9:30 pm. Open most holidays, including Christmas and New Year's for dinner.

Prices: Traditional Japanese: Lunch entrees, $10 - $25; Dinner entrees, $20 $33; Hibachi: Lunch entrees, $11 - $32; Dinner entrees, $13 - $38. They have an hibachi children's menu. Sunday Brunch, $20 per adult and $10 for children under 11.

Albas (Italian)

400 North Main Street

Port Chester, NY 914.937.2236

www.albasrestaurant.com

Our best experience here was at a wine-tasting dinner party. Our visits as regular diners left us less impressed. The decor, intended to resemble a New England Inn, seems dark and drab. Of all the dishes we tried, our favorite was the Ceasar salad for two, prepared at our table.

Hours: Lunch, weekdays, noon - 2 pm; Dinner, Monday - Thursday, 5:30 - 10 pm, Friday and Saturday to 11 pm.

Prices: Dinner entrees, $18 - $31

Alpen Pantry (Delicatessen)

23 Arcadia Road, Old Greenwich, 637.3818

Nice take-out sandwich selection.

Hours: Monday - Saturday, 9 am - 5 pm.

Arcadia Coffee Company (Coffee) *
20 Arcadia Road, Old Greenwich, 637.8766
www.arcadiacoffee.com
"Let's meet at Arcadia." This is the local friendly coffee house where you can take your newspaper and relax with a good cup of coffee and a sandwich. The walls are decorated with works for sale by local artists. Arcadia is a venue for many author book discussions. Teenagers enjoy meeting here to listen to music performed by young-adult bands. Check the website for upcoming events.
Hours: Monday, 6:30 am - 5 pm; Tuesday - Friday, 6:30 am -9 pm; Saturday & Sunday, 7 am - 5 pm.
Note: During the summer these hours may vary.

Applausi Osteria (Italian) *
199 Sound Beach Avenue, Old Greenwich, 637.4447
www.OsteriaApplausi.com
One of the three successful Marchetti-Tarantino family restaurants is located right in the heart of Old Greenwich. Perfect for diners wishing to have a leisurely conversation and very good meal in a refined atmosphere. You will find lots of interesting choices, but with Maria still making most of the pastas, be sure to order a pasta like the Fettuccine with artichokes and truffles.
Hours: Lunch, weekdays, noon - 2:30 pm;
Dinner, Monday-Saturday, 5:30 pm - 10 pm;
(Friday & Saturday until 10:30 pm).
Prices: Lunch entrees, $8 - $17; Dinner entrees, $18- $33.

Arcuri's (Pizza)
• 178 Sound Beach Avenue, Old Greenwich, 637.1085
• 226 East Putnam Avenue, Cos Cob, 869.6999
Extensive selection of specialty pizzas. They are well-known for their good salads.
Hours: Open every day from 11 am - 9:30 pm;
Friday and Saturday until 10 pm.

Asiana Cafe (Asian) *

130 East Putnam Avenue, 622.6833

Ready for a savory twist on PanAsian food? Don't expect their dishes (Vietnamese, Chinese, Thai and Japanese) to be like you have had in other restaurants. My Szechuan spicy beef was oh-so-good. They also make great satay, tempura shrimp and papaya salad. The helpings are generous and the service attentive. The atmosphere is minimalist modern. In the summer you can dine outside.

Hours: MondayThursday, 11 am - 10 pm;

Friday & Saturday, 11 am - 11 pm; Sunday, noon 10 pm.

Closed Thanksgiving and Christmas (maybe).

Prices: Lunch entrees, $7 to $8; Dinner entrees, $11 - $21.

Augie's (American, Casual)

136 River Road Extension, Cos Cob, 862.0640

In a hidden-away location, just off the Post Road, Augie's (formerly Mianus River Tavern) is a fun place to go when you are in the mood for a casual evening out. Although there are a number of entrees, the tavern fare portion is the most popular. Enjoy a hamburger or a yummy steak sandwich.

Hours: Sunday Thursday, 11:30 am - 10 pm;

Friday and Saturday, 11:30 am - 11 pm.

The bar is open until 1am during the week and until 2 am on weekends.

Prices: Dinner, entrees, $8 - $24; Tavern fare, $8 - $10.

Aux Délices (Delicatessen, Eat In, French-American) *

- 1075 East Putnam Avenue, Riverside, 698.1066
- 3 West Elm, Greenwich, 622.6644

For delivery orders call 326.4540 x 115 or 101

www.auxdelicesFoods.com

Provencal-style food with an American twist prepared under the direction of talented Chef Debra Ponzek. Delicious gourmet take-away food. Both locations have a few tables- grab one for a quick breakfast or late lunch. They also have excellent hors d'oeuvres. In our 2005 Hors D'Oeuvres Tasting Contest they received top scores. They have a weekday home delivery service and will deliver your order even when you are not home, packaged to keep the food at the proper temperature.

Greenwich Hours: weekdays, 7 am - 6:30 pm:

Saturday, 8 am - 6:30 pm; Sunday, 9 am - 4 pm.

Riverside Hours: Monday - Saturday, 7:30 am - 6:30 pm; Sunday, 7:30 am - 5 pm.

Prices: Lunch entrees, $5.95 - $12; Dinner entrees, $9.50 - $30.

Baang Café (Asian Fusion, AsianFrench) *
1191 East Putnam Avenue, Riverside, 637.2114
www.DecaroRestaurantGroup.com
Just because they can't hear you when you call in for a reservation and the wait staff has learned to lip read, doesn't keep this noisy, lively, starkly modern restaurant from continuing to be highly popular. It is less noisy around 6:30 but the volume turns up steadily through the evening as the younger crowd arrives. The rare tuna, crispy spinach and grilled Shang-hai beef are all very good and beautifully presented. Outdoor dining in the summer.
Hours: Lunch, weekdays, noon 2:30 pm;
Dinner, Monday - Thursday, 6 pm - 10 pm
Friday & Saturday, 6 pm - 11 pm.
Reservations are only accepted for parties of six or more, so arrive early, especially on Friday and Saturday nights.
Prices: Lunch entrees, $20 - $25; Dinner entrees, $40 - $45.

Balducci's (Delicatessen, Grocery)
1050 East Putnam Avenue, Riverside, 637.7600
www.Balduccis.com
One of a large chain of sophisticated gourmet delis and country shops for fruits, vegetables and unique foods. Balducci's carries hundreds of imported and American cheeses. Don't go in hungry.
Hours: every day, 8 am - 8 pm, Sunday to 7 pm.

Barcelona (Spanish) *
• 63 North Main Street, South Norwalk, CT, 203.899.0088
• 18 West Putnam Avenue, Greenwich, 983.6400
www.barcelonawinebar.com
We first enjoyed this authentic tapas restaurant near the SoNo theaters in Norwalk. It's still there, so have fun in Norwalk or in Greenwich. The Greenwich bar is lively. There is an excellent wine list, with over 30 wines by the glass. We love most of the tapas. Try the mouth-watering gambas, the empanadas, scallops, asparagus, goat cheese, potato tortilla and the Argentine grill. For dessert, try the chocolate indulgence.
Greenwich Hours: Lunch, weekdays, noon -3 pm;
Dinner, Sunday -Thursday, 5 pm -10 pm, Friday & Saturday, to 11 pm. (Bar is open Friday & Saturday until 2 am). Closed on major holidays.
Norwalk: No lunch, hours are usually the same for dinner
Prices: Lunch entrees, $8 - $15; Dinner entrees, $20 - $30; tapas $4 - $14.
Directions to SoNo location: I-95 North, Exit 14, R at stop sign, L at 2nd traffic light into SoNo Plaza.

Baskin-Robbins (Ice Cream)

www.BaskinRobbins.com
- 146 Sound Beach Avenue, Old Greenwich, 637.0480
  Hours: every day, 11 am-10 pm
- Dunkin' Donuts, 375 Putnam Avenue, Cos Cob, 869.7454
  Hours: every day, 5 am - 11 pm

Beach House Café (American, Casual)

220 Sound Beach Avenue, Old Greenwich, 637.0367
www.beachhousecafe.com
The decor is light, bright, cheerful and comfortable. A large portion of the restaurant is devoted to a bar populated by a sophisticated, youthful crowd. Food is served continuously from noon on, making it a good choice for a late lunch or early dinner. The service is friendly. Live music on Thursday, Friday and Saturday evenings after 10pm.
Hours: Sunday - Thursday, 11:30 am - 11 pm (bar open till 12:30 am);
Friday & Saturday, 11:30 am - 12 am (bar open till 1:30 am);
Sunday brunch starts at 11 am.
Prices: Lunch entrees $9 - $15; Dinner entrees $19 - $25.

Beehive (American, Casual)

30 Old Route 22, Armonk, 914.765.0688
For those in northwest Greenwich, Armonk is only about 10 to 15 minutes away. A large menu with large servings of a number of American, Italian & Continental dishes. We liked the tuna and moussaka. Our friends (who go there often) order the veal meatloaf when it is on the menu.
Hours: Open every day, Monday - Thursday, 11 am - 9 pm,
Friday and Saturday, to 10 pm; Sunday 9 am to 9 pm.
Prices: Lunch entrees, $8 - $12; Dinner entrees, $16 - $30.

Bella Nonna (Italian)

371 East Putnam Avenue, Cos Cob, 869.4445
Casual dining in a friendly, family-oriented restaurant, serving thin crust pizzas and traditional Italian cuisine. They have a children's menu. While children may be chowing down on pizza, we relish their specials.
Hours: Open every day. Lunch, 11:30 am - 3 pm;
Dinner, 3 pm - 11 pm. Make reservations for 4 or more.
Prices: Lunch entrees, $6 - $12; Dinner entrees, $12 - $20,
Pizzas start at $8.

Bengal Tiger (Indian) *
144 East Post Road, White Plains, NY, 914.948.5191
www.bengalTiger1.com
The formally dressed waiters and colorful fabric decorations make this the prettiest Indian dining in the area. The food has been getting rave reviews since 1975. We agree the food is very, very good. Is it excellent? We are not so sure. But we love eating here and it is a great place to introduce a guest to Indian cuisine.
Hours: Open every day: Lunch 11:30 am - 2:30 pm;
Dinner, Sunday - Thursday, 5 pm - 10:30 pm,
Friday & Saturday, until 11 pm.
Prices: Lunch buffet, weekdays, $13, weekends, $15 - $18; Dinner entrees,$14 - $28.

Beyond Bread (Fast Food, Bakery)
214 Sound Beach Avenue, Old Greenwich, 637.2543
Who would ever dream that croissants as divine as the ones in Paris are being made on Sound Beach Avenue? Harvey, the baker, often begins his day at midnight so you can have fresh croissants, pain au chocolate, Danish pastries and many other breads right out of the oven by 6 am. Insiders also know that this tiny shop, with its few tables, is a good place for soup and sandwich at lunch. Be sure to order ahead for their quiche and pie.
Hours: Closed Mondays; Tuesday-Saturday, 6 am - 4 pm;
Sunday, 6 am - 1 pm.

Bernard's (French) **
20 West Lane, Ridgefield, CT, 203.438.8282
www.BernardsRidgefield.com
We wish it were closer. While Chef/Owner Bernard Bouissou works his magic culinary skills, his wife, Sarah, greets and charms their guests. The menu varies with the season. On one occasion there was a large selection of truffle dishes and game meats - elk, buffalo, antelope. It is certainly worth a trip for special occasions or a romantic dinner. Piano music, fresh flowers, and the attractive inn-style dining room set the mood. The service is sweet, but not as polished as one would expect.
Hours: Lunch, Tuesday - Saturday, noon - 2:30;
Sunday Brunch, noon - 2:30 pm;
Dinner, Tuesday - Saturday, 6 pm - 9 pm (Friday & Saturday to 10 pm)
Sunday, 5 pm - 8:30 pm.
Prices: Dinner entrees, $26 - $36.

Bistro Bonne Nuit (French) *
12 Forest Street, New Canaan, 203.966.5303
http://www.culinarymenus.com/bistrobonnenuit.htm
White tablecloths and fresh flowers give a dressy flair to this intimate, bistro. Julia Child would have loved their cassoulet, as well as many of their typical French dishes.
Hours: Monday- Thursday, 5 pm - 9:30 pm;
Friday & Saturday, 5:30 - 10 pm; Sunday, 5 pm - 8 pm.
Prices: Dinner entrees, $25 - $38.

Blue Hill at Stone Barns (American, New) **
630 Bedford Road, Pocantico Hills (Tarrytown), 914.366.9600
www.BlueHillStoneBarns.com; www.BlueHillFarm.com
By all means worth the trip. This unique restaurant was converted from a stone barn once owned by the Rockefellers. It is surrounded by a working farm which provides many of the ingredients, which are picked fresh each day. Top chefs are in the kitchen creating innovative, fantastic cuisine. You need to make a reservation well in advance. Arrive early so you can take a walk around the pretty grounds. Dress code: business casual.
Hours: Closed Monday & Tuesday. Lunch, Sunday 11:30 am - 2 pm;
Dinner Sunday, Wednesday & Thursday, 5 pm to 10 pm,
Friday & Saturday until 11 pm.
Prices: Dinner, three course $65; four course $75.

Boston Market (FastFood)
1345 East Putnam Avenue, Old Greenwich, 637.4088
www.BostonMarket.com
Homestyle cooking in a fast-food setting.
Hours: every day 11 am - 10 pm.

TIP: CONNECTICUT IS A WINE-DOGGY-BAG-STATE

Public Act No. 03-228 and 04-33 (call for copy) allows a restaurant, cafe or hotel dining room patron to remove one unsealed bottle of wine for off-premises consumption provided the patron has purchased a full course meal and consumed a portion of the wine with such meal. The bottle that is removed must be securely sealed and placed in a bag by restaurant personnel. New York is also a Wine-Doggy-Bag State.

Boxcar Cantina (Southwestern)

44 Old Field Point Road, 661.4774

http://www.boxcarcantina.com/

Popular, informal, and childfriendly, this restaurant is an incredible hit in town. It was conceived as an homage to all of the Route 66 Cantinas of the Southwest, serving a mix of high quality, ultra-fresh Mexican and Southwestern food. We are hooked on their posole soup, Mexican pizza and salmon burritos. Choose from an original menu of homemade margaritas.

Hours: Lunch, weekdays, 11:30 am - 3 pm; Dinner, Monday Thursday, 5:30 pm - 9:30 pm; Friday & Saturday, 5:30 pm - 10:30 pm; Sunday, 4:30 pm - 9 pm. Reservations are accepted only for large parties. On Friday and Saturday nights, be sure to arrive early.

Prices: Lunch entrees, $11 - $16; Dinner entrees, $12- $22.

Bruckner's (Fast-Food, vegetarian) *

1 Grigg Street, 422.6300

www.bruckners.com

Just off the Avenue, this friendly, small restaurant has quick service and tasty, healthy wraps and soups. It is the "in" place for a good takeout lunch. They will even deliver your breakfast. A few tables are also available. The owner/chef Richard Fertig has an impressive ability to spice his food just right. They have excellent vegetarian/vegan food as well as smoothie power drinks.

Delivers breakfast weekdays, 8 am - 10 am.

Hours: weekdays, 7 am - 4:30 pm; Saturday, 8 am - 4 pm.

Prices: Entrees, $6 - $8.

Brasitas (Latin-American) *

954 East Main Street, Stamford, CT, 323.3176

www.Brasitas.com

Without Linda and Don saying we must meet under the plastic palms, we would never have discovered this funky, fun, thriving restaurant. It is the kind of place you would pass if you didn't know. We are not the first to discover it. Their valet parking lot is full of sports cars. You must make a reservation. Whether you order the Coconut Shrimp or salmon, you are sure to be delighted. As you sip your Mojitos and Margaritas you will forget you are on the Post Road.

Prices: Lunch entrees, $8 - $14; Dinner entrees, $15 - $25.

Hours: weekdays, 11 am - 10pm; Saturday, 11 am - 11pm; Sunday, 12:30 pm - 10 pm.

Brewhouse (American, Casual) *

13 Marshall Street, South Norwalk, CT, 203.853.9110

www.SonoBrewHouse.com

When you feel like a casual evening in a friendly, informal restaurant, this is the place. In some ways reminiscent of an upscale German beer hall, this large, comfortable restaurant attracts the young at heart. There is a nice selection of casual foods on the menu, and of course, a large selection of beers. Try the beer burger or wiener schnitzel. The seafood chowder is a winner as is the apple strudel. Be sure to order the strudel in advance as it takes 20 minutes to prepare.

Hours: Lunch, Monday Sunday, 11:30 am - 5 pm;

Dinner, Monday - Thursday, 5 pm - 10 pm;

Friday & Saturday, 5 pm - 11 pm; Sunday, 4 pm - 9 pm.

Prices: Lunch entrees, $8 - $13; Dinner entrees, $9 - $24.

Directions: I-95 N to exit 14, go straight to light; R on West, L on North Main, L on Marshall.

(La) Bretagne (French)

2010 West Main Street(US-1 just across the Greenwich border), Stamford, CT, 324.9539

For a restaurant to stay in business for more than 30 years, they have to offer consistently good food and pleasant hospitality. The interior is dimly lit and eating here is like taking a step back in time. The dishes are traditional French. The staff is attentive and formally attired. This may be a good choice for entertaining aunts, uncles and parents.

Hours: Lunch, Monday - Saturday, noon - 2:30 pm;

Dinner, Monday - Saturday, 6 pm - 9:30 pm.

Prices: Lunch entrees, $16 - $21;Dinner entrees, $21 - $45.

Buffalo Wild Wings (American Casual)

44 Westchester Avenue, Port Chester, NY, 914.690.9453

www.BuffaloWildWings.com

A sports bar chain located at the movie theater complex, where beer is more important than the food.

Hours: Monday-Thursday, 11 am - 1 am;

Friday & Saturday to 2 am; Sunday to midnight.

Prices: Entrees, $4 - $13.

Cafeteria at Greenwich Hospital (American, Casual)
5 Perryridge Rd, 863.3000
Located on the ground floor of the Helmsley Pavillion.
The food is simple, freshly-prepared and satisfying. The portions are generous and well-priced. It is a real find for someone on a limited budget.
Hours: Everyday, Breakfast, 6:30am - 10.45am;
Lunch, 11:30am - 2:30pm; Dinner, 3:30 pm - 7 pm.
Prices: Entree with two vegetables, $6; 30% off for seniors.

Capriccio (Ice Cream)
189 Bedford Street, Stamford, 356.9819
Gelato to die for, tucked inside a small pizza café. Our favorite is the hazelnut.
Hours: every day, 11 am - 10:30 pm, (Friday & Saturday until midnight).
Directions: I-95 N to exit 8, L on Atlantic, continue on Atlantic which becomes Bedford as it crosses Main.

Carvel (Ice Cream)
604 North Main Street, Port Chester, NY, 914.939.1487
www.Carvel.com
Located just on the border of Greenwich and Port Chester on US-1, this standby is open seven days a week. If you like hot fudge sundaes the way we do, Wednesday is your day. You can get two for the price of one.
Hours: Sunday - Thursday, 10 am - 10 pm;
Friday & Saturday, 10 am - 11 pm.
Prices: Medium Hot Fudge Sundae, $4

Cava (Italian, Wine Bar)
2 Forest Street, New Canaan, CT 203.966.6946
www.CavaWineBar.com
Entering this just-below street level, brick-faced space you have the feeling of dining in a private wine cellar (albeit a large one that seats 60). A good place to go when you want to relax, unwind, have a good glass of wine and a pleasant meal.
Hours: Lunch, Tuesday - Friday, noon to 3 pm;
Dinner, everyday, 5 pm - 10pm, Friday and Saturday to 11pm.
Prices: Pizza, $11 - $13; entrees, $17 - $31;
wine by the glass, $7.50 - $15.

Centro Ristorante (Italian) *

323 Pemberwick Road (at The Mill), Glenville, 531.5514
www.centroRistorante.com
Bright, cheery, and popular with an unpretentious atmosphere . Just right
when you hunger for homemade pastas and a good glass of wine from
their extensive list. Request the outdoor patio overlooking the waterfall
and order one of their raviolis. Some of our friends go just for the des-
serts. Child-friendly with crayons.
Hours: Lunch, Monday - Saturday, 11:30 am - 3 pm,; pizzas & light fare,
Monday - Saturday, 3 pm - 5:30 pm;
Dinner, Monday - Thursday, 5:30 pm - 10 pm,
Friday & Saturday, 5:30 pm - 11 pm, Sunday 5 pm - 9:30 pm.
Prices: Lunch entrees, $8 - $14; Dinner entrees, $8 - $17.

(Le) Château (French)

Junction of Routes 35 and 123, South Salem, NY, 914.533.6631
www.lechateauny.com
A spacious, elaborate restaurant about thirty minutes from Greenwich,
on the grounds of the 32-acre, 1907 J.P. Morgan estate. It is perfect if you
are wishing for a romantic setting for a large party or just a night out
with a close friend. The food is classic French. The rack of lamb is a good
choice as is the chocolate souffle (order the souffle early).
Hours: Sunday brunch (usually January - April), 11:30 - 3 pm;
Dinner, Tuesday - Friday, 5:30 pm - 9 pm, Saturday seatings at 6 and 9,
Sunday, 2 pm - 9 pm. Reservations in advance are a must, as is a jacket
and tie. Closed Mondays and New Year's Day.
Prices: Sunday Brunch, $35 ; Dinner entrees, $29 - $35.
Directions: Merritt Parkway N to exit 38, 123 N, R on Rte 35.

TIP: THE BEST CHOCOLATE TRUFFLES AND VANILLA ICE CREAM IN GREENWICH

We held a Tasting Contest to choose the best chocolate truffles and
vanilla ice cream. Over a hundred people participated. The winner
of the chocolate category was: Bridgewater Chocolate, Brookfield,
CT, 203.775.2286, Cold Stone Creamery, 79 East Putnam Avenue,
302.3300, came in first for their ice cream. For all the ratings of the
truffles and ice cream go to www.greenwichguide.com.

RESTAURANTS

Chez Jean-Pierre (French)
188 Bedford Street, Stamford, 357.9526
www.chezjeanpierre.com
A charming restaurant serving traditional French dishes. During warm weather you can sit on the sidewalk and watch the people go by. Inside the original, crowded dining room, you would think you were in a Paris bistro. The new addition lacks ambiance. The service is friendly. Unfortunately, the food is inconsistent. The escargots are an excellent choice for appetizer. Choose the tenderloin, cassoulet, duck á l'orange or tuna and you will leave with a smile on your face. The desserts should be skipped. A wide selection of wines by the glass. The menu changes five or six times a year.
Hours: Lunch, Monday - Saturday, noon - 3pm;
Dinner, Monday - Thursday, 6 pm 10 pm
(Friday, Saturday to 10:30 pm, Sunday to 9:30 pm);
Closed Memorial Day, Christmas & NewYear's & Labor Day.
Prices: Lunch entrees, $9 - $24; Dinner entrees, $25 - $30.
Directions: Directions: I-95 N to exit 8, L on Atlantic, continue on Atlantic which becomes Bedford as it crosses Main.

Chicken Joe's (TakeOut)
235 East Putnam Avenue, Cos Cob, 861.0075
Great fried chicken, chicken bits, french fries, potato cones and onion rings. Strictly takeout. A teenage favorite.
Hours: Weekdays 6 am - 6:30 pm; Saturday 6 am - 4:30 pm; Sunday 8 am - 3 pm.

Ching's Table (Asian)
64 Main Street, New Canaan, CT 203.972.2830
www.ChingsRestaurant.com
This is a popular New Canaan restaurant with entrees similar to those at Penang Grill which has the same ownership. We found the service very attentive and the food equally good. We like the Satay chicken, Vietnamese salad, the Pad Thai with shrimp, lemon grass chicken and wok beef tenderloin. Reservations accepted for parties of four or more. On busy nights, consider takeouts as the wait can be long.
Hours: Open every day for lunch and dinner.
Monday - Thursday, 11 am - 10 pm; Friday & Saturday, 11 am - -11 pm; Sunday, noon to 10 pm. Closed Thanksgiving.
Prices: Lunch entrees, $10 - $15; Dinner entrees, $12 - $21.
Directions: Exit 13 L at the light R onto West Norwalk Rd. Straight 4 miles. Enter New Canaan. Ching's on R side across from Town Hall.

Chocopologie (American, Casual) *

12 South Main Street, South Norwalk, 203.838.3131
www.chocopologie.com
If chocolate is your passion, as it is ours, this small restaurant in the front of a Knipschildt's chocolate factory is a must. When our tasting experts, Matthew and Cameron, gave it thumbs up, we knew this restaurant was destined for success. The menu includes soups, salads, quiches, omelets, as well as a variety of savory crepes and, of course, luscious chocolate desserts. Try their crepe with strawberries in green peppercorn jus and chocolate love for dessert.
Hours: Wednesday, 11 am- 9 pm; Thursday, 11 am - 10 pm;
Friday & Saturday, 11 am- midnight, Sunday, 10 am-5 pm.
Prices: Entrees, $5 - $17

Chola (Indian)

107-109 Greenwich Avenue, 869.0700
www.FineIndianDining.com
This restaurant, hidden away upstairs next to the back of CVS, has good, mildly flavored Indian dishes. There are entrees from many Indian regions, including a large selection of vegetarian (including vegan) dishes, which are our favorites. We like the navratan Korma, baingan bhartha and aloo gobi palak.
Hours: Lunch, every day, noon - 2:30 pm;
Dinner, every day, 5 pm - 10 pm.
Prices: Lunch boxes to go, $7 - $10; Lunch entrees, $9 - $12;
Dinner entrees, $10 - $24.

City Limits (American) *

135 Harvard Avenue (at La Quinta), Stamford, 348.7000
www.citylimitsdiner.com
"A restaurant, disguised as a diner." This large diner, with its whimsical decor, serves upscale casual and comfort food. Try their chicken-corn quesadilla, corned beef hash, shrimp or curry chicken wrap and Valrhona pudding. If you are looking for a good early morning breakfast (orange-lemon waffles or country breakfast) or a late night meal give them a try. They have a children's menu.
Hours: Lunch menu from 11 am - 4 pm.
Dinner, Sunday - Thursday, 7am - 11pm;
Friday & Saturday, 7am - midnight.
Prices: Lunch wraps, sandwiches and burgers, $7 - $12;
Dinner entrees, $13 - $26.
Directions: I-95 N to exit 6, R on Harvard.

Cobble Stone (American, Casual)

620 Anderson Hill Road, Purchase, NY, 914.253.9678
www.cobblestonethecreek.com
Open since 1933, this informal, pub-style restaurant is more than just a college hang-out. It is fun for any age - a good choice before a SUNY concert. It has been owned and run by five generations of the same family. Try the onion soup, crab cakes, or one of their many hamburgers. For dessert, have their Oreo cookie madness. There is a children's menu.
Hours: Sunday brunch, 11:30 am - 3 pm; Lunch, Monday - Saturday,11:30 am - 5 pm, Sunday, 3pm - 5pm; Dinner, Sunday-Wednesday, 5pm-9pm, Thursday-Saturday, 5 pm - 10 pm. Late night drinks and light meals, 10 am - midnight (12:30 on Friday and Saturday).
Prices: Brunch, $8 - $12; Lunch entees, $4 - $13;
Dinner entrees, $7 - $18; Late night entrees, $8 - $.13.
Directions: King Street to Anderson Hill Road, just past SUNY Purchase on the left.

Cold Stone Creamery (Ice Cream) *

79 East Putnam Avenue, 302.3300
www.ColdStoneCreamery.com
Who doesn't have fun while eating ice cream? This franchise has a formula for success: stores are popping up all over the United States. You choose all your favorite sweet treats (from nuts to gummy bears) and they mix them in the ice cream, and if you tip they'll burst into song. They took first place during our 2004 Ice Cream Tasting Party.
Summer Hours: Sunday, noon - 10 pm;
Monday - Thursday, 2 pm - 10 pm; Friday & Saturday, noon - 11 pm.
Winter Hours: Sunday - Thursday, noon - 10 pm; Friday & Saturday, until 11 pm.

Cosi (Fast Food)

129 West Putnam Road, 861.2373, Catering: 203.861.2674
www.GetCosi.com
Pronounced Cozy, a restaurant popular in Manhattan, has found its niche in Greenwich. Lots of room to sit down, good soup, salad and sandwiches.
Hours: Monday - Thursday, 6:30 am 10 pm, Friday to 11 pm,
Saturday, 7:30 am 11 pm, Sunday 7:30 -9 pm.

Crab Shell (Seafood)

46 Southfield Avenue, Stamford, 967.7229

www.crabshell.com

Good casual seafood in a nautical setting. During the summer evenings, especially the weekends, it is a meeting ground for the 30 to 50-something crowd. From May to September the restaurant expands onto a huge outdoor deck - The Crab Shack - which can accommodate over 200. The Crab Shack has its own late night menu and a live band most weekends. The band schedule is on their website.

Hours: Open every day: Lunch, 11 am - 3 pm;

Dinner, Sunday-Thursday, 5 pm - 9:30 pm, Friday -Saturday, 5 -10pm; During the summer the bar is open to 1:30 am or later and the kitchen often stays open until they run out of food.

Prices: Lunch entrees, $10 -$25; Dinner entrees, $11-$30 (kids $9)

Directions: At Stamford Landing, near Dolphin Cove. I-95 N to exit 7, R on Southfield.

(La) Crémaillère (French) *

46 Bedford/Banksville Road, Banksville, NY, 914.234.9647

www.cremaillere.com

For years we have had an on/off affair with this restaurant. This should be expected for a restaurant open since 1947. We are happily back on. Expect attentive service, fine wines with refined French food in a dressy, romantic setting. Jackets and ties are expected. Many Greenwich couples have become engaged in this restaurant. They are making a name for themselves with their homemade sorbets and ice cream.

Hours: Lunch, Thursday - Saturday, noon - 2:30 pm ;

Dinner, Tuesday - Saturday, 6 pm - 9:30 pm; Sunday, 1 pm - 8 pm. Closed Monday.

Prices: Lunch is prix-fixed at $36; Dinner entrees, $32 $45.

Directions: Four miles N of the Merritt on North Street.

Culinary Institute of America Restaurants

1946 Campus Drive, Hyde Park, NY, 845.471.6608

www.ciachef.edu

- American Bounty (American, New) **
- Ristorante Caterina de Medici (Italian) **
- Escoffier (French) **

Superb dining, illustrating the quality of this renowned cooking school. Food, ambiance and service are all top notch. The Craig Claiborne Bookstore is located on the first floor of Roth Hall. We hope a lot of these chefs are attracted to the Greenwich area. Reservations well in advance are a must, even if you are going for lunch. The dress code is business casual. No jeans or sneakers.

Hours: Lunch, 11:30 am - 1 pm; Dinner, 6:30 pm - 8:30 pm.
Medici is open weekdays only,
Escoffier and Bounty are open Tuesday - Saturday.
Prices: Bounty, Lunch entrees, $12 - $21, Dinner entrees, $18 - $26;
Medici, Lunch entrees, $14 - $18, Dinner entrees, $14 - $20;
Escoffier, Lunch entrees, $16 - $25, Dinner entree, $24 - $28.
Directions: About 1.5 hours north on I-684 & Route 9 N.
Detailed directions are on their website.

Dakshin (Indian) *

68 Broad Street (corner of Summer), Stamford, 964.1010
www.coromandelcuisine.com/stamford/index.html
Hungry for Indian cuisine? Want to know where connoisseurs of fine Indian food dine? Want to be able to have a conversation? This colorful, spacious restaurant, with its delicious specialities from many regions and its attentive staff will capture you.
Hours: Lunch, every day, noon - 2:30 pm;
Dinner every day , 5 pm - 10 pm.
Prices: Lunch buffet, $11; Dinner entrees, $12 - $23.

Darlene's Heavenly Desires (Ice Cream, Chocolates) *

185 Sound Beach Avenue, Old Greenwich, 622.7077
www.darlenesheavenlydesires.com
In summer, you will see happy people licking cones outside this shop filled with delicious chocolates, gelato, Coney Island custard and Weight Watchers ice cream. In our Tasting Contest, Darlene's Sedutto ice cream scored at the top. Sedutto comes in about 34-flavors. After eating a cone, you'll decide to take some home.
Hours: Every day, Summer, 11 am to 10 pm; Winter, 11 am to 8 pm.

Doral Arrowwood Atrium (Sunday Brunch)
975 Anderson Hill Rd, Rye Brook, NY, 914.939.5500
www.DoralArrowWood.com
The Atrium is a large restaurant in a resort hotel. One side is all windows looking over the lovely golf course, the other side, for Sunday brunch, is a banquet of foods. With such great variety, there is something for all tastes. Live music plays in the background, as a magician tours the tables showing young and old a good time. Large groups are easily accommodated.
Hours: Sunday Brunch seatings, 11:45 am & 1:45 pm
Brunch: $32.50

(The) Drawing Room (Tea)
5 Suburban Avenue, Cos Cob, 661.3737
Tucked around the corner from the Post Road, near the Cos Cob Library is the perfect place for light lunch and/or afternoon tea. This small, cheerfully decorated tea room serves tea, hot chocolate, finger sandwiches, scones and desserts. The staff are tea experts who can help you make delightful tea choices. Having tea and browsing through the adjoining antique store, make this a fun and civilized break in the day.
Official tea time is considered to be 11 am - 4 pm.
Hours: Tuesday - Saturday, 8 am - 5 pm.
Prices: Petit Afternoon Tea, $12, Grand Afternoon Tea, $24.

Dressing Room (American Casual)
27 Powers Court, Westport, CT, 203.226.1114
(located next to the Westport County Playhouse)
www.DressingRoomHomeGrown.com
This Newman's Own-sponsored restaurant, specializes in cooking American heritage recipes with locally grown, organic food.
Hours: Lunch, Wednesday - Sunday, 11:30 am - 3 pm; Dinner, Tuesday - Sunday, starting at 5 pm.
Prices: Dinner entrees, $20 - $28.

Dunkin' Donuts (Coffee, Ice Cream)
• 375 East Putnam, Cos Cob, 869.7454
  This location also sells Baskin-Robbins, ice cream.
• 271 West Putnam Avenue, Greenwich, 869.5791
www.DunkinDonuts.com
We are addicted to their coffee. Be sure to try their summer coffees.
Hours: Open every day, 5 am - 11 pm.

Ebb Tide Seafood (Seafood)

1 Willet Avenue (just at the River),Port Chester, NY 914.939.4810
This is a find - casual dining on picnic tables overlooking the river - hidden at the end of Willet Avenue. The seafood is fresh and very good. Stand in line to place your order and your freshly prepared selections such as oysters, chowder, fish & chips, or lobster will arrive at your table.
Hours: Open all year and every day except Monday.
Lunch, noon - 4 pm; Dinner, 5 pm - 9 pm.
The hours can vary, so it is wise to call ahead. No reservations.
Prices: $7 - $25, based on market prices.

Edo (Japanese, Steak)

140 Midland Avenue (shopping center next to Home Depot), Port Chester, 914.937.3333
 A large restaurant with 11 hibachi tables each seating 8 people. The cooking process, done in front of you, is very dramatic- perhaps too the-atrical. If you are thinking of hosting a children's party around a hibachi table, you will have plenty of room here and the children will enjoy the show.
Hours: Monday-Thursday, 5:30 pm to 10 pm;
Friday & Saturday, 5:30 pm to 11 pm;
Sunday Lunch, noon - 3, Dinner, 4 pm to 9 pm.
Prices: Entrees, $15 - $29.

Elm Street Oyster House (Seafood) **

11 West Elm Street, 629.5795
www.elmstoysterhouse.com
Their raw bar and chowders are hard to beat. We have yet to be disap-pointed. You will like the creative recipes and yummy desserts. Try their wasabi sesame crusted tuna or the Lobster Paella. The panfried oysters are top-rate for an appetizer. This small, lively restaurant is a great place to meet after work and to stay for dinner.
Hours: Monday - Thursday, 11:30 am - 10 pm;
Friday & Saturday, 11:30 am - 11 pm; Sunday, noon - 9 pm.
Closed on major holidays. They accept lunch, but not dinner reserva-tions. For dinner, arrive before 7 pm or after 9 pm, otherwise expect to wait at their active bar.
Prices: Entrees, $23 - $29, Salads and Sandwiches, $8- $18.

(My) Favorite Place (American, Casual)

1 Strickland Avenue, Cos Cob, 869.1500

Order from the counter and take it home or sit down at one of the few tables. They even have curbside pickup. This is a home-town, casual restaurant at its best. Besides the good salads and popular hamburgers (our favorite is "white heat"), we like the homemade potato chips, and the chicken chili. This is a kid-friendly place.

Hours: Monday - Wednesday, 10 am - 4 pm;

Thursday & Friday, 10 am - 8pm; Saturday & Sunday, 11 am - 4 pm.

Prices: Entrees, $5 - $10; Kids menu $2 - $5.

(Le) Figaro (French)

327 Greenwich Avenue, 622.0018

www.figarobistro.com

Le Figaro calls itself a Paris bistro and nothing could be more descriptive. From the moment you enter you feel like you are in France, albeit in a rather elegant bistro. The service is friendly and at the pace you would expect in France. The food is casual French. Three scallops for an entree seems small, other entrees are ample.

Hours: Sunday Brunch, 11 am - 3 pm;

Lunch, Monday - Saturday, noon - 2:30 pm;

Dinner, Monday - Thursday, 5:30 pm - 9:30 pm;

(Friday & Saturday until 10:30 pm); Sunday, 5 pm - 9 pm.

Prices: Lunch entrees, $ 11 - $22; Dinner entrees, $18 - $29.

F.I.S.H. Fox Island Seafood House (Seafood) *

102 Fox Island Rd, Port Chester, NY, 914.939.4227

www.fishfoxisland.com/home.htm

Finding this trendy, waterfront restaurant is part of the fun. In this unique location, you will discover inventive, ultrafresh seafood, served by a friendly staff. The menu changes weekly.

Hours: Summer: Lunch, Wednesday - Sunday, 11:30 am - 3 pm;

Dinner, Monday- Thursday, 5:30 pm - 10 pm,

Friday & Saturday until 11pm; Sunday, 5 pm - 9 pm.

Closed Monday & Tuesday during Fall & Winter.

Prices: Entrees, $12 - $27; They sometimes offer a free bottle of wine for your table if you order by 6:30.

Directions: Route 1 South through Main street in Port Chester to Grace Church Street, L on Fox Island.

RESTAURANTS

Fjord Sunday Brunch (American)
143 River Road, Cos Cob, 800.925.2622
www.fjordcatering.com
Brunch cruises sail from Cos Cob harbor year round. This is an especially nice way to experience the Greenwich waterfront, while eating French toast and smoked fish. Of course, you need a reservation.
Hours: Sail at 11:30 am, Return at 2 pm.
Price: $64 per adult, $25 per child.

Fonda La Paloma (Mexican)
531 Post Road, Cos Cob, 661.9395
Rarely do restaurants survive a decade. This one has been here for over thirty years! Our waiter had been working there for twenty-six years and they have a loyal following despite the dated decor. On Friday and Saturday evenings they have a strolling Mariachi band. The guacamole is good, the mole poblano is no longer the mole of our memory, unfortunately.
Hours: Lunch, weekdays, noon 2:30 pm;
Dinner, Monday - Thursday, 5 pm - 9:45 pm;
Friday & Saturday, 5 pm -10:45 pm; Sunday, 5 pm - 9 pm.
Prices: Lunch entrees, $5 - $13; Dinner entrees, $11 - $23.

Frank's (Italian)
23 Putnam Avenue, Port Chester, NY 914.939.8299
This popular pizza take-out has a dining room with cloth napkins, pretty plates and friendly service. We were wowed by the quality and variety of their freshly prepared entrees. We especially like the garlic balls, eggplant parmigiana and the fettuccine Alfredo.
Hours: Monday-Thursday, 10:30 am to 10 pm;
Friday & Saturday until 10:30 pm. Closed Sunday.

Frankie & Louie's (Italian)
414 Willet Avenue, Port Chester, NY 914.939.0202
Casual dining where pasta dishes are the strong suit of the kitchen. Portions are plentiful, so arrive hungry! Take advantage of their special nights, such as "Pasta Madness" or "Ravioli Night".
Hours: Open every day, 11am - 11pm.
Prices: Entrees, $12 - $17; Sunday Pasta Madness, $11;
Thursday Ravioli Night, $12;
Wednesday Family Night, 2 - 4 people for $25.

Gaia (American, New)

253 Greenwich Avenue, 661.3443

www.GaiaRestaurant.com

Gaia, named after the goddess of mother earth, is in a splendid setting, a beautifully restored bank with high vaulted ceilings. You will be cared for by an attentive, well-trained serving staff. The chef, Frederic Kieffer, is known for his unique cooking in "mason jars." Who would think you would want to dine out in a spiffy restaurant and have a jar of macaroni and cheese, but their macaroni with Gruyère and truffles is an all-time favorite. However, most of the dishes we liked the best were not in jars. If noise is a factor, plan to arrive early.

Hours: Lunch, weekdays, 11:30 am - 5 pm, Brunch Saturday and Sunday, 11:30 - 4 pm; Dinner, everyday, 5:30 pm 10 pm; Friday & Saturday to 11pm.

Prices: Lunch entrees, $13 - $26, Price fixed, 2-course; $22, 3-course, $27; Dinner entrees, $25 - $40.

Garden Café at Greenwich Hospital (American, Casual)

5 Perryridge Road, 1st Floor, Watson Pavillion, 863.3000

The hospital's garden café is a good place to lunch, whether you are visiting someone or not. Diners can enjoy a surprisingly good salad or sandwich as well as garden views through floor-to-ceiling windows, and in good weather, from the trellised bluestone terrace. This welcoming addition was donated by the Victor Borge family. The café is also accessible from the street.

Hours: weekdays, Breakfast, 8 am- 11 pm, Lunch, 11:15 am - 3 pm.

Prices: Lunch entrees , $6-$8

Garden Catering (TakeOut)

www.GardenCatering.net

If you like fried chicken, don't miss this takeout. Everyone loves the potato cones.

• 185 Sound Beach Avenue, Old Greenwich, 698.2900

Hours: weekdays, 6 am - 7 pm; Saturday, 6 am - 6 pm; Sunday, 6 am - 5 pm.

• 177 Hamilton Avenue, Byram, 422.2555

Hours: weekdays, 6 am - 7:30 pm; Saturday, 6 am - 5 pm; closed Sunday

• 140 Midland Avenue, Port Chester, 914.934.7810 or 7852

Hours: Monday - Saturday, 6:30 am - 7 pm, Sunday; 7 am - 6 pm.

Garelick & Herbs (Delicatessen) *

48 West Putnam Avenue, 661.7373

A sophisticated deli. It has a wide selection of first-rate, ready-to-serve dishes. Primarily a takeout store, although there are places to sit for the lucky few who get there first.

Hours: weekdays, 7 am - 7 pm; Saturday, 8 am - 6 pm;
Sunday, 9 am - 5 pm.

Gates (American)

10 Forest Street, New Canaan, CT, 203.966.8666
http://www.culinarymenus.com/gates.htm

An informal standby for over twenty-five years. On a back street, this large, gaily decorated, cheerful restaurant, is a popular place to have lunch if you are shopping in New Canaan. Service is good humored and youthful. The menu is strong on burgers, salads and wraps as well as some more sophisticated entrees.

Hours: Lunch, every day 11:30 am - 3:30 pm;
Dinner, Monday Thursday, 5:30 pm - 10 pm;
Friday & Saturday, 11 pm; Sunday, 4:30 pm - 9:30 pm.
Prices: Lunch entrees, $7 - $11; Dinner entrees, $7 - $19.
Directions: Merritt Parkway N to exit 36, L on CT 106 (which become Main Street), R on East , L on Forest.

Ginger Man (American, Casual)

64 Greenwich Avenue, 861.6400

A lively burger / beer place in a classic, upscale tavern atmosphere. Twenty-one beers on tap and fifty beers in the bottle. If you stop here and you are not in the mood for a burger or fish and chips, have the delicious pear salad.

Hours: Monday - Thursday, 11:45 am - 10 pm;
Friday & Saturday until 11 pm, Sunday until 9 pm.
Prices: Lunch entrees, $10 - $15; Dinner entrees, $10 - $30.

Giorgio's (Italian)

64 Merritt Street, Port Chester, NY, 914.937.4906 or 1096

Good service and good Italian food in a romantic, rather out-of-the-way location. It is a favorite restaurant of some of our friends. Quiet enough that you can actually have a conversation. Small enough that you should be sure to make a reservation. Like the restaurant the menu is small. Be sure to try their angel hair bolognese (an appetizer large enough for a main course) or the delicate veal picata.

Hours: Lunch, weekdays, noon - 3 pm;

Dinner, every day, 5 pm - 10 pm (Friday & Saturday to 11 pm).

Prices: Lunch entrees, $18 - $20; Dinner entrees, $18 - $34.

Directions: Post Road to Main Street in Port Chester, R on Westchester Avenue, L on South Regent Street, R on Ellendale (just past Piero's Restaurant).

Gofer Ice Cream (Ice Cream)

522 East Putnam Avenue, 661.9080

www.GoferIceCream.com

Good hard, soft ice cream, and gelato. We are fans of their Razzles.

Summer Hours: Monday - Thursday, noon 9:45 pm,

Friday & Saturday 12:30 pm - 10 pm, Sunday, 12:30 pm - 10:30 pm.

Winter/Fall Hours: Monday - Saturday, 12:30 pm - 9:30

(Friday & Saturday to 10:30 pm), Sunday, 1:30-9 pm.

Glory Days (Diner, American, Casual)

Previously know as the Colonial Diner, a.k.a. Greenwich Diner

69 East Putnam Avenue, 661.9067

A welcoming diner, with a celebrity-studded clientele, that has been open since 1923. It was completely rebuilt in 2002 with a sleek new look. Nick, the friendly owner, has operated the restaurant for over 15 years. He keeps prices low and serves hearty portions. This is what a diner is supposed to be. Everyone has their favorites here; we particularly like their Greek salad and baklava. It is a popular late-night meeting place for students.

Hours: Open 24 hours a day, every day, even holidays.

Lunch hours, 11 am - 3 pm. They will deliver locally. No reservations.

Prices: Breakfast entrees, $2 - $5; Lunch entrees, $4 - $7;

Dinner entrees, $8 - $15.

Greenwich Health Mart (Vegetarian)
30 Greenwich Avenue, 869.9658
In the back of this health product store, is a very small vegetarian food bar, serving soups, salads, wraps and sandwiches. They have good tofu chili and organic fruit smoothies.
Hours: Monday - Wednesday 8:30 am - 5:30 pm;
Thursday 8:30 am - 7:30 pm; Friday 8:30 am - 5:30 pm;
Saturday 8:30 am - 5 pm; Sunday, 11 am - 3 pm.
Prices: Sandwiches, $5 - $7.

Habana (LatinAmerican, new)
70 North Main Street, South Norwalk, CT, 203.852.9790
Enjoy the festive atmosphere, while dining on contemporary latin cuisine. Patrons having a good time make the restaurant noisy. This may be more because of the good Mojitos and sangria rather than the food, which unfortunately seems to be slipping.
Hours: Dinner, every night, 5 pm - 11 pm. Reservations are a good idea.
Prices: Dinner entrees, $14 - $22.
Directions: I-95 North, Exit 14, R at stop sign, L at 2nd traffic light into SoNo Plaza.

HäagenDazs (Ice Cream)
374 Greenwich Avenue, 629.8000
It's a toss up between a hot fudge sundae or a chocolate-laced cone filled with creamy dulce de leche.
Hours: everyday, 11 am - 10 pm.

Horseneck Tavern (American, Casual)
338 West Putnam Avenue, 661.8448
The motto of this restaurant is "good food and good times!" Step inside this old-fashioned restaurant and bar and you will meet residents who have been going there for generations. This is the place to have a burger, served by a friendly staff.
Hours: everyday, 11:30 am -10 pm (Sunday until 9 pm);
Bar is open until crowd leaves.
Prices: Entrees, $6 - $14.

Hostaria Mazzei (Italian)

25 South Regent Street, Port Chester, NY 914.939.2727

Regulars are greeted at the door with a hug and waiters remember what their customers like in this long-standing, large comfortable southern Italian restaurant. Lots of people choose to have birthday parties and special occasions here. Easy, ample parking. Fish, like Bronzini, rather than pasta, is the better choice.

Hours: Lunch, weekdays, noon - 2:30;

Dinner, every day, 5 pm - 11 pm (Sunday, 4 pm - 9 pm).

Prices: Lunch entrees, $6 - $17, Lunch 3-course prix-fixe, $20;

Dinner entrees, $17 - $29. Specials may be more.

Directions: Follow Post Road to Main street in Port Chester. At 3rd light, R on Westchester, at 4th light, L on South Regent.

Hunan Cafe (Chinese) *

1233 East Putnam Avenue, Riverside, 637.4341

Well-prepared, authentic Chinese cuisine. If you are planning a multi-course feast with entrees such as Peking duck, place this meal in their hands and you will have a first-rate experience. On Sundays, they have a habit-forming dim sum brunch, which we highly recommend.

Hours: weekdays, 11:30 am - 9:30 pm, weekends until 10 pm.

Prices: Lunch entrees, $5 - $7; Dinner entrees, $8 - $18.

Hunan Gourmet (Chinese)

68 East Putnam Avenue, 869.1940

www.greenwichhunangourmet.com

A Chinese restaurant with white tablecloths and an elegant flair. Just thinking about their shredded pork with dried bean curd or grilled sea bass with ginger makes us hungry. The staff is especially nice to children, making it a popular family place.

Hours: Monday - Thursday, 11:30 am - 10 pm; Friday, 10 am - 11 pm; Saturday, noon - 11 pm, Sunday, noon - 10 pm; Lunch is served every day until 3 pm.

Prices: Lunch entrees, $8 $18; Dinner entrees, $12 $18.

Free delivery with a minimum purchase of $20.

IHOP (American, Casual)

2410 Summer Street, Stamford, 324.9819
www.ihop.com
As you probably know, IHOP, a.k.a. International House of Pancakes, is the place for chocolate pancakes and every imaginable breakfast treat.
Hours: Open every day from 7 am - 10 pm.
Directions: Merritt Parkway N to exit 34, R on Long Ridge which becomes Summer.

Jean-Louis (French) **

61 Lewis Street, 622.8450
www.RestaurantJeanLouis.com
Still our favorite French restaurant. This is an artfully simple, intimate and refined restaurant, not a large, grandiose one. You will be delighted with Jean-Louis Gerin's new French cuisine. He was recently named by the James Beard Foundation as the best chef in the Northeast. His skillfully prepared dishes are made from ingredients as fresh as spring. The service is intended to make you feel special and comfortable, due in large part to Linda Gerin's gracious hospitality. The menu degustation is always a great choice.
Hours: Lunch, weekdays, noon - 2 pm, no lunch in June, July & August; Dinner, weekdays, seating starts at 5:45 pm; Saturday, seatings at 6:15 & 8:40 pm. Be sure to make reservations.
Prices: Lunch entrees, $19 - $21, (2-course prix fixe, $29); Dinner entrees, $31 - $40, (Prix fixe menus, $49 & $95).

Jimmy's Grill (Fast-Food)

101 Field Point Road, Parking Lot of Greenwich Town Hall
An outdoor stand (mobile van). They have yummy chili dogs, chicken souvlaki and Philly cheese steaks, all for very reasonable prices. When you are in a hurry for lunch, remember Jimmy's. They even serve breakfast for people on the go.
Hours: weekdays, 8 am - 2 pm, though these hours seem flexible.

Jordan's Hilltop Restaurant (American-Lebanese, Casual)

632 Anderson Hill Rd, Purchase, NY, 914.253.9055

www.JordansHilltop.com

The extensive menu is what you might expect in a diner. The ambiance in this 100-year old restaurant is casual, cozy and fun. There is something for everyone on the menu. A lot of people come for the burgers. We come for their yummy Lebanese-Mediterranean dishes.

Hours: Open daily, 11 am - 10 pm.

Prices: Lunch entrees, $5 - $19; Dinner entrees, $6-$18.

Katzenberg's Express (Fast Food)

342 Greenwich Avenue, 625.0103

A New York-style deli with a wide selection of sandwiches. Primarily takeout, but there are a few places to sit. Not only is this a kid-friendly place, it's baby-friendly too. Ask for the Katzy's Babies Menu; it features applesauce and mashed potatoes.

Hours: weekdays, 8 am - 5 pm; Saturday, 10 am - 5 pm;
Sunday, 10 am - 4 pm.

Kazu (Japanese)

64 North Main Street, South Norwalk, CT, 203.866.7492

Very near the Norwalk movies. Order the movie box, it has a tasty sampling of their Japanese specialties. The sushi or teriyaki are good choices. We like the mix on the menu of traditional Japanese and creative Asian dishes.

Hours: Lunch, weekdays, noon - 2 pm; Dinner, weekdays, 5:30 pm - 10:00 pm; Friday & Saturday, 5:30 pm - 11 pm; Sunday, 5 pm - 9:30 pm.

Prices: Lunch entrees, $12 - $16; Dinner entrees, $15 - $28.

Directions: I-95 North, Exit 14, R at stop sign, L at 2nd traffic light into SoNo Plaza

Kira Sushi (Japanese) *
4 Lewis Court, 422.2990
This Armonk sushi restaurant has opened a second venture in a hidden space just off of Greenwich Avenue. The decor with its remarkable rock-water wall, is attractive and soothing. The miso soup and seaweed salad are superb, as are the beef teriyaki and chicken tempura. As you might expect, the sushi and their special rolls, such as the iridescent Kira Wasabi roll, get high marks. Only the Bento was a disappointment.
Hours: Monday-Thursday, 11:30 am to 10 pm; Friday until 11 pm; Saturday, noon to 11 pm; Sunday, noon to 10 pm.
Prices: Sushi plates, $18 - $25; special rolls, $8 - $16, entrees, $12 - $23.

Kit's Thai Kitchen (Thai) *
927 High Ridge Road, Turn of River Shopping Center 329.7800
www.KitsThaiKitchen.com
A find! Tiny spot in a shopping center with mouth-watering curries and chicken. They use organic products and are not afraid to make spicy dishes. Pleasant seating outside and tables inside. There is nothing better than their Chicken Satay or Sum Tum (Papaya Salad). You can't go wrong with their curries or Pad Thai.
Hours: everyday, 11 am - 10 pm, Sunday to 9 pm.
Prices: Entrees, $11 - $23.
Directions: Merritt Pkwy N to exit 35, R on High Ridge.

(The) Kneaded Bread (Fast Food, Bakery)
181 North Main Street, Port Chester, NY, 914.937.9489
www.kneadedbread.com
A first-rate bread bakery. Every day they bake over 17 varieties of crusty, European-style breads. They also have croissants, Danish, and sandwiches. Make their fresh donuts a Sunday morning treat. There are a few seats, so stop in for a good coffee and sandwich. Be sure to order holiday breads in advance. They only accept cash or local checks.
Hours: weekdays, 7 am - 5 pm; Saturday, 8 am - 4 pm;
Sunday, 8am - 1pm.

KU (Japanese)

85 East Putnam Avenue, Cos Cob, 422.6310
Stylish and modern with an open kitchen and sushi bar. It is quieter than many Greenwich restaurants, but too dimly lit for our taste. Chefs are from Tokyo and the service is attentive. They are at their best when you have sushi or sashimi, although we also like the Chilean sea bass.
Hours: Lunch, weekdays, noon - 2:30 pm;
Dinner, Sunday - Thursday, 5 pm to 10 pm,
Friday & Saturday, until 10:30 pm.
Prices: Lunch, entrees $13 - $19, Bento boxes $12-15;
Dinner, entrees $17 $27, sushi $4-$16.

Landmark Diner (Diner, American, Casual)

31 East Putnam Avenue, Cos Cob, 869.0954
Lucky Greenwich to have two good diners. Landmark and Glory Days. They have the same owners. Landmark serves a wide variety of hearty breakfast and dinner dishes, including a yummy spinach pie and our always favorite Greek salad. Expect reasonable prices, large servings and friendly service.
Hours: everyday, 6 am - 11 pm. No reservations.
Prices: Breakfast, $3 - $8; Lunch & Dinner, $3 - $16.

L'Escale (French, Mediterranean) *

500 Steamboat Road, 661.4600
http://www.lescalerestaurant.com/
L'Escale, French for "port of call," evokes good memories of dining along the French Riviera. What better style restaurant to be on our Greenwich waterfront! In the summer the terrace is the perfect spot to dine - especially for a Sunday Brunch. This bright, airy restaurant has nicely spaced tables allowing diners to have good conversations and a good time. Although the service is sometimes wonderful, it is sometimes pitiful. Don't go for afternoon tea.
Prices: Lunch entrees, $12 - $25; Dinner entrees, $17 - $32;
Afternoon Tea, $35; Brunch, $36.
Hours: Breakfast, everyday, 7 am - 10 am;
Lunch, Monday - Saturday, 11:30 am - 2:30;
Dinner, Sunday - Thursday, 5 pm - 10 pm,
Friday & Saturday, until 11 pm; Sunday Brunch, 11:30 am - 3 pm.

Little Thai Kitchen (Thai) *
21 St. Rochs Avenue, 622.2972
www.LittleThaiKitchen.com
http://www.culinarymenus.com/restaurants/littlethaikitchen.htm
A tiny jewel of a place (5 tables), serving some of the best Thai cuisine outside of Bangkok, is tucked away on St. Rochs. If you don't like your food spicy, you will have to tell them. We love their Nau Nam tok (beef salad), Mee Grob (Thai crispy noodels), Pad Thai noodles as well as their curries, particularly the Thai Massaman and Thai green curry. We suspect that the Thai iced tea may be an acquired taste.
Hours: Lunch, every day, 11 am - 2:30 pm,
Saturday & Sunday, noon - 2:30 pm;
Dinner, Monday - Thursday, 4:30 pm - 9:30 pm;
Friday & Saturday, 5 pm - 10 pm; Sunday, 5 pm - 9 pm.
Prices: Lunch entrees, $7 -$12; Dinner entrees, $10 - $30.

Longford's (Ice Cream) *
4 Elm Place, Rye, New York, 914.967.3797
www.longfordsicecream.com
Longford's ice cream factory is on Wilkins Street in Port Chester. Many clubs and high quality restaurants in and around Greenwich are supplied by Longford's. Fortunately, Longford's has one ice cream parlor just a short distance away in downtown Rye. Fill your freezer with ice cream, ice cream pies and sorbets. We haven't tasted a flavor we didn't like. In our Tasting Contest, they scored at the top.
Hours: Every day, noon-9 pm (Friday & Saturday, until 10pm).
Directions: US-1 South (Boston Post Road West) through Port Chester. Just past the intersections of I-287 and I-95, R on Purdy, L on Purchase, L on Locust, R on Theodore, R on Elm.

Long Ridge Tavern (American, Casual)
2635 Long Ridge Road, Stamford, 329.7818
www.LongRidgeTavern.com
Dating from the 1880s, this charming country restaurant gives you a sense of stepping back into history. If you are looking for tavern fare such as Chicken Pot Pie, Yankee Pot Roast or Bread Pudding, you won't be disappointed. They have live entertainment on Friday & Saturday evenings: check their website for details. They have a dining room minimum of $15 per person.
Hours: Lunch, every day, noon - 3 pm;
Dinner, Monday - Thursday, 3 pm - 9 pm (Friday & Saturday, to 10 pm).
Prices: Lunch entrees, $10 - $16; Dinner, $13 - $28.
Directions: Merritt N to exit 34, L on Long Ridge.

MacDuffs Public House (Pubs, British/Scottish) *

99 Railroad Avenue, 422.0563
www.MacDuffsPub.com
When you are yearning for bangers and mash, fish and chips or simply a first class burger, you will love this trendy, pub-style restaurant across from the movie theater. Cheers to the two Brunswick graduates who knew Greenwich would enjoy a lively pub.
Hours: Lunch, Monday - Thursday & Sunday, 11:30 am - 1 pm;
Friday & Saturday, to 2 pm;
Dinner, Monday - Thursday & Sunday, 5 pm - 9 pm,
Friday & Saturday to 10 pm.
Prices: Entrees, $10 - $27

MacKenzie's Grill Room (American, Casual, Pub) *

148 Sound Beach Avenue, Old Greenwich, 698.0223
www.mackenziesgrillroom.com
Casual, friendly restaurant and bar, with good food, celebrating its 13th year. The perfect place to watch a game. Sit at the bar or a table and try the nachos, skins or wings, or choose a booth and have a tasty meal. Try their steak au poivre - we love it. For dessert have the Lava cake or Mac's mud pie. On weekends, MacKenzie's is a "hot spot" and may be crowded and lively. Starting at 9 pm on Thursdays they have live entertainment.
Hours: Lunch, every day, noon - 4pm; Dinner, every day 4pm-10pm (Friday & Saturday to 11pm).
Open most holidays. Reservations accepted for 6 or more.
Prices: Lunch entrees, $6 - $12; Dinner entrees, $7 - $26.

McDonald's (Fast Food)

- 268 West Putnam Avenue, 629.9068
- 1207 East Putnam Avenue, Riverside, 637.8598
Hours: Open every day, 6 am - midnight.

Match (American, New) *

98 Washington Street, South Norwalk, CT 203.852.1088
www.matchsono.com
For two years, Connecticut Magazine readers have voted Match the Best Restaurant in Fairfield County. As a result of Chef Matthew Storch's innovative creations, this restaurant continues to grow in popularity, so be sure to reserve. Match has a trendy, happy atmosphere with helpful, efficient service and good food.
Hours: Dinner, everyday, 5 pm - 10 pm, Friday & Saturday, until 11pm.
Prices: Dinner entrees, $21 - $37.
Directions: I-95 N, exit 14, R on West Avenue, L at fork onto Main Street, L onto Washington.

Meigas (Spanish, New) **

10 Wall Street, Norwalk, CT, 203.866.8800
www.meigasrestaurant.com
Chef Luis Bollo, a top Spanish chef, is creating exciting new Spanish cuisine. Count on a pleasant evening. The decor is simple and classic, the service attentive and the food artfully prepared and delightful.
Hours: Closed Monday and most major holidays.
Lunch, Tuesday - Friday, noon - 2:30 pm;
Dinner, Tuesday - Thursday, 5:30 pm - 9:30 pm;
Friday & Saturday until 10:30 pm, Sunday until 8:30 pm.
Paellas are usually available only on Sunday.
Prices: Lunch entrees, $15 - $26; Dinner entrees, $27 - $38; Paellas, $24 - $29.
Directions: I-95 N to Exit 16, L off the exit, L on Wall, entrance on Hugh St.

MeliMelo (French, Casual, Ice Cream) *

362 Greenwich Avenue, 629.6153
www.MeliMeloCreperie.com
A tiny, always popular, always crowded restaurant with French casual foods such as yummy onion soup and crepes. Our favorite, however, is their croque monsieur. The fresh fruit sorbets are to die for. These are the best sorbets in town. The Owner, Chef Marc Penvenne, is very gracious as well as talented. The weekend breakfast menu features delicious omelets. This is where Holly met Tod.
Hours: every day, 10 am - 10 pm. No reservations.
Prices: Entrees, $5 - $11.

Mirage Cafe (American, New) *
531 North Main Street, Port Chester, NY, 914.937.3497
www.cafemirageny.com
A relaxed restaurant, with funky decor and excellent dishes. The chef-owner, calls his menu a melting pot of Caribbean, French, Asian, Cajun and American cuisines. Especially popular for late night dining, you will have fun at this restaurant. Try the wonderful steak au poivre or steak diable. Their lemon grass shrimp and southwestern tuna are also good choices. It can be very noisy inside. In the summer, escape the noise and dine on the terrace.
Hours: Lunch, weekdays, 11:30 am - 4 pm;
Dinner, weekdays, 4 pm - midnight, Saturday 6 pm - midnight.
It is a small restaurant, advance reservations are recommended - especially for weekends.
Prices: Lunch entrees $7 - $14; Dinner entrees, $17 - $24.

Mediterraneo Restaurant (Italian) *
366 Greenwich Avenue, 629.4747
http://www.mediterraneoofgreenwich.com/
Lively, bustling, welcoming. Lots of people seem to order their pizzas and spaghetti, but the kitchen can turn out really good seafood dishes as well. The terrace provides an interesting perspective on life along Greenwich Avenue and also allows you to have a conversation. Popular Terra, has the same ownership.
Hours: Lunch, Monday Saturday, noon 2:30 pm (Saturday until 3 pm);
Dinner, Monday Saturday, 5:30 pm 10 pm; Sunday, 5 pm 9:30 pm.
Reservations are usually required.
Prices: Lunch entrees, $16 - 26, Dinner entrees, $16 - $30,
Pizzas, $13 to $15.

(The) Melting Pot (Swiss, Fondue)

14 Grove Street, Darien, CT, 203.656.4774
www.MeltingPot.com

Don't expect to dash in and have a quick fondue. This large restaurant chain-over 300 are scattered across the US, is for "an experience", a date or better yet a party. The "experience" will take, at least, two hours. The menu offers an extensive array of choices, great for some, daunting for others. A long dark hall leads to a variety of private alcoves. Our friends in Switzerland surely could not imagine what has happened to the traditional fondues we savored in the Alps. A whole new genre of fondues is on the menu in this entertaining, if not traditional, restaurant. After trying some of the unusual combinations we settled on the traditional Emmenthaler cheese fondue and one of the chocolate fondues (original or pure chocolate or flaming turtle) as our favorites. They have an extensive wine list and entertainment on Friday nights.

Hours: Dinner, Monday - Thursday, 5 pm - 10 pm,
Friday, Saturday & Sunday, 5 pm - 11 pm.

Prices: Cheese fondue, $16; Entree fondues, $18 - $50,
Chocolate Fondues, small - $18, regular - $32. Four-course dinners for two (The Big Night Out) $96 to $100 per couple.

Morton's of Chicago (Steak) *

377 North State Street (Swiss Bank Center), Stamford, 324.3939
www.mortons.com

A carnivore's paradise with excellent service. If the menu presentation doesn't turn you into a vegetarian, you will find the steak as good as it gets. Forget the seafood and the sauces, this restaurant is all about the cuts and quality of their beef. Choose creamed spinach as a side and the hot chocolate cake (not the souffles) for dessert. A popular place for the business crowd on expense accounts.

Hours: No Lunch; Dinner, Monday - Saturday, 5 pm -11 pm;
Sunday, until 10 pm.

Prices: Entrees, $25 - $84. All side dishes are a la carte.

Directions: I-95 N to exit 8, immediate L on Atlantic, immediate L on State. Valet Parking.

Nuage (Asian Fusion, JapaneseFrench) **
203 East Putnam Avenue, Mill Pond Plaza, 869.2339
www.nuagerestaurant.com
This small restaurant, with its unpretentious decor, has a menu of sophisticated and artistically presented dishes that diners with discriminating taste rave about. The noise level is relatively low, making it a pleasant place to have a conversation. We recommend the seven-course tasting menu—and the delicious chocolate pyramid for dessert.
Hours: Lunch, weekdays, 11:45 am to 2:30 pm;
Dinner, every night, 5:30 pm - 10 pm, Friday & Saturday to 11 pm,
Sunday to 9:30 pm.
Prices: Lunch entrees, $15 - $25; Dinner entrees, $22 - $78; five course tasting menu, $65 and up, seven course tasting menu, $80 and up.

Ocean 211 (Seafood) **
211 Summer Street, Stamford, 973.0494
http://www.ocean211.com/
Located in a townhouse in the heart of downtown Stamford, this is a perfect choice for pre-theater dining. The menu is small, but we loved everything, making you forgive the pricy menu and paper table cloths. They say the Crab cakes are the best in Fairfield county, and we agree. Their creative preparations of fresh fish have earned them acclaim as one of the best seafood restaurants in the area. For a good dining experience ask to be seated upstairs, even if they frown at your request.
Hours: Lunch, weekdays, noon - 2:30 pm;
Dinner, Monday - Thursday, 5:30 - 10 pm,
Friday and Saturday until 11pm.
Prices: Lunch entrees, $18 - $30; Dinner entrees, $29 - $42.
Directions: I-95 N to exit 8, L on Atlantic, L on Broad, L on Summer.

Ole Mole (Mexican) *
130 High Ridge Road, Stamford, 461.9962
www.ole-mole.com
This very small restaurant with its rather unimposing exterior is the best Mexican restaurant in our area. Their authentic cuisine is fresh and healthy. Be sure to try their Ole Mole salad or mole poblano. There is very limited seating, so come early or plan to make this a takeout dinner.
Hours: Monday - Thursday, 11:30 am - 9:30 pm;
Friday & Saturday, until 10 pm; Sunday, 11:30 - 9 pm.
Prices: Entrees, $12 - $16.
Directions: Merritt Parkway N to exit 35, R on High Ridge (restaurant is in shopping center across from Borders Books).

Oriental Gourmet (Chinese) *

214 Sound Beach Avenue, Old Greenwich, 637.1010

For years Olivia and her family have been traveling across town to eat in their favorite Chinese restaurant, where they always order Szechuan Dumplings and Sesame Chicken. Old Greenwich residents have long been in the know about the very good food in this modest restaurant. Eat-in or takeout, this is a real find. This restaurant was the launching place for the owners of Penang and Asiana.

Hours: Monday - Saturday, 11 am - 10 pm; Sunday, noon - 10 pm.

Prices: Entrees, $9 - $14.

Panda Pavilion 3 (Chinese)

420 West Putnam Avenue, 869.1111

We always feel relaxed at this well-priced Chinese restaurant with friendly service. This is a good place for little ones to learn to use chop sticks. Try our favorites: sesame chicken, spicy broccoli, orange beef, ginger beef or the house special bean curd. Free delivery for orders of $20 and over.

Hours: Monday - Thursday, 11:30 am - 9:30 pm;

Friday & Saturday, noon - 10:30 pm; Sunday, noon - 10 pm.

(Lunch is served until 3 pm).

Prices: Lunch entrees, $6 - $10; Dinner entrees, $10 - $28.

Pacifico (Seafood) *

316 Boston Post Road, Port Chester, NY, 914.937.1610

When you are in the mood for a fun evening with terrific food, try this modern, funky restaurant. The excellent "NuevoLatino" seafood is the work of Rafael Palomino, chef and owner of Sonora. The attentive wait staff clearly enjoy their work. The ebony squid ink fettuccini and seared yellow fin tuna are two of our favorites among many of his dazzling creations.

Hours: weekdays, Lunch 12 pm-3 pm;

Dinner 5 pm-10 pm (Friday and Saturday till 11pm); Sunday 3pm - 10pm.

Prices: Appetizers $7 - $10; Lunch entrees, $10 - $20;

Dinner entrees, $18 to $24.

Directions: US-1 almost to the end of Port Chester.

Paesano's Deli (Delicatessen)

146 Mason Street, 625.0040

Popular for breakfast. Fast friendly service. Limited seating.

Hours: Monday - Saturday, 7 am - 5 pm.

Panera (Fast Food) *
10 Westchester Avenue, Port Chester, NY, 914.939.0079
www.Panerabread.com
Located at the movie complex in Port Chester, their soups and sandwiches are a delight. Order at the counter, then have a seat in the large airy dining space and wait for your name to be called. We wish they had shorter lines, although the wait does afford time to decide what to order.
Hours: Monday - Thursday, 6 am - 9 pm;
Friday, Saturday & Sunday, 7 am - 8 pm.

(La) Panètiere (French) **
530 Milton Road, Rye, NY, 914.967.8140
www.lapanetiere.com
For 21 years, one of Westchester County's best, only fifteen minutes away, serving classic French food in an attractive Provençal-style dining room. Relatively quiet, you can have a conversation. For that special evening, the decor, attentive service and delightful food make this restaurant a perfect choice. We recommend the July 14 (Bastille Day) tasting menu. Jackets required, ties preferred.
Hours: Lunch, Tuesday - Friday & Sunday, noon - 2:30 pm;
Dinner, Monday to Saturday, 6 pm - 9:30 pm;
Sunday, 5 pm - 8:30 pm.
Advance reservations recommended, no minimum.
Prices: Lunch entrees, $10 - $18 (appetizer size portions) ;
Dinner entrees, $25 - $36; Tasting menu: 2 course, $52;
3 course, $65; 5 course, $78 or $123 with wine.
Directions: I-95 S to exit 19, R on light to Milton Rd.

Pantanal (Brazilian, Steak)
29 North Main Street, Port Chester, NY, 914.939.6894
A Brazilian restaurant with an earthy flair and generous servings of beans and rice. Entering from the front (Main Street) you will make your way past the bar and pool tables to find a white tableclothed dining room with a friendly wait staff. This restaurant is all about meat. Try their smoked sausage appetizer and the speciality, Rodizio.
Hours: Lunch, Tuesday - Sunday, noon - 3 pm;
Dinner; weekdays, 5 pm - 10:30 pm; Lunch/Dinner,
weekends, noon - 11:30 pm.
Prices: Lunch, weekday specials, $9 - $11 (lunch buffet $9);
Dinner entrees, $17 - $30.

Paradise Bar & Grill (Seafood)

78 Southfield Avenue (Stamford Landing), Stamford, 323.1116
www.paradisebarandgrille.com
Located on the water at the Stamford Landing, near Dolphin Cove. Eating here is like stepping into a tropical island restaurant. In summer, dine open-air on the boardwalk. Try the charcoal-broiled fish entrees. The pizzas are another good choice. Children are welcome.
Hours: Lunch everyday, noon - 3pm; Dinner, every day, 5 pm - 10 pm; Sunday, until 9:30 pm.
During the winter, they may be closed Sunday & Monday evenings and Saturday lunch. In the summer, reservations are accepted for eight or more. In the winter, reservations are accepted for two or more.
Prices: Lunch entrees, $11 - $25, Sunday Brunch, $12 - $15;
Dinner entrees, $9 - $34.
Directions: I-95 N to exit 7, R on Greenwich Avenue, next light is intersection of Greenwich Avenue/Selleck/Southfield. Stamford Landing is .2 miles on the left.

Pasquale Ristorante (Italian)

2 Putnam Avenue (border of Greenwich), Port Chester, NY, 914.934.7770
This family-style restaurant serves traditional southern Italian food in a friendly homespun atmosphere. Stepping into the shoes of the diners to understand the steady following, we realized that dining is not always about the food. One dish we all starred was the Pollo alla Francese.
Hours: Lunch, Tuesday - Friday, noon - 3 pm;
Dinner, Tuesday - Thursday, 4 pm 10 pm, Friday until 11 pm,
Saturday, 3 pm 11 pm; Sunday, 1 pm 9 pm; Closed Monday.
Prices: Lunch entrees, $9 - $13; Dinner entrees, $12 - $26.

Pasta Nostra (Italian)**

116 Washington Street, Norwalk, CT, 203.854.9700

www.PastaNostra.com

You must dine at this restaurant. The spartan, simple decor sends a clear message, this place is about food and service. And, its inventive, continually changing menu is brilliant. If it says the best stuffed pepper you will ever eat, it is. Skip the chicken and devour the seafood. The yummy pastas are only background. Beware: reservations are usually necessary but owner, Chef Bruno often requires a $25 credit card deposit in case you don't show or don't cancel by 3 pm. American Express cards are not accepted.

Hours: Dinner only, Wednesday - Saturday, 6 pm closing.

Prices: Entrees, $20 - $37.

Directions: I-95 North to exit 14, R on Fairfield (first street), bear left at fork on to Washington.

Pasta Vera (Italian) *

48 Greenwich Avenue, 661.9705

www.pastavera.com

This popular, casual restaurant is noted for its homemade pastas. But that doesn't mean pasta is the only tasty choice. We like their other dishes too. First-time visitors should try their homemade ravioli or seafood special. It's a great place for a late lunch. For takeouts, they have a variety of fresh, ready-to-go selections. Order by 4 pm and they will deliver free of charge.

Hours: Take-out, Monday - Saturday, 7 am - 10 pm;

Lunch, Monday - Saturday, 11:30 - 3 pm;

Dinner, Monday - Saturday, 5 pm - 10 pm, Sunday, 4 pm - 9 pm.

Open most holidays, with no vacation closings.

Reservations are accepted for parties of six or more.

Prices: Lunch entrees, $9 - $13; Dinner entrees, $15 - $28.

Pellicci's

96 Stillwater Avenue, Stamford, CT 323.2542

After almost 60 years serving bountiful family-style meals, we agree with Gene Scarpella, Pellicci's knows how to do it. Tucked away on a side street where you might not expect to find a bustling large restaurant, you will be greeted by friendly valet parking in a secure parking lot. Expect good food in this informal, friendly place. First time visitors should try their "Family Style Dinner".

Hours: Everyday, 11:30 am - 11 pm; Sunday, kitchen closes at 10 pm.

Prices: Entrees, $9 to $19, Family style per person $16.

Penang Grill (Asian)
55 Lewis Street, 861.1988
Casual dining with very good PanAsian food. When you want something flavorful and unique, head to this small, established restaurant. The service is friendly and attentive. The refreshing mango chicken is our favorite. Popular for takeout.
Hours: Monday - Thursday, 11 am - 10 pm;
Friday & Saturday, 11 am - 11 pm; Sunday, noon - 10 pm.
Lunch menu is served until 3 pm.
Table space is limited. No reservations accepted.
Prices: Lunch entrees, $7 - $8; Dinner entrees, $12 - $20.

Per Voi (Italian)
23 North Main Street, Port Chester, NY 914.937.3200
When you are in the mood for Frank Sinatra, good home-made marinara sauce in an old fashioned, comfortable surrounding, Per Voi (For You) is for you. This 12-year old Port Chester mainstay can seat 130 people and on weekends it is often full. If you have a favorite dish which is not on the menu, ask the chef to make it for you.
Hours: Monday - Thursday, 11:30 am -11 pm;
Friday, Saturday, Sunday, 5 pm - midnight.
Prices: Entrees, $5 - $30.

Pierangelo (Italian)**
355 Greenwich Avenue, 869.3411
The decor in this 10-table restaurant is sophisticated and puts you in the mood for a nice experience. Usually it is quiet enough to have a conversation. A devoted following keeps this warmly lit restaurant busy. On Sundays, we found the service annoyingly slow. On other days it has been fabulous. We especially like the tuna, salmon, fettuccini and chicken with goat cheese. Good wine list with many choices by the glass.
Hours: Open every day, Lunch, noon - 3pm;
Dinner 5:30 - 10 pm.
Prices: Lunch and Dinner entrees, $20 - $40.

TIP: TOUR GREENWICH KITCHENS
Often in June, the Old Greenwich-Riverside Community Center (OGRCC), has organized a tour of the ultimate kitchens in Old Greenwich and Riverside. Luncheon in a private home can be ticketed separately. For more information contact the OGRCC office at 637-3659.

Piero's (Italian)

44 South Regent Street, Port Chester, NY, 914.937.2904

Casual, off-the-beaten-path Italian. This little restaurant, with decor that doesn't seem to change, has a loyal following. They like being greeted by the owner and being treated like family by the waiters.

Hours: Lunch, Tuesday - Friday, noon - 2:30 pm;
Dinner, Tuesday - Thursday, 5 pm 9:30 pm;
Friday, 5 pm - 10:30 pm; Saturday, 2 pm - 10:30 pm;
Sunday, 2 pm - 9:30 pm.

Prices: $15 - $21. Visa and Master Card only.

Directions: US-1 S thru Port Chester, R on Westchester, L on South Regent.

Pizza Express (Pizza) *

160 Hamilton Avenue, 622.1693

The Winner! This friendly, small neighborhood pizzeria won the Town competition for the best pizza. They have free delivery and will fax you their menu. Try their homemade soup or ravioli.

Hours: Monday Saturday, 10 am - 10 pm; Sunday, 11 am - 10 pm.

Pizza Factory (Pizza)

380 Greenwich Avenue, 661.5188

Not everyone can agree on the best pizza place, but Pizza Factory's pizza is always competing for the top of the list. Be sure to try their gorgonzola salad and four cheese pizza. They have table service, carry out and delivery. They accept credit cards or a Greenwich check.

Hours: everyday, 11:30 am - 10 pm.

Pizza Glenville (Pizza) *

243 Glenville Road, 532.1691

Glenville residents, as well as people all over town, love Glenville Pizza. It is one of the few places serving by the slice. They were one point from winning the town pizza contest. No deliveries. No credit cards, but they will accept a check.

Hours: Monday - Saturday, 10:30 am - 10:30 pm; Sunday, noon - 10 pm.

Pizza Hut (Pizza)

19 Glenville Street, 531.4411

They may be a chain, but we still like their pan pizza.
Major credit cards accepted. No deliveries.

Hours: Sunday - Thursday, 11 am - 10 pm (Sunday from noon); Friday & Saturday, 11 am - 11 pm.

Pizza Post (Pizza)

522 East Putnam Avenue, 661.0909
A local favorite. No deliveries. No credit cards, but they accept checks.
Hours: Monday - Thursday, 11 am - 10 pm;
Friday & Saturday, 11 am - 11 pm; Sunday, noon -10 pm.

Planet Pizza (Pizza)

28 Railroad Avenue, 622.0999
Traditional New York City-style pizzeria in a central Greenwich location next to the theater. Try their "penne planet." Clean, well-lighted dining area. They will deliver.
Hours: Monday - Thursday, 10 am - 11 pm;
Friday & Saturday, 10 am - midnight; Sunday, 10 am - 10:30 pm.

Plateau (Asian)

25 Bank Street, Stamford, 961.9875
http://www.culinarymenus.com/plateau.htm
Sophisticated, minimalist decor, friendly service and good cuisine make this South Asian restaurant a good choice. The food is a mix from Malaysia, Vietnam and Thailand. We like the sesame tofu and basil shrimp. Please don't leave without having fried bananas for dessert.
Hours: Lunch, weekdays, 11:30 am to 3 pm,
Saturday and Sunday from from 12:30 pm;
Dinner, Monday - Thursday, 5 pm - 10 pm,
Friday and Saturday 3:30 - 11:30pm; Sunday, 3:30 pm - 10 pm.
Prices: Lunch entrees, $7 - $12; Dinner entrees, $8 - $25;
Pre-theater menu, $25.

Plum Pure Foods (TakeOut) *

236 East Putnam Avenue, Cos Cob, 869.7586
www.PlumPureFoods.com
Plum provides delicious takeout foods made primarily from natural products grown locally. They have something for everyone: soups, sandwiches and hot entrees. The owners aim to please with their food and their service. One evening I called at closing time just before a major holiday. They happily agreed to stay open until I arrived. They are exceptional caterers. Plum scored at the top during our 2005 Catering Contest.
Hours: Closed Sunday & Monday; Tuesday-Friday, 7:30 am - 6:00 pm, Saturday, 8:30 am-3:30 pm.

Polpo (Italian)**

554 Old Post Road # 3, Greenwich, 629.1999
www.polporestaurant.com
This out-of-the-way Italian Restaurant is a popular Greenwich destination for those in the know. It is located in a charming 100 year-old stone house. The restaurant has good vibes. The ambiance is warm, the service is attentive and gracious. Diners always seem to be in a festive, noisy mood. Quieter tables are upstairs. The lively piano music is downstairs. Allow time for making decisions- the menu is filled with excellent choices. Don't miss the polpo (octopus) appetizer.
Hours: Monday - Thursday, 11:45 am - 10 pm;
Friday, until 11 pm, Saturday, 5 pm - 11 pm, Sunday, 3 pm - 10 pm.
Prices: Entrees, $19 - $36.

Pomodoro (Italian)

1247 East Putnam Avenue (Riverside Shopping Center), 698.7779
www.pomodoroRiverside.com
Friendly, casual, family dining. A popular spot with youngsters. If there were a contest for the largest portions, this small, charmingly decorated restaurant would win. With their generous portions, your leftovers will likely feed you the next day.
Hours: Monday - Thursday, 11 am - 10 pm;
Friday & Saturday, 11am - 11 pm; Sunday, 11 am - 10 pm.
Prices: Lunch, Subs & Wraps, $8 - $11; Medium Pizzas, $12 - $15;
Dinner entrees, $8 - $18. They have a children's menu.

Porterhouse (Steak)

124 Washington Street, South Norwalk, CT, 203.855.0441
www.PorterhouseRestaurant.com
Steaks and desserts, served in a warm, friendly atmosphere. They have an excellent wine list. Favorites here - the calamari with chili sauce and porterhouse steaks.
Hours: Lunch, weekdays noon - 4 pm;
Dinner, Monday - Thursday, 4 pm 10 pm; Friday & Saturday, 4 pm - 11 pm, Sunday, 4 pm - 9 pm.
Prices: Lunch entrees, $10 - $16 (wraps and salads);
Dinner entrees, $21 - $41.
Directions: I94 N to exit 14, R on Fairfield (first street), bear L at fork onto Washington.

Putnam Restaurant (American, Casual)

373 Greenwich Avenue, 869.4683

This inexpensive, informal hometown restaurant, with clouds painted on the ceiling, has been in business since 1955. We hope it stays. Their menu is like a diner's with a large number of selections. Their specials are always a good choice. We also like the Gorgonzola salad and Fettuccine Alfredo. Remember to stop here for a traditional breakfast.

Hours: Every day, even most holidays, 7 am - 10 pm.

Prices: Entrees, $10 - $16.

Q (American, Casual, Barbeque) *

112 North Main Street, Port Chester, NY, 914.933.7427

www.QrestaurantAndBar.com

We are grateful to Jeffrey and Jennifer Kohn, owners of the terrific Kneaded Bread, for opening another top-notch place. They went on a 25-restaurant barbecue tasting journey before opening Q, a slightly Spartan barbecue restaurant (order at the counter and they bring the food to your table). Thank heavens they took this journey and now we can satisfy our cravings for authentic pulled pork and beef brisket. For sides, order the biscuits, collard greens and the baked beans.

Hours: Monday - Saturday, noon - 9:30 pm (Friday and Saturday to 10:30); Sunday, 1 pm to 9 pm.

Prices: Sides, $3 - $8; Entrees, $8-$20.

Quattro Pazzi (Italian)

165 Fillow Street, Norwalk, CT

(At the Oak Hills Public Golf Course), 203.855.1800

www.QuattroPazzi.com

This large restaurant overlooks the Norwalk Town Golf course. Eating here gives one the distinct impression of dining at a private country club. Unfortunately the service and food are not on par with the attractiveness of the restaurant.

Hours: Closed Monday: Tuesday - Saturday, 11 am - 10 pm; Sunday, 11 am - 9 pm.

Prices: Entrees, $16 - $27.

RESTAURANTS

Quattro Regali (Italian)*
245 Hope Street, Stamford, 964.1801 or 249.2665
A wonderful pasta restaurant tucked away in the Glenbrook area of Stamford. This place hits the spot when we want to have a hearty bowl of pasta with friends. This restaurant is small, popular, noisy, and lots of fun. Try the fettuccini á la Mitty or Capellini Poverino.
Hours: Lunch, Tuesday Friday, 11:30 am - 3 pm;
Dinner, Tuesday Friday, 5 pm - 10 pm; Saturday, 5 pm - 10:30 pm;
Sunday, 5 pm - 9 pm.
Main course price range: Lunch, $8 - $15; Dinner, $13 - $25.
Directions: I-95 N to exit 8, stay straight on South State Street, L on Canal, R on Tresser (US-1), L on Glenbrook Rd, continue straight onto Hope.

Ramen Stand (Japanese)
Behind Fjord Fisheries, 137 River Road, Cos Cob, 661.5006
Run by Mr. Isal Kato, the Fjord Fisheries sushi chef. When the red lanterns are lit, drive behind the fish shop and you will find him serving bowls of soup over ramen noodles under an outdoor tent.
Hours: Tuesday - Sunday, 6 pm to 9:30 pm (may be closed in the Winter)
Prices: $7.50 per bowl.

Rebecca's (American, New) **
265 Glenville Road, 532.9270
www.rebeccas.moonfruit.com
www.rkateliers.com
One of the best restaurants in town. This Manhattan-chic restaurant run by a husband and wife team is tucked in southwestern Greenwich. It serves modern American cuisine with a French flair. Rebecca Kirhoffer has assembled a sophisticated wine list to match her husband Chef Reza Khorshidi's awesome food. The service is sometimes impervious. The restaurant has a sleek modern look, complete with a large window that allows you to see the kitchen.
Hours: Lunch, Tuesday - Friday, 11:30 am - 2:30 pm;
Dinner, Tuesday - Thursday, 5:30 pm -9:30 pm;
Friday & Saturday, 5:30 pm - 10:30 pm.
Be sure to make a reservation well in advance (a month's notice wouldn't hurt), although you might be able to drop in and eat at the bar.
Prices: Lunch entrees, $25 - $25; Dinner entrees, $34 - $50.

River Cat Grill (American, New)

148 Rowayton Avenue, Rowayton, CT, 203.854.0860
www.rivercatgrill.com

If you have memories of the Greenwich Boxing Cat, you will find many similarities here. Like the Boxing Cat, there is an eclectic menu, but we recommend the tasty thin crust pizzas. They have a large selection of wines by the glass. If you are in Rowaton, you will enjoy this cozy, cheery spot. Check website for music schedule.

Hours: Lunch, Tuesday - Friday & Sunday, 11:30 am - 3 pm;
Dinner, Monday - Saturday, 5:30 pm - 10 pm
(open to 10:30 pm on Friday & Saturday); Sunday, 5 pm - 9 pm.
The bar stays open later.

Prices: Lunch entrees, $12-$16; Dinner entrees, $12 $37, pizzas $11 - $13 Wine by the glass, $7 - $18.

Directions: I-95 N, exit 12, Rte 136 toward Rowayton.

Rodney's Roadhouse (Fast Food)

Glenville Road

Nothing beats a tasty hot dog. Do you like your's with chili, mustard, cheese, relish or all of the above? Joe Kralik serves hotdogs, hamburgers, steak sandwiches and more from his roadside lunch stand nestled in the pretty little park on Glenville Road.

Hours: summertime, weekdays, 10 am - 2:30 pm.

Roger Sherman Inn (Swiss)

195 Oenoke Ridge Road (Route 124), New Canaan, CT,
203.966.4541
www.rogershermaninn.com
Built in the 1700s, it is one of the oldest and prettiest inns in Fairfield County. The Swiss owners serve continental cuisine with Swiss specialties. Try the sliced tenderloin of veal with mushroom cream sauce. Be sure to order the superb chocolate souffle in advance. On Sunday evenings, November through March, they serve raclette and fondue. The inn is well equipped for elegant parties. It can accommodate groups from 8 to 180 guests. Ask to see their typical wedding banquet menu.
Hours: Breakfast for guests only;
Lunch, Tuesday - Saturday, noon to 1:45,
Sunday brunch, 11:30 - 2pm (not served January March);
Dinner, weekdays, 6pm - 8 pm; weekends, 6 pm - 9:30 pm.
It's wise to make reservations in advance.
Prices: Lunch entrees, $13 - $19; Dinner entrees, $26 - $38;
Sunday brunch, prix fixe $36 per person,
Sunday Raclette / Fondue, $43 per person.
Directions: Merritt N exit 37, L onto Rte 124 N 2 miles, Rte 124 makes a right at Cherry Street. Next L (light) on Main continue on 124 for 1 mile. Inn is on the right.

Rotisserie (American, Casual, Fast-Food)

280 Railroad Avenue, Greenwich, 661.0100
www.willmortonsrotisserie.com
As soon as we tasted the North Carolina-style pulled pork sandwich, we predicted this small, "quick-casual" restaurant would soon be a US chain. Will Morton knows what people want - healthy food, good flavors and reasonable prices.
Hours: Monday - Saturday, Lunch 11:30 am - 2 pm;
Dinner, 5 pm - 9 pm.
Prices: Sandwiches and Entrees, $9 -$14; wine by the glass, $7 - $9.
They accept Master Card & Visa.

Rowayton Seafood Company (Seafood) *

89 Rowayton Avenue, Norwalk, CT, 203.866.4488

www.coastalprovisions.com/rowaytonseafoodrestaurant.htm

Small and popular, informal and relaxed, just right for summer dining. A good place to bring landlocked visitors for lobster and a view of the water. If you're not in the mood for lobster, try their seafood stew, grilled tuna or fresh oysters.

Hours: Lunch, every day, 11:30 am - 3 pm; a limited menu is sometimes available from 3 pm - 5 pm;

Dinner every day. Sunday - Thursday, 5pm - 9:30pm (Friday & Saturday until 11 pm).

On weekends, be sure to make reservations well in advance.

Prices: Lunch entrees, $11 - $17; Dinner entrees, $23 - $30; Lobster $26 per pound.

Directions: I-95 N to exit 12, Rte 136 towards Rowayton for 1.5 miles to stop sign, 500 yards on R.

Savvy (American, New) *

26 Locust Avenue, New Canaan, CT, 203.972.3303

www.savvy-restaurant.com

When you want to dine in a lively, noisy, bustling restaurant and need a menu to satisfy different tastes, head to Savvy. You will be pleased with the welcoming service and the creative dishes, many of which have a European accent. Save room for the mighty good desserts. The decor is as modern as the food. If you are yearning for conversation and weather permits, dine on the outside terrace.

Prices: Lunch entrees, $10 - $15; Dinner entrees, $23 - $34.

Hours: Lunch, Monday - Saturday, noon - 2:30;

Dinner every day, 5pm - 10pm, Sunday to 9pm.

TIP: GREEK FESTIVAL

In October every year, the Church of the Archangels, (Bedford & Third Streets), Stamford CT has a festival with authentic Greek food. To find out the exact date or request a take out, call 348.4216.

Silvermine Tavern (American, Casual)

194 Perry Avenue, Norwalk, CT, 203.847.4558, 888.693.9967
www.SilvermineTavern.com
A 15 - 20 minute drive from Greenwich, this 18th century Colonial inn, situated right on the river, is a very good choice for Sunday brunch. The reasonably priced buffet has a selection of dishes to delight everyone. We especially enjoy their French toast, yogurt with strawberry preserves and their justifiably famous buns. The atmosphere is informal and children are always welcome. The inn is very spacious, but it is also popular, so arrive early.
Hours: Lunch, Monday - Saturday, noon - 3:00 pm;
Sunday Brunch, 11 am - 2:30 pm;
Dinner, Wednesday-Thursday, 6 pm - 9 pm;
Friday & Saturday, 6 pm-10pm; Sunday, 3:30 pm - 9pm;
Brunch reservations given only for parties of seven or more.
The Dining room is often closed on Tuesdays and is closed Monday in January through April.
Prices: Sunday brunch is $21 for adults, $9.95 for children ages 5 - 10, children under 5 are free; Lunch entrees, $10 - $16;
Dinner entrees, $19 - $31.
Directions: Merritt Parkway N to Exit 40A, R on Main Street, R on Perry Avenue. R on Silvermine Road.

Skylight Café (American, Casual)

YWCA, 259 East Putnam Avenue, 869.6501
A well-priced, bright and sunny eatery run by Mary & Martha's Catering. You can enjoy a continental breakfast, a healthy lunch or just grab a freshly baked muffin. They make the best chicken-salad sandwich in town. Once a month they serve afternoon tea. Call for dates and reservations. Children are always welcome! No credit cards.
Hours: weekdays, 9 am - 6 pm, Saturday, 9 am - 1pm.

Smokey Joe's BarBQ (American, Casual, Barbeque) *

1308 East Main Street (US-1), Stamford, 406.0605
This is the best Texas BarBQ this side of Fort Worth. Casual and inexpensive, Smokey Joe's offers a great variety of meats, gumbos and side dishes, in a cafeteria-style restaurant setting. The servings (on paper, not porcelain) are large, especially the Texas size. Order their beef brisket and pulled pork, with a side of collard greens and sweet potato fries.
Hours: Monday - Thursday, 11:30 am - 9:30 pm; Friday & Saturday, 11:30 am - 10:30 pm; Sunday, 11:30 am - 9:30 pm.
Prices: Sandwiches, $3 - $8; two-meat combos, $10 - $14.
Directions: I-95 N to exit 9, R on US-1.

Solaia (Italian)*

363 Greenwich Avenue, 622.6400

www.SolaiaEnoteca.com

Right on the avenue is an active "enoteca" - an Italian wine bar with small plate tastings. The wine list is extensive and many good wines are offered by the glass. The service is cheery and food in the small 10-table wine cave is creative and flavorful. Yummy soups and tastings are fun to share.

Hours: every day, noon - 10 pm (Friday & Saturday until 11 pm).

Prices: Entrees, $15 - 30. Wine by the glass, $10 - $15, but one wine is an astonishing $77 a glass.

SoNo Baking Company & Café (Fast Food, Bakery)

101 South Water St., South Norwalk, 203.847.7666

www.sonobaking.com

A dear friend and food writer, first introduced us to this place, saying "its amazing, full of some of the most delicious pastries and breads I have ever tried." Soups and sandwiches are good here, too. Its not surprising, the owners are John Barricelli, Senior Food Editor for Martha Stewart Living and Margot Olshan, Commissary Chef for Martha Stewart.

Hours: Closed Monday: Tuesday - Saturday, 7 am - 6 pm;

Sunday, 7 am-5 pm.

Prices: Sandwiches, $5 - $8.

SoNo Seaport Seafood (Seafood)

100 Water Street, South Norwalk, CT, 203.854.9483

www.sonoseaportseafood.com

A very informal, fun spot on the water to have lobster or fish and chips. Bring your children. Nice outside deck with raw bar.

Hours: every day. November - April, 11 am - 9 pm;

May - October, 11 am - 10 pm.

Reservations accepted for parties of six or more.

Main course price range: $8 - $20, market for lobster, crab & mussels.

Directions: I-95 N, exit 14, turn R. Go straight to intersection of Washington and Water, R before the bridge. Restaurant is 100 yards on the L in SoNo Square.

Sonora (LatinAmerican, new) *

179 Rectory Street, Port Chester, NY, 914.933.0200
www.sonorany.com and www.pasioncatering.com
We continue to sing the praises of this popular, out-of-the-way restaurant. The total experience—unique decor, skillful service, and "LatinAmerican food with a flair"—makes us happy. Start with the fresh guacamole followed by one of their many fish entrees or the Cuban Chicken. Be sure to save room for passion fruit flan. To add to the fun, Chef Palomino teaches cooking classes, and on Wednesday nights he has price fixed tapas and wine dinners.
Prices: Lunch entrees, $9 - $17, Dinner entrees, $21 - $29,
Price fixed Wed dinner, $45.
Hours: Lunch, Tuesday Friday, noon - 3 pm;
Dinner, everyday, 5 pm - 10 pm (Friday & Saturday until 11 pm).
Directions: Post Road to Main Street in Port Chester. R on Rectory.

Splash Café (Seafood)

Inn at Long Shore, 260 South Compo Road, Westport, CT, 203.454.7798
www.DecaroRestaurantGroup.com
A Baang relative with the same delicious eclectic Pacific Rim menu. A lovely setting on the water, which makes this a good summer destination. During the winter when you cannot dine outside, it may not be worth the trip. Enjoy dishes like Chilean sea bass baked in a banana leaf, Ahi Tuna or Shanghai beef. Located in a town park, the Inn has a great outdoor terrace right along the water with a bar and live music. It's a great place to watch the sunset. The bar is open late and is an evening hot spot.
Hours: Summer: Lunch, Monday - Saturday, noon - 2:30 pm;
Dinner, every night, 5 pm - 9 pm, Friday & Saturday until 11 pm;
Sunday, 5 pm - 9 pm.
Winter: Closed Mondays: Sunday Brunch, 11 am - 3 pm;
Dinner, Tuesday - Saturday, 5:30 pm - 10 pm,
(Friday & Saturday to 11 pm), Sunday, 5 pm - 9 pm.
Prices: Lunch entrees, $11 - $18; Sunday Brunch buffet, $30 per person, Children age 12 & under, $15 (Brunch is more expensive on holidays); Dinner entrees, $21 - $38.
Directions: I-95, exit 17, 2 lights to stop sign, L onto Riverside Avenue, R onto Bridge. R at first light after bridge, R at 1st light (look for golf course).

Starbucks (Coffee)
- 301 Greenwich Avenue, 661.3042
- 60 East Putnam Avenue, 629.0432
- 147 East Putnam Avenue, Cos Cob, 661.1543
- 1253 East Putnam Avenue, Riverside, 698.1790

www.starbucks.com
One of the few places you can get your coffee made with soy milk.
Hours: Monday Saturday, 5:30am - 10 pm
(Friday & Saturday until 11 pm); Sunday, 7 am - 10 pm.

Streets of London (Seafood, Fast Food)
456 Main Avenue (Route 7), Norwalk, CT, 203.846.9560
The best fish and chips this side of London, served in a fast food atmosphere. Other English specialties such as shepherd's pie and steak and kidney pie are also available. Foods are fried in corn and canola oils. Many of our English friends require a weekly dose.
Hours: every day, 11 am - 9 pm.
Directions: Exit 15 Route 7 stay on all way (to end) R down hill DMV in front make a R and SOL on L side next to Kinkos.

Subway Sandwich (Fast Food)
(Top of Avenue) 28 Greenwich Avenue, 622.1515
(Bottom of Avenue) 401 Greenwich Avenue, 422.2218
www.Subway.com
Here's the place for those famous sandwiches made with bread freshly baked on the premises.
Hours: every day, 9 am - 10 pm.

Sundown Saloon (American, Casual)
403 Greenwich Avenue, 629.8212
www.sundownsaloon.com
This is an interesting combination of an adult bar and an informal, cute restaurant serving casual food with a western theme. There is a special menu for "little dudes." Be sure to order the lemonade. The friendly staff, and crayons for writing on the tablecloths, make this a good choice for the whole family. The bar is a popular afterwork meeting place after work.
Hours: Lunch, every day, 11:30 am - 5 pm; Dinner, everyday, 5 pm - 11 pm (Friday & Saturday until midnight). Do not accept reservations.
Prices: Lunch entrees, $8 - $13; Dinner entrees, $10 - $20.

T Party Antiques and Tea Room (Tea)

2 Squab Lane, Darien, 203.662.9689
www.TPartyAntiques.com
Oh, what a delightful place for tea. The setting is an 1890 farmhouse, filled with charming childhood antiques and tea collectibles. Invite a special friend, daughter or granddaughter, and have a "Grand Afternoon Tea" with a variety of tiny sandwiches, freshly baked scones, clotted cream and jam and sweets you will adore. You will leave with a smile and a memory to keep forever. Be sure to make a reservation.
Hours: Wednesday - Friday, seatings, noon & 2 pm;
Saturday, seatings 1 pm & 3 pm.
Prices: Petit Afternoon Tea, $12, Grand Afternoon Tea, $17.

Taco Bell (Fast Food)

1371 East Putnam Avenue, Old Greenwich, 698.2290
www.TacoBell.com
Hours: Open every day, 8 am-1 pm,
Friday and Saturday to 2 pm(drive thru)

Tandoori (Indian)

- 163 North Main Street, Port Chester, NY, 914.937.2727 *
- 1114 East Putnam Avenue (next to Howard Johnson's in Riverside), 637.4110

www.Tandooritasteofindia.com
It's nice to have good Indian restaurants close by. Try their fixed price buffet lunch on weekdays. Their chicken tikka masala and shrimp malabar are favorites. We always order sweet lassi. Given the choice, we prefer the Port Chester location.
Hours: Sunday brunch, noon 2:30;
Lunch, Monday - Saturday, buffet, noon - 2:30 pm;
Dinner, every day, 5 pm - 10 pm.
Prices: Lunch buffet, $10; Dinner entrees, $14 - $20;
Weekend buffet, $12.

Telluride (American, New) *
245 Bedford St, Stamford, 357.7679
www.telluriderestaurant.com
Innovative western cuisine in a casual, Western mountain ambiance with friendly service. Dip your bread in the salsa and have a good time. Our favorites are the informal foods such as Boulder crab cakes, cowboy empanadas, smoky mountain pizza or pistachio crusted chicken salad with pears. The extensive wine list offers 25 wines by the glass. We like the wine recommendations written on the menu for each dish.
Hours: Lunch, weekdays, 11:30 am - 4:30 pm;
Dinner, weekdays, 5 pm - 10 pm; Saturday 5 pm - 11 pm;
Sunday, 5 pm - 9 pm. Closed on major holidays.
Reservations: 6 or more for lunch; no limit for dinner.
Prices: Lunch entrees, $12 - $21; Dinner entrees, $12 - $48;
7oz glass of wine, $8 - $18.
Directions: I-95 North to Exit 8 Atlantic St. At the light at the end of the ramp go L onto Atlantic St. Follow until it becomes one way Bedford Street. Telluride is one block up on the R. They have parking in the front and the rear but it is still difficult to find a spot.

Tengda Asian Bistro (Japanese, Asian)
21 Field Point Road, 625.5338
http://www.tengdaasianbistro.com
The decor is hip factory, with lots of metal, noise, and typically filled with chic clientele in a festive mood. The sushi, which includes many special creations such as our favorite, the magical roll, is popular. If you are not having sushi, we recommend skipping the other entrees and having the Tengda Classics- generous servings of tempura, teriyaki or mango chicken. We like the cheerful, fast-paced service.
Hours: Lunch, every day, 11:30 to 3 pm, starts noon on Sunday;
Dinner, every day 5 pm to 10:00 pm, Friday & Saturday to 11:30 pm.
Prices: Lunch boxes, $9 - $14, Lunch entrees, $7 - $11;
Dinner entrees, $15 - $20, sushi, $5 - $18.

Terra Ristorante Italiano (Italian)

156 Greenwich Avenue, 629.5222

Walking along Greenwich Avenue, it's hard to escape the wonderful smells coming from their woodburning ovens serving up Northern Italian food such as our favorite the Pollo Arrosto. A lively, hip trattoria. If you want to escape the noise, dine on the terrace.

Hours: Lunch, Monday - Saturday, 11:30 - 3 pm;

Dinner, Monday - Saturday, 5 pm - 10 pm (Friday & Saturday to 11 pm);

Sunday, 6 pm - 9:30 pm

Small menu available 2:30 pm -5:30 pm.

Prices: Lunch entrees, $11 - $22; Dinner entrees, $15 - $38, Pizzas, $13 to $15.

Thali (Indian, Fusion) **

87 Main Street, New Canaan, CT 203.972.8332

www.thali.com

This is not just another Indian restaurant. A waterfall rolls across the ceiling of what was formerly a bank. Expect delightful, unusual flavors. Many of the dishes seem to be a fusion of French and southern Indian with a touch of whimsy. Our mouth waters at the mention of their chat appetizers particularly the ragda patties, jalapeno nan and the Navrattan Korma. Yes, their chicken tikka masala is also very good. David Rosengarten says this is the best Indian restaurant in the U.S. We haven't tried them all, but he could be right.

Hours: Lunch, everyday, noon - 2:30 pm;

Dinner, Monday - Thursday, 5 pm - 10 pm,

Friday & Saturday, 5 pm - 11 pm, Sunday, 4 pm - 9 pm;

Prices: Dinner entrees,$13 - $20; Sunday Brunch, $17.

Top Dog (Fast Food)
118 River Rd. Ext., near E. Putnam Ave., Cos Cob, 203.661.0573
Don't think for a second that Greenwich residents, age 2 to 92, aren't fond of good hot dogs. This friendly little "diner style" restaurant has been recognized as one of the best hot dog places on the East Coast. So take a stool and enjoy their onion rings, sweet potato fries and dogs with or without chili.
Hours: every day, 11 am - 7 pm (Friday, Saturday & Sunday until 6 pm).

That Little Italian Restaurant (Italian)
228 Mill Street, Byram, 531.7500
Tucked away on a small street in the Byram neighborhood of Greenwich, this cute restaurant has a loyal following despite its timidly flavored cuisine. It is a comfortable place for families, where children enjoy large plates of spaghetti and meat balls. Shrimp Scampi and Penne Florentine are also favorites. Paul Vitiello, owner, received the Chambers 2005 Small Business Award.
Hours: Closed Monday: Lunch, Tuesday - Friday, 11:30 am - 2:30 pm;
Dinner, Tuesday - Sunday, 5 pm - 9:30 pm
Friday & Saturday until 10:30 pm.
Reservations are accepted for parties of 6 or more.
Prices: Lunch, entrees, $10 - $15;
Dinner, entrees, $13 - $23, medium pizzas, $10 - $15.

Thataway Cafe (American, Casual)
409 Greenwich Avenue, 622.0947
www.ThatawayCafe.com
A popular, pub-style, casual restaurant located at the end of the Avenue. The large outdoor patio is a delightful place to dine in the summer. Try the Avenue Sandwich or Whichaway Burger. Top the evening off with Appleberry Crumb Pie or Oreo Decadence. Tuesdays and Sundays are Karoke night. Thursday evenings from 9 pm to midnight is Jam Night (Sporting events may interfere with Karoke and Jam).
Hours: Lunch, every day, 11:30 am - 5 pm
(Sunday Brunch, 11 am - 3 pm);
Dinner, Monday, Thursday, 5 pm - 11 pm
(Friday & Saturday until midnight).
Bar is open until 1 am, Monday to Sunday, Saturday until midnight.
Reservations are accepted for parties of 6 or more.
Prices: Lunch, entrees, $10 - $12; Dinner, entrees, $10 - $25.

Thomas Henkelmann (French) **
(at the Homestead Inn), 420 Field Point Road, 869.7500
www.ThomasHenkelmann.com
Nestled in Belle Haven, in a lovely, formal inn with antiques and a garden setting, there is a restaurant with delicious contemporary French food. We rate this as one of Greenwich's best. The owner and chef, Thomas Henkelmann, is regarded as one of the premier chefs in the US. The wait staff is attentive, polite and informed. Men should wear a jacket and tie.
Hours: Breakfast only for the inn guests;
Lunch, weekdays, noon - 2:30 pm;
Dinner, every day, 6 pm - 9 pm; Closed the first two weeks in March. Closed Sundays from mid-July through August.
Make reservations well in advance.
Prices: Lunch entrees, $35 - $55; Dinner entrees, $55 - $75.

Upper Crust Bagel Company (American, Casual)
197 Sound Beach Avenue, Old Greenwich, 698.0079
www.UpperCrustBagel.com
A good place to sit down and chat while having a deli sandwich and a fruit smoothie. They have tasty old-fashioned kettleboiled and hearthbaked bagels, as well as gourmet spreads and coffees. They accept checks but no credit cards.
Hours: weekdays, 6 am - 4pm;
Saturday, 7 am - 4 pm; Sunday, 7 am - 3pm.

Utsav (Indian)
19 High Ridge Road (Bulls Head Shopping Center),
 Stamford, CT 359.8977
This small Indian "bistro" is a pleasant find. Stylish, attentive service and good dishes make a happy evening. Their meat dishes are either lamb or chicken. They have a nice selection of vegetarian specials, our favorite is the Avial Malabar.
Hours: Open everyday: Lunch buffet, 11:30 am - 3 pm;
Dinner, 5 pm - 10 pm.
Prices: Lunch boxes to go, $8 - $10, Lunch Buffet $9 - $10;
Dinner entrees, $12 - $20.

Valbella (Italian)**

1309 East Putnam Avenue, Riverside, 637.1155
http://www.valbellact.com/
Excellent Italian food in a dressy decor. Everyone gets good service, even the celebrities who dine here frequently. There is something wonderful on the menu for everyone. Top off your meal with a chocolate souffle. They have a spectacular wine cellar with 850 wines to choose from. A Town favorite and our vote as the best Italian restaurant in town. If only it were less noisy. Reservations required.
Hours: Lunch, weekdays, 11:30 am - 3:30 pm;
Dinner, Monday - Saturday, 5 pm - 10 pm (11 pm Friday and Saturday).
Prices: Lunch entrees, $15 - $20; Dinner entrees, $24 - $40.

Versailles (French) *

315 Greenwich Avenue, 661.6634
A small, very French bistro with a front counter full of pastries and croissants that will make your day worth living. Just the right place to meet a friend for lunch to enjoy a quiche and a selection from their repertoire of desserts. We have an excuse for trying the desserts. We hope you can figure one out too. The good food and atmosphere are reminiscent of our Paris favorites.
Hours: Breakfast, weekdays, 7:30 am - 11 pm (Saturday starts at 8 am);
Lunch, everyday, noon - 3 pm (Sunday Brunch 11 am - 4 pm);
Dinner, everyday, 5:30 pm - 8 pm.
Prices: Breakfast entrees, $8 -10; Lunch, set menu at $17 or $11 - $15; Dinner entrees, $20 - $28.

Villarina's (TakeOut, Italian)

551 East Putnam Avenue, Cos Cob, 422.0174
On your way home, grab a dinner like eggplant rollatini, lasagna, or stuffed pork chops for your family or guests. Everyone will think you are a great cook!
Hours: Closed Sunday: Weekdays, 10:30 am - 7 pm;
Saturday, 11 am - 6 pm.

Vuli (Italian)

Stamford Marriott, 2 Stamford Forum (Atlantic Street), 323.5300
www.vulirestaurant.com
The gimmick of this restaurant is that it rotates (very slowly) on top of the Marriott Hotel. Unfortunately, its views do not show much of downtown Stamford. We find the food uneven and the service indifferent. Live music nightly. Dress is upscale, jackets preferred.
Hours: Lunch, weekdays, 11:30 am - 5 pm;
Dinner, Monday - Thursday, 5 pm - 10 pm;
Friday & Saturday 5 pm - 11 pm.
Prices: Lunch entrees, $17 - $26, Dinner entrees, $22- $36.
Directions: I-95 N to exit 8, L on Atlantic.

Wasabi Chi (Asian Fusion, Japanese-French) *

2 South Main Street, South Norwalk, CT, 203.286.0181
www.wasabichi.com
When you enter a trendy restaurant, where the bar is prominent and colorful drinks are being served, you don't always expect the food to be stunning. But we loved the food, even without drinks. The creative combinations were fresh and fun. By all means have the tuna pizza. We also recommend the wasabi calamari and the scallops.
Hours: Lunch, weekdays, noon to 2:30 pm;
Dinner, Sunday - Thursday, 5 pm - 10 pm, Friday & Saturday, to 11 pm.
Prices: Lunch entrees, $13 - $15 ; Dinner entrees $21 - $55 (Kobe steak), small plates, $11 - $18.

Waterfront Grille (American, Casual)

42 Westchester Avenue, Port Chester, NY 914.933.2606
Located right next to the movie theater complex, we were hoping to find a new seafood restaurant. What we found was a dark, giant sports bar, lounge serving casual food.
Hours: Every day, 11:30 am to 10:30 pm, bar open later.
Prices: Lunch entrees, $6 - $15; Dinner entrees, $10 - $30.

Waterfront Roasters Café (Coffee)

106 Purdy Street, Port Chester, NY 800.690.7230
The Café of Empire Coffee, a company roasting five million pounds a year, is bound to draw you inside by aroma alone. Drinking coffee in the building where it is roasted will bring your coffee tastes to a new level. How could it be fresher? The café has sandwiches and a good selection of tea, too.
Hours: Monday - Saturday, 7 am - 6 pm, Sunday, 10 am - 5 pm.

Wendy's (Fast Food)

420 West Putnam Avenue, Greenwich, 869.9885
www.Wendys.com
This is the only fast food burger place with a drive-through in Greenwich.
Hours: Every day, 10 am - midnight.

Whole Foods (TakeOut, Grocery)

90 East Putnam Avenue, 661.0631
www.wholefoods.com
This mostly organic grocery store has a first class deli. On a recent evening, we served their lemon pepper rotisserie chicken, sesame green beans, mixed green salad and corn bread. Everyone loved it! Don't miss their authentic Indian dishes.
Hours: Everyday, 8 am - 10 pm.

Wild Ginger (Asian, Fusion) *

328 Pemberwick Road (at the Mill in Glenville), 531.3322 or 3289
www.WildGinger-CT.com
You will find this unique restaurant, with its trendy decor and inventive food, a happy discovery. The food is up to the fun. In the summertime it is pleasant to dine outside. We recommend their tuna pizza and Chilean sea bass. We are especially fond of their luncheon set menu.
Hours: Lunch, weekdays, 11:30 - 3 pm, Saturday, noon - 3 pm;
Dinner, Monday - Saturday, 5 pm - 10 pm, Sunday, 4:30 pm to 9:30 pm.
Prices: Lunch entrees, $14 - $18; Dinner entrees, $20 - $29.

Winfields at the Hyatt (American) *

Hyatt Regency, 1800 East Putnam Avenue, Old Greenwich,
637.1234 / reservations, 409.4400
www.greenwich.hyatt.com
Set in a beautifully converted publishing building, this is not a typical hotel nor do they serve typical hotel fare. The Hyatt demonstrates what good hotel dining can be. The indoor garden with water, flowers and very high ceilings gives the feeling of dining outdoors, even in the middle of the winter. The buffet lunches and Sunday brunch are first rate.
Hours: Everyday and all holidays: Breakfast, 6:30 am - 10:30 am;
Lunch, Monday - Saturday, 11:30 am - 2:30 pm,
Sunday brunch, noon - 3 pm; Dinner, 5 pm - 10 pm.
Reservations are a good idea, especially for Sunday brunch.
Prices: Breakfast entrees, $4 - $15; Lunch entrees, $10 - $19;
Dinner entrees, $12 - $26;
Brunch price fixed - Adults, $44, Children ages 5 - 12, $30,
Children under 5 are free.

Xaviar's (American, New) **

506 Piermont Avenue, Piermont, NY, 845.359.7007
www.xaviars.com
Rockland County's best. Just twenty-five minutes from Greenwich across the Tappan Zee Bridge. This intimate, romantic restaurant serves contemporary cuisine. It is the Hudson Valley's most celebrated restaurant. Piermont has a number of very good art galleries so arrive in time to visit them and don't miss the Piermont Flywheel Gallery, which we think has the best artists. Don't even consider going without making reservations well in advance.
Hours: Lunch, Friday and Sunday, noon - 2 pm,;
Dinner, Wednesday - Friday, 6 pm - 9 pm;
Saturday seatings, 6 pm or 9 pm, Sunday, 5 pm - 8 pm.
Prices: Lunch, price fixed at $35; Dinner, price fixed, $70; wine, $12 glass.
No credit cards are accepted, only cash or check.
Directions: I-95 S to I-287 W, cross the Tappan Zee Bridge and take first exit for Rte 9W West, left when you see the signs to Piermont, follow the road downhill to the Hudson River and turn right.

For early childcare and after school programs, see CHILDREN, Childcare
For enrichment opportunities, including language schools, see CHILDREN
Pre-school programs are usually very popular. You should contact the school
well in advance to make sure you have reserved a place. Usually programs
are halfday until the child is four years old.

Banksville Nursery School

12 Banksville Road, 661.9715
Children, ages 3 - 4. Creative movement classes. Morning and afternoon
sessions available. Closed during the summer.

Bridges

Old Greenwich Civic Center, Harding Road, 637.0204
Children, ages 2 - 4. New theme each month. Morning and afternoon
sessions.

Brunswick Pre-school

100 Maher Avenue, 625.5800
www.brunswichschool.org
Boys age 4. Admission to pre-K usually ensures admission to the school.

Children's Day School

139 East Putnam Avenue, 869.5395
Children, 6 weeks 6 years. All-day, year-round childcare and pre-school
located in the Second Congregational Church. Emphasizes cooperation
and integration of projects.

Christ Church Nursery School

254 East Putnam Avenue, 869.5334
Children, ages 2 - 5. Blend of enrichment and free play. Kindergarten
alternative, 9 am - 1:30 pm.

Clover Hill Early Childhood Learning

572 Roxbury Road Stamford CT, 661.1073
www.cloverhillschool.org
Children, ages 14 months to 4 years.

Convent of the Sacred Heart Early Learning Program

1177 King Street, 531.6500
www.cshgreenwich.org
Girls, ages 3 - 4; Half-day program for 3-year-olds optional; 4-year-olds, full day. Grounded in the Roman Catholic tradition, although 35% of students are not Catholic.

Family Center

40 Arch Street, 869.4848
www.familycenters.org
Children, ages 3 - 4. An all-day, year-round childcare and pre-school. 5:30 pm pickup available. Learn-through-discovery approach.

Giant Steps Head Start at Wilbur Peck Court

869.2730 Ages: 3 - 4.

Kids Corner Head Start at Armstrong Court

869.2730 Ages: 3 - 4.

First Church Pre-school

108 Sound Beach Avenue, Old Greenwich, 637.5430
www.firstchurchpreschool.org
Children, ages 3 - 4. Hours: 9 am - 11:30 am or 12:30 pm - 3 pm. Some preference is given to church members. Summer camp program for ages 3 - 4.

First Presbyterian Church Pre-school

37 Lafayette Place, 869.7782
www.fpcg.org/ns/school.htm
Children, ages 2 - 4. Morning and afternoon classes.
Also 2 x 2 program, 2 days per week. Enrichment programs change every 6 - 8 weeks. Art Scampers summer camp for ages 3 - 6.

Greenwich Academy

200 North Maple Avenue, 625.8900
www.greenwichacademy.org
Girls, ages 4 - 5. Morning and afternoon sessions.
Admission to pre-K usually ensures admission to the school.

pre-school

Greenwich Catholic School
471 North Street, 869.4000
www.greenwichcatholicschool.org
Children, ages 4 - pre-K. Pre-K is a structured program with academics for 4-year-olds. Little Angels is a play group for younger children. Admission to these programs does not ensure admission to the school.

Greenwich Country Day
401 Old Church Road, 863.5600
www.greenwichcds.org
Starting at age 3. Admission to pre-K usually ensures admission to the school. Summer camp for children ages 4 - 5.

Greenwich Kokusai Gakuen
Worldwide Children's Corner
521 East Putnam Avenue, 629.5567, 618.0790
www.greenwichkokusai.com
Children, ages 2 - 5 years. Full-day program.

Greenwich Pre-school Clinic
Riverside Elementary School
90 Hendrie Avenue, 637.5412
www.greenwichschools.org/aboutdistrict/pre-school.htm
Greenwich runs a pre-school for ages 3 - 4.
Greenwich Pre-school Program, 637.2892

North Greenwich Nursery School
606 Riversville Road, 869.7945
Children, ages 2 - 5. Halfday program with optional extended-day available. Computers integrated into program. US Gymnastic Academy is at the same location and can provide afternoon classes.

Putnam Indian Field School
101 Indian Field Road, 869.0982, 661.4629
www.pifs.net
Co-ed pre-school, children, ages 2 - 5.
Summer camp program for ages 2 - 6.

Round Hill Nursery School

466 Round Hill Road, 869.4910
www.roundhillnurseryschool.com
Children, ages 2 - 4. Fifty years of giving children a love of going to school. Computer training and special teachers for music and art.

St. Catherine's

6 Riverside Avenue, Riverside, 637.9549
Children, ages 2 - 4. Age 2, 1 - 3 pm; ages 3 - 4, 9 am - 12:30 pm.

St. Agnes Pre-school

247 Stanwich Road, 869.8388
Children, ages 2 yrs - 9 mos 5. Flexible 3, 4 or 5 day a week programs. Half-day programs with extended-day options. Summer camp program.

St. Paul's Christian Nursery School

286 Delavan Avenue, 531.5905
Children, ages 3 - 4; 9 am - 11:30 am. Religious values stressed.

St. Paul's Day School

200 Riverside Avenue, Riverside, 637.3503
Children, ages 2 - 5. Non-sectarian, with enrichment program for older children. Summer camp program for ages 3 - 6.

St. Savior's Nursery School

350 Sound Beach Avenue, Old Greenwich, 698.1303
Children, ages 2 yrs 5 mos - 5-years-old. Non-denominational. Summer camp program for ages 3- 5.

Selma Maisel Nursery School

Temple Sholom, 300 East Putnam Avenue, 622.8121
Children, ages 2 - 5. "Mommy & Me" program for 2 and under. Programs with Judaic content.

Stanwich School Pre-Kindergarten

257 Stanwich Road, 532.0035
www.stanwichschool.org

pre-school

Tiny Tots

97 Riverside Avenue, Riverside, 637.1398
Children, ages 3 - 5. Residential setting. One of the oldest nursery schools
in town. Summer camp program for ages 2 years 9 months - 6

Whitby School

969 Lake Avenue, 869.8464
www.whitbyschool.org
Children, ages 1 - 5 years. One of the oldest American Montessori schools.
Summer camp program for ages 3 - 5.

YMCA Rainbow Connection Pre-school

40 Gold Street, Byram, 869.3381
Children, ages 2 years 9 months - 5 years, 9 am - 1 pm. Follows public
school calendar. Offers enrichment curriculum.

YWCA 123 Grow/Beginnings

259 East Putnam Avenue, 869.6501 x 221
www.ywcagreenwich.org
Children, ages 15 months - 3 years; toddlers, 9 am - 11:30 am;
age 2, 9 am - 11:30 am or noon - 3 pm.

YWCA Tinker Tots

259 East Putnam Avenue, 869.6501 x 241
www.ywcagreenwich.org
Children, ages 3 - 4. Half-day program for age 2; ages 3 - 4, full-day, 7:30
am - 6 pm. Enrichment programs. Summer camp.

private / parochial

Greenwich has an abundance of excellent private schools. Typical annual tuition is $9,000 to $15,000, depending upon the grade. Private schools typically have more applicants than they have spaces. It is prudent to apply early. Private schools often have one or more open houses for parents of prospective attendees. Many offer extended-day programs or early dropoff for their pre-schoolers. More details are available on our website: www.greenwichliving.com

Brunswick School

100 Maher Avenue, 625.5800
www.brunswickschool.org
Boys, pre-K (age 4) through 12th grade.

Chabad Gan of Greenwich

75 Mason Street, 629.9059
Contact: Maryashie Deren, Director of Education
Pre-school

Convent of the Sacred Heart

1177 King Street, 531.6500
Sr. Joan Magnetti - Headmistress
www.cshgreenwich.org
Girls, pre-K (age 4) through 12th grade.

Eagle Hill

45 Glenville Road, 622.9240
Dr. Mark J. Griffin - Headmaster
www.eaglehillschool.org
Coed, ages 6 - 16. A school for bright children with learning disabilities. Day and 5-day boarding. Student faculty ratio is 4:1.

French-American School

Admissions Office, 914.834.3002 ext. 233
www.fasny.org
The pre-school is in Scarsdale, the elementary in Larchmont and the secondary in Mamaroneck.

private / parochial

German School
50 Partridge Road, White Plains, 914.948.6513
www.dsny.org
The German School is an independent bilingual (German/English) international school which teaches classes according to German as well as American standards. The elementary school includes grade K (for five-year-olds) through grade 4 and the secondary school includes grade 5 through 12.

Greenwich Academy
200 North Maple Avenue, 625.8900
Molly H. King - Head of School
www.greenwichacademy.org
Girls, pre-K (age 4) through 12th grade.

Greenwich Country Day
Old Church Road, 863.5600
Adam Rohdie - Headmaster
www.greenwichcds.org
Co-ed, pre-K (age 3) through 9th grade.

Greenwich Catholic School
471 North Street, 869.4000
Genevieve Madonna - Principal
www.greenwichcatholicschool.org
Co-ed, pre-K (age 4) through 8th grade.

Greenwich Japanese School
15 Ridgeway, 629.9039
www.gwjs.org
Co-ed, grades 1 - 9.

Stanwich School
257 Stanwich Road, 542.0000, admissions 542.0035
Patricia Young - Headmistress
www.stanwichschool.org
A thriving co-educational independent day school, founded in 1998 by the former head of the lower school at Greenwich Academy. It currently serves students in grades Kindergarten through 8. The school intends to add a grade each year through Grade 12.

private / parochial

Westchester Fairfield Hebrew Academy
270 Lake Avenue, 863.9663
Nora Anderson - Head of School
www.WFHA.org
Co-ed, grades K - 8. Founded in 1997, Westchester Fairfield Hebrew Academy serves 110 students. It is a Jewish community day school with a curriculum in general and Judaic studies. It includes children from all branches of Judaism.

Whitby School
969 Lake Avenue, 869.8464
Dr. Michele Monson - Head of School
www.whitbyschool.org
Co-ed, grades pre-K - 8. Founded in 1958, it is one of the oldest Montessori schools in the country. During the summer Whitby conducts a drama day camp for ages 8 - 16.

TIP: THE ENCHANTED FOREST

Each year in early November, the Junior League organizes a magical display of beautifully decorated Christmas trees and gingerbread houses, all donated by Greenwich organizations and individuals. The auction of these items helps support the good works of the Junior League. This is a fun event for the whole family. Call 869.1979 for details.

public school information

www.greenwichschools.org
Greenwich public schools rank among the best in the nation and are consistently ranked the best in Fairfield County. In addition to their other fine programs, Greenwich schools have outstanding ESL (English as a second language) programs for all grades K through 12.

Greenwich has 11 elementary, 3 middle, 1 high school and an alternative high school, Arch School, for students who need special attention. 40% of the graduates go to the "Most Competitive Colleges." The school budget is more than $70 million. The average class size is 20 and over 90% of the teachers have masters' degrees. To attend you must be a Greenwich resident.

The elementary schools serve students in grades K - 5, the middle schools serve students in grades 6 - 8; and the high school serves students grades 9 - 12. Schools open for students around Labor Day and close in the middle of June.

Board of Education
290 Greenwich Avenue, Havemeyer Building
Weekdays, 8am - 4pm 625.7400
Call 625.7400 for school district information.
Call 625.7447/6 for brochures and pamphlets.
Superintendent, Betty Sternberg.

Before and AfterSchool Child Care Programs
Ten of the elementary schools offer before and after-school programs for enrolled students. These programs are paid for by the parents. Children can usually be dropped off at 7:30 am and must be picked up by 6 pm. There is often a waiting list, so apply early. Some of the schools also offer enrichment programs where children can take computer or other classes. Call your elementary school to see what programs they sponsor. For other programs, see CHILDREN, Childcare or Pre-schools.

public school information

Kindergarten

To register for kindergarten, your child must have reached the age of five on or before January 1 of his or her kindergarten year. Parents must provide a birth certificate and proof of residence. Your child must also have a complete physical examination and a record of immunizations.

School Closings

www.greenwichschools.org

If schools are closed for snow, or if opening is delayed, listen to Greenwich Radio WGCH (1490). Announcements begin at 6:30 am. You may also find information on cable channel 12.

School Bus Information

625.7449

Call for information on school bus pickup times and locations. If your child is young and other children are not nearby, you can often get the school bus to stop in front of or near your home. Bus service is provided for students who live beyond these distances:

Grades K - 5, one mile from the school;

Grades 6 - 8, one and a half miles from school;

Grades 9 - 12, two miles from school.

TIP: GREENWICH THEATREGOERS

A non-profit group sponsored by the Greenwich Education Association who organize bus trips to New York City theaters three times a year. There is a $25 one-time fee to be put on the mailing list. Director Mary Ruth Allen, 629.2297

public elementary

Cos Cob Elementary School
300 East Putnam Avenue, Cos Cob, 869.4670
Philip M. Brown, Principal (415 students, 8:45 am - 3:15 pm)

Glenville Elementary School
33 Riversville Road, 531.9287
Marc D'Amico, Principal (429 students, 8:30 am - 3 pm)

Hamilton Avenue Elementary School
184 Hamilton Avenue, 869.1685
Dr. Damaris Rau, Principal (255 students, 8:15 am - 2:45 pm)

International School at Dundee
55 Florence Road, Riverside, 637.3800
Teresa Ricci, Principal (345 students, 8:45 am - 3:15 pm)

Julian Curtiss Elementary School
180 East Elm Street, 869.1896
Nancy Carbone, Principal (351 students, 8:15 am - 2:45 pm)

New Lebanon Elementary School
25 Mead Avenue, Byram, 531.9139
Gene Nyitray, Principal (237 students, 8:15 am - 2:45 pm)

North Mianus Elementary School
309 Palmer Hill Road, Riverside, 637.9730
Bonnie Butera, Principal (436 students, 8:45 am - 3:15 pm)

North Street Elementary School
381 North Street, 869.6756
Elisabeth Burfeind, Principal (474 students, 8:45 am - 3:15 pm)

Old Greenwich Elementary School
285 Sound Beach Avenue, Old Greenwich, 637.0150
Patricia Raneri, Principal (413 students, 8.45 am - 3.15 pm)

SCHOOLS

public elementary

Parkway Elementary School
141 Lower Cross Road, 869.7466
Paula Bleakley, Principal (354 students, 8:45 am - 3:15 pm)

Riverside Elementary School
90 Hendrie Avenue, Riverside, 637.1440
John Grasso, Principal (471 students, 8:45 am - 3:15 pm)

public middle

Central Middle School
9 Indian Rock Lane, 661.8500
Carol Walsh, Principal (730 students, 7:45 am - 2:35 pm)

Eastern Middle School
51 Hendrie Avenue, Riverside, 637.1744
Ralph Mayo, Principal (709 students, 7:45 am - 2:35 pm)

Western Middle School
Western Junior Highway, 531.5700
Stacy Gross, Principal (594 students, 7:45 am - 2:35 pm)

public high

Arch School
289 Delavan Avenue, 532.1956
Barbara Varanelli, Program Administrator (8 am - 2 pm)
The Arch School is an alternative high school for students who need special attention.

Greenwich High School
10 Hillside Road, 625.8000
Alan Capasso, Headmaster (2,695 students, 7:30 am - 2:15 pm)

Seniors in Greenwich typically stay actively involved in the community, often serving on town boards, the RTM, and philanthropic organizations. Many of our volunteer organizations are run by the retired presidents and leaders of major companies. This wealth of talent of our senior leaders is a significant reason Greenwich is America's number one town. Most senior citizens continue living in their own homes by utilizing the many services the town has available.

For information on medical resources, see the HEALTH section.

TIP: THE SAVVY SENIOR

This quarterly publication of the Greenwich Commission on Aging is filled with information on Greenwich programs and topics of interest to seniors. Call 622.3992 or email sdeibler@greenwichct.org to be added to the mailing list.

Commission on Aging

622.3992

www.eldercare.gov

Located in the Senior Center, the Commission on Aging provides information and written materials on a variety of issues of interest to seniors. Commission staff provides information and referral services and locates resources. Ask to be on the mailing list for "The Savvy Senior."
Hours: weekdays, 8 am - 4 pm.

Greenwich Hospital

863.3000

www.greenhosp.org

Provides community outreach by offering support groups, health screenings and community health education.

Greenwich Senior Services

Local: 625.6577, Long Distance: 866.309.1966
Community Answers: 622.7979
www.CommunityAnswers.org

A valuable point of contact for all local services for seniors can be found on the Community Answers home page or by calling the numbers above. Gathering this information was the joint initiative of the United Way of Greenwich, Commission on Aging and Community Answers.

Infoline

In Connecticut dial 211 (outside CT 260.522.4636)
www.infoline.org

A 24-hour confidential information, referral, advocacy and crisis help line. Caseworkers have information about hundreds of services, including health, transportation, housing, safety, employment, support services, counseling, financial/legal services and activities.

Senior Health Fair

Contact Greenwich Commission on Aging for details.
The Commission on Aging, Department of Health and Greenwich Hospital join together once a year in October to provide free tests and helpful information.

clubs & organizations

Generations

863.4375

A free membership program for people 50 years and older, run by the Greenwich Hospital Healthy Aging department. They provide seminars on various medical and wellness topics.

Glenville Senior Citizens

Western Greenwich Civic Center

Contact: Bernice Carroll, President, 637.0134

A social club for seniors in the Greenwich area, they have fun meeting and taking trips. Tell a club member you would like to join.

Greenwich Old Timers Athletic Association

PO Box 558, Greenwich 06836

Dr. Jeff Ranta, President, 637.8119

Erf Porter, First Vice President, 698.0352

A large social club for men interested in sports. They provide scholarship help and support youth sports in Greenwich.

Greenwich Seniors Club

John Titsworth, President 531.6618

Jean Connaughton, Membership, 637.1251

A social club for area residents over 55. Meetings are held once a month at Saint Mary's Parish on Greenwich Avenue.

Red Hat Society

Fullerton, CA, 714.738.0001

www.RedHatSociety.com

The Red Hat Society began as a result of a few women deciding to greet middle age with verve, humor and elan. To contact one of the local chapters use the website.

Local Greenwich Chapters:
• All Ahead Reds,
• Red Hot Babes of Greenwich
• Scarlot Harlots of Greenwich
• The Chickahominy Chicks

clubs & organizations

Retired Men's Association

YMCA, 50 East Putnam Avenue
James Fahy, President, 531.6075
John deCsepel, Program Chairman, 637.1293
Sponsored by and located at the YMCA, this active group of retirees hold weekly business meetings with interesting speakers. They also have special interest trips. Members volunteer many hours of community service work annually. Membership is for retired men in the Greenwich area, 55 and older and is by invitation.

TIP: TOUR GREENWICH GARDENS

Each year in June, the Garden Education Center organizes a tour of some of Greenwich's most special, private gardens. Call 869.9242 for details.

continuing education

The internet and email have sparked a communications revolution among seniors who find it the easiest way to stay connected with their family and interests. In addition to the extensive list of courses given by Greenwich Continuing Education, and other resources described in CONTINUING EDUCATION, there are a number of senior-oriented programs.

Diane McKeever, CPP

www.dianemckeever.com

If you want to learn a Microsoft program, you should enroll in one of Diane's Continuing Education classes at the Greenwich High School. But if you don't have the time, she gives private lessons for students of all levels - she is a CPP (Certified Patient Person).

DeCaro Associates

3 Sweet Briar Lane, Cos Cob, 943.4705

Noted Greenwich website designers, responsible for many of Greenwich's best websites, help seniors with computer problems at discounted prices.

Lifetime Learners Institute

Norwalk Community College, 188 Richards Avenue, 203.857.3330
office: Room W013, West Campus, Lower Level
www.LifeTimeLearners.org
email: info@LifeTimeLearners.org

A fabulous organization, affiliated with the Elderhostel Institute Network. It is an independent continuing education program within NCC. To join you must be over 50 and want to continue learning. Dues are $25 per academic year. Members can choose from over 40 courses for $15 per course. Members also have free use of the well-equipped college fitness center.

Norwalk Community College

Norwalk, CT, 203.857.7060 or 203.857.7080
www.ncc.commnet.edu

This community college allows seniors age 62 and older to audit any course free of charge. For more details on the college see the entry in ADULT CONTINUING EDUCATION.

continuing education

SeniorNet

Greenwich Senior Center 299 Greenwich Avenue
Contact Fred Elser 622.3993
www.seniornet.org/usa/greenwich
The Greenwich chapter of SeniorNet is a non-profit organization with the basic goal of teaching seniors to use and to enjoy computers. Classes for seniors, 50 and older, are taught by senior volunteers.

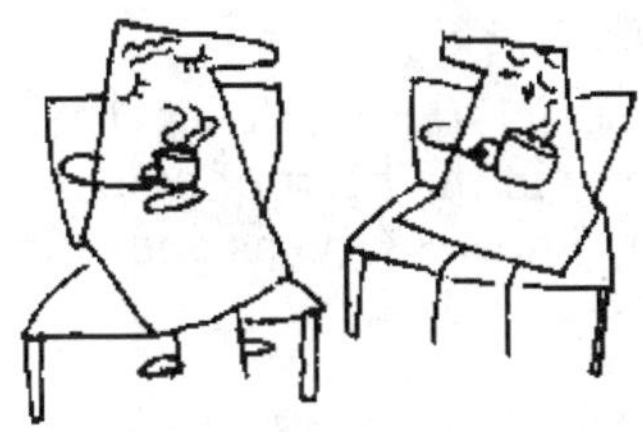

TIP: ROUND HILL COUNTRY DANCING

www.roundhill.net
The Round Hill Country Dancers meet on the second Saturday of every month at the Round Hill Community House, 397 Round Hill Road, from 8 pm to 11 pm. This multi-generational group welcomes singles and couples, beginners and advanced. There is a lesson before the program begins.
Call 914.244.7248.

According to the town's 1998 Plan of Conservation and Development, the Housing Authority has 291 independent living units for seniors with low income and who are over 62.

Medicare Ratings for Nursing Homes

www.Medicare.gov

On Medicare.gov's home page is a link to addresses and ratings for nursing homes in the USA. There are 23 nursing homes listed within 10-miles of the Greenwich zip code 06830. The top rating is 5 stars. Nathaniel Witherell has a five-star rating.

(The) Mews

(Bolling Place, 869.9448

Assisted living for seniors 55 and over. The Mews is a managed-care residential community in the heart of downtown Greenwich, very close to the town's Senior Center. 88 rooms and suites are available at affordable rates.

Hill House

10 Riverside Avenue, 637.3177

37 one-bedroom apartments for the healthy elderly. Residence is open to any able-bodied person over age 62 who meets income guidelines.

Nathaniel Witherell

70 Parsonage Road, 618.4227 www.witherell.org

The town is considering several options for rebuilding or renovating our Town-owned nursing home. Nathaniel Witherell cares for 202 residents both long term and short term re-habilitation. They have a large Alzheimer program. Admission preference is given to Greenwich residents, but because the facility is almost always 100% occupied, it is wise to call 618.4200 for an application well in advance of expected need.

Parsonage Cottage

88 Parsonage Road, 869.6226   www.Parsonagecottage.org

A charming residence for 40 seniors. It is funded by low income tax credits, the Town of Greenwich, CDBG and private donations. It is on land leased from Nathaniel Witherell, but it is a separate operation.

Call-A-Ride

37 Lafayette Place, Collyer Center, 661.6633
Non-profit organization. Residents 60 years or older can call for a ride anywhere in Greenwich for any purpose. Please give them 24 - 48 hours notice.
Hours: weekdays, 9 am - noon and 12:30 pm - 3:15 pm.

Comfort Keepers

17 Heronvue Road, Greenwich, 629.5209 or 899.0465
www.comfortkeepers.com
A national franchise that offers non-medical services to those who might not otherwise be able to live independently. They provide services such as in-home meal preparation, grocery shopping, transportation, house-keeping and companionship. Dennis and Marian Patouhas decided to buy the franchise for this much-needed business in Greenwich. Comfort Keepers charges between $20 and $22 per hour. They have a staff of about 40.

Friendly Connections

20 Bridge Street, 661.8841
www.familycenters.org
Family Centers, Inc. provides three Friendly Connections programs:

• Telephone Groups

This program brings seniors(or those who have difficulty getting out) together on the telephone for a variety of recreational, support and discussion groups. All groups are conducted over the phone and are facilitated by a moderator. There are more than 50 groups scheduled each month. They are a great way to meet new friends and stay connected.

• Friendly Callers

Professionally trained volunteers make daily calls to elderly, homebound or isolated individuals. Telephone Reassurance provides an opportunity to have a friendly chat, stay in touch and feel safer at home. They can also provide medication reminders and a "safety check," when requested. Calls are made every day from 9 am - 9 pm.

• Friendly Visitors

This program provides volunteers to visit seniors.

Greenwich Adult Day Care

125 River Road Extension, 622.0079

www.gadc.org

Day programs designed to give home caregivers a day off and participants a day filled with socialization, activity and fun. GADC has completely renovated a wonderful new center at the historic 1927 Railroad Pump House on the Mianus River in Cos Cob. The renovation creates a facility designed specifically for adult day care. With more than 8,000 square feet of space, the facility will have capacity for 75 clients a day.

Jewish Family Services of Greenwich

One Holly Hill Lane, 622.1881

www.jfsgreenwich.org

A free service for Greenwich residents over 60, providing grocery shopping for the home-bound; also, carpentry, minor plumbing and snow shoveling.

Kindness Counts

Teacher leader, Jonathan Guyot Smith, 531.5700

www.kindnesscounts.com

A Western Middle School student-run program. Students prepare and deliver meals to residents in senior housing facilities.

Meals onWheels

869.1312

Non-profit organization prepares and delivers to homes of anyone recovering from illness or an injury, regardless of age.

$7 per day for two meals, one hot and one cold.

Hours: weekdays, 8 am - 1 pm.

Memory Lane Productions

Harriet Feldman, 531.1323

A former volunteer with the Greenwich Library's Oral History Project, Harriet helps families record their history through a written version or compact disc or both.

services

Red Cross Transportation Services

99 Indian Field Road, 869.8444

www.greenwich.ctredcross.org

The transportation service is one of the many superb Red Cross programs. Volunteers, using Red Cross vehicles, provide transportation for Greenwich residents to and from health care and rehabilitation appointments.

Senior Center

299 Greenwich Avenue, 622.3990

www.greenwichct.org/ParksAndRec/prFacilityPrograms.asp

Stop in to see the monthly bulletin board of activities for Greenwich seniors 55 and older. There are a lot of activities going on! Recent listings included: "Qigong" Chinese exercises, chess and bridge instruction, a luncheon cruise, trips to the opera, ice cream socials, painting, shopping center trips and a brown bag auction. Free classes (in conjunction with Greenwich Continuing Education) were being held in line dancing, writing short stories, writing your memoirs and sewing.

Hours: weekdays, 9:00 a.m. to 4:00 p.m.

Supermarketing for Seniors

One Holly Hill Lane, 622.1881

One of the wonderful Jewish Family Service programs to help homebound older residents of any faith. They will arrange grocery shopping on a weekly basis, and this kind service is free.

TAG (Transportation Association of Greenwich)

13 Riverside Avenue, 637.4345

Non-profit organization operates a fleet of 15 specially modified vehicles. They drive elderly and disabled people of all ages to health, social and educational organizations in Greenwich and neighboring communities. TAG operates Monday - Saturday, 6 am - 6:30 pm.

Tax Counseling for Seniors

Volunteer counselors provide free tax return assistance to Seniors starting in mid-February. On Mondays and Fridays, from 9 am to 1 pm, they are at the Greenwich Senior Center (299 Greenwich Avenue). On Wednesdays from 1 pm to 4 pm, they are at Town Hall (101 Field Point Road). Counselors are required to pass an examination administered by the IRS.

services

USE Utilize Senior Energy

Greenwich Senior Center, 299 Greenwich Avenue, 629.8032

This non-profit "employment agency" is run by volunteers from the basement of the Senior Center. This brilliant organization founded in 1977 by Viola Caldwell allows retired seniors to continue working and provides an excellent resource for the community. It is a good place to find all manner of help: receptionists, business consultants, painters, baby sitters, etc.

Hours: Weekday, 9:30 am to 12:30 pm.

Weekend Lunch Bunch

Greenwich Hospital, 863.3690

Anyone age 55 or older can enjoy a $5 4-course meal in the cafeteria. Call and you will know the menu for the weekend.

Hours: Saturday & Sunday, noon - 2 pm.

YMCA Exercise Programs

50 East Putnam Avenue, 869.1630

www.gwymca.org

The Y offers a number of programs tailored to the needs of seniors, including walking, stretching, resistance training and swimming.

TIP: SCULPTURES IN GREENWICH

Greenwich has 30 outdoor sculptures. Some are tucked away in parks, some are in public buildings. Have fun on a sculpture hunt. Stop in the Greenwich Arts Council (second floor of 299 Greenwich Avenue) and ask for the map of sculpture locations.

This section was under the heading HOME in previous editions of the guide.
To rid yourself of furry or feathery visitors see ANIMALS, WILDLIFE & ANIMAL RESCUE.
For home delivery of groceries, see FOOD.
For Car Rentals, see AUTOMOBILES.
For Travel Agents, see TRAVEL.
For Ticket Agencies, see CULTURE.
For Baby Sitting See CHILDREN.

art

Art Shops are in STORES.

Fine Arts Conservation Laboratory

107 Orchard Street, Stamford, 323.3225
Efrem Capestany is an art conservator. His business is geared towards serious art collectors wishing to preserve paintings.

Library Lending Art Program

Greenwich Library, 622.7900
The Lending Art Program of the Library has an extensive collection of artworks acquired by the Friends of the Library. It is available to all patrons and can be checked out on a short-term or long-term basis.

blueprints

Greenwich Blue Print Company

255 Greenwich Avenue, 869.0305
Friendly quick service. This upstairs blueprint company is known to architects and builders. It is the perfect source for homeowners to get copies of their plans.

child safety

Children under the age of one need to be in a rear facing car seat. Children between the ages of one and seven need to be in car seats. The Greenwich Fire Department, 622.8087, will help you install or inspect your seat. Call for an appointment.

Child Proofers Inc

540 W Boston Post Rd, Mamaroneck, NY, 914.381.5106
www.babypro.com

Protecta Child Pool Fencing

www.protectachild.com
The local distributor is Art O'Neill, 800.778.8411.
The main number is 800.992.2206.

chimney cleaning

You should have your chimneys cleaned every three years. This business seems to attract con men, so be sure you know who is coming into your home. We recommend the following cleaning services:

Bill Ingraham

Cos Cob, 869.5242.

Chimney Swifts

Cos Cob, 661.7243

computers

To recycle used computers, see Cristina Foundation under RECYCLING

Canaan Technology

194 Main Street, Norwalk, CT 203.847.2444
www.Canaantechnology.com
Canaan Technology specializes in services to individuals and small-to medium-size businesses wanting technology solutions from design and sales, to installation and support. They are a solution provider, not a hardware or software retailer.
Hours: weekdays, 9 am - 5 pm. Service is available 24 hours a day, every day of the year.

Computer Guru

Stamford, CT 325.8935, 800.983.2111
Nicholas Guild repairs, troubleshoots, and solves PC computer problems. Joan, one of our clients, loved the way he set up her computer and got her back into action following her move.

Computer Super Center

103 Mason Street, 661.1700
They sell and service computers as well as HDTV and Audio equipment. They service Apple - Sony - BOSE - Shure - HP - Lenovo (IBM) - Fujitsu and OKI.

Decaro Associates

203.943.4705
Fred DeCaro is a technology consultant used by the Town and many Greenwich businesses and individual residents. He gives seniors a discount.

Angie's List

888-944-5478
www.AngiesList.com
A website that rates service providers and has customer comments (good and bad) about their services. One annoyance is you have to register to use the site.

Better Business Bureau
Wallingford, CT 203.269.2700
www.ctbbb.org

Franklin Report
www.FranklinReport.com
The Franklin Report rates service providers (aka contractors) by price and quality. We have found their ratings to be reliable. However, most contractors charge more when they are busy and less when they are not, so be sure to get at least two estimates.

TIP: OLD GREENWICH MEMORIAL DAY PARADE
This annual event began in 1923. It draws thousands of people to the parade down Sound Beach Avenue and to the ceremony afterwards in Binney Park. Attending this wonderful town event, organized by the Sound Beach Volunteer Fire Department, will make you glad to be part of the community.

firewood

Firewood by Gus

(also called Connecticut Demolition)
2 Apple Tree Lane, Riverside, 637.5804
They will stack for an extra charge.

Buzz and Ray

(also called Ray's Lawn Service)
31 St. Rochs Place, 862.9271
They will stack for an extra charge.

landscape contractors & tree services

Round Hill Tree Service

1 Armonk Street, Greenwich, 531.5759
Rick Masi will make sure your dead trees are cut down, your limbs are trimmed back and your yard sprayed for mosquitos.

TIP: LEAF BLOWER RULES

A blower can be operated weekdays, 8 am - 6 pm; weekends & holidays, 9 am - 3 pm.

money & banking

Greenwich has been invaded by banks. We counted 25, but one authoritative source said 33. In any event, we understand that at least 3 more banks are coming. With so many on Greenwich Avenue, we may have to change the street's name to Bank Street.

For as long as we can remember, Greenwich residents have preferred to work with in-town banks. Friendly hellos and loans from bankers who know and work in the community are a much more civilized way to bank than dealing anonymously with a big, inflexible institution. Greenwich is fortunate to have two locally owned hometown banks. Drop in and say hello.

(The) Greenwich Bank & Trust Company

A Division of Connecticut Community Bank
- 115 East Putnam Avenue, 618.8900 (main branch)
- 22 Railroad Avenue, 983.3370
- 1103 East Putnam, Riverside, 698.4030
- 273 Glenville Road, 532.4784

www.ccbankonline.com

While you are there, use the foreign currency ATM at the main branch to get any money you need for your next trip.

Hours: Monday - Thursday, 8:30 am - 4 pm; Friday, 8:30 am - 5 pm; Saturday 9 am - noon. The Glenville branch is not open on Saturday.

(The) Bank of Greenwich

165 Mason Street, 629.8400

www.TheBankOfGreenwich.com

This recently opened bank was founded by highly respected local residents, who care about our community.

Hours: weekdays 8:30 am - 4 pm; Thursdays until 6 pm; Saturday, 9 am - 12 pm.

moving, packaging & storage

Your move depends on the people assigned to your job. We sure hope you get the best. Perhaps it will help if you tell them you will be reporting both good and bad news to us. To check on a moving company and any complaints that have been filed, call the Department of Transportation at 860.594.2870. They are very helpful.

Alexander Services

Call Shawn Alexander at 888.656.6838, 203.324.4012.
They are the mover of choice for many antique shops.

Callahan Brothers

133 Post Road, Cos Cob, 869.2239
They are the local agent for Joyc- Lines and have been a fixture in Greenwich for many years. When you need to move across the country or across the world, give them a call.

Joe Mancuso Moving

Joe Mancuso, 914.937.2178
An excellent resource when you are making a local move.

Mail Boxes Etc

- 15 East Putnam Avenue, 622.1114
- 1117 East Putnam Avenue, 698.0016

Mail box rentals, packing, crating and shipping, even Notary services.
Hours: weekdays, 9 am - 6 pm; Saturday, 10 am - 2 pm.

Morgan Manhattan Moving & Storage

16 Bruce Park Avenue, 869.8700
www.morganmanhattan.com
A regional moving company with corporate headquarters in Greenwich.

Packages PlusNMore

Mill Pond Shopping Center, 215 East Putnam Ave,
 Cos Cob, 625.8130
An up-scale packing and shipping company, that will not only ship packages for you, but will pickup a package from your home or office upon request.
Hours: weekdays, 5:30 am - 7 pm; Saturday 5:30 am - 5:30 pm;
Sunday 5:30 am - 5 pm.

moving, packaging & storage

Tilford Piano Movers

Days:203.426.8625, evenings after 7 pm: 203.743.6107
They specialize in local and long distance piano moving.

Two Men and A Truck

28 Knight Street, Norwalk, CT, 203.831.9300
www.twomenandatruck.com
This is a locally owned mover franchised by a national company. We are impressed with their careful and courteous ways.

Westy Self Storage (866.229.3789)

• 80 Brownhouse Road, Stamford, CT, 961.8000
• 351 North Main Street, Port Chester, NY, 914.937.2222
www.westy.com
Convenient, clean, secure, private storage rooms.

Gerhard Feldmann

208 East 70th Street, NYC 10021
212.717.2907, Cell: 917.686.5946
Specialist for Bösendorfer pianos, but does all makes. Expensive, good choice for professional pianists who tax their instruments through heavy practicing.

Robert Marullo

869.4943
This popular, talented piano teacher at Greenwich Academy, also gives private lessons. We strongly recommend him for lessons as well as piano repairs, tuning and reliable advice about purchases.

Piano Service

Ken Svec, 359.2231
Ken tunes pianos and is an excellent consultant if you wish to buy or sell a piano.

Tilford Piano Movers

Days:203.426.8625, evenings after 7 pm: 203.743.6107
They specialize in local and long distance piano moving.

TIP: GREENWICH ARTS COUNCIL CONCERTS

For a lovely evening, be sure to attend one of the three concerts sponsored by the Greenwich Arts Council. These free concerts are held during the summer months. Call 622.3998 for details.

recycling

The Public Works department of the Town has a good description of your options:
http://greenwichct.org/PublicWorks/pwWARecycling.asp

Blue Bins

Recycling is now mandated by the state, but it is interesting to note that thanks to Mariette Badger and the active Greenwich Recycling Advisory Board of community volunteers, Greenwich recycling has been organized for over twenty-five years. Our recycling program saves the Town money and protects the environment. Each week at a designated day and time, the Town picks up recyclables and brings them to the Holly Hill Transfer Station. To get your blue bin(s) and recycling details, call 622.0550, week-days, 9 am - 3 pm. Blue Bins cost $10.

Cell Phones

Collection boxes are located all over town for old Cell phones, PDAs, Pagers and chargers. Check the Public Works site www.greenwichct.org/ParksAndRec/ParksandRec.asp for their location or call Sally Davies, Chair of the Greenwich Recycling Advisory Board, at 629.2876. This equipment is refurbished and used for 911 phones for women in crisis. Older equipment is sent to countries where the technology is less advanced. Support this program. Collection boxes are available to put in your own work place.

Christmas Trees

Between December 26th and January 5th, you can bring your un-decorated tree to Bruce Park, Byram Beach or Greenwich Point and the tree will be chipped and transported by the town. Of course, you can bring your tree at any time to the Holly Hill recycling facility. The idea that the tree will be recycled back to nature lifts our spirits.

recycling

Computer Donations

Resources for donating old computers are listed below. Be sure to check their policy and drop-off times in advance.

- **Cristina Foundation**
  500 West Putnam Avenue, 863.9100
  www.Cristina.org

National Cristina Foundation (NCF) is a not-for-profit organization that provides computer technology to people with disabilities and economically disadvantaged persons. How wonderful that they are working to ensure that used computer technology resources that no longer meet an individual's needs are given a second productive life. They only accept more recent computers under 5 years old. Systems must have a hard drive, monitor, keyboard, & mouse.

- **Good Will** (under 6 years old), 363.5228
- **Salvation Army** (under 6 years old), 800.958.7825
- **Greenwich Hospital Thrift Shop** (under 3 years old), 869.6124

Hazardous Waste

Whenever you wish to dispose of items such as bug spray, engine oil, old paint cans or other items which are not part of the normal recycling program, call Department of Public Works at 869.6910, 622.7838 or 622.7740.

Holly Hill Recycling Facility (aka The Dump)

Holly Hill Lane, 622.0550

Greenwich has one of the world's best dumps. You have to see it to believe it. On any given day, you may see BMWs and Mercedes dropping off items. The "in" decal for your car is a dump permit. Permit applications are available at the Holly Hill entry gate. To get one of these valuable permits, you must show proof of residency, as well as valid vehicle registration and insurance.

Hours: weekdays, 7 am - 3 pm; Saturday, 7 am - noon.

recycling

i-SOLD-it (eBay Consignment)
• 607 Main Ave (Rt. 7 across from the DMV), Norwalk, 203.845.0290
• 1299 North Ave (Quaker Ridge Shopping Cntr), New Rochelle, NY 914.636.1981
www.isoldit.com
A chain of 180 stores, helping people sell their items on eBay. They photograph, write copy, ship and collect payment for you. The item must sell for, at least, $75. Their commission is 33% - 25% of the money received, depending upon the value of the item.
Hours: Norwalk, Monday- Saturday, 10 am - 7 pm.
Hours: New Rochelle, Tuesday - Friday, 10 am - 6 pm; Saturday to 5 pm.

Leaf Collection
Town leaf collection is limited to all properties on PUBLIC STREETS ONLY in building zones R20 (half-acre) and below. Many residents with one or more acres compost on their own property. For a schedule of leaf collection, call 622.7718, 618.7698 or watch for the schedule printed by the Greenwich Time in the fall.

refuse collectors

Garbage collection is done by independent contractors. New residents may call the Greenwich Independent Refuse Collectors Association at 622.0050 to find out which collector services their home. When you move to a home be sure to ask the former owner or a neighbor who is servicing their home.

rug & dry cleaning

Berger Cleaners
282 Mason Street, 869.7650
A good choice for your curtains and draperies.
Hours: weekdays, 7 am - 6:30 pm; Saturday, 7:30 am - 4:30 pm.

Brighton Cleaners
25 Glenville Street, 531.5679
146 Sound Beach Avenue, Old Greenwich, 698.1135
Reliable dry-cleaning on their premises. They offer same day service.

Carpet Ron
Ron Laroche, Stamford, 359.4285
Recommended by our friends as a good rug cleaner.

Katie's Cleaners
138 East Putnam Avenue, Cos Cob, 863.0960
weekdays, 7 am - 6:30 pm; Saturday, 8 am - 5 pm.
All work done on the premises. Tony likes his shirts done here!

Thomas Dry Cleaning and Chinese Hand Laundry
68 Lewis Street, 869.9420
A good choice for fine linens and tablecloths.
Hours: weekdays, 7:30 am - 6 pm; Saturday, 7:30 6 pm.

Triple S Carpet and Drapery Cleaners
400 West Main Street (Post Road), Stamford, 327.7471
They clean draperies and upholstery and will come to the house to clean rugs and upholstery. They do a great job of cleaning and/or repairing rugs.
Hours: weekdays, 8 am - 5:30 pm; Saturday, 8 am - 1:30 pm.

furniture restoration

Paul Kechejian

71 Orchard street, Cos Cob, cell: 914.227.3153
Many residents remember the antique shop, Provence de France, which was on Greenwich Avenue for 20 years. Paul was responsible for their refinishing. Fortunately for us, Paul is still polishing, refinishing and repairing antique and modern furniture.

Raphael's Furniture Restoration

655 Atlantic Street, Stamford, 348.3079
www.raphaelsfurniture.com
They will repair and restore just about any piece of furniture, but they specialize in the restoration of eighteenth and nineteenth century antiques. Call for an appointment.
Hours Summer: Tuesday -Thursday, 8 am - 5 pm;
Friday, 8 am - 3 pm; Saturday, 8 am - noon.
Hours Labor Day to Memorial Day: Tuesday - Friday, 8 am - 5 pm;
Saturday, 8 am - noon.
Directions: I95 North to Exit 7 (Greenwich Avenue), straight to 4th light, R on Atlantic, 5th building
on the R.

Wood Den

266 Selleck Street, Stamford, 324.6957
Wood and metal furniture stripping. Chair caning and furniture repairs.
Hours: Tuesday, Wednesday & Friday, 9 am - 5 pm; Thursday, 8 am - 8 pm; Saturday, 9 am - 3:30 pm.
Directions: I95 N to exit 6, straight to 2nd light, R on West to Selleck.

home delivery

For home delivery of groceries, see FOOD.

Berman Newspaper Delivery

323.5955

Depending upon where you live, Berman will deliver to your home between 5 and 6 am, where you want it, all of the major papers including: *The New York Times*, *Financial Times* and *USA Today*. The local papers come out too late for this delivery, so unless you want these papers a day late, you should contact them directly: Greenwich Time, 625.4400; Greenwich Post, 861.9191; Greenwich Citizen, 750.5313.

Deliver Ease of Greenwich

622.3040, 532.0370

www.deliverease.com

Hours: every day, 8 am - 9 pm.

For $8 for every 15 minutes of travel time, this reliable service will pamper your every need. They promptly deliver to or pick up from your door just about anything you can imagine: aspirin from your drugstore, poster board for a project, food from your favorite restaurant, forgotten dry cleaning, a late video, or just a cup of Dunkin' Donuts' coffee. Why not send a gift to cheer up someone at the hospital?

locks & keys

Charles Stuttig

158 Greenwich Avenue, 869.6260

A fixture in Greenwich for many years, they provide a wide variety of locks and safes. Whether you have an emergency or just need a key replaced, they can be counted on and trusted.

Hours: weekdays, 7:30 am - 5:30 pm.

Greenwich Lock and Door

280 Railroad Avenue, 622.1095

www.greenwichLockandDoor.com

A reliable local source for architectural hardware, doors, security products and lock-smithing. Good customer service.

Hours: Monday & Wednesday, 7 am - 4 pm;
Tuesday, Thursday & Friday, 8 am - 4 pm.

media room design & installation

The following stores are described in SHOPPING
* Audiocom, 321 Greenwich Avenue, 552.5224
* Bang & Olufsen
        Harvey Electronics, 19 West Putnam Avenue, 622.0324
* Best Buy , 330 Connecticut Avenue, Norwalk, CT, 203.857.4543
* Circuit City, 44 Connecticut Avenue, Norwalk, CT 203.866.3600
* CompUSA, Norwalk and White Plains
* Computer Super Center, 103 Mason Street, 661.1700

EPI

538 Route 22, Pawling, NY, 845.855.5785
www.episi.com
Pawling may not seem nearby, but they do a lot of high quality work in Greenwich. They are a great resource for system integration and home theaters. They have their own electrician specialists working with them.

Performance Imaging (Electronics - Audio/Visual)

550 West Avenue, Stamford, 862.9600 or 504.5200
www.performanceimaging.net
They have temporarily given up their showroom, but they are still a terrific source for system integration, home theater design and installation.

repairs

For furniture repairs see Furniture Restoration above.

Action Appliances
Bill Miles, 698.0211
If you have washers, dryers, dishwashers, ranges or refrigerators that aren't working, call Bill. For 16 years Bill has rescued many a home-owner.

American Typewriter
Route 202, New Milford, CT, 860.354.6903
David Morrill repairs typewriters and sells refurbished ones. One of the last places around to do this work.
Hours: weekdays, 10 am - 4 pm.

Appliance Servicenter of Stamford
15 Cedar Heights Road (off High Ridge Road), Stamford, 322.7656
If you can carry it, they can probably repair it. In addition they service stoves, refrigerators, washers and dryers in your home.
Hours: weekdays, 8:30 am - 5:30 pm, Saturday, 8:30 am -1:30 pm.
Directions: Merritt Parkway N to exit 35, R on High Ridge, in about a mile R on Cedar Heights (at the Mobile Station).

Clock Repairs
Darien, CT 203.655.2100
Many antique clocks in our area may have come from the Village Clock Shop. The owner no longer sells clocks, but Karen is ready to repair your valuable clock.

Dean's China & Glass Restoration
324 Guineviere Ridge, Cheshire, CT, 800.669.1327, 203.271.3659
Send them a photo of your broken or chipped piece and they will give you an estimate.

Detail Painting & Repairs
Norwalk, CT
Marcos Souza, 203.846.1157, Cell: 203.515.8256
If you need an expert interior or exterior paint job, if you need your gutters cleaned or minor carpentry, you will not find a nicer person to work with.

repairs

EnviroShield

Stratford, CT, 203.380.5644
www.enviroshield.com
A totally trustworthy group to call if you have any concerns about mold abatement, testing, removal or installation of oil tanks or remediation of areas contaminated by petroleum or other chemicals.

TV Repair

54 Hamilton Street, Stamford, 323.2683
Ed Fraioli and Len DiChiara repair Camcorders, VCRs, and TVs (including plasma). Before throwing out your television, give these repairman a call. They charge a flat fee for repairs rather than an hourly rate.
Hours: weekdays, 9 am - 5 pm; Saturday, 9 am - 1 pm. Be sure to make an appointment.

Greenwich Metal Finishing

300 West Main Street, Stamford, 977.0494
If you have an ailing silver piece or chandelier, you may want to visit these metal artisans. They polish, replate, refinish and even fabricate metal items. They will completely refinish and rewire your chandelier.
Hours: weekdays, 7:30 am - 4 pm.

Graham Company

Mark Graham, 800.942.5575
Mark actually lives in Florida, but comes to Greenwich about once a month. His whole business is repairing and installing ceiling fans.

Greenwich Window Doctor

Andrew Coviello, 531.4485
www.GreenwichWindowDoctor.com
Replacement windows are not always necessary or desirable when you can rehabilitate your older windows. Since 1989 Andrew has been repairing broken cords, re-chaining, unsticking and repairing old windows.

Jason, The Handyman, Inc.

17 Cognewaugh Rd, Cos Cob 625.0411
If you need a mirror hung, gutters installed or cleaned, walls painted, tile regrouted, or an electrical outlet installed, call Jason Wahlberg. Reasonably priced and offers senior discounts. If he can't do it, he'll recommend someone who can.

repairs

Longo's RentaTool
263 Selleck Street, Stamford, 975.0569
A do-it-yourselfer's paradise.
Hours: weekdays, 7:30 am - 5 pm; Saturday, 8 am - noon.

Nimble Thimble
21 Putnam Avenue, Port Chester, NY, 914.934.2934
The resource for home sewing needs. Lots of fabrics, notions, and quilting supplies and sewing machines. This is the place to have your sewing machine repaired.
Hours: Monday - Saturday, 10 am - 5 pm.

Occhicone
42 North Main Street, Port Chester, NY, 914.937.6327
Expert repairs, by Italian craftsmen, for high quality leather items, such as handbags, briefcases, leather apparel, suitcases and shoes. They can make just about anything look new.
Hours: Monday - Saturday, 8 am - 5 pm.

Oops, I broke it!
Tablescraps, Cheshire, CT, 800.801.4084
www.tabletopdesigns.com
If you are missing a piece of china, crystal or silver from your collection, this is a good place to find a replacement. Call, visit their website or email them at lenox@ntplx.net.
If for some reason Tablescraps can't help you, try these out-of-the-area replacement services:
• Clintsman International, 800.781.8900
• Pattern Finders, 631.928.5158
• Replacements Ltd, 800.737.5223

Ultrawiz Electronics
20 Henry Street, 532.0175
www.UltraWiz.com
Have you ever wondered how to get a plasma or projection television repaired? Greenwich residents are lucky to have Ultrawiz, a factory authorized service center for most plasma TVs. They also repair VCRs, camcorders and hi-fi equipment.
Hours: weekdays, 9 am - 5 pm, Saturday, 9 am - 1 pm.

See also Locks and Keys above

TIP: FINDING TAG SALES
Tag sales a.k.a. Estate Sales (but not called Garage Sales) are a popular Greenwich weekend pastime. The Friday and weekend Greenwich Time newspaper lists tag sale locations. Greenwich Radio (869.1490) has a Saturday morning trading post from 7 am - 8 am. It's a free way to find items to buy or sell. They also announce tag sales.

security

Advanced Electronic Systems (AES)

16 Brookfield Street, Norwalk, CT 203.846.0700
www.AdvancedElectronicSystems.net
They have been helping Greenwich residents with alarm systems for over 30 years. Howard Friedman can be counted on to help you choose the right system.

Dark House Service

622.8000
If residents notify the police that they will be away for an extended period of time, Greenwich police will patrol the area with an extra-cautious eye. You can also hire an off-duty police officer to personally check your home each day when you are away.

Kennedy Security Services

58 East Elm Street, 661.6814
For extra security while you are away from home, Kennedy Security has been serving Greenwich residents for over 40 years.

PI Security

Stamford, CT, 203.869.9300
A high-end, completely trustworthy, alarm system distributor/installer that can meet anyone's needs.

tailors, dressmakers & cobblers

Aptons
24 Field Point Road, 661.3877
Stylish ready-made and custom clothing. David Proudfit (yes, this is his real name and it fits) was for many years the expert tailor at Richards. For men and women caring about fabric, style and a great fit, you will really enjoy the experience here. The tailor shop is below the showroom.
Hours: Weekdays 9 am - 6 pm; Saturday, 9 am - 6 pm; Sunday, noon - 5 pm.

Coppola
347 Greenwich Avenue, 869.2883
Just the right place for suit alterations. Buy a tux while you are there.

Greenwich Shoe Repair
15 East Elm Street, 869.2288
Hidden in an alley off of East Elm, George Togridis has been mending Greenwich shoes for over 15 years.
Hours: Monday - Saturday, 8 am - 5 pm.

Nibia Stezano, Master Seamstress
629.5474
www.nibiastezano.com
Nibia works out of her attic studio in Cos Cob. She is an extremely skilled dressmaker capable of designs from scratch. She is also willing to do small alterations for both men and women.

Ted The Tailor
2 Church Street, 869.5699
They have been tailoring in Greenwich since 1948. They do everything from alterations to custom suits. They also work on leather.
Hours: weekdays, 8:30 am - 6 pm; Saturday to 5 pm.

A more complete list is in NUMBERS YOU SHOULD KNOW, or online at www.GreenwichLiving.com/contacts_relocation.htm

Greenwich Telephone System

Greenwich is on the border between Verizon (formerly Bell Atlantic, formerly Nynex) and AT&T (formerly SNET, formerly SBC) coverage areas. Old Greenwich exchanges (637 & 698) are covered by AT&T. From there you can dial many Connecticut 203 numbers directly. The rest of Greenwich is controlled by Verizon. This means that many numbers outside of Greenwich require you to dial 1.203 first.

Most Stamford numbers do not require the 203 prefix, but information for Stamford requires you to dial 203.555.1212. Greenwich information can be accessed by dialing 411. We have tried to organize the numbers in this guide to make it clear when you have to dial 203 (if you are in the Verizon coverage area) or when you can simply dial the local number.

Aquarion (formerly Connecticut-American Water Company)

www.aquarion.com

869.5200 (office)

203.445.7310, 800.732.9678 (emergency),

800.292.2928, 800.732.9678 (customer service),

AT&T/SNET/SBC: Old Greenwich exchanges 637 & 698

From AT&T coverage area, dial 811 for repairs; from out-of-state, 800.453.7638 (Customer Service); 203.420.3131 (repairs) or 611 from cell phone

www.snet.com

www.sbc.com

Cablevision of Connecticut

348.9211, 203.846.4700

www.cablevision.com

www.optimum.com

Connecticut Natural Gas

869.6900 (customer service)

869.6913 (repair & emergency)

www.cngcorp.com

utilities

Northeast Utilities / Connecticut Light & Power
800.286.2000 (main), 800.286.5000 (Customer Service, emergencies)
www.nu.com
Our local power company.

Verizon: Greenwich, Byram, Cos Cob, Glenville & Riverside
869.5222 (new service)
661.5444 (repairs), 611 (cell phone)
625.9800 (customer service)
www.bellatlantic.com
www22.verizon.com

Antiques

A Woodhouse
Antique & Artisan Center (See Stamford Antique Area)
Braswell Galleries
Federalist
Greenwich Oriental Art
Guild Antiques
Harborview Center for Antiques
HenriBurton French Antiques
Hiden Galleries (see Stamford Antique Area)
Lynda Willauer Antiques
Quai Voltaire Antiquites
Rinfret Home & Garden
Rue Faubourg St. Honoré
Shippan Center for Arts & Antiques
Stamford Antiques Center (See Stamford Antique Area)
Vallin Galleries
Wyler

ART - Galleries

Abby M Taylor Fine Art
Bendheim Gallery
Cavalier Galleries
Flinn Gallery
Miranda Arts
Quester Gallery
Silvermine Guild Arts Center
Zorya Fine Art

ART- Supplies

Friedman
Michaels

ART- Framing

Friedman
J Pocker & Son
Left of The Bank
Miranda Art
Red Studio

Boating

(See Fitness & Sports for boating instruction and information)
Beacon Point Marine
Landfall Navigation
Rex Marine Center

Books

(See Section Books for donations and book sales)
Barnes & Noble
Borders Books
Borders Express
Gift Shop at Christ Church
Diane's Books of Greenwich
Just Books

CHILDREN (and youth)
Clothing, Shoes & Gifts
Babies "R" Us
Carter's
Gap
Beame & Barre
Best & Co.
Buy Buy Baby
Candy Nichols
Chilly Bear
Julia B Boutique
L'Enfance Magique
Lilly Pulitzer
Little Eric
Love
Petit Bateau
Petit Patapon
Rags
Talbots Kids & Babies
Wishlist

CHILDREN
Furniture & Equipment
Babies "R" Us
Kids Home Furniture
Bellini
Buy Buy Baby
Go To Your Room
Great Outdoor Toy Company
Kid's Supply Co.
Wendy Gee!

CHILDREN -Toys
Dianne's Doll Shoppe
Fun House
Graham's
Hobby Center
Love
Right Start
Smart Kids Company
Toys "R" Us
Whimsies Doll House

CLOTHING Men
(Shoes & Accessories and Department Stores are listed separately)
Aptons
Brooks Brothers
Banana Republic
Fila
Gap
J Crew
Land's End
Lucky Jeans
Michaels Men's Formal Wear
Richard's
Rugby
Scoop
Threads & Treads
Syms
Vineyard Vines

Gifts Shops (including Dishes & Crystal)

06830 Gifts
Baccarat
Cherry Blossoms
CM Almy
Connecticut Store (The)
Georg Jensen
Gift Shop at Audubon Center
Gift Shop at Bruce Museum
Gift Shop at Christ Church
Gift Shop at Greenwich Hospital
Gift Shop at Hyatt Hotel
Greenwich Exchange for
   Women's Work
Hoagland's of Greenwich
House Warmings
L'Occitane
Michaelangelo of Greenwich
Quelques Chose
Sophia's Great Dames
Tallow's End
Tiffany & Co.

HEALTH - Equipment, Furniture & Products

Pharmacies, vitamins, exercise equipment, glasses, hearing aids, physical therapy and medical equipment are reviewed in a the separate section - HEALTH.
Spas are reviewed in the separate section - GROOMING

HOME - Appliances and Cookware

Bed, Bath & Beyond
Cook & Craft
Crate & Barrel
Greenwich Kitchen Store
Harris Restaurant Supply
Reo Appliances
Williams-Sonoma

Parties

(See separate section on Entertaining for services including Caterers)
East Putnam Variety
Fiesta Place
Party City
Party Paper & Things
Party Warehouse
Strauss Warehouse
Tallow's End

Pets

(Services and information are listed in the separate section ANIMALS)
Canine Corner
House of Fins
Pet Pantry

Pharmacies *(See HEALTH)*

Photography

(Photographers have a separate section)
Camera Wholesalers
Images
Ritz Camera Center

Shopping Centers and Outlets

ABC Carpet Warehouse Outlet Store
Clinton Crossing Premium Outlet
    Mall
Galleria Shopping Center
J. McLaughlin Outlet Store
Liberty Village Outlet Mall
Lillian August Outlet Store
Ridgeway Shopping Center
Stamford Town Shopping Center
Tangier Outlet Shopping Center
Westchester Mall
Woodbury Commons Outlet Mall

Toys *(See Children-Toys)*

Sewing & Needlework

Knitting Niche
Nimble Thimble
Village Ewe

Shoes & Accessories - Men & Women

Anne Klein
Ann Taylor
Athlete's Foot
Coach
Cochni
DSW
Foot Solutions
In Things
Kate Spade
New York Running Company
Plaza Too
Richard's
Shoes N More
Threads & Treads
Talbots
Unisa

STORE INDEX

by category

Sporting Goods (Equipment & Clothing)

(Boating is listed separately)

All Sports Apparel
Athlete's Foot
Bedford Sportsman
Beval Saddlery
BikeEx
Bodd
Bruce Park Sports
Chilly Bear
Compleat Angler
Custom Golf of Connecticut
Cycle Dynamics
Darien Golf Center
Darien Sport Shop
Dave's Cycle & Fitness
De Mane's Golf Inc.
Eastern Mountain Sports
EuroChasse
Greenwich Bicycles
Greenwich Golf Fitting Studio
Gordon's Gateway to Sports
Griffin & Howe
Hickory & Tweed
Instant Replay
New York Running Company
Orvis
Outdoor Traders
Recreation Showroom
Rex Dive Center
Riders Up
Rink & Racquet
Skaters Landing
Sportif Ltd.
Sportsman's Den
Stamford Archery & Firearms
Threads & Threads

Stationery & Greeting Cards

Kate's Paperie
Packages PlusNMore
Papyrus (The)
Saint Clair
Staples

Thrift

Act II Consignment Shop
Goodwill
Greenwich Hospital Thrift Shop
MerryGoRound
Neighbor-to-Neighbor
Rummage Room
Salvation Army

06830 Gifts (Gift Shops)

522 East Putnam Avenue (Indian Field Plaza, Cos Cob), 340.2963
www.06830gifts.com
Charming baby gifts and housewarming gifts, many with a Greenwich theme. The shop promotes local products and artists.
Hours: Tuesday - Saturday, 10 am - 6 pm.

A Woodhouse (Antiques-Silver & Jewelry)

7 West Putnam Avenue, 422.2500
Founded in 1690 in London. This shop specializes in antique and second-hand sterling silver items such as: tea sets, candle sticks and serving pieces.
Hours: Tuesday - Saturday, 10 am - 5 pm.

ABC Carpet Warehouse Outlet (Home Decorating)

1055 Bronx River Avenue (at Bruckner Boulevard),Bronx, NY, 718.842.8770
www.ABCHome.com
A wonderland of rugs and carpets. ABC has been selling off-price rugs at its huge Bronx warehouse for five years. The company has expanded the space and filled it with bed linens, furniture and accessories. Bargain hunters can buy ABC's merchandise for 20 percent to 70 percent off downtown prices. You can park in a secure parking lot attached to the building.
Hours: Monday - Saturday, 10 am - 7pm; Sunday, 11 am - 6 pm.

Aby M Taylor (Art)

43 Greenwich Avenue, 622.0906
www.amtFineArt.com
At the top of the Avenue, this gallery focuses on 19th and 20th century American and European paintings and sculpture by known artists. Prices range from $4,000 to $495,000.
Hours: weekdays, 10 am - 5 pm; Saturday, 11 am - 5 pm.

Albe Furs & Outerwear (Clothing-Women)

1212 E Putnam Avenue, 637.3883
www.albefurs.com
They have stores in Westport and New Canaan as well as Greenwich. They store, clean, restyle, repair and appraise furs.
Hours: Monday - Saturday, 10 am - 6 pm, during the winter they may be open Sunday.

Accessory Store (Home - Accessories)
69 Jefferson Street, Stamford, 327.7128
www.StamfordShades.com
Dealers and decorators use this store and you should, too. They have a large selection of lamp shades and chandelier parts. They also have many lamps, display stands and more, all at great prices.
Hours: Monday - Saturday, 10:30 am - 5:30 pm; Sunday, noon - 5 pm.
Directions: I-95 N to Exit 8, R on Canal (second light), L on Jefferson.

Ace Hardware of Cos Cob (Hardware)
136 East Putnam Avenue, Cos Cob, 869.9254
Right next to the Food Mart, this convenient, small hardware store has been helping residents for over 70 years. As you can imagine, after this length of time, they have what you need.
Hours: Monday - Saturday, 8 am - 6 pm, Sunday, 9 am - 4 pm.

Ada's Variety Shop (candy)
112 Riverside Avenue (Corner of Chapel Lane & Riverside Ave)
637.0305
An old fashioned candy store loved by children and their children.
Hours: weekdays, 7:30 am - 5 pm; weekends, 7:30 am - 2 pm.

All Sports Apparel (Sporting Equipment & Clothing)
146 Sound Beach Avenue, Old Greenwich, 698.3055
www.allsportsapparel.com
Apparel for most sports, even yoga. Team licensed products including hats and jerseys. They also carry field hockey and lacrosse equipment.
Hours: weekdays, 10 am - 5 pm; Saturday, 10 am - 3 pm.

Alma Workshop (Jewelry)
4 Grigg Street, 869.0113
Just off Greenwich Avenue, this small workshop has jewelry designed for easy wear and compliments.
Hours: Thursday, Friday & Saturday, 10:30 am - 6 pm.

Angela Moore (Jewelry-Women & Youth)
254 Sound Beach Avenue, Old Greenwich, 698.3254
www.angelamoore.com
Colorful hand-painted beaded necklaces and bracelets to make everyday dressing fun. They also carry clothing accessories to go with the jewelry.
Hours: Monday - Saturday, 9:30 am - 5:30 pm.

Ann Sacks Tile & Stone (Home-Decorating)
23 East Putnam Avenue, 622.8884
www.annsacks.com
A showroom filled with pretty tiles - many unique, such as pebble, wood or concrete.
Hours: weekdays, 9 am - 5 pm.

Ann Taylor (Clothing - Women)
200 Greenwich Avenue, 661.6455
www.anntaylor.com
High-end casual and professional clothing and shoes.
Hours: Monday - Saturday, 10 am - 6 pm; Thursday until 7pm; Sunday, noon - 5 pm.

Anna Banana (Clothing-Children)
248 Sound Beach Avenue, Old Greenwich, 637.0128
Kathy O'Malley of Hoagland's, has gifted Greenwich with the most cheerful, adorable clothing shop for babies and young children imaginable. Fashions are by designers such as: Ralph Lauren, Lili Gaufrette, Charlie Rocket, Hartstrings and E-Land.
Hours: Monday - Saturday, 9:30 - 5:30.

Anne Fontaine (Clothing - Women)
234 Greenwich Avenue, 422.2433
www.annefontaine.com
Originally from Paris, with stores on Madison Avenue and in SoHo, this woman's boutique specializes in black and white. You will find an assortment of sophisticated, trendy and top-of-the-line blouses for all occasions.
Hours: Monday - Saturday 10 am - 6 pm; Sunday noon - 5 pm

Anne Klein (Shoes & Accessories-Women)
120 Greenwich Avenue, 622.4655
www.AnneKlein.com
Luxury accessories for the well dressed woman, such as handbags, shoes, scarves and glasses.
Hours: Monday - Saturday, 10 am - 6 pm (Thursday until 7 pm); Saturday, noon to 5 pm.

Antan (Home Decorating- lamps & shades)

1075 East Putnam Avenue, Riverside (above Aux Delices), 698.3219
www.antanantiques.com
If you see a lamp shade in a very pretty color, it may be from Monique Olmer's shop. For over 20 years, she has been providing Greenwich with unique lamps and shades.
Hours: Tuesday - Saturday, 10:30 am - 5 pm.

Anthropologie (Home Furnishings & Clothing - Women)

480 West Putnam Avenue, 422.5421
www.anthropologie.com
A retailer of high-end casual clothing. Though mainly women's apparel and accessories, the store also sells furniture and home furnishings. The company prides itself on its one-of-a-kind items.
Hours: Monday - Saturday, 10 am -7 pm; Sunday, noon - 6 pm.

Apadana (Home Decorating - Carpets)

539 East Putnam Avenue, Cos Cob, 422.0700
www.ApadanaInc.com
Apadana's presence in Greenwich is fairly new, but New Yorkers have known them for 20 years. They have antique and reproduction carpets in modern and traditional patterns.
Hours: Monday - Saturday, 10 am - 6 pm.

Aptons (Clothing - Men & Women)

24 Field Point Road, 661.3877
Stylish ready-made and custom clothing. David Proudfit (yes, this is his real name and it fits) was for many years the expert tailor at Richards. For men and women caring about fabric, style and a great fit you will really enjoy the experience of shopping here. The tailor shop is below the showroom.
Hours: Weekdays 9 am - 6 pm; Saturday, 9 am - 6 pm;
Sunday, noon - 5 pm.

AT Proudian (Home-Decorating, Oriental Rugs)

120 East Putnam Avenue, 622.1200
www.atproudian.com
A family-owned dend operated Oriental rug business. They have been in Greenwich since 1974 and have a good reputation. A source for cleaning, repair and appraisal.
Hours: Monday - Saturday, 10 am - 5 pm (Saturday to 4 pm).

Atelier Constantin Popescu (Music)

1139 East Putnam Avenue, Riverside, 637.7421

www.atelierconstantinpopescu.com

Sells, repairs and rents string instruments. Constantin Popescu is a graduate of both the Bucharest Conservatory in Romania and of Juilliard School of Music. Constantin is the Principal Bassist of the Greenwich Symphony. The Riverside School of Music is located above his store.
Hours: weekdays, 10 am - 6 pm; Saturday, 10 am - 2 pm.

Athlete's Foot (Shoes)

73 Greenwich Avenue, 629.3338

www.theathletesfoot.com

A locally run chain store. Their goal is to be the definitive expert on athletic footwear. And, indeed they have a very good selection of shoes.
Hours: weekdays, 9:30 am - 7 pm; Saturday, 9:30 am - 6 pm;
Sunday, 11:30 am - 5 pm.

Audiocom (Electronics Audio/Visual)

321 Greenwich Avenue, 552.5224

www.audiocomhifi.com

Previously in Old Greenwich since 1968. They sell high quality audio, video and home automation equipment from their lower level 5,000 square foot space now on the Avenue. They have equipment you may not see anywhere else. They will design and install your home theater.
Hours: weekdays, 10 am - 5 pm; Saturday, 10 am - 4 pm.

TIP: BABY STORES ON CENTRAL PARK AVENUE

It's worth the drive to visit these baby stores which you will find along both sides of the street: Central Park Avenue is approximately 20 minutes away, (which runs through Yonkers and Scarsdale in Westchester County NY). You'll find everything you need for your children. Bring a lot of energy—it's going to be an exhausting day! Directions: I-95 S to 287 W to exit 4 (RT-100A), L off Ramp towards Hartsdale. At 3rd main intersection R on Central Park Avenue.

Avenue News (Newspapers & Magazines)
375 Greenwich Avenue, 629.2429
A popular shop with friendly service and magazines on every topic. Stop in while you are on the Avenue or heading to the train station for a cold drink, snack or headache remedy.
Hours: every day, 5 am - 9:30 pm.

Babies 'R 'Us (Children)
2700 Central Park Ave., Yonkers, NY, 914.722.4500
www.babiesrus.com
Mega baby store selling toys, bedding, furniture. This is just one of the baby stores on Central Park Avenue in Yonkers.
Hours: Monday - Saturday, 9:30 am - 9:30 pm, Sunday, 11 am - 7 pm.
Directions: I-95 S to exit 21, I-287 W to exit 8 (Westchester Avenue towards White Plains), follow NY119 to Bronx River Parkway S, from Bronx River Parkway take ramp towards Scarsdale/Ardsley, R on Ardsley Rd, L on NY100 S/Central Park Avenue.

Baccarat (Gifts, Crystal)
236 Greenwich Avenue, 618.0900
www.baccarat.fr
A table set with their French luxury crystal is very special. They also have a selection of pretty vases and giftware.
Hours: Monday - Saturday, 10 am - 6 pm;
Sunday (December only) noon - 5 pm.

Baker Furniture (Home, Furniture)
200 Greenwich Avenue, 862.0655
www.bakerfurniture.com
Now you can buy directly what once was the exclusive province of interior designers. Furniture, fabrics and accessories with a timeless elegance.
Hours: Monday - Saturday, 10 am - 6 pm (Thursday until 8 pm);
Sunday, noon - 5 pm.

Banana Republic (Clothing, Men & Women)
254 Greenwich Avenue, 622.9199
www.bananarepublic.com
They sell the Gap's higher end casual career clothing. Most of the clothes are rather trendy. In the US there are over 400 Banana Republic stores.
Hours: Monday - Saturday, 10 am - 7 pm; Sunday, 11 am - 6 pm.

Bang & Olufsen - Harvey Electronics (Electronics - Audio/ Visual)
19 West Putnam Avenue, 622.0324
www.bangolufsen.com http://www.bangolufsen.com/sw6060.asp
www.HarveyElectronics.com
Bang & Olufsen has been creating exceptional music and audio systems for over 75 years. Their cutting-edge Danish designs are so attractive they have been on display at the Museum of Modern Art. They have a combined store with Harvey Electronics where you will find stereos, speakers, televisions and telephones.
Hours: Monday Saturday, 10 am - 6 pm.

The Barn (Home Furnishings- Fabrics)
50 Hurd Avenue, Bridgeport, CT, 203.334.3396
If you want to see a wide variety of fabrics, visit this old barn with 20,000 square feet of well priced bolts: silks, linens, velvets, cottons. You can also get upholstered headboards and throw pillows.
Hours: Monday - Saturday, 10 am - 5 pm.

BCBG Max Azria (Clothing, Women)
200 Greenwich Avenue, 861.7303
www.bcbg.com
Bon Chic Bon Genre caters to modern women who want trendy, chic, unique fashions at reasonable prices. Their upscale garments are in the Max Azria Collection.
Hours: Monday - Saturday, 10 am - 6 pm; Sunday, 11 am - 6 pm.

Beacon Point Marine (Boating)
49 River Road, Cos Cob, 661.4033
http://www.boats.com/sites/beaconpointmarine
New and used recreational and fishing boats, storage and service.
Hours: Monday - Saturday, 10 am - 5 pm.

Beads in the Loft (Jewelry)
3 Lewis Street, 861.0086
Beads in the Loft carries handmade custom jewelry. Unlike other jewelry stores, customers can also design their purchases themselves. They have beads of every color and size, and everything in the store is made from semi-precious stones, precious stones and fresh water pearls, using 18 and 24karat gold and sterling silver.
Hours: Tuesday - Saturday 10 am - 5 pm.

Beame & Barre (Clothing-Children, Dance wear)
352 Greenwich Avenue, 622.0591
Dance wear to suit even the most discriminating ballerina's tastes. Plus exercise wear, skating attire and costumes.
Hours: weekdays, 10 am - 5:30 pm; Saturday, 10 am - 5 pm.

Bed Bath & Beyond (Home, Accessories)
• 2275 Summer Street (Ridgeway Shopping Center), Stamford 323.7714
• 25 Waterfront Place, Port Chester, NY, 914.937.9098
www.bedbathandbeyond.com
A huge store with medium-to-high quality items for the bedroom, bathroom, plus the dining room and kitchen. They operate 819 stores. Their main competitor is Linens n Things.
Stamford Hours: Monday-Saturday, 9 am - 9 pm;
Sunday, 9:30 am - 6 pm.
Port Chester Hours: Monday - Saturday, 9 am - 9:30 pm,
Sunday, 10 am - 7 pm.

Bedford Sportsman (Fishing, Equipment & Clothing)
25 Adams Street, Bedford Hills, NY, 914.666.8091
www.bedfordsportsman.com
Specializes in freshwater fly and spin fishing equipment. A good resource for New York watershed streams. They teach fly fishing during the summer and they have a full range of guide services.
Hours: Tuesday - Friday, 9 am - 6 pm (Thursday's until 7 pm); Saturday, 9 am - 5 pm; Sunday, 9 am - 3 pm.

Bellini Juvenile Designer Furniture (Children - Furniture)
• 495 Central Park Avenue, Scarsdale, NY, 914.472.7336
• 984 High Ridge Road, Stamford, CT, 703.2084
www.bellini.com
Wellmade baby and teen furniture.
Scarsdale Hours: Monday - Saturday, 10 am - 6 pm
(Thursday until 7 pm); Sunday, noon - 5 pm.
Stamford Hours: Monday - Saturday, 10 am - 5 pm
(Saturday until 6 pm); Sunday, noon - 5 pm.

Bendheim Gallery (Art)

299 Greenwich Avenue, 622.3998

http://www.greenwicharts.org/currentshow.asp

Inside the Art Center, the Arts Council gallery has interesting exhibits you will not want to miss.

Hours: weekdays, 10 am - 5 pm (Thursday until 7 pm);Saturday, noon - 5 pm.

Best & Co (Clothing -Children)

289 Greenwich Avenue, 629.1743

www.bestnco.com

This is a sophisticated children's department store serving children from infancy through the early teenage years. In addition to clothing, the store offers layette registry, home furnishings for children and gifts.

Hours: Monday - Saturday, 10 am - 6 pm.

Best Buy (Electronics)

330 Connecticut Avenue, Norwalk, CT, 203.857.4543

www.bestbuy.com

Best Buy has a 45,000 square foot store just down the street from arch rival Circuit City. Best Buy is the largest retailer of consumer electronics in the US. Circuit City is the next largest.

Hours: Monday Saturday, 10 am - 9:30 pm; Sunday, 11 am - 7 pm.

Directions: I-95N to exit 13, R on Connecticut Avenue.

Betteridge Jewelers (Jewelry)

117 Greenwich Avenue, 869.0124

www.betteridge.com

A third-generation family-owned business; buying, selling and collecting some of the finest jewelry. The shop specializes in fine timepieces, rare and exceptional stones, estate jewelry and pearls, plus a broad collection of classic and contemporary jewelry and silver to suit a diverse clientele. They carry many renowned brands, such as Cartier and Van Cleef & Arpel. Totally trustworthy with excellent service and repair, as well as appraisal services.

Hours: Tuesday - Saturday, 9 am - 5 pm. (Call for holiday hours).

Beval Saddlery (Sporting Equipment & Clothing - Riding)

50 Pine Street, New Canaan, CT, 203.966.7828
www.beval.com
English saddlery and clothing. They do a good job of fitting a saddle to you and your horse.
Hours: Monday-Saturday, 9 am - 5 pm (Thursday until 8 pm).
Directions: Merritt Parkway N to Exit 37, L onto Route 124. At light (Gulf station on right), L on Cherry Street. Go straight through the light, Cherry Street will turn into Pine Street.

Blinds To Go

411 Westport Avenue, Norwalk, 203.840.1357
www.Blindstogo.com
One of a 120 superstores providing blinds and shades of all descriptions. They claim to be the largest retailer of these items in the world.
Hours: Monday-Tuesday, 10 am - 7pm; Closed Wednesday; Thursday-Saturday, 10 am -7 pm; Sunday, noon - 5 pm.

Bloomingdale's (Department Store)

175 Bloomingdale Road, White Plains, NY, 914.684.6300
www.Bloomingdales.com
A large stand-alone store, with lots of parking. Bloomingdale's is a chain of upscale American department stores owned by Federated Department Stores, which is also the parent company of Macy's. Bloomingdale's has 36 stores nationwide. It competes on an average price level with Nordstrom and slightly below that of Saks Fifth Avenue and Neiman Marcus.
Hours: Monday - Saturday, 10 am - 9 pm (Friday & Saturday until 10 pm); Sunday, 11 am - 7 pm.
Directions: I-95 S to I-287 W to exit 8 (Westchester Avenue), L on Bloomingdale.

Bodd (Sport Clothing - Women)

181 Greenwich Avenue (second floor), 983.5470
www.BoddFitness.com
Stylish exercise wear for women. They also have exercise classes.
Hours: weekdays, 8 am - 11 am; Saturday, 9 am - 11 am.

Braswell Galleries (Antiques)

737 Canal Street, Stamford, 327.5101
www.braswellgalleries.com
Located in the Stamford antique district, browse through the antiques in the Estate Center and the Gallery Shop. The Gallery typically has the mid-level antiques. The Estate center specializes in higher level antiques. Buyers can also have fun taking part in their auctions, which are held once or twice a month. Leave a silent bid or attend the auction and you may be able to purchase the item you want at a very competitive price.
Hours: Monday - Saturday, 10:30 am - 5:30 pm;
Sunday, 11 am - 5 pm.
Braswell Galleries is home to Braswell Galleries Estate Center, The Gallery Shop and Stamford Auction.

Brooks Brothers (Clothing - Men & Women)

181 Greenwich Avenue, 863.9288
www.brooksbrothers.com
This 12,000 sq. ft. store carries classic men's, women's and boy's clothing. Brooks has 240 stores and is the oldest men's clothier in the US
Hours: weekdays, 10 am - 7 pm, Thursday until 8 pm; Saturday, 10 am - 6 pm; Sunday, noon - 6 pm.

Bruce Park Sports (Sporting Equipment & Clothing)

104 Mason Street, 869.1382
Team uniforms and equipment for most sports.
Hours: weekdays, 9 am - 5:30 pm; Saturday, 9 am - 5:30 pm.

Burlington Coat Factory (Department Store)

74 Broad Street, Stamford, CT, 363.0450
www.Coat.com
This national chain has 360 stores. They have branched out since their founding in 1924 and now sell women's apparel, including suits, shoes and accessories. They even have a baby department and sell linens. All items are sold at a discount to its principle competitors, TJ Maxx and Filene's Basement.
Hours: Monday - Saturday, 9:30 am - 9 pm; Sunday, 11 am - 6 pm.

Button (Home - Accessories)

125 East Putnam Avenue, 6613540

www.buttonhomestyle.com

As its website says, "interesting things for interesting homes." You'll find everything from an assortment of candles and drawer liners, to pillows, home design books, colorful place settings and even a few pieces of furniture.

Hours: weekdays, 10 am - 5:30 pm; Saturday, 11 am - 5 pm.

Buy Buy Baby (Children)

1019 Central Park Avenue, Scarsdale, NY, 914.725.9220

www.buybuybaby.com

Everything for children ages 0-3. It's a large store so wear comfortable shoes!

Hours: Monday Saturday, 9:30 am - 9:30 pm; Sunday, 11 am - 7 pm.

Directions: I-95 S to 287 W to exit 4 (RT100A), L off ramp towards Hartsdale. At 3rd main intersection R on Central Park Avenue.

Camera Wholesalers (Photography)

1034 High Ridge Road, Stamford CT, 357.0467

www.CameraWholesalers.com

A family-owned store that has been in business since 1978. They are authorized dealers for almost all makes of cameras and many are in stock. They have a knowledgeable staff to help you make selections.

Hours: weekdays, 9 am to 6 pm (Thursday to 9 pm); Saturday, 10 am - 6 pm.

Candy Nichols (Children & Youth - Clothing)

- 59B Purchase Street, Rye NY, 914.967.2288
- 67 Elm Street, New Canaan, CT 203.972.8600

This children's store is run by local moms, for moms who don't want to pay high prices. They know what kids in our schools think is "cool", and they select their merchandise to suit them. For years Candy Nichols had a shop in Greenwich. Devotees have followed them to Rye and New Canaan. They have children's clothing, toys and accessories from infants to girls' sizes 7 - 14 and boys' sizes 8 - 20.

Hours: Monday - Saturday, 9:30 am - 5:30 pm.

The Canine Corner (Pets)

177 Sound Beach Avenue, Old Greenwich, 637.8819
For your dog or your dog-loving friends, this is THE gift shop.
Hours: Tuesday - Friday, 10 am - 6 pm; Saturday, 9 am - 5 pm.

Carters (Children - Clothing)

2329 Summer Street (Ridgeway Shopping Center), Stamford
975.9725
www.carters.com
Mothers love this store for good buys for newborns, toddlers and kids
(through size 7). This is where you will find all of the basics.
Hours: Monday - Saturday, 9 am - 9 pm; Sunday, 10 am - 6 pm.

Cashmere Inc. (Clothing - Women)

55 E. Putnam Avenue, 552.1059
They have a wide selection of sweaters, dresses, scarves, gloves and
friendly help.
Hours: Monday - Saturday, 9:30 am - 5:30 pm. Open Sundays noon 5 pm
in December.

Cavalier Galleries (Art)

405 Greenwich Avenue, 869.3664
www.cavaliergalleries.com
Ronald Cavalier specializes in painting and sculpture by contemporary
artists working in a representational style. You may already have smiled
at one of the gallery's lifelike sculptures on a sidewalk in Greenwich or
Stamford. Prices range from $100 to $100,000.
Hours: Summer: Monday - Saturday 10:30 am - 6 pm; Sunday by appointment. Winter: Monday - Saturday, 10 am - 6pm; Sunday, 11 am - 5
pm.

Ceramic Design (Home - Decorating)

26 Bruce Park Avenue, 869.8800
The store is larger than it appears. They have a good selection of tiles
and knowledgeable help.
Hours: weekdays, 9 am - 5 pm; Saturday, 10 am - 4 pm.

Cherry Blossoms (Flowers and Gifts)

2 Lewis Court, 869.2733

When Marcy Imbert said she had a lifestyle store, our curiosity was piqued. They have a mixture of gifts and flowers, even fine French Mariage Freres tea. We were seduced by a tiny Lady Slipper orchid.

Hours: Monday - Saturday, 9:30 am - 5 pm.

Chillybear (Clothing & Sports Equipment- Youth)

401 Greenwich Avenue, 622.7115 or 888.463.2707

www.chillybear.com

A store for the hip young adolescent. Filled with the latest garb as well as skateboards, inline skates and accessories. Very nice customer service.

Hours: Monday - Saturday, 10 am - 6 pm; Sunday, noon - 5 pm.

Christopher Fischer (Clothing - Women)

103 Greenwich Avenue, 861.7400

Cashmere clothing designed with style.

Hours: Monday - Saturday, 10 am - 6 pm

Circuit City (Electronics)

- 44 Connecticut Avenue, Norwalk, CT 203.866.3600
- 220 Main Street, White Plains, NY, 914.272.1060

www.circuitcity.com

Circuit City is the #2 US electronics retailer. Best Buy is #1. They are known for their broad selection of audio and video equipment and competitive pricing.

Hours: Monday - Thursday, 10 am to 9:30 pm;

Friday & Saturday, 10 am -10 pm; Sunday 1 pm to 8 pm

Directions: I-95 N to exit 13, R on Connecticut Avenue.

Claire Maestroni (Home-Furnishings, curtains)

135 Mason Street, 422.0567

www.clairemaestroni.com

Ready-made and custom draperies and valances, using French and Italian fabrics. Some Italian lighting fixtures.

Hours: Monday - Saturday, 10 am - 5 pm.

Classic Sofa (Home Furniture)

79 East Putnam Avenue, 863.0005

www.classicSofa.com

This is a custom sofa store; any size, any shape, any fabric. Select a model from the many samples in the showroom or show them a picture, choose your fabric and size. Within two weeks after the fabric arrives, the sofa will be in your home.

Hours: Monday - Saturday, 10 am - 6 pm.

Clinton Crossing Premium Outlets (Outlet Mall)

Route 81, Clinton, CT, 860.664.0700

www.premiumoutlets.com

The largest outlet center in Connecticut, they have seventy upscale stores. If you have time, have dinner at the nearby Inn at Chester, 318 West Main Street (Rts 145 & 81), Chester, CT, 860.526.9541 www.innatchester.com or at the top-rated French Restaurant Du Village, 59 Main Street (at Maple Street), Chester, CT, 860.526.5301. www.RestaurantDuVillage.com

Regular Hours: Monday - Saturday, 10 am - 9 pm; Sunday, 10 am - 6 pm.

Holiday Hours: (December only) Monday Saturday, 9 am - 9 pm;

Sunday 9 am - 7 pm.

Directions: I-95 N exit 63.

CM Almy (Gifts-Religious)

228 Sound Beach Avenue, 637.2739

www.Almy.com

A supplier of clerical attire, the front of this shop is filled with Christian books and gifts.

Hours: weekdays, 10 am - 5 pm; Saturday, 10 am - 2 pm.

Coach (Accessories- Women)

243 Greenwich Avenue, 629.6228

www.coach.com

For 65 years, this company has been a leading handbag designer. One of the hallmarks of the Coach company is their policy which states that any Coach product may be repaired for the life of the product by simply shipping it back to the home office for a nominal fee, with a note or letter stating the problem. Its main competitors are Louis Vuitton (Westchester Mall) and Kate Spade.

Hours: Monday - Saturday, 10 am - 6 pm; Sunday, noon - 5 pm.

Cochni (Clothing-Women, Shoes & Accessories)

6 Greenwich Avenue, 422.0970

At the top of the Avenue, almost on the sidewalk level, is a large boutique with fun items such as unbelievable belt buckles, jeweled slippers, cashmere sweaters with embroidery & trim, and a selection of silk scarves. All at reasonable prices.

Monday - Saturday, 10 am - 6 pm; Sunday, noon - 5 pm.

Cocoon (Home-Furniture, Home-Accessories)

83 Greenwich Avenue, 622.3138

www.cocoon-group.com

When you enter this store, you are going to say "wow" as you are greeted by unusual, pottery, trays, dishes, art objects and furniture in striking colors. All beautifully made from shells, bamboo and many other elements from nature.

Hours: Monday - Saturday, 10 am - 6 pm; Sunday, 11 am - 5 pm.

Colony Florist (Florist)

315 Greenwich Avenue, 227.7836

www.colonyflorist.org

A family-owned shop giving Greenwich residents personal service for 50 years. If you grew up in Greenwich, it is likely your first corsage came from Colony. They do a lot of custom work. They will even decorate your Christmas tree as well as your mantel and banister.

Hours: Monday - Saturday, 8 am - 5:30 pm (Saturday until 4 pm)

Computer Super Center (Electronics - Computer)

103 Mason Street, 661.1700

For friendly help and expert advice on PCs and Apples try the Super Center. A good selection of hardware and software. They also sell and service Sony LCD home theater equipment.

Hours: weekdays, 9 am - 6 pm; Saturday, 10 am - 5 pm.

Compleat Angler (Fishing Equipment & Clothing)

172 Heights Road, Darien, CT, 203.655.9400 or 877.329.2753

www.compleatangler.com

A large selection of flyfishing and light tackle spinfishing equipment as well as outdoor clothing. Ask about their lessons and guide service.

Hours: Monday - Saturday, 9:30 am - 6 pm (Thursday until 8 pm); Sunday, 11 am - 4 pm.

The Connecticut Store (Gifts)

120140 Bank Street, Waterbury, CT, 800.474.6728

www.theconnecticutstore.com

This store specializes in items made in Connecticut. This is a great resource if you are looking for a unique gift. Best of all, you can buy almost everything from their website without making a trip. We especially like the blazer buttons from the Waterbury Button Company, their selection is amazing.

Hours: Tuesday - Saturday, 9:30 am - 5 pm.

Directions: I84 East exit 22. L on South Main, L at next light, then L again.

The Container Store (Home Furnishings)

145 Westchester Avenue (next to the Westchester Mall), White Plains, NY 914.946.4767

www.containerStore.com

A 25,000 square foot store designed to help you organize your life and hopefully the life of your college student.

Hours: Monday - Saturday, 9 am - 6 pm; Sunday, 10 am - 6 pm.

Cook and Craft (Home - Cooking Equipment)

27 Arcadia Road, Old Greenwich, 637.2755

www.cookandcraft.com

This shop has a whole range of high quality kitchen essentials. The cookware, knives, utensils, gadgets, cookbooks and gourmet pantry items are selected by the owner, an ex-chef of ten years. They have a bridal registry.

Hours: Monday - Saturday, 10 am - 5 pm. (Seasonal, hours vary).

Cos Cob Farms (Flowers)

6163 East Putnam Avenue, Cos Cob, 629.2267

Fresh fruit, vegetables and flowers at reasonable prices.

Hours: Monday - Saturday, 8 am - 7 pm; Sunday 9 am - 6 pm.

Costco (Grocery & Department Store)

1 Westchester Avenue, Port Chester, NY, 914.935.3103

www.costco.com

You have to buy a membership to shop at this international chain, but that hasn't kept this megastore, a.k.a. warehouse, from being a Greenwich hit. From pesto in their grocery section to a DVD player to a refrigerator, this huge store tries to give good value. If you want an expensive electronic item or a large quantity of a staple, this could be your best bet. If you want to run in quickly to get something, forget it.

Hours: weekdays, 10 am - 8:30 pm, Saturday, 9:30 am - 6 pm, Sunday, 10 am - 6 pm.

Country Floors (Home- Decorating)

12 East Putnam Avenue, 862.9900

www.countryfloors.com

A large store with a good selection of all styles and prices, recognized by House and Garden as (Best of the Best, 2004). One of six locations throughout the USA.

Hours: weekdays, 9 am - 5:30 pm.

Crate & Barrel (Home Furniture and Cookware)

125 Westchester Avenue (Westchester Mall) White Plains, NY 914.682.0900

www.CrateAndBarrel.com

A chain specializing in housewares, indoor and outdoor furniture and home accessories. Much of the merchandise is direct from Europe. Their major competitors are IKEA, Pottery Barn and Williams-Sonoma.

Hours: Monday - Saturday, 10 am - 9 pm; Sunday, noon - 6 pm.

Curtain Works of Greenwich (Home-Decorating, Draperies)

30 East Putnam Avenue, 622.2354
www.CurtainWorksofGreenwich.com
The perfect place to find ready-made curtains that have the designer look at reasonable prices. There are over 100 fabrics to choose from. Many of the silks are from India. They provide measuring services and hardware.
Hours: Monday - Saturday, 9:30 - 5:30.

Custom Golf of Connecticut (Golf Equipment)

2770 Summer Street, Stamford, 323.7888, or 800.804.5754
www.golfpsychos.com
Wide variety of golf clubs for sale or rent and some clothing. They do repairs and re-gripping.
Hours: weekdays, 10 am - 6 pm (Thursday until 7 pm in summer); Saturday, 9 am - 5 pm.
Directions: I-95 N to Atlantic Street exit 8, L on Atlantic (becomes Bedford), past Stop & Shop, L and next L onto Summer.

Cycle Dynamics (Bicycles)
BikeEx

12 Riversville Road, Glenville, 532.1718
Ken Adler used to work at Buzz's Cycle Shop before he started Cycle Dynamics, a full service sales and service store. Ken also operates BikeEx, a mobile repair shop that will come to your home to tune-up or repair your bicycles.
Hours: weekdays, 10 am - 6 pm; Saturday, 10am - 5 pm.

Darien Golf Center (Sporting Equipment & Clothing -Golf)

233 Post Road, Darien, CT, 203.655.2788
www.dariengolfcenter.com
Excellent selection of golf equipment and men's clothing. Very helpful service.
Hours: Monday - Saturday, 9 am - 5:30 pm; Sunday, 10 am - 3:30 pm.
Directions: I-95 N to exit 13, L on Post Rd.

Darien Sport Shop (Clothing - Men, Women, Children)
1127 Post Road, Darien, CT 203.655.2575
www.DarienSport.com
Good-looking sports attire. They also carry a limited supply of Boy and Girl Scout uniforms.
Hours: Monday - Saturday, 9 am - 5:30 pm; Thursday until 8:30 pm.
Directions: I-95 N to exit 11, toward Darien, keep L and merge on US-1 (Post Road).

Dave's Cycle and Fitness (Bicycles & Exercise)
78 Valley Road, Cos Cob, 661.7736
www.davecycle.com
A good source for bike rentals and exercise equipment.
Hours: Tuesday - Wednesday 10 am - 6pm; Thursday, 10 am - 8 pm; Friday, 10 am - 6 pm; Saturday, 9 am - 5 pm; Sunday, 11 am - 4 pm.

De Mane's Golf (Golf Equipment)
35 Chapel Street, Byram, 531.9126
www.demanegolf.com
Golfers in the know visit Rick's shop for custom clubs and repairs.
Hours: Tuesday - Saturday, 10 am - 5 pm.

Decorators Secret (Home Furnishings- Fabrics)
735 Canal Street, Stamford, CT, 323.5093
www.TheDecoratorsSecret.com
A warehouse filled with discounted bolts of fabric from overstocks at New York trade showrooms. A good place to buy your fabric. We recommend you use your own upholsterer.
Hours: Monday - Saturday, 10:30 am - 5:30 pm; Sunday, noon - 5 pm.

Design Within Reach (Home-Furniture)
86 Greenwich Avenue, 422.2013
www.dwr.com
A small chain dedicated to classic, modern furniture, most from known designers. Their goal is to provide furniture traditionally found only in design showrooms.
Hours: Monday - Saturday, 10 am - 6 pm (Thursday to 7 pm); Sunday, noon - 5 pm.

Diane's Doll Shoppe (Dolls)

227 Mill Street, 531.3370

www.dianesdollshoppe.com

A darling collection of play and collector dolls. Sweet faces so lifelike, they encourage you to pick them up and cuddle them. A delight for collectors and the little girl in your life.

Hours: Tuesday - Saturday, 10 am - 5 pm.

Dighton Rhode (Clothing-Women)

5 Lewis Street, 622.4600

Beautiful designer clothing, in an elegant small shop just off the Avenue.

Hours: Monday - Saturday, 10 am - 6 pm.

Dinoffer (Luggage)

344 Greenwich Avenue, 622.8238

www.dinoffer.com

Luggage, briefcases, handbags, wallets and photo albums. This family-owned, high quality, high-end shop carries Longchamps, Agresti, Daines & Hathaway, Hartmann and Tusting.

Hours: Monday - Saturday, 10 am - 6 pm (Thursdays until 8 pm between Thanksgiving and Christmas).

Drapery Exchange (Home Furnishing - Drapery)

1064 Boston Post Road, Darien, CT, 203.655.3844

What a great idea! A consignment shop for beautiful draperies. Some almost new. None over 3 years old.

Hours: weekdays, 10 am - 5 pm; Saturday, 10 am - 1 pm.

DSW (Shoes-Men & Women)

5 Westchester Avenue (The Waterfront), Port Chester, NY
 914.690.2841

www.DSWshoes.com

The Designer Shoe Warehouse has more that 30,000 pairs of adult men's and women's shoes in an amazing variety of styles.

Hours: Monday - Saturday, 9:30 am - 9:30 pm; Sunday, 11 am - 6 pm.

Duxiana Beds (Home - Beds)
15 West Putnam Avenue, 661.7162
www.DuxBed.com
Made in Sweden with several layers of springs, Dux beds are guaranteed for 20 years and cost between $5,350 and $9,100 for a king-size bed and between $2,500 and $3,000 for a single. Owners of these beds tell us they are worth the price.
Hours: Monday - Saturday, 10 am - 6 pm; Sunday, noon - 5 pm.

East Putnam Variety (Magazines & Newspapers)
Whole Foods shopping Center, 88 East Putnam Avenue, 869.8789
This conveniently located shop has magazines, cards, newspapers, and a myriad of party goods, including a fabulous balloon selection. Great customer service.
Hours: Monday - Saturday, 7 am to 10 pm.

Eastern Mountain Sports (Sporting Equipment & Clothing)
952 High Ridge Road, Stamford, 461.9865
www.ems.com
A general purpose chain sports store with an emphasis on camping, climbing and kayaking. A good place to find out about climbing and kayaking instruction.
Hours: weekdays, 9 am - 9 pm; Saturday to 7 pm; Sunday, 11 am - 5 pm.
Directions: Merritt Parkway N to exit 35. R on High Ridge.

Elsebe (Clothing - Women)
51 East Putnam Avenue, 869.4760
Elegant casual and business attire from well known designers. Elsebe, the owner, gives great personal attention. She is very good at helping you find just the outfit you need.
Hours: Monday - Saturday, 10 am - 5:30 pm.

Estate Treasures of Greenwich (Consignment - Furniture)
1162 East Putnam Avenue, Riverside, 637.4200
www.EstateTreasures.com
An antique consignment shop which has a wide selection of jewelry and china. A good source for silver services and serving pieces. A large number of tables and desks, although some are high quality reproductions (always marked as reproductions).
Hours: Monday - Saturday, 10 am - 5:30 pm; Sunday, noon - 5:30 pm.

Ethan Allen (Home - Furniture)

2046 West Main, Stamford, 352.2888

www.EthanAllen.com

This 30,000 square-foot store is the company's largest to date. Its collections are divided between informal and classic. They carry just about everything for a home, including a large selection of furniture, window treatments, area rugs and accessories.

Hours: Monday Saturday, 10 am - 6 pm (Tuesday & Thursday, until 8 pm); Sunday, noon - 5 pm.

Directions: Just over the Greenwich border on US-1.

EuroChasse (Sporting Equipment & Clothing)

398 Greenwich Avenue, 625.9501

www.eurochasse.com

Two floors of fascinating gifts and fashionable men's and women's sporting apparel. If you plan to hunt in Europe, this is a must. They also have serious fly fishing equipment and gifts just right for your sporting friends. A good place to get your hunting license.

Hours: Monday - Saturday, 10 am - 6 pm.

Evelyn (Florists - Artificial Flowers)

14 West Putnam Avenue, 661.6743

An abundance of silk flowers so real you will almost smell the fragrance.

Hours: Monday - Saturday, 10 am - 5:30 pm.

Farrow & Ball (Home Furnishing- Wallpaper & Paint)

32 East Putnam Avenue, 422.0990

www.Farrow-Ball.com

A favorite of designers, this shop is open to everyone. The soft and classic patterns of the wallpaper are color coordinated with their paints. Paints are available in many colors and finishes.

Hours: weekdays, 9 am - 6 pm; Saturday, 10 am - 5 pm.

Fashion Light Center (Home - Lighting)

168 West Putnam Avenue, 869.3098

A handy local resource for bulbs, lampshades, lamps, chandeliers and repairs.

Hours: Monday - Saturday, 9 am - 5:30 pm.

Federalist (Home - Furniture)

365 Greenwich Avenue, 625.4727

www.thefederalistonline.com

Not antiques, but only experts would know it. The shop is filled with fine reproductions of 18th century furniture and accessories.

Hours: Monday - Saturday, 10 am - 6 pm; and by appointment.

Feinsod (Hardware)

268 Sound Beach Avenue, Old Greenwich, 637.3641

43 N Main St , Port Chester NY 914.939.3872 www.servistar.com or www.feinsodhardware.com

Friendly, well-stocked hardware store run by people who take customer service that extra step. They even repair storm windows and screens.

Hours: Monday - Saturday, 8 am - 5:30 pm; Sunday, 9 am - 2 pm.

Femmegems (Jewelry)

19A East Putnam Avenue, 861.2531

www.femmegems.com

A pleasant place to try out your own skills at jewelry designing. You can start fresh or re-design something you already own. They also have pretty, pre-made baubles for gifts, just right for bridesmaids.

Hours: Monday - Saturday, 10:30 am - 6 pm;

During holidays, Sunday, noon - 5 pm.

Fiesta Place (Parties)

985 East Main Street, Stamford, 961.0034

They sell party favors including piñatas of all kinds.

Hours: Monday - Saturday, 9 am - 8 pm.

Fila (Clothing - Men & Women)

348 Greenwich Avenue, 661.7625

www.fila.com

Italian athletic clothing retailer, with nine stores in the US. They have outfits for running, golf, tennis and general fitness. Great tennis shirts.

Hours: Monday - Saturday, 10 am - 6 pm; Sunday, noon - 5 pm.

Flinn Gallery (Art)
At Greenwich Library, 101 West Putnam Avenue, 622.7900
This attractive gallery, sponsored by the Friends of Greenwich Library, has rotating exhibits selected by a jury. The Gallery also hosts the annual juried exhibition of the Greenwich Art Society.
Hours: Monday - Saturday, 9 am - 5 pm (Thursday, 10 am - 8 pm); Sunday 1 pm 5 pm. Closed on Sundays in July and August.

Floor Covering Warehouse (Home - Carpets)
112 Orchard Street, Stamford, 323.3113
www.floorcoveringwarehouse.org
Tucked away, yet close to Greenwich, this family-owned rug and carpet store has good prices and good service.
Hours: Tuesday - Friday, 8:30 am - 4:30 pm;
Saturday, 8:30 am - 3:30 pm.
Directions: I-95 N to exit 7; R on Greenwich Avenue, R on Homestead, L on Orchard.

Flowers By George (Florist)
7 Strickland Road, Cos Cob, 661.0850
Volunteers in the Hospital rave about their pretty arrangements.
Hours: Tuesday - Saturday, 10 am - 5 pm.

Foot Solutions (Shoes - Men & Women)
168 South Ridge Street, Rye Brook, NY, 914.939.6565
www.footsolutions.com/ryebrook
One of a large chain of stores solely devoted to making sure you have shoes that fit properly. They also make orthotics.
Hours: weekdays, 10 am - 6 pm; Saturday, 10 am - 4 pm.

Forest and Field Outdoor (Sporting Goods)
4 New Canaan Ave, Norwalk CT, 203.847.4008
www.forestandfield.com
A 12,000 square foot firearm store representing a great number of manufacturers. They have a 14-point shooting range and offer pistol certification courses.

Fortunoff (Department Store)

1 Maple Avenue, White Plains, NY, 914.287.8700
(Between Westchester Mall and Bloomingdale's
www.fortunoff.com
A Manhattan-based retailer of jewelry, furniture, housewares and table settings.
Hours: Monday - Saturday, 10 am - 9 pm; Sunday, 11 am - 6 pm.
Directions: I-287 exit 8, L on Westchester Avenue, L on Bloomingdale Road.

Friedman, A.I. (Art Supplies)

431 Boston Post Road, Port Chester, NY, 914.937.7351
www.aifriedman.com
Discount art and craft supply store frequented by many local artists. Large selection of quality pre-made frames and mats.
Hours: weekdays, 9 am - 8:30 pm; Saturday, 9 am - 6 pm;
Sunday, 10 am - 6 pm.

The Funhouse (Toys)

236 Sound Beach Avenue, Old Greenwich, 698.2402
This is a store where you may happily take your children. They have a great variety of small, inexpensive items. Parents fill their party bags here. Good place to find a unique or hard-to-find gift. The staff couldn't be friendlier. They will suggest age-appropriate gifts, sure to please.
Hours: weekdays, 10 am - 6 pm; Saturday, 10 am - 5 pm.

Gabby (Clothing, Women)

70 Greenwich Avenue, 661.5044
This woman's boutique carries good quality and stylish sweaters, jackets, blouses and pants. The service is friendly and the atmosphere is very appealing. If you quickly need to find something to wear for dinner on Friday night, you should give this place a try.
Hours: every day, 10 am - 5:30 pm.

Galleria (Shopping Center)

100 Main Street, White Plains, NY, 914.682.0111
http://www.galleriaATwhiteplains.com/static/node1792.jsp
The anchor stores are Sears (914.644.1400), Macys (914.946.5015), Old Navy (914.682.0482) and H&M (914.422.3777). Sears bought Lands End in 2002 and has a Lands End store at this location.
Hours: Monday - Saturday, 10 am - 9:30 pm; Sunday, 11 am - 7 pm.

Gap (Clothing-Baby, Youth, Adult)
264 Greenwich Avenue, 625.0662
www.Gap.com www.babygap.com, www.gapkids.com
The Gap targets teenagers - 40s. Its merchandise is divided between career clothing and trendy attire and includes maternity. Its lower price line is sold at Old Navy (an anchor store in the Ridgeway Shopping Center and in the Galleria). Banana Republic carries their higher end casual career clothing. A department in the store is for infants up to about 36 months.
Hours: Monday - Saturday, 9 am - 7 pm; Sunday, noon - 6 pm.

Georg Jensen (Jewelry, Gifts)
160 Greenwich Avenue, 661.6195
www.GeorgJensen.com
Jewelry, watches and cutlery with their unique Danish flair. Their stainless steel cutlery is a favorite of brides.
Hours: Monday - Saturday, 9:30 am - 5 pm.

Gift Shop at Audubon Center
613 Riversville Rd, 869.5272
The perfect place to find nature objects, field guides and books. Many unique gifts for children and adults.
Hours: Every day, 9 am - 5 pm.

Gift Shop at Bruce Museum
1 Museum Drive, 869.0376
www.brucemuseum.org
This attractive, high-quality store is filled with unique gifts from around the world, including many with educational value and an excellent selection of books. Merchandise complements the Museum's current exhibits. Be sure to attend their holiday gift bazaar.
Hours: Tuesday Saturday, 10 am - 5 pm; Sunday, 1 am - 5 pm.

Gift Shop at Christ Church
254 East Putnam Avenue, 869.9030
This is the "in" place to go when you need a special gift with meaning. Marijane Marks and her helpful staff have a fine selection of books, gifts, jewelry and greeting cards. During holidays, gifts cascade out of the shop, making the store a joy to visit.
Hours: Tuesday - Saturday 10 am - 5 pm; Sunday 10 am - 1 pm.

Gift Shop at Greenwich Hospital

5 Perryridge Road, 863.3371

www.greenhosp.org

They have a wide array of gifts for patients, including pretty planters and beautiful nightgowns. The items selected by the volunteer staff have made this shop a place to go whether or not you are visiting in the hospital. Selections are well-priced and tax free. All profits go the hospital.
Hours: weekdays, 9:30 am - 8 pm; Saturday, 10 am - 5 pm; Sunday, noon - 6 pm.

Gift Shop at Hyatt Regency

1800 East Putnam Avenue, Old Greenwich, 637.1234

Hotel guests love this shop, but we also dash there when we need a gift with "Greenwich" on it. Best buy: their silk ties!
Hours: Everyday, 8 am - 8 pm.

Go To Your Room (Children, Furniture)

234 Mill Street, Byram, 532.9701

www.go2uroom.com

Children's rooms do not have to be boring. Fernando Martinez, an Argentine furniture designer, creates colorful, whimsical furniture which will make any child smile.
Hours: Monday - Saturday, 10:30 am - 5 pm.
After 5pm by appointment only.

Gordon's Gateway to Sports (Sports Equipment)

217 East Putnam Avenue (Mill Pond Shopping Center), 661.1824

After 35 years of operation, this sports store is still going strong. They are well-known for their racquet sports. They will restring your old racquet or lend you a new one to demo. They carry swimming attire for serious swimmers. They are experts at lacrosse equipment. During the winter they have an extensive ski department. Expect friendly service.
Hours: Monday - Saturday, 9 am - 5 pm (Thursday until 8 pm); Sunday, noon - 5 pm.

Grahams's Toys (Children-Toys)

60 Greenwich Avenue, 983.6800
www.GrahamsToys.com
A barber shop for children that has developed into a unique toy store. We love their interesting children's books. They still have a barber shop in the back.
Hours: Monday - Saturday, 10 am - 5 pm (Tuesday & Friday until 6 pm).

Great Stuff (Clothing-Women)

321 Greenwich Avenue, 861.6872
Eclectic selections with a flair - informal and formal, with lots of possibilities for evening wear.
Hours: Monday - Saturday, 10 am - 6 pm; Sunday, noon - 5 pm.

Great Outdoor Toy Company (Children - Equipment)

9 Kings Highway, Westport, CT, 203.222.3818
www.thegreatoutdoortoycompany.com
Playhouses, hoops, trampolines, red wood swing sets with interchangeable parts, allowing you to make your own fun designs.
Hours: Monday - Saturday, 9 am - 5 pm.
Directions: I-95 N to Exit 17. L at exit, R on Sylvan Road, R on Rt 1, L on Kings Highway N.

Greenwich Bicycles (Bicycles)

189 Greenwich Avenue (behind Saks Fifth Avenue), 869.4141
www.greenwichbikes.com
This large store has all the right equipment and a very helpful website to review before you shop for a bike.
Hours: weekdays, 10 am - 6 pm; Saturday, 9:30 am - 5:30 pm.

Greenwich Exchange for Women's Work (Gifts)

28 Sherwood Place, 869.0229
This small shop, whose mission is to help others help themselves, has reasonably priced, handmade items. If you want to give a gift to a newborn or young child, you will adore their hand-knit sweaters and smocked dresses.
Hours: weekdays, 10 am - 4 pm; Saturday 10 am - 1 pm.

Greenwich Furs (Clothing-Women)

5 West Putnam Avenue, 869.1421

Since 1948 this furrier has been helping Greenwich residents select, repair, remodel and store their furs.

Hours: weekdays, 10 am - 5 pm; Saturday, 11 am - 5 pm.

Greenwich Golf Fitting Studio (Golf Equipment)

222 Mill Street, Byram, 532.4810

www.Greenwichgolf.com

Jacques Intriere repairs your clubs or fits custom golf clubs to make you a better golfer.

Hours: Monday 11 am - 6 pm;

Tuesday, Wednesday, Thursday, 10 am - 7pm;

Friday, 1 pm - 6 pm; Saturday, 9 am - 5 pm.

Hours may vary, call store for information.

Greenwich Hardware (Hardware)

- 195 Greenwich Avenue & Liberty Way Parking Area, 869.6750
- Banksville Home Center, 914.234.2000

www.greenwichhardware.com

Anyone moving into town will find this a valuable resource. A helpful place to call when you have forgotten something: they will deliver it to you. Greenwich Hardware has a 10,000 sq. ft store at Banksville Home Center Complex. A great resource for back-country residents. This is the place to go for your John Deere mower.

Hours: Greenwich: Monday Saturday, 7:30 am - 5:30 pm;

Sunday, 9 am - 4 pm.

Banksville: Monday - Saturday, 7:30 am - 5 pm; Sunday, 10 am - 4 pm.

Greenwich Hospital Gift Shop Flowers (Florist)

5 Perryridge Road, 863.3371

The gift shop keeps a selection of fresh flowers in vases. Call and they will immediately deliver a bouquet to your favorite patient.

Hours: weekdays, 9:30 am - 8 pm; Saturday, 10 am -5 pm;

Sunday, noon - 6 pm.

Greenwich Lock and Door (Home-Hardware)
280 Railroad Avenue, 622.1095
www.greenwichLockandDoor.com
A reliable local source for architectural hardware, doors, security products and lock-smithing. Good customer service.
Hours: Monday & Wednesday, 7 am - 4 pm;
Tuesday, Thursday & Friday, 8 am - 4 pm.

Greenwich Kitchen Store (Home, Cooking Equipment)
118 Greenwich Avenue, 983.3165
www.gkworks.com
When you need a gift for someone who enjoys cooking, this shop has a wide selection of upscale kitchen-related products and specialty food items. A good place to buy an expresso coffee maker.
Hours: Monday - Saturday, 9:30 am - 5:30 pm;
Sunday 11 am - 4 pm.

Greenwich Music (Music)
1200 East Putnam Avenue, Riverside, 869.3615
www.greenwichmusic.com
Their store is filled with sheet music and instruments. They have a large selection of guitars & drums and a helpful staff. A full line of instruments are available for rent; a great way to discover if that instrument is right for you or your child. They have a music school (Fraioli School of Music) next door where they give lessons for the instruments they carry.
Hours: Monday - Thursday, 10 am - 7 pm;
Friday & Saturday, 10 am - 6 pm; Sunday, noon - 4 pm.

Greenwich Orchids (Florist)
106 Mason Street, 661.5544
Grown in a local greenhouse, the orchids are exquisite. They have many varieties, some with unusual colors. They also make lovely flower arrangements.
Hours: Monday - Saturday, 9 am - 6 pm.

Greenwich Oriental Art (Antiques)
7 East Putnam Avenue, 629.0500
www.greenwichorientalart.com
A mixture of old and modern oriental art.
Hours: Monday - Saturday, 10 am - 5:30 pm.
Sunday by appointment only.

Griffin & Howe (Sporting Equipment and Clothing -Guns)
340 West Putnam Avenue, 618.0270
www.griffinhowe.com
Excellent sporting firearms, clothing and accessories. This is the place where serious skeet and trap shooters buy their shotguns. They also have shooting schools and coaching.
Hours: Monday - Wednesday, 10 am - 6 pm; Thursday, 11 am - 8 pm; Friday, 10 am - 6 pm; Saturday, 10 am - 5 pm.

Guild Antiques (Antiques)
384 Greenwich Avenue, 869.0828
www.guildantiques.com
Owned by long-term Greenwich residents, Regina and George Rich. They carry a large selection of 18th and 19th fine English antiques. Their other two shops are on Madison Avenue on the upper east side of Manhattan.
Hours: Monday - Saturday, 10 am - 5 pm.

Harbor View Antiques Center (Antiques)
101 Jefferson Street, Stamford, 325.8070
www.harborviewantiques.com
70 dealers displaying their antiques in a large show area.
Hours: Monday - Saturday, 10:30 am - 5:30 pm; Sunday, noon - 5 pm.
Directions: I-95 N to exit 8, R on Canal (at second light), L on Jefferson.

Harris Restaurant Supply (Home - Cookware)
25 Abendroth Avenue, Port Chester, NY, 914.937.0404
www.hrsfoodservice.com
Commercial restaurant supplier which also allows the general public to buy supplies. Cooks go crazy here.
Hours: weekdays, 9 am - 4 pm; Saturday, 9 am - 2 pm.

Helen Ainson (Clothing, Women)
1078 Post Road, Darien, CT, 203.655.9841
www.HelenAinson.com
For over 25 years Helen Ainson has helped ladies in our area look their best at special occasions. When you discover you are soon to be "mother of the bride," you will like their friendly, knowledgeable advice and fashions from over 150 manufacturers.
Hours: Monday - Saturday, 9:30 am - 5:30 pm.
(Tuesday & Thursday until 7 pm).
Directions: I-95 N to exit 11, one block north.

HenriBurton French Antiques (Antiques)

382 Greenwich Avenue, 661.8529

18th and 19th century French country antiques and accessories. A specialty is 19th century gold leaf mirrors.

Hours: Monday - Saturday, 10 am - 5 pm.

Hickory & Tweed (Skiing Equipment & Clothing)

410 Main Street, Armonk, NY, 914.273.3397

www.hickoryandtweed.com

A wide selection of skis, boots and clothing. Good technical help. When you are planning to buy equipment, this store is definitely worth the trip.

Hours: weekdays, 10 am - 5:30 pm (Thursdays until 8 pm); Saturday, 9:30 am - 5:30 pm; Sunday, noon - 4 pm

Directions: 95 S to 287 W to 684 N to Y38. Bear right to Rt 225, 2nd light R off Rt 128 (Main Street).

Hoagland's of Greenwich (Gifts)

175 Greenwich Avenue, 869.2127

www.Hoaglands.com

A first-class gift shop owned for years by a Greenwich resident with exquisite taste. This is THE place for brides and grooms to register. In addition to their crystal, china and silver, they have charming baby gifts.

Hours: Monday - Saturday, 9 am - 5:30 pm.

Hobby Center (Toys)

405 East Putnam Avenue (Cos Cob Plaza), Cos Cob, 869.0969

For years, kids in Greenwich have been rewarded for cleaning their room or finishing their homework with a trip to Ann's Hobby Center. Rockets and radio-controlled boats are current favorites. No matter what your hobby, they are likely to have what you need.

Hours: Monday - Saturday, 9:30 am - 5:30 pm

Home Boutique of Greenwich (Home Accessories)

14 Lewis Street, 869.2550

When you feel like treating yourself or want to create a picture-perfect bedroom, visit this shop filled with pretty linens.

Hours: Monday - Saturday, 9:30 am - 5:30 pm.

Home Depot (Hardware)
www.homedepot.com
They have 40,000 brand names to choose from.
• 600 Connecticut Avenue, Norwalk, CT, 203.854.9111
Hours: Monday - Saturday, 6 am - 10 pm; Sunday, 7 am - 9 pm.
Directions: I-95 N to exit 13, R on US-1 (Connecticut Avenue).
• 150 Midland Avenue, Port Chester, NY, 914.690.9755
Hours: Monday - Saturday, 7 am - 10 pm; Sunday, 9 am - 6 pm.
Directions: I-95 S to exit 21, immediate R on Midland Avenue.

Home Depot Expo (Home, Decorating)
8 Joyce Road, New Rochelle, 914.637.5600
www.expo.com
If you are decorating or re-decorating your house, you owe it to yourself to go there to get ideas or to buy quality home accessories. Their contracting and design services can be slow.
Hours: weekdays, 10 am - 9 pm; Saturday, 10 am - 9 pm;
Sunday, 11am - 6 pm.
Directions: I-95 exit 16, L at first light, go under RR at second light L, 100 yards on L.

Home Goods (Home - Accessories)
High Ridge & Cold Spring Road, Stamford, 964.9416
www.homegoods.com
When you are ready to accessorize a room, this store is a must. Casual, fun items at great prices.
Hours: Monday - Saturday, 9:30 am - 9:30 pm; Sunday, 11 am - 6 pm.
Directions: Merritt Parkway N to exit 35, R on High Ridge.

Home Works (Home, Fabric)
509 North Main Street, Port Chester, NY 914.934.0907
When you want to redo your window draperies or upholster a chair, they are a good resource for your fabric.
Hours: Weekdays, 10 am - 5 pm (Thursday until 7 pm).

House of Fins (Pets)
99 Bruce Park Avenue, 661.8131
www.houseoffins.com
Everything you need to make a successful aquarium and good advice as well.
Hours: Monday - Saturday, 10 am - 7 pm; Sunday, noon - 5 pm.

Housewarmings (Home-Furniture & Gifts)
235 Sound Beach Avenue, 637.5106
Unique home furnishings and decorative accessories. Comfortable furniture with a choice of fabrics.
Hours: Monday - Saturday 10 am - 5:30 pm.

IKEA (Home, Furniture)
www.Ikea.com
A huge store, with moderate prices and several grades of Scandinavian designed furniture and housewares. Popular with Europeans. There is a supervised children's play area. A good place to go when you are on a limited budget and need to furnish a home or dorm room quickly.
Stores are closed on Thanksgiving Day, Christmas Day and Easter Sunday.
• 1000 Center Drive, Elizabeth, NJ, 908.289.4488 (44 miles)
Hours: weekdays, 10 am - 9 pm; Saturday 9 am - 9 pm; Sunday, 10 am - 8 pm.
Directions: I-95 S across the George Washington Bridge to the New Jersey Turnpike exit 13A then follow signs.
• 450 Sargent Drive, New Haven, CT, 203.865.4532 (51 miles)
Directions: I-95 N Exit 46, L onto Long Wharf Drive, L onto Canal Dock Rd, R onto Sargent Drive.

Images (Photography-Frames)
202 Sound Beach Avenue, Old Greenwich, 637.4193
www.imagescenter.com
In addition to framing your photographs, they restore damaged photographs by removing scratches, tears and stains, enhance photographs to reduce redeye or correct color and brightness, and, of course, enlarge, crop or add a border. No negative is required.
Hours: Monday - Saturday, 10 am - 6 pm.

In Things (Shoes & Accessories-Women)
354 North Main Street (Steilmann Building), Port Chester, NY 914.934.9006
www.inthingscorp.com
Unique shawls, footwear, purses and jewelry from India.
Hours: Monday - Saturday, 11 am - 6 pm.

Innovation Luggage (Luggage)
17 East Putnam Avenue, 869.5322
www.InnovationLuggage.com
A national chain carrying luggage, casual bags, business cases and travel accessories. Nice selection and very helpful service.
Hours: weekdays, 9 am - 6 pm; Saturday, 9:30 am - 6pm; Sunday, noon -5 pm.

Instant Replay (Sporting Goods - Hockey)
1054 Hope Street, Stamford, CT, 322.7502
Located across from the Stamford Twin Rinks, is a shop where parents in the know can save money outfitting their family with every thing they will need for playing hockey or baseball. They have a wide selection of new and used equipment.
Hours: weekdays, 10 am - 7 pm (Friday until 6 pm); Saturday, 9 am - 5 pm; Sunday, 11 am - 4 pm.

Irresistibles (Clothing-Women)
335 Greenwich Avenue, 869.2230
www.Irresistibles.com
Contemporary Sportswear for women. At a holiday luncheon, 6 out of 10 ladies had purchased their pretty decorated sweaters at this shop.
Hours: Monday - Saturday, 9:30 am - 6 pm; Sunday, noon - 5 pm.

J Crew (Clothing, Men & Women, Youth)
126 Greenwich Avenue, 661.5181
www.jcrew.com
A large store with preppy-casual men and women's clothing. Check out "Crew Cuts" for children.
Hours: Monday - Saturday, 10 am - 7 pm; Sunday, 11 am -6 pm.

J Pocker & Son (Art-Framing)
175 West Putnam Avenue, 629.0811
www.JPocker.com
A family business since 1926. Good suggestions for appropriate frames and mats. They have a large portfolio of limited edition prints.
Hours: Tuesday - Saturday, 10 am - 5:30 pm.

JSJ Window Treatments (Home - Decorating)

3 Strickland Road, Cos Cob, 661.5123

A reliable source for blinds, shades and shutters. They carry Hunter Douglas. Shades can be cut on the premises.

Hours: weekdays, 9 am - 5 pm; Saturday, 10 am - 2 pm.

Julia B. Boutique (Clothing-Women & Children)

70 Arch Street, 422.2216

It is clear that Julia Manina has exquisite taste. Fitted women's shirts, sweaters (even made-to-order cashmeres) and classic children's clothing.

Hours: Monday - Saturday 10 am - 5 pm.

Julia B. Home (Home-Accessories, Gifts)

44 West Putnam Avenue,

The custom designed linens, towels, pillows and more will surely impress.

Hours: Monday - Saturday, 10 am - 5 pm.

Juliska (Home Furnishings)

465 Canal Street, Stamford, CT 316.9118

www.Juliska.com

Stores all over the USA, like Saks, Neiman Marcus and Michael C Fina, carry this distinctive glassware. This flagship store has scrumptious table settings and dramatic pieces.

Hours: Monday - Saturday, 10 am - 5 pm.

Kate & Leo (Children-Clothing & Furniture)

28 Bruce Park Avenue, 629.8340

www.KateAndLeo.com

The creation of a Greenwich family, this delightful shop is a favorite of Greenwich mothers when they want something unique or special for their newborn to 3-year-old child. The good news, for those who have not planned far enough ahead, they can deliver furniture within a few days.

Hours: weekdays, 10 am - 6 pm; Saturday, 10 am - 5 pm.

Kate's Paperie (Stationery)

125 Greenwich Avenue, 861.0025

www.KatesPaperie.com

Whether you're looking to design an invitation for a baby shower, birthday party or wedding, you will be impressed with the variety of creative and custom options. This store also carries an assortment of lovely calendars, stationery, paper, photo albums, arts and crafts supplies and much, much more. Remember to stop here when you need a gift.

Hours: weekdays, 9:30 am - 6 pm; Saturday, 10am - 6pm; Sunday, 12 pm - 5 pm.

Kate Spade (Accessories- Women and Home)

271 Greenwich Avenue, 622.4260

www.KateSpade.com

Women's specialty shop selling chic handbags, shoes, and home accessories.

Hours: Monday - Saturday, 10 am - 6 pm; Sunday, noon - 5 pm.

Kenneth Lynch & Sons (Garden Accessories)

84 Danbury Road, Wilton, 203.762.8363

www.klynchandsons.com

If you are looking for an elaborate fountain, pretty garden bench, statuary, topiary, weathervane or sundial, this will be paradise for you. The Lynch family has been crafting garden ornaments for over sixty years. Ornaments are made to order. Their extensive catalog is available for $15 softcover or $25 hardcover.

Hours: weekdays, 8:30 am - 5 pm.

Directions: Merritt Parkway N to exit 39 (Norwalk), N on Rte 7.

Kids Home Furniture (Children - Furniture)

11 Forest Street, Stamford, 327.1333

www.babyandtoy.com

Baby and teen furniture and accessories at reasonable prices.

Hours: Monday - Saturday, 10 am - 5 pm (Thursday until 7 pm).

Directions: I-95 N to exit 8, L at light, pass 3 lights, L on Forest.

Kid's Supply Co. (Children - Furniture)
14 Railroad Avenue, 422.2100
www.KidsSupply.com
It's fun to visit this store selling beautiful, well-built, kid's furniture and decorative accessories and linens.
Hours: weekdays, 9:30 am - 5:30 pm; Saturday, 10 am -5 pm.

Kinko's / FedEx (Office Services)
- 48 West Putnam Avenue, Greenwich, 863.0099
- 980 High Ridge Road, Stamford, CT, 968.8100
www.kinkos.com
FedEx Kinko's offers a wide variety of production and finishing services, as well as FedEx shipping, however they're most known for making photocopies. The primary clientele consists of small business and home office clients.
Greenwich Hours: weekdays, 8 am - 8 pm; Saturday 10 am - 6 pm.
Stamford Hours: Monday, 7 am - midnight;
Tuesday, Wednesday, Thursday, open 24 hours;
Friday, midnight - 11 pm; Saturday & Sunday, 7 am - 11 pm.

Klaff's (Home - Decorating)
28 Washington Street, South Norwalk,
800.552.3371 or 203.866.1603
www.klaffs.com
A tremendous selection of indoor and outdoor lighting fixtures, door hardware, bathroom fixtures. They even have kitchen cabinets, tile and mirrors.
Hours: Monday - Saturday, 9 am - 5:30 pm; Thursday, until 8 pm.
Directions: I-95 N, exit 14. R at the top of the ramp, down hill, bear L at 1st light, go straight through 2nd light. Klaffs is 1 block on R.

Kmart (Department Store)
399 Tarrytown Rd, White Plains, NY, 914.684.1184
www.Kmart.com
Discount store, owned by Sears, which competes with Wal-Mart and Target: Clothing, footwear, bedding, furniture, jewelry, electronics and housewares. They are a primary source for Martha Stewart & Jaclyn Smith brands.
Hours: every day, 8 am - 10 pm.

The Knitting Niche (Sewing & Needlework)

115 Mason Street, 869.6205

www.KnittingNiche.com

This store offers everything to fulfill your knitting needs and desires. Whether you're a beginner or advanced, you will feel inspired here. There is an impressive assortment of yarn, and the sales team is enthusiastic. They also hold group and private knitting classes.

Hours: Monday, Wednesday, Thursday, 9:30 am - 5:30 pm; Tuesday, 9:30 am - 7:30 pm; Friday & Saturday, 10 am - 5 pm.

Knoyzz (Clothing-Youth & Women)

375 Greenwich Avenue, 340.2405

www.knoyzz.com

Pronounced "noise", this East Coast hip store for teens and those who consider style "not an age but just an attitude" carries 20 lines of jeans and brands such as Elvis Denim, Blue Cult, Junkfood, Rebel Yell and People for Peace.

Hours: Monday - Saturday, 10 am - 6 pm (Thursday until 7 pm); Sunday, noon - 5 pm.

Kohl's (Department Store)

431 Post Road (Shopping Center), Port Chester, NY 914.690.0107
www.Kohls.com

More of a J. C. Penney than a Caldor, they sell men's and women's clothing and accessories as well as some household items at discounted prices.

Hours: Monday - Saturday, 8 am - 10 pm; Sunday, 9 am - 9 pm.

Directions: Follow US-1 through the main part of Port Chester.

Landfall Navigation (Boating)

151 Harvard Ave, Stamford, 487.0775

www.landfallnavigation.com

Henry Marx, the owner, is very knowledgeable and helpful. If you have a boat, he has what you need: charts, supplies or just information. Be sure to get a copy of his catalog. They have excellent nautical gifts.

Hours: weekdays, 9 am - 5 pm; Saturday 9 am -noon.

SHOPPING

Landmark Document Services (Office Services)

375 Fairfield Avenue, Stamford, 325.4300

www.landmarkprint.com

Our favorite place for large volume printing. They are very careful and easy to work with. Their reasonable prices don't hurt, either.

Hours: weekdays, 8 am - 5:30 pm.

Land's End @ Sears (Clothing - Men & Women)

100 Main Street (Galleria Shopping Center), White Plains, NY

www.landsend.com

Casual clothing for women, men and youth. Land's End has opened shops in a number of Sears stores.

Hours: Monday - Saturday, 10 am - 9 pm; Sunday, 11 am - 7 pm.

L'Enfance Magique (Clothing -Children)

236 Greenwich Avenue, 625.0929

Pretty French clothes accent this shop for babies and young children.

Hours: Monday - Saturday, 10 am - 5:30 pm; Sunday, noon - 5 pm. Closed on Sundays during the summer.

LF (Clothing-Women)

319 Greenwich Avenue, 629-6193

www.lfstores.com

LF wants to be an alternative to mainstream brands. With their California ultra-hip merchandise, we think they have met their goal. We recently overheard a customer in Pucci boots, exclaim "That's cool" when examining a $180 pair of jeans.

Hours: Monday - Saturday, 10 am - 6 pm (Thursday until 7 pm); Sunday, noon - 5 pm.

Liberty Village (Outlet Mall)

1 Church Street, Flemington, NJ, 908.782.8550

www.premiumoutlets.com

Shop until you drop. There are more than 120 outlet stores in a number of outlet centers in Flemington. Sixty of the shops are in Liberty Village.

Hours: Sunday - Wednesday, 10 am - 6 pm; Thursday - Saturday, 10 am - 9 pm.

Directions: I-95 to I-287 W to I-287 S to Rte 202 W.

L'Occitane (Gifts, Cosmetics)
236 Greenwich Avenue, 422.0234
www.usa.loccitane.com
Fragrances, candles and body care products with the soft scents of southern France.
Hours: Monday - Saturday, 10 am - 6 pm; Sunday, noon - 6 pm.

The Light Touch (Home - Lamps)
12 Lewis Street, 629.2255
When you are looking for a lamp or lamp shade with character, be sure to stop in here.
Hours: Monday - Saturday, 10 am - 5:30 pm.

Lillian August (Home - Furniture)
• 19 West Elm Street, Greenwich, 629.1539
• 32 Knight Street, Norwalk, CT, 203.847.3314
www.lillianaugust.com
Sofas, chairs and desks designed by Lillian August. The Norwalk store, their Flagship Store, is housed in a converted factory. It has 60,000 square feet of selling space, double the size of the next largest store.
Greenwich hours: Tuesday - Saturday, 10 am - 6 pm.
Norwalk hours: Monday - Saturday, 10 am - 7 pm; Sunday 11 am - 6 pm.

Lillian August Outlet Store (Home - Furniture)
85 Water Street (SoNo Square), South Norwalk, CT, 203.838.0153
www.lillianaugust.com
Sofas, chairs and desks designed by Lillian August.
Hours: Monday - Saturday, 10 am - 6 pm (Thursday until 7 pm);
Sunday, noon - 6 pm.
Directions: I-95 N to exit 14, R on West, bear left at fork onto North Main, cross intersection with Washington street, L on Haviland, R on South Water.

Lilly Pulitzer (Clothing - Women, Children)
92 Greenwich Avenue, 661.3136
www.LillyPulitzer.com
Popular since the 1960's. Lots of pink and green and pretty colors for upscale casual women and children. Totally charming mother - daughter dress alikes.
Hours: Monday - Saturday, 10 am - 6 pm; Sunday, noon - 5 pm.

Little Eric (Children - Shoes)
15 East Elm Street, 622.1600
A children's shoe store with high quality dress and play wear. A helpful sales staff eliminates the usual shoe-shopping hassles.
Hours: Monday Saturday, 9 am - 6 pm; Sunday 11 am - 5 pm.

Lord and Taylor (Department Store)
110 High Ridge Road, (at convergence of Long and High Ridge Roads) Stamford, 327.6600
www.LordAndTaylor.com
A large full-service, stand-alone store, with easy parking and well priced attractive, up-scale fashions for men and women 35 and up. Father and son, Robert and Richard Baker of Greenwich, purchased the chain in 2006. They intend to keep the store thriving.
Hours: weekdays, 10 am - 9:30 pm; Saturday, 10 am - 8 pm; Sunday, 11 am - 7 pm.
Directions: Merritt Parkway to exit 34, R on Long Ridge, watch for sign on L.

Love (Children - Toys & Clothing)
22 West Putnam Avenue, 422.0900
www.ShopWithLove.net
Kristin Fine selects only children's items she loves. Toddlers like their moms to shop here so they can play in their special area.
Hours: Tuesday - Saturday, 10 am - 5 pm.

Lucky Jeans (Clothing-Men, Women)
244 Greenwich Avenue, 861.4039
www.LuckyBrandJeans.com
This large retro-shop is filled with garments reminiscent of the Jack Kerouac era. Everything from the shop's decor to the music is designed to make the 60's ooze from the clothing. Denim makes up most of their business. Lucky Brand Jeans first became popular due to the words, "LUCKY YOU" being stitched into the fly of every pair. They try to have the right pair of jeans for every body type. From their start in 1990 they have expanded to 110 stores.
Hours: Monday - Saturday, 10 am - 7 pm; Sunday, noon - 6 pm.

Lush (Cosmetics)

89 Greenwich Avenue, 629.5874

www.Lush.com

At first glance, you may think this is a fruit and vegetable shop. Instead, these colorful concoctions are soap and skin care products. Stop by and see why this large British chain, with its fresh, hand-made cosmetics has such a wide appeal.

Hours: weekdays, 10 am - 6 pm (Thursday till 7 pm);
Saturday, 11 am - 7 pm; Sunday, 11 am - 4 pm.

Lux Bond & Green (Jewelry)

169 Greenwich Avenue, 629.0900

www.LBGreen.com

They carry David Yurman jewelry and Steuben gifts.

Hours: Monday - Saturday, 9:30 am - 5 pm.

Lynda Willauer Antiques (Antiques)

115 Mason Street (Village Square), 661.8022

www.LyndaWillauerAntiques.com

This store is filled with Chinese Export Porcelain and many other highly sought-after porcelains. If you are not already a collector, visit this store and you will be hooked. We love the blue and white!

Hours: Late September to late June,
Monday - Saturday, 10 am - 4:30 pm. Closed July and August.

Lynnens (Home - Accessories, linen)

278 Greenwich Avenue, 629.3659

www.lynnens.com

Since 1980 this high-end bed, bath, linen and nightwear store has been a real favorite of Greenwich residents. Lynne Jenkins has stocked her store with luxury products from around the world. Their specialties are service and customizing linens.

Hours: Monday - Saturday, 9:30 am - 5:30 pm.

Lynnens Too (Home- Accessories, linen)

1 Bruce Place (in the basement around the corner from Best & Company), 983.6763

An outlet for discontinued items from Lynnens on Greenwich Avenue. Most of the merchandise is ½ off. Cash and checks only. No returns.

Hours: Monday - Saturday, 9:30 am - 5:30 pm.

McDermott Paint & Wallpaper (Home - Decorating)
35 Spring Street, 622.0699
If you are planning to do any of your own home painting, you can count on good advice and products from this longtime Greenwich shop. If you are trying to match a color, take a sample and they can duplicate it with their computer.
Hours: Monday - Saturday, 7:30 am - 5 pm.

J. McLaughlin (Clothing - Women)
45 East Putnam Avenue, 862.9777
Primarily women's informal preppy clothing - "stylish, but not stuffy"
Hours: Monday - Saturday, 10 am - 6 pm.

J. McLaughlin Outlet Store (Clothing - Women)
68 Water Street, South Norwalk, CT, 203.838.8427
www.jmclaughlin.com
An outlet for their clothing.
Hours: Monday - Saturday, 10 am - 6 pm; Sunday, noon - 5 pm.
Directions: I-95 N to exit 14, R on West, bear L at fork onto North Main, cross intersection with Washington Street, L on Haviland.

McArdleMacMillen Florist & Garden Center (Florist)
48 Arch Street, 661.5600, 800.581.5558
www.mcardles.com
Many pretty dinner tables are adorned with their arrangements. A good place to buy flowers (they have a large selection), corsages and plants. Come early on weekends during the garden season, as it is always busy or place an order on their website. They have a newsletter filled with helpful gardening tips. Be sure to get on their mailing list.
Hours: Monday - Saturday, 8 am - 5:30 pm;
Sunday, May & June, 9 am - 1 pm.

Macy's (Department Store)
Stamford Town Center, 964.1500
www.macys.com
Macy's holds a special place in many people's hearts. Macy's opened in 1858. The company is now part of Federated Department Stores and competes on an average price level above Kohl's, J.C. Penney, and Sears, and below Nordstrom and sister chain Bloomingdale's.
Hours: weekdays, 10 am - 9:30 pm; Saturday, 10 am - 8 pm;
Sunday, 11 am - 7 pm.
Directions: I-95 N to exit 8, L on Atlantic, R on Tresser, L onto ramp.

SHOPPING

Malia Mills (Clothing-women's swimwear)

16 Greenwich Avenue, 622.3137
www.maliamills.com
Swimwear designed to make women feel good about shopping and wearing a bathing suit.
Hours: Monday - Saturday, 10 am - 6 pm.

Marshalls (Department Store)

- 2235 Summer Street (Ridgeway Shopping Center), Stamford, CT
        356.9667
- 20 Waterfront Place, Port Chester, NY, 914.690.9380

http://www.marshallsonline.com/off_price.asp
Marshalls and TJ Max have the same parent company and have similar product assortments. Marshalls sells brand name and designer clothing at off-prices. They carry clothing for men, women, kids, and teens. They also carry footwear, bedding, furniture, jewelry and housewares.
Hours: Monday - Saturday, 9:30 am - 9:30 pm; Sunday, 11 am - 6 pm.

Michaels (Craft Supplies)

- Ridgeway Shopping Center, 2233 Summer Street, Stamford
        978.0026
- 27 Waterfront Place, Port Chester, NY, 914.937.3060

www.michaels.com
A large arts and craft store. A favorite source for scrapbook makers.
Hours: Monday - Saturday, 9am - 9pm; Sunday, 10am - 7pm.

Michelangelo of Greenwich (Gifts)

353 Greenwich Avenue, 661.8540, 800.677.4490
www.mikegifts.com
Wide selection of clocks, crystal, pewter, brass and silver which they will engrave for personal or corporate gifts. They have produced awards for the Super Bowl and the Pebble Beach Golf Tournament.
Hours: Tuesday - Friday, 10 am - 6 pm; Saturday 10 am - 5 pm.

Michael's Men's Formal Wear (Clothing-Men)

121 Greenwich Avenue, 625.8175
For years Greenwich men have been renting and buying formal wear here.
Hours: Monday - Saturday, 9:30 am - 5:30 pm (Thursday until 7 pm)

Miranda Arts (Art)

6 North Pearl Street, Suite 404E, Port Chester, NY, 914.935.9362
www.MirandaFineArts.com
Art Gallery featuring local artists. Patricia Miranda teaches painting and gilding techniques to adults and youth. She does museum quality framing and frame repair.
Hours: Wednesday - Saturday, 11 am - 5 pm.

The Music Source (Music)

1345 East Putnam Avenue, Old Greenwich, 698.0444
They carry a wide selection of sheet music as well as strings and other small items. They also give lessons.
Hours: weekdays, noon - 5 pm; Saturday 10 am - 2 pm.

Neiman Marcus (Department Store)

Westchester Mall in White Plains, 914.428.2000
www.NeimanMarcus.com
An upscale, specialty, retail department store which competes with Bloomingdale's, Nordstrom, and Saks Fifth Avenue.
Hours: weekdays, 10 am - 8 pm; Saturday, 10 am - 7 pm;
Sunday, noon - 6 pm.
Directions: I-95 S to I-287 W to exit 8 (Westchester Avenue), L on Bloomingdale or L on Paulding.

New York Running Company (Sporting Goods, Clothing)

2 Greenwich Avenue, 861.7800
www.TheRunningCompany.net
The Running Company started in Princeton New Jersey in 1998. Their goal is to cultivate all of their customers into long-time believers in the sport of running and a healthy life style. They carry most major running, walking and cross training shoes, as well as spikes, classy apparel and accessories.
Hours: weekdays, 10 am - 7 pm; Saturday, 10 am - 5 pm;
Sunday, noon - 5 pm.

Nimble Thimble (Sewing)

21 Putnam Avenue, Port Chester, NY, 914.934.2934
The resource for home sewing needs. Lots of fabrics, notions, and quilting supplies and sewing machines. This is the place to have your sewing machine repaired.
Hours: Monday - Saturday, 10 am - 5 pm;
Closed on Mondays in July and August.

Nordic Stove & Fireplace Center (Home - Accessories)

220 Harvard Avenue, Stamford, 406.9881
www.nordicstoveandfireplace.com
Everything you might want for your fireplace. Good customer service.
Hours: Tuesday - Friday, 10 am - 5 pm; Saturday, 9 am - 4 pm.

Nordstrom (Department Store)

Westchester Mall in White Plains, 914.946.1122
www.Nordstrom.com
An upscale department store with clothing, footwear, accessories, hand-bags, jewelry, cosmetics and home furnishings. The company competes at an average price level above J.C. Penney, Macy's, and Sears, on par with Bloomingdale's, but below that of Neiman Marcus and Saks Fifth Avenue.
Hours: Monday - Saturday, 10 am - 9 pm; Sunday, 11 am - 6 pm.
Directions: I-95 S to I-287 W to exit 8 (Westchester Avenue), L on Bloomingdale or L on Paulding.

Norwalk Mattress Company (Home Furnishings)

145 West Cedar Street, Norwalk, CT, 203.866.6913
www.NorwalkMattress.com
Nearby is a mattress company that will custom make any size, any level of comfort or type of mattress, including space-age memory foam. Within 10 days you will have the mattress on your bed, all at very competitive prices.
Hours: Monday - Saturday, 9 am - 5 pm.

Old Navy (Department Store)

- 2175 Summer Street (Ridgeway Shopping Center), Stamford, CT
    325.4088
- 100 Main Street (Galleria Shopping Center), White Plains, NY,
    914.682.0469

www.oldNavy.com
Owned by the Gap which also owns Banana Republic. Their clothing is trendy and more affordable than the Gap or Banana Republic or competi-tors such as American Eagle (Stamford Center). They have specialized sections for infants, boys, girls, men and women, including a collection of business clothes for women.
Stamford Store Hours: Monday - Saturday, 9 am -9 pm;
Sunday, 10 am - 6 pm.

Omni Fitness (Health - Exercise Equipment)
20 Railroad Avenue, 422.2277
www.omnifitness.com
A wide selection of high-end fitness equipment at reasonable prices and very nice people to work with.
Hours: weekdays, 10 am - 7 pm, Thursday until 8 pm; Saturday 10 am - 6 pm; Sunday, 11 am - 5 pm.

Orvis Company Store (Sporting Equipment & Clothing- Fishing)
432 Boston Post Road, Darien, CT, 203.662.0844
www.orvis.com
Clothes, luggage and fishing equipment for the well-attired fisher. They also have a large book and video selection as well as a guide service.
Hours: Monday - Saturday, 10 am - 6 pm (Thursday until 8 pm); Sunday, noon - 5 pm.
Directions: I-95 N, exit 13, L on Post Road, 1 mile on L.

Outdoor Traders (Sporting Equipment & Clothing)
55 Arch Street, 862.9696
www.OutdoorTraders.com
Outfitters for just about any outdoor trip or trek.
Hours: Monday - Saturday 10 am - 6 pm; Sunday 11 am - 5 pm.

Out of the Box (Clothing- Women)
73 Greenwich Avenue, 625.9696
You will be happy you climbed the stairs to find this out-of-the-ordinary clothing store. Jill duPont's name for the store is just right. You will love the jackets and the gorgeous fabrics. You will also love the prices. She has a workshop for alterations and custom work. If she doesn't have your size, she can usually get it.
Hours: Monday - Saturday, 10 am - 5:30 pm.

Packages PlusNMore (Office Services & Cards)
Mill Pond Shopping Center, 215 East Putnam Ave, Cos Cob, 625.8130
One of the few places that carries Greenwich gift items including postcards with local scenes. An up-scale packing and shipping company, that will not only ship packages for you, but will pickup a package from your home or office upon request.
Hours: weekdays, 5:30 am - 7 pm; Saturday 5:30 am - 5:30 pm; Sunday 5:30 am - 5 pm.

Papyrus (Stationery)

268 Greenwich Avenue, 869.1888

www.PapyrusOnline.com

Papyrus, formerly The Papery, has more than 150 stores nationwide selling fine custom social stationery and invitations. If you want a traditional or an out-of-the ordinary invitation, you will have fun here. The staff is extraordinarily talented at helping you choose and design invitations. You will be sending more greetings to your friends when you see their large selection of high-end greeting cards. They also sell Godiva Chocolates.

Hours: weekdays, 9:30 am - 6 pm; Saturday, 10 am - 6 pm; Sunday, noon - 5 pm.

Parfumerie Douglas (Cosmetics)

96 Greenwich Avenue, 625.9392

Large selection of brand name cosmetics, skincare products and perfumes. The courteous staff is quite willing to help you sample new products or pick out a gift.

Hours: Monday - Saturday, 9 am - 6 pm; Sunday, 11am - 5 pm.

Party City (Parties)

535 Boston Post Road, Port Chester, NY, 914.939.6900

www.partycity.com

A giant store with an impressive inventory of party supplies. Like the Strauss Warehouse Outlet, they have a very large assortment of Halloween costumes during the season.

Hours: Monday - Saturday, 9 am -9 pm; Sunday, 10 am - 6 pm.

Party Paper and Things (Parties)

410 East Putnam Avenue , 661.1355

An excellent selection of high quality party paper goods, wrapping paper, disposable serving dishes and lots of balloons. They will deliver for a very modest fee.

Hours: weekdays, 10 am - 5:30 pm; Saturday, 10am - 5pm.

Party Warehouse (Parties)

24 Harbor View Avenue, Stamford, CT, 203.967.3313
They say they are the largest discount party Super Store, and we believe it. Besides a large selection, they have very good customer service. When we needed some special order items they went out of their way to make sure we received them on time.
Hours: weekdays, 10 am - 6 pm (Thursday until 7 pm);
Saturday, 9:30 am - 5 pm; Sunday, 11 am - 4 pm.

Patio.Com (Home - Furniture)

600 East Putnam Avenue, Cos Cob, 869.3084
www.Patio.com
Primarily outdoor furniture, they also sell a variety of sports equipment such as pool tables and ping pong tables.
Hours: Monday - Saturday, 10 am - 6 pm; Sunday noon - 5 pm.

Pastiche (Clothing-Women)

250 Sound Beach Avenue, Old Greenwich, 637.4444
Designer casual clothing with a fashionable dressy flair.
Hours: Monday - Saturday, 9:30 am - 5:30 pm.

Patricia Gourlay (Clothing - Women)

45 East Putnam Avenue, 869.0977
www.PatriciaGourlay.com
Brides-to-be love this fine lingerie shop. This is also a good place to find the right bra. Wonderful customer service! They are more conservative than their advertisements would indicate.
Hours: Monday - Saturday, 9:30 am - 5:30 pm

Penny Weights (Jewelry)

124 Elm Street, New Canaan CT, 203.966.7739
www.pennyweights.com
This is a great place to find an inexpensive piece of jewelry for a teenager. Most of the jewelry is silver. The sales staff is friendly and helpful. The prices are terrific.
Hours: Tuesday - Saturday, 10 am - 6 pm; Thursday until 8 pm;
Sunday, 12 pm - 5 pm.

Pet Pantry (Pets)
290 Railroad Avenue, 869.6444
Large store with a gigantic inventory. Friendly, helpful service. Our Jack Russell, Daisy, loves going here to pick her own dog food and meet new friends.
Hours: Weekdays, 8 am - 8 pm; Saturday, 8 am - 6 pm; Sunday 9 am - 6 pm.

Petit Bateau (Clothing - Children)
84 Greenwich Avenue, 622.8300
www.PetitBateau.com
Created in France in 1893, Petit Bateau has one of their adorable baby boutiques on Greenwich Avenue. This store carries clothes for newborns and children up to 18 years. They have everything from the cutest tshirts and hats, to blouses, pants, jumpers, jackets and pajamas for boys and girls.
Hours: Monday - Saturday 10 am - 6 pm; Sunday, noon - 5 pm.

Petit Patapon (Clothing - Children)
271 Greenwich Avenue, 861.2037
www.petitpatapon.com
Lovely playwear for young children. The whimsical and pastel-colored outfits will make you smile.
Hours: Monday - Saturday, 9:30 am - 6 pm; Sunday, noon - 5 pm

Petticoat Lane (Clothing Women)
347 Greenwich Avenue, 863.0045
www.BagShop.com
One of our familiar shops that has been on the Avenue a long time. They have a large selection of handbags and lingerie.
Hours: Monday - Saturday, 9 am - 6 pm; Sunday, noon - 5 pm

Pier 1 Imports (Home - Accessories)
2300 Summer Street, Stamford, 325.1035
www.pier1.com
Affordable chain carrying everything for the home, from table linens to wicker furniture and throw pillows. They operate 1,200 stores.
Hours: weekdays, 9 am - 9 pm; Saturday, 10 am - 9 pm; Sunday, 1 pm - 7 pm.

Plaza Too (Shoes, Women)

68 Greenwich Avenue, 618.1023

www.PlazaToo.com

A great place for women's shoes! They offer many different styles with a variety of price ranges. You will also find handbags, stockings, socks, jewelry and accessories. Their sales almost always have great buys.
Hours: weekdays 9 am - 6:30 pm; Saturday 9 am - 6 pm; Sunday, noon -5 pm.

Pottery Barn (Home - Furniture)

Stamford Town Center, 324.2035

www.PotteryBarn.com

www.PotteryBarnKids.com

This fresh, appealing furniture is very popular in Greenwich. They have a strong emphasis on bed, bath, dining as well as adorable furniture for children.
Hours: weekdays, 10 am - 9 pm; Saturday, 10 am - 8 pm; Sunday, noon - 6 pm.
Directions: I-95 N to exit 8, L on Atlantic, R on Tresser, L onto ramp.

Post Road Iron Works (Home - Accessories)

345 West Putnam Avenue, 869.6322

Serving Greenwich since 1927, although they do more mundane iron work, they are the local resource for ornamental welding. They also sell a good selection of fireplace accessories and can order weathervanes.
Hours: weekdays, 7:30 am - 5:30 pm; Saturday, 8 am - noon.

Quai Voltaire Antiques (Antiques)

378 Greenwich Avenue, 618.9777

www.qvantiques.com

Late 17th and early 19th century French Antiques selected by the owner, Guy Flichy, on his frequent trips to France.
Hours: Monday - Saturday, 10 am - 6 pm.

Quelques Choses (Gifts)

259 Sound Beach Avenue, Old Greenwich, 637.5655
Hidden in an alley way is this tiny shop brimming with charming gifts you won't see anywhere else.
Hours: Monday - Saturday, 10ish - 5 pm.

Quester Gallery (Art)

279 Greenwich Avenue, 629.8022

www.QuesterGallery.com

Quester also has a location in Stonington, CT. They specialize in fine 19th and 20th century marine art. This gallery is full of beautiful paintings. Prices range from $2,500 to $100,000, though most of the paintings seem to be in the higher range. They have an exceptionally informative website, with pictures of many of their paintings.

Hours: Monday - Saturday, 10am - 6pm.

Radio Shack (Electronics)

• 1265 East Putnam Avenue

(Riverside-Thruway Shopping Center) 637.5608

• 160 East Putnam Avenue, Cos Cob, 661-2212

www.RadioShack.com

Radio Shack operates over 3,000 stores. If you need a telephone or telephone supplies, a strange battery, or if you are not sure where to find some piece of electronic equipment, they will probably have it.

Hours: Monday - Saturday, 9 am - 8 pm (Riverside is open to 9 pm); Sunday, 11 am - 6 pm.

Rags (Children & Youth - Clothing)

73 Greenwich Avenue, 869.0915

Chic outfits for trendy youths. Lots of good-looking corduroys and jackets. Affordable prices.

Hours: Monday - Saturday, 9 am - 6 pm; Sunday, noon to 5 pm.

Recreation Showroom (Sporting Equipment - Games)

250 Indian River Road, Orange, CT, 203.891.9633

www.RecreationShowroom.com

A variety of games and game tables including over 30 different pool tables on display. They also have a large assortment of camping equipment.

Hours: Monday - Saturday, 10 am - 6 pm (Thursday, until 8 pm); Sunday, 11 am - 4 pm.

The Red Studio (Art - Framing)

39 Lewis Street, 861.6525

The frames are often works of art in themselves. They also sell prints and old drawings.

Hours: Monday - Saturday, 10:30 am - 5:30 pm.

Reflection (Clothing-Youth)

116 Greenwich Avenue, 629.2010
Attractive, fashionable clothes for young people at college tuition prices.
Hours: Monday - Saturday, 9:30 am - 6 pm (Thursday till 7 pm); Sunday, 11:30 am - 6 pm.

Relax the Back (Health, Furniture)

367 Greenwich Avenue, 629.2225
www.relaxtheback.com
For people seeking relief and prevention of back and neck pain, they offer attractive posture and back support products and self-care solutions.
Hours: Monday - Wednesday, 10am - 5:30pm;
Thursday - Saturday, 10am - 6pm.

Reo Appliances (Home - Appliances)

233 East Avenue, East Norwalk, CT, 203.838.7925
www.reoappliances.com
Large selection of major appliances at competitive prices. Lots of personal service.
Hours: Monday - Saturday, 9 am - 5 pm; Thursday, 9 am - 7:30 pm. Closed Sunday.
Directions: I-95 N to exit 16, South on East Avenue.

Restoration Hardware (Home - Accessories & Furniture)

239 Greenwich Avenue, 552.1040
www.restorationhardware.com
An American chain with 133 stores. A very upscale, trendy store with a combination of decorative hardware and furniture based on period designs. It is fun to stroll through. The merchandise changes frequently.
Hours: Monday - Saturday, 9 am - 7 pm (Thursday until 8 pm);
Sunday, 11 am - 6 pm.

Rex Dive Center (Sporting Equipment-Diving)

144 Water Street, Norwalk, CT, 203.853.4148
www.rexdivecenter.com
The place to go for your scuba equipment. You will be greeted by a friendly, knowledgeable staff. They provide lessons for beginners.
Hours: Weekdays, 11 am - 7 pm; Saturday, 9 am -5 pm;
Sunday, noon - 5 pm.
Directions: I-95 N to Exit 14, R on Fairfield Avenue (which turns into Washington Street), R on Water.

Rex Marine Center (Boating)

144 Water Street, Norwalk, CT, 203.866.5555

http://www.rexmarine.com

If you are looking for a small boat or boating paraphernalia, they are worth a visit.

Hours vary, call ahead.

Directions: I-95 N to Exit 14, R on Fairfield Avenue (which turns into Washington Street), R on Water.

Riverside Floor Covering (Home Decorating)

5 Riverside Lane, Riverside, 637.3777

A small showroom brimming with carpet choices from many manufacturers. They have been helping Greenwich residents for years.

Hours: weekdays, 9:30 am - 5 pm; Saturday, 9:30 - noon.

Richard's of Greenwich (Clothing, Men & Women)

359 Greenwich Avenue, 622.0551

www.mitchellsonline.com

A Greenwich classic carrying fine quality men's and women's clothing from the world's leading designers. Nowhere in the world can you find better customer service.

Hours: Monday - Saturday, 9:30 am - 6 pm; Thursdays, until 8 pm.

Ridgeway Shopping Center (Mall)

2235 Summer Street, Stamford

The anchor stores in this updated 400,000 square foot center are Marshall's, Old Navy and Michael's. It has a very large Bed, Bath and Beyond as well as a huge Super Stop & Shop.

Hours: Monday - Saturday, 9:30 am - 9 pm. Bed, Bath and Beyond is open Sunday, 9:30 am - 6 pm.

Directions: Merritt Parkway N to exit 34, R on Long Ridge which becomes Summer.

Right Start (Toys)

42 West Putnam Avenue, 422.2525

A local resource for educational toys, books and videos. They also have car seats, strollers and much more. Mothers have fun meeting each other here.

Hours: Monday - Saturday, 10 am - 6 pm; Sunday, 11 am - 5 pm

Rinfret Home and Garden (Home - Furniture & Accessories)

354 Greenwich Avenue, 622.0204

Classic English antique and reproduction furniture and accessories. If you are wondering what is "Classic Greenwich Style", you will want to visit this store and buy a copy of Cindy Rinfret's book.

Hours: weekdays, 10 am - 6 pm (Saturday to 5 pm).

Rink and Racquet (Sporting Equipment)

24 Railroad Avenue, 622.9180

Hockey (field & ice), figure skating, baseball, softball, lacrosse, roller blades, team uniforms. If they don't have what you need for ice hockey, it is probably not made.

Hours: weekdays, 9 am - 5:30 pm; Saturday, 9 am - 5 pm.

Ring's End Lumber (Hardware)

181 West Avenue, Darien, 203.655.2525

www.ringsend.com

A large supplier of lumber, hardware and building materials. Good displays of kitchens and windows. If possible, shop on weekdays; they are very busy on the weekends.

Hours: Monday - Saturday, 7 am - 5 pm (Thursday until 8 pm).

Directions: I-95 N to exit 10, L on Noroton, R on West.

Ritz Camera (Photography)

82 Greenwich Avenue, Greenwich, 869.0673

www.ritzcamera.com

Part of a large chain of camera stores. They have an extensive selection of cameras and batteries for watches as well as cameras. They do one-hour photo developing or you can e-mail your pics to www.RitzPix.com for prints in one hour you can pick up at the store. If you buy a camera, they will give you free class lessons.

Hours: weekdays, 8:30 am - 6:30 pm; Saturday, 10 am - 5 pm.

Ronnie's News (Magazines & Newspapers)

26 West Putnam Avenue, 661.5464

A convenient place to find your favorite magazines and newspapers.

Hours: weekdays, 5 am - 6 pm; Saturday, 6 am - noon.

Roundabout (Clothing-Women)

48 West Putnam Avenue, 552.0787

Clothes must be from a well-known designer, in perfect condition, and less than 2 years old to be consigned. The store also buys show and end-of-season stock from designers.

Hours: Monday- Saturday, 10 am - 5 pm.

Rue Faubourg St. Honore (Home - Accessories & Antiques)

44 West Putnam Avenue, 869.7139

For over 30 years this small shop has supplied antique lighting fixtures and fireplace accessories to Greenwich mansions and vintage homes.

Hours: weekdays, 9:30 am - 5 pm; Saturday, 9:30 am - 4 pm.

Rugby by Ralph Lauren (Clothing-Men & Women)

195 Greenwich Avenue, 861.7053

www.Rugby.com

Polo shirts, sweaters, denim wear with sporty prep-school look, targeted for men and women ages 18 - 25. Rugby was launched in 2004. The line's post-prep look has edgier styling and slightly lower price points than the signature Polo Ralph Lauren brand. Their shopping bags can be seen all over town.

Hours: Monday - Saturday, 10 am - 6 pm; Sunday, noon - 5 pm.

Rye Ridge Tile (Home-Decorating)

520 North Main Street, Port Chester, 914.939.1100

www.RyeRidgeTile.com

The 6,000 sq. foot showroom is covered with a great variety of tile patterns from 75 different manufactures, making it easy to visualize choices. They also have the Villeroy & Boch line of very modern plumbing fixtures.

Hours: Monday - Saturday, 9 am - 5 pm, Wednesday to 7 pm, Saturday to 4 pm.

Saint Clair (Stationery)

23 Lewis Street, 661.2927

www.theresesaintclair.com

Going to Cartier's for fine stationery is not necessary if you live in Greenwich. For many years Greenwich residents have shopped here for their invitations and elegant stationery. Stop in and see the range of things they can do.

Hours: Monday - Saturday, 9:30 am - 5:30 pm.

Saks Fifth Avenue (Department Store)

www.saks.com

An upscale clothing store. It competes on a price level with Neiman Marcus, Bergdorf Goodman and Lord and Taylor and above Bloomingdale's and Nordstrom.

- 205 Greenwich Avenue, 862.5300
  Hours: Monday - Saturday, 10 am - 6 pm, Sunday, noon - 5 pm.
- Stamford Town Center, 323.3100
  Hours: Monday & Thursday, 10 am - 8 pm; Tuesday, Wednesday, Friday & Saturday, 10 am - 6 pm; Sunday, noon - 6 pm.

Sam Bridge Nursery & Greenhouses (Home - Gardening)

437 North Street, 869.3418

www.sambridge.com

A family-run operation that has been welcoming Greenwich residents to their greenhouses since 1930. Many of the more than 100,000 plants available are grown in their own greenhouses. They offer classes on topics such as perennial gardening and pruning. You can select live or cut Christmas trees, which they will deliver to you when you are ready.

Hours: Closed Sunday; Monday - Saturday, 8:30 am - 5 pm.

Saturnia (Clothing - Women & Youth)

39 Lewis Street, 625.0390

www.shopsaturnia.com

A favorite clothes store of the younger set. A good place to find a cute dress, leather pants or the perfect sweater.

Hours: weekdays, 9:30 am - 5:30 pm; Saturday, 10 am - 5 pm.

Safavieh (Home - Furniture & Rugs)

248 Atlantic Street, Stamford, 327.4800

www.safaviehhome.com

Oriental rugs galore and lots of quality English, French and American reproduction furniture from firms such as Kindel, Baker, Widdicomb, Henredon and others. They have parking behind the store.

Hours: Monday - Wednesday, 10 am - 7 pm; Thursday 10 am - 8:30 pm; Friday & Saturday, 10 am - 6 pm; Sunday 11 am - 6 pm.

Directions: I-95 N to exit 8 (Atlantic Street), L on Atlantic.

Scoop (Clothing, Men & Women)
283 Greenwich Avenue, 422.2251

www.scoopnyc.com

From Manhattan to Greenwich Avenue, this clothing store has trendy and fun pieces designed to attract men and women of all ages, but perhaps the 12 to 25 year-olds are happiest here. You'll find everything from shirts, shoes, jewelry, hats, t-shirts and handbags.
Hours: Monday - Saturday 10 am - 6 pm, Thursday until 8 pm; Sunday noon - 5 pm.

Sea Cloth (Home-Accessories, Fabric)
107 Greenwich Avenue, 422.6150

www.SeaCloth.com

A shop showcasing their own fabric designs - vibrant colors and bold prints. You may buy the textiles by the yard or they will provide custom drapery or upholstery services. Their pretty place mats, pillows and table-top accessories are hard to resist.
Hours: Monday - Saturday, 10 am - 6 pm.

Sears (Department Store)
100 Main Street (Galleria Shopping Center), White Plains, NY
914.644.1400

www.Sears.com

Home furnishings, home improvement, appliances, electronics, clothing, including a Land's End Store. They own the brands: Kenmore, Craftsman & DieHard. Sears competes with Macy's, pricing below Bloomingdale's, Nordstrom and Saks and above JC Penny and Kohls.
Hours: Monday - Saturday, 10 am - 9 pm; Sunday, 11 am - 7 pm.

Sephora (Cosmetics)
75 Greenwich Avenue, 422.2191

www.sephora.com

A vast selection of men's and women's beauty products are displayed in this large, airy store. There are eight make-up stations, with consultants to help you bring out your inner self.
Hours: Monday - Saturday, 10 am - 6 pm; Sunday, noon - 5 pm.

Shippan Center for Arts and Antiques (Antiques)

614 Shippan Avenue, Stamford, 353.0222
www.shippancenter.com
One of a cluster of 5 antique centers in Stamford. They have 125 dealers.
Hours: Monday - Saturday, 10 - 5; Sunday, noon - 5 pm.
Directions: I-95 N to exit N to exit 8, R on Canal.

Shoes N More (Shoes)

251 Greenwich Avenue, 629.2323
A fun assortment of boys and girl's clothing, sizes 2T - 16. They have an excellent shoe selection including Astor, Elefanter, Nike and Merrill. They carry some western boots and accessories. Twice a year they have a very good shoe sale (summer & after Christmas).
Hours: Monday - Saturday, 9 am - 7 pm; Sunday, 11 am - 6 pm.

Shanti Bithi Nursery(Home, Gardening)

3047 High Ridge Road, Stamford, 329.0768
www.shantibithi.com
Wonderful greenhouse of bonsai trees as well as supplies and lessons to create your own bonsai. They also have a nice selection of Asian garden ornaments. They teach beginning, intermediate and advanced bonsai classes, most are on the weekend.
Hours: Monday - Saturday, 9 am - 5 pm.
Directions: Merritt Parkway N to exit 35, L on High Ridge, about 5miles on the right.

The Side Door (Clothing-Women)

248 Mill Street, Byram, 532.5606
Casual wear for the busy woman, at reasonable prices. Lots of samples and manufacturer's closeouts.
Hours: Monday, 10:30 am - 3:30 pm;
Tuesday - Saturday, 10:30 am - 5 pm.

Simon Pearce (Home - Accessories)

325 Greenwich Avenue, 861.0780
www.simonpearce.com
Beautiful handblown glass, pottery, lamps and furniture. Very reasonable prices for the quality.
Hours: Monday - Saturday, 10 am - 6 pm; Sunday, noon - 5 pm.

Silvermine Guild Arts Center (Art)

1037 Silvermine Road, New Canaan, CT, 203.966.9700

www.silvermineart.org

The Silvermine Arts Center has been a gathering place for artists and art lovers for almost 100 years. The Silvermine galleries have 20 shows each year in addition to the juried annual Art of The Northeast, held late in April. Silvermine offers a great many lectures, workshops and art classes. During the summer they run Art Day Camps for children ages: 5 - 8, 8 - 12 and 14 - 17.

Skaters Landing (Sports: Equipment and Clothing)

242 Mill Street, Byram, 542.0555

www.Skaterslanding.com

When you buy your skating equipment from a skating instructor like Mark Magliola, you know you are getting expert advice. This shop has everything you need for figure skating; skates, costumes, blades and sharpening. Make appointments for fittings and while-u-wait sharpening.

Hours: Tuesday, noon - 5 pm; Wednesday, noon - 3 pm;

Thursday, noon - 7 pm; Friday, noon - 4 pm;

Saturday, 9:30 am - 5 pm; Sunday, 1 pm - 5 pm.

Sleepy's (Home- Furniture and Furnishings)

• 159 West Putnam Avenue, 869.5255

• 1340 East Putnam Avenue, Old Greenwich, 637.8571

www.sleepys.com

A large chain of mattress shops, carrying most major brands.

Hours: weekdays, 10 am - 9 pm; Saturday, 10 am - 8 pm;

Sunday, 11 am - 7 pm.

Smart Kids Company (Toys)

17 East Elm Street, 869.0022

www.SKToys.com

The toys in Mary De Silva's shop may look like a lot of fun, but most have been selected to help in your child's growth and educational development through play. This local shop has a global clientele from the website.

Hours: Monday - Saturday, 9 am - 6 pm; Sunday, 11 am - 5 pm.

Smith & Hawken (Home - Indoor, Outdoor Furniture)
30 East Avenue, New Canaan, CT, 203.972.0820
www.SmithandHawken.com
Upscale store selling stylish garden furniture and some home furnishings.
Hours: Monday - Saturday, 10 am - 6 pm; Sunday, 11 am -5 pm
Directions: Merritt Parkway N to exit 37, L on Rte 124/South Street, R on Elm, L on Main, R on East.

Sophia's Great Dames (Clothing, Women & Gifts)
1 Liberty Way, 869.5990
Wonderful shop for vintage clothing, antiques, collectibles, gifts and costume rentals. Fun to visit.
Hours: Monday - Saturday, 10 am - 5:30 pm; open later during holidays.

Sound Beach Sportswear (Clothing - Women & Children)
239 Sound Beach Avenue, Old Greenwich, 637.5557
The sportswear is an interesting mix of casual dressiness. They also carry adorable infant and children's wear and some matching mother-daughter sweaters. Expect a friendly reception in this family-owned business.
Hours: weekdays, 10 am - 6 pm; Saturday, 10 am - 5 pm.

Sportif Ltd (Clothing, Sports)
41 Greenwich Avenue, 629.8874
www.sportifltd.com
A large selection of sporting goods and clothing including, skiing, snowboarding, tennis and in-line skating.
Hours: weekdays, 9:30 am - 6 pm; Saturday, 9:30 - 5:30 pm;
Sunday, noon - 5 pm.

Sportsman's Den (Fishing)
33 River Road, Cos Cob, 869.3234
Supplies and classes on angling and fly fishing. One visit and you will be hooked. Captain Bill Harold is the best saltwater guide in the area. Get your fishing license here. They also carry heritage kayaks and kayaking accessories.
Hours: weekdays, 9 am - 5 pm, Monday until 2 pm;
Saturday, 8 am - 5 pm; Sunday, 8 am - 2 pm.

Stamford Antique Area (Antiques)

Tucked away in converted manufacturing buildings are five collections of antique dealers with enough collectibles and antiques to suit just about anyone. With antiques from over 350 dealers, it's hard to imagine anyone not finding something they want. A great outing for the antique enthusiast.

- **Antique and Artisan Center,** 69 Jefferson Street, 327.6022
  www.antiqueandartisancenter.com
  Look in the Modernism Room and see their collection of 20th Century "antiques-in-the-making." 150 dealers.
- **Hiden Galleries**, 481 Canal Street, 323.9090
  www.hidengalleriesantiques.com
- **Stamford Antiques Center**, 735 Canal Street, 888.329.3546
  www.antiquesinstamford.com

Hours: Monday - Saturday, 10 am - 5:30 pm; Sunday, noon - 5 pm.
Directions: I-95 N to Exit 8, R on Canal (at 2nd light), continue straight or L on Jefferson.

Stamford Archery & Firearms (Sporting Goods)

379 Shippan Avenue, Stamford, CT 348.2221
An extensive supply of bows, arrows and rifles. Ask about archery instruction.
Hours: weekdays, 11 am - 6 pm (Thursday to 8 pm);
Saturday, 10 am - 5 pm.

Stamford Town Center (Shopping Center)

Stamford, CT 324.0935
www.ShopStamfordTownCenter.com
A large, attractive 23-year old mall with plenty of brand name shops (such as: Pottery Barn, Banana Republic, Limited, Brookstone, Mikasa, Sharper Image and Williams-Sonoma). Macy's (964.1500) and Saks Fifth Avenue (323.3100) are the anchor stores.
Hours: weekdays, 10 am - 9 pm; Saturday, 10 am - 8 pm;
Sunday, noon - 6 pm.
Directions: I-95 N to exit 8, L on Atlantic, R on Tresser, L onto ramp.

Staples (Office Supplies)

1297 East Putnam Avenue, 698.9011
www.staples.com
Office supplies of every sort. This store also carries electronics and office furniture. Yes, they have staples, too!
Hours: weekdays, 8am - 9pm; Saturday, 10 am - 9 pm;
Sunday, 10am - 6pm.

Steilmann (Clothing - Women)

354 North Main Street, Port Chester, NY 914.939.1500
www.steilmann.de
This is a huge warehouse of classic European-style clothing. Steilmann is a German Company.
Hours: Everyday, 11 am - 6 pm, Thursday until 7 pm.

Steven B. Fox (Jewelry)

8 Lewis Street, 629.3303
A full service family-owned jewelry store specializing in precious jewels, pearls, watches, estate jewelry and objets d'art. Repairs done on the premises. They make estate purchases.
Hours: Monday - Saturday, 9:30 am - 5 pm;
Sunday noon - 5 pm, from Thanksgiving to Christmas.

Stickley (Home-Furniture)

50 Tarrytown Road, White Plains, NY 914.948.6333
www.stickley.com
Stickley mission furniture and fine English reproduction furniture.
Hours: Monday - Saturday 10 am - 5:30 pm; Monday & Thursday until 9 pm; Sunday, noon - 5 pm.
Directions: I-95 S to exit 21 (I-287 W); I-287 W to exit 8 (Westchester Ave); continue on Westchester Avenue which becomes Tarrytown Rd (NY119).

Strauss Warehouse Outlet (Parties)
140 Horton Avenue, Port Chester, NY, 914.939.3544, 7132
www.straussoutlet.com
Gift wrapping, party favors, balloons, paper goods, just about anything you might want for a party at great prices. They carry a huge selection of Halloween costumes during October.
Hours: weekdays, 9 am - 7 pm; Saturday, 9 am - 5 pm;
Sunday, 10 am - 3 pm.
Directions: Post Road to Main Street in Port Chester, R on Wilkins, L on Locust, R on Horton (Horton is one way).

Charles Stuttig Locksmith (Hardware)
158 Greenwich Avenue, 869.6260
A fixture in Greenwich for many years, they provide a wide variety of locks and safes. Whether you have an emergency or just need a key copied, they can be counted on and trusted.
Hours: weekdays, 7:30 am - 5:30 pm.

Super Handy Hardware (Hardware)
1 Riversville Road, Glenville Center, 531.5599
A good old-fashioned hardware store with most everything you would need for light and heavy-duty home projects, barbecue grills and more. What is wonderful, you can stop in, tell one of the dear sales people what you want and they will find it for you immediately.
Hours: Monday - Saturday, 8 am - 5 pm; Sunday, 9 am -1 pm.

Syms (Clothing - Youth, Men, Women)
295 Tarrytown Road, Elmsford, NY, 914.592.2447
www.Syms.com
Off-price children's, men's and women's designer and brand name clothing, in a warehouse setting.
Hours: Monday - Saturday, 10 am - 9 pm (Saturday to 8:30 pm);
Sunday, 11 am - 5:30 pm.

Tahiti Street (Clothing- women's swimwear)
113 Greenwich Avenue, 622.1878
www.tahitistreet.com
Perfect for a trip to the Caribbean or to look elegant on the beach. You can purchase bathing separates in different sizes.
Hours: Monday - Saturday, 10 am - 5 pm.

Talbots (Clothing - Women)
151 Greenwich Avenue, 869.7177
www.talbots.com
Talbots has classic clothes for business women of all ages as well as a good sportswear line. They have an extensive women's petite department.
Hours: Monday - Saturday, 9:30 am - 6 pm (Wednesday & Thursday until 7 pm); Sunday, noon - 5 pm.

Talbots Kids & Babies (Clothing- Children)
165 Greenwich Avenue, 869.6770
A mix of casual and dressier classic children's clothes. Sizes from newborn to 12 years old.
Hours: Monday - Saturday, 9:30 am - 6 pm; (Wednesday & Thursday until 7 pm); Sunday, noon - 5 pm.

Tallows End (Gifts)
41 East Elm Street, 661.5903
The largest selection of candles in the area, all shapes, sizes and scents. They also have a nice selection of gifts.
Hours: weekdays, 9:30 am - 5:30 pm; Saturday, 9:30 am - 5 pm.

Tangier Outlet Center (Mall -Outlet)
Westbrook, CT, 866.665.8685
www.TangierOutlet.com
With 65 stores, it is just barely smaller than Clinton Crossing and only a few miles away. If you are in the area, you should stop by.
Hours: April - December: Monday Saturday, 10 am - 9 pm; Sunday, 10 am - 6 pm. January - March, Monday- Saturday, 10 am - 6 pm.
Directions: I-95 N to exit 65, L on Flat Rock Place.

Target (Department Stores)
21 Broad Street, Stamford, CT 388.0006
www.Target.com
This discount department store is the 6th largest retailer in the US with 1,494 stores. They are the 3rd largest seller of music in the US. Target competes with Wal-Mart and Kmart. Since its founding in 1962, it has differentiated its stores from its competitors by offering what it believes is more upscale, trend-forward merchandise at low cost.
Hours: Monday - Saturday, 8 am - 10 pm; Sunday, 8 am - 9 pm.

Theory (Clothing- Women)

396 Greenwich Avenue, 422.0020

www.theory.com

You can't go wrong with the high-quality clothes from Theory. Perfect for business and social attire. This store has wonderful suits and blouses for women as well as dresses, sweaters, slacks, shoes and bags. There is also a small men's section.

Hours: Monday - Saturday 10 am - 6 pm; Thursday until 7 pm; Sunday noon - 5 pm.

Threads and Treads (Sporting Equipment and Clothing)

17 East Putnam Avenue, 661.0142

www.threadsandtreads.com

Entry forms for the latest races are available here. This is a good source for biking, swimming and running attire. They sponsor the Road Hogs www.roadhogs.org which conducts classes for runners, cyclers and swimmers, of all ages and abilities.

Hours: Monday - Saturday, 9:30 am - 6 pm; Sunday, noon -3 pm.

Tiffany & Co (Jewelry, Gifts)

140 Greenwich Avenue, 661.7847

www.tiffany.com

This famous store has a nice collection of jewelry and giftware, as well as helpful sales people.

Hours: Monday - Saturday, 10 am - 6 pm; Sunday, noon - 5 pm.

Tory Burch (Clothing-Women)

255 Greenwich Avenue, 622.5023

www.ToryBurch.com

Sportswear, swimwear, shoes, bags and jewelry by a New York designer.

Hours: Monday - Wednesday, 10 am - 6 pm; Thursday, 10 am - 7pm; Saturday, 10 am - 6 pm; Sunday, noon - 5 pm.

TJ Maxx (Department Store)

330 Connecticut Avenue & Route 1, Norwalk, CT, 203.854.9890

www.TJMaxx.com

The largest off-price apparel retailer in the US with over 700 stores. Merchandise is normally 20-50% below regular department store prices. In this 25,000 square foot store, they sell just about everything, from clothing and footwear to bedding, furniture, jewelry and housewares.

Hours: Monday-Saturday, 9:30 am - 9:30 pm; Sunday, 11 am - 6pm.

Toys "R" Us (Toys)

59 Connecticut Avenue, Norwalk, CT, 203.852.6988
www.Toysrus.com
A typical mega toy store.
Hours: Monday - Saturday, 10 am - 9 pm; Sunday, 10 am - 6 pm.
Directions: Just off I-95, exit 14.

Trezure (Women - Clothing & Accessories)

253 Mill Street, Byram, 531.3101
Artist, Trez Topo, has a selection of trendy clothing for the young and young at heart. Her shop, a showroom for local artists, is fun to visit.
Hours: Tuesday - Saturday, 11 am - 5 pm.

Tulips Greenwich (Florist)

91 Lake Avenue (at the Lake Avenue Circle), 661.3154
European floral design shop known for its creative and innovative bouquets of Dutch and French flowers.
Hours: weekdays, 9 am - 5 pm; Saturday 10 am - 4 pm.

Tumi (luggage)

289 Greenwich Avenue, 861.2920
www.tumi.com
Traveling is a hassle. Why not, at least, go in style. Attractive and distinctive luggage, wallets, business cases. Even some sportswear.
Hours: Monday - Saturday, 10 am - 6 pm; Sunday, noon - 5 pm.

Unisa (Shoes & Accessories - Women)

85 Greenwich Avenue, 422.2959
A factory store with stylish, casual shoes, handbags, belts and accessories at reasonable prices.
Hours: Monday - Saturday, 10 am - 6 pm; Sunday, noon - 5 pm.

United House Wrecking (Home - Furniture)

535 Hope Street, Stamford, 348.5371
www.unitedhousewrecking.com
An unusual source for the unusual. Thirty-thousand square feet of inventory with everything from collectibles to antiques to architectural items to junk. Don't miss it.
Hours: Monday - Saturday, 9:30 am - 5:30 pm; Sunday, noon - 5 pm.
Directions: I-95 N to exit 9, Make first 2 lefts onto Rt 1, at 2nd light R on Courtland (Rt 106), L on Glenbrook, R on Hope.

Vallin Galleries (Antiques)
516 Danbury Road (Route 7), Wilton, CT, 203.762.7441
www.valingalleries.com
Located far from the source of these antiques is a quaint saltbox filled with a collection of Asian art, some rare, all beautifully displayed.
Hours: Call store.
Directions: Merritt Pkw. N to exit 39 (Norwalk) or I-95 N to exit 15, Rte 7 N.

Veronique (Clothing-Women's Maternity)
14 Railroad Avenue, 625.8620
www.veroniquematernity.com
To find this upscale Manhattan maternity shop, you have to go through the Kids Supply store next to the Greenwich railroad station. Mothers-to-be appreciate their selection of casual, business and dress-up fashions.
Hours: weekdays, 9:30 am - 5:30 pm; Saturday, 10 am - 5 pm.

Victoria's Secret (Lingerie)
200 Greenwich Avenue, 661.0158
www.VictoriasSecret.com
A popular chain shop with lingerie and fashionable pajamas.
Hours: weekdays, 10 am -7 pm; Saturday, 10 am - 6 pm; Sunday, noon - 5 pm.

Village Ewe (Sewing)
244 Sound Beach Avenue, Old Greenwich, 637.3953
www.thevillageewe.com
Beware of stopping here unless you are ready to get hooked on needlepoint. Individual lessons for beginners can be arranged. Group classes are offered in the fall and spring. They are a full service needlepoint studio with over 1,500 handpainted canvases.
Hours: Monday - Saturday, 10 am - 5:30 pm.

Vineyard Vines (Clothing-Men, Women, Children)

145 Greenwich Avenue, 661.1803
www.VineyardVinesByRichards.com
www.VineyardVines.com
Greenwich residents are proud of this 5,000 square foot shop filled with colorful, informal, delightful clothing. Shep and Ian Murray of Greenwich began their company a few years ago by creating unique ties - worn by presidents, celebrities and many Greenwichites. You will love this shop.
Hours: Monday - Saturday, 10 am - 6 pm (Thursdays to 8 pm); Sunday, 11 am - 5 pm.

WalMart (Department Store)

680 Connecticut Avenue, Norwalk, CT, 203.854.5236
www.Walmart.com
Founded in 1962, it is the largest retailer in the world. They are also the largest grocery retailer and the largest toy retailer in the US with an estimated 22% of the toy business.
Hours: every day, 7 am - 10 pm.

Waterworks (Home - Decorating)

23 West Putnam Avenue, 869.7766
www.waterworks.com
High-end bathroom and kitchen fixtures as well as a very nice selection of tiles. Excellent customer service.
Hours: weekdays, 9 am - 5 pm; Saturday, 10 am - 4 pm.

Weber Fine Art (Art)

24 West Putnam Avenue, 422.5375
www.Artnet.com/weberfineart.html
Modern post-war and contemporary art.
Hours: Tuesday - Saturday, 11 am - 5 pm.

Wendy Gee (Children- Furniture)

42 Greenwich Avenue, 422.2811
www.wendygee.com
Wendy Gee provides a colorful assortment of home accessories, furniture and gifts. They offer creative decorating ideas and reasonable prices.
Hours: Monday - Saturday, 9:30 am - 6 pm; Sunday noon - 4 pm. Closed Sundays in July and August.

Wendy's Closet (Clothing, Women)
375 Greenwich Avenue, 622.7130
A nice mix of trendy casual and business outfits.
Hours: Monday - Saturday, 10 am - 6 pm.

Westchester Mall (Mall)
White Plains, NY, 914.683.8600
www.simon.com or www.simon.com/mall/directory.aspx?ID=105
An even larger mall than the Stamford Town Center boasting over 150 fine upscale stores including: Carte & Barrel, Pottery Barn Kids, Louis Vuitton, Gucci, Apple, Brooks Brothers, Tumi, Sony Style and P.F. Chang's China Bistro. Neiman Marcus (914.428.2000) and Nordstrom (914.946.1122) are the anchor stores. Hours: Monday Saturday, 10 am - 9 pm; Sunday, 11 am - 6 pm.
Store hours may vary.
Directions: I-95 S to I-287 W, exit 8 (Westchester Avenue), L on Bloomingdale or on Paulding.

Whimsies Doll House & Miniature Shop (Toys)
18 Lewis Street, 629.8024
The ultimate dollhouse store.
Hours: Monday - Saturday, 10 am - 6 pm.

Williams-Sonoma (Home Cookware)
• 100 Greyrock Place (Town Center), Stamford, CT, 961.0977
• 125 Westchester Avenue (Westchester Mall), White Plains, NY, 644.8360
www.Williams-Sonoma.com
Speciality cookware and housewares as well as a variety of gourmet foods that are difficult to find elsewhere. They teach cooking classes as well.
Hours: Monday - Saturday, 10 am - 9 pm; Sunday, 11 am - 6 pm.

Wishlist (Clothing-Youth)
350 Greenwich Avenue, 629.4600
www.wishlistgirl.com
Stylish clothing, nicely displayed, for sophisticated teens and pre-teens.
Hours: weekdays, 10 am - 6 pm, Thursday until 7 pm;
Sunday, noon - 5 pm.

Woodbury Commons (Mall, Outlet)
Harriman, NY, 845.928.4000
www.premiumoutlets.com
A huge outlet location with over 220 stores, including Burberrys and Brooks Brothers. Definitely worth the 60-minute drive. If you go to the website first and sign up for a coupon book, it can really pay off.
Hours: every day, 10 am - 9 pm.
Directions: Take I-95 to I-287 W across the Tappan Zee Bridge and follow I-87 N (New York State Thruway) to exit 16. R at the exit. You can't miss it.

Wyler (Antiques)
40 West Putnam Avenue, 622.2390
This jewel of a shop has 19th and 20th century English silver and fine porcelain.
Hours: Tuesday - Saturday, 10 am to 5:30 pm.

Zorya (Art)
38 East Putnam Avenue, 869.9898
www.ZoryaFineArt.com
Emerging and established Ukrainian artists.
Hours: Tuesday - Saturday, 11 am - 7 pm.

Zyns News (Magazines & Newspapers)
345 Greenwich Avenue, 661.5168
This store has the largest selection of magazines and newspapers in Fairfield County. For many years, Greenwich residents have loved finding all of their favorite publications here.
Hours: every day, 6 am - 9 pm; Sunday, until 6 pm.

SINGLES

According to the 2000 US Census, Greenwich has an adult population of 54,557 of which 16,533 are singles. If you are single, no matter what your age or life style, there are many ways to meet others. In addition to joining one of the numerous volunteer organizations, there are a variety of organized social events.

Capers Singles

PO Box 2126, Westport, CT, 06880, 203.227.4513
www.Capers-Singles.com
A Greenwich-based, for-profit singles club, created by Jim Godbout. It conducts respected, upscale, dressy singles events all over lower Fairfield County for ages 30 to 50+. Even when held in towns such as Westport, a great many of the attendees are from Greenwich.

Cotton Club

at Christ Church, 245 East Putnam Avenue, 869.6600
Barbara Reid, CoPresident, 914.202 7649
E-Mail: barbara@reid.net
www.christchurchgreenwich.com
A social club, with approximately 350 members, for singles of all faiths, ages 40 and up. Members participate in a variety of activities, from hiking and tennis to attending the theater and polo matches. Be sure to get their newsletter.

Greenwich Jaycees

PO Box 232, Greenwich, 06836, 358.3134
www.greenwichjaycees.org
Membership is open to young professionals ages 21-39. This group has a good time working together on fund rasing events for worthy charities in Greenwich. They organize the annual Greenwich Road Rally, www.GreenwichRoadRally.com

Greenwich Reform Synagogue Singles

Rabbi Richard Chapin, 629.0018
www.grs.org
Comprised of men and women in their 30s, 40s and 50s. Meetings are at private clubs in Fairfield and Westchester County.

Pinnacle Ski and Sports Club

Jason Sliss, President, 203.353 1781
Eric Zuidema, Vice President Membership, 203.451.8990
E-Mail: ezski@optonline.net
www.pinnacleski.org
Non-profit social and recreational organization founded in 1990 which sponsors year-round activities: ski and snowboarding trips in the winter and a variety of other sports, excursions, and events during the rest of the year. It has around 270 single and family members from the Fairfield / Westchester area ranging in age from 21 to 70.

Singles Under Sail

Contact: Kelly Barney 929.6886
www.singlesundersail.org
Social events for singles who love sailing.

Ski Bears of Connecticut

11 Wall Street (entrance in rear), Norwalk, CT 203.838.8801
www.skibears.org
Erin Cuniffe, Membership Chair
A ski and social club for singles and married adults. Membership is open to anyone over 21. Emphasis is on outdoor activities.

Westport Singles

Unitarian Church, Westport, CT, (203.227.8173: Recording)
www.westportsinglesct.org
Don Smith, President
A non-profit singles group, with about 800 members, sponsoring programs at various locations in Fairfield County. Ask for their newsletter.

Young Friends of the Bruce

For information call Whitney Lucas Rosenberg, Membership Manager, 869.6786 XT 366.
A Bruce Museum membership group for singles and couples, ages 20's, 30's, and 40's. Enjoy quarterly get-togethers to mingle in a cultural setting. Members and their guests enjoy exhibition tours, wine tastings, and cocktail receptions. Events are held on certain Thursdays.

TEENS/YOUNG ADULTS

The Department of Parks and Recreation has a great many athletic programs for teens. www.greenwichct.virtualtownhall.net/Public_Documents/ GreenwichCT_ParkRec/GreenwichCT_Recreation/programs/youth. For instance, the Skate Park (described in PARKS & BEACHES) is good place for teens to meet.

Ambassadors in Leotards

Contact: Felicity Foote, 869.9373

For twenty-four years, Felicity, director of the Greenwich Ballet Workshop, has taken a group of accomplished 14 to18-year-old dancers to Europe to dance for charitable events. Auditions are required.

Arch Street Teen Center

100 Arch Street, 629.5744

www.ArchStreet.org

Founded in 1991, Arch Street (also known as the Greenwich Teen Center, Inc.) is a refurbished warehouse right on the harbor. Whether at the dance floor and bandstand or the upstairs snack shop with booths, Arch Street provides teens with the opportunity to be together in a healthy environment. Arch Street is more than just a place to hang out, the Center provides everything from college application advice and counseling help, to opportunities for teens to participate in community service projects or to learn leadership skills. Although there is an adult board, the teens run Arch Street through the teen board. This board has sixty members, from 9th to 12th grades, and has representatives from both private and public schools. Arch Street is open to Greenwich students from 7th through 12th grade.

Boys and Girls Club

4 Horseneck Lane, 869 3224

www.bgcg.org

This club is awesome. The totally renovated facility has a gymnasium, game room, library, swimming pool, and the skating rink used for ice skating in winter, and roller skating/street hockey or basketball during other seasons.

Members must be Greenwich residents or have a parent working in town. Transportation by bus or van is provided to and from several areas around town including Central and Western Middle Schools. The membership fee for ages 6-18 is $20 per year for residents or $120 for nonresidents. The Club also has 77-acre preserve, Camp Simmons, for summer teen activities.

Boy Scouts

869.8424

www.greenwichbsa.com

Boy Scouts, for boys in 6th grade until their 18th birthday; Venturing and Exploring, co-ed programs for high school students, ages 14 - 20.

Greenwich Cotillion

www.jlgreenwich.org

Greenwich still has a Cotillion every year at the beginning of summer for young ladies who wish to debut. The Cotillion, sponsored by the Junior League of Greenwich, is often described as a "fun party with dignity," but perhaps is more accurately described as a series of dignified fun parties. Attendance is by open invitation on a first-come, first-serve basis. Some years you need to send in your check and application the moment it is received; other years there is less demand and the event fills up more slowly. To be included on the mailing list, contact the Junior League at 869.1979.

Girl Scouts

800.882.5561

www.gscswct.org

They offer a broad range of activities for girls. Greenwich has 60 troops with some 750 girls and 500 plus registered, trained adults. Cadettes, grades 7 - 9 (ages 11 - 14); Seniors, grades 9 - 12 (ages 14 - 17).

Junior Educator Program, Bruce Museum

Bruce Museum, 1 Museum Drive, 869.0376

Contact Jennifer Josef at extension 323

www.BruceMuseum.org

High school students are trained to teach young children in the Museum's Neighborhood Collaborative program. Topics covered relate to the Museum's exhibits, such as turn of the century American art, costal ecology and Native American baskets techniques.

airports

The Verizon yellow pages has handy airport maps of La Guardia (LGA), Kennedy (JFK) and Newark (EWR).

Kennedy Airport (JFK)
Queens, NY, 718.244.444
www.panynj.gov

La Guardia Airport (LGA)
Queens, NY, 718.533.3400
www.panynj.gov

Newark Airport (EWR)
Newark, NJ, 973.961.6000
www.panynj.gov
Of the major New York City airports, Newark in New Jersey takes the longest to get to (80 minutes). Newark Airport is somewhat less congested than the other two. In addition, flights out of Newark are sometimes less expensive, especially for Continental Airlines.

Westchester County Airport (HPN)
White Plains, NY,
Airlines: 914.995.4860; Operations: 914.995.4850
www.co.westchester.ny.us/airport
This airport is located on upper King Street. It is newly renovated and has good parking facilities. Commercial flights are limited and somewhat more expensive than those from the major NYC airports, but nothing could be easier or more convenient. Airlines that fly out of Westchester are: Air Canada, AirTran, American Airlines, Continental, Delta, Northwest, United (Chicago), & US Air.
Directions: Glenville Road to King Street; R on King; L at light to Rye Lake Rd.

airport flight delay information

FAA Flight Delay Information

www.fly.faa.gov/flyfaa/usmap.jsp
A good source of independent information for airports around the country. Even if NY airports are clear, if the hub of the airline you are using is experiencing delays, your flight is likely to be delayed.

USA Today

www.usatoday.com/travel/flights/front.htm
This site provides real time flight information.

airport parking

Parking long term or overnight at short term airport parking lots is not recommended for new or late model cars. To be sure, use one of these private lots. The cost seems to be about the same, the service better and your car safe.

Avistar Airport Valet Parking

800.621.7275, Newark: 973.297.0430
www.avistarparking.com
Avistar operates out of Kennedy, La Guardia and Newark. If you fly out of one airport, but return to another, they will transfer your car and have it waiting for you. Their website has good instructions to each of their airport locations. You must make a reservation in advance.

Skypark

Newark Airport, 973.624.9000, 800.PICK U UP
www.sunmetrosys.com/skypark
SkyPark is self-parking with frequent shuttle service to the airport. SkyPark has the bonus of giving you a free stay after ten visits. A reservation is not required.
Directions: Follows signs from I-95 (the New Jersey Turnpike) to Newark Airport, exit at Hayes Street onto Route 1 S. Skypark is on the R.

airport transportation

CT Limousine Service

800.472.5466

www.CTlimo.com

If you are traveling alone, this may be your least expensive way to get to La Guardia, Kennedy or Newark airports. Pick up at the Stamford Marriot.

Eveready (Yellow) Cab Company

At Cos Cob RR Station, 869.1700

Greenwich Police

622.8006, 8015

A Greenwich off-duty policeman will drive you to any of the NY area airports and pick you up in your own car. This is often less expensive than a limousine service.

Greenwich Taxi

At Greenwich RR Station, 869.6000

An old stand-by for getting around town or to the train station - call ahead and make a reservation to be picked up. This is a good way to get to Westchester Airport, LaGuardia or Kennedy. Greenwich Taxi is open until 1:30 am.

Red Dot Airport Shuttle

800.673.3368

Transportation to and from Kennedy and La Guardia airports from the Hyatt Regency in Greenwich.

Rudy's Limousine Service

869.0014

A comfortable, reliable service. When several people travel together, this is a wise choice. Their drivers are very professional and pleasant.
Hours: 24 hours a day every day.

clubs

AAA / CT Motor Club

623 Newfield Avenue, Stamford, 765.4222

www.aaa.com

The Place to get your International Drivers's License or other help for a trip.

Hours: weekdays, 8:30 am - 5:30 pm, Saturday 8:30 am - noon.

Directions: I-95 N to exit 8, follow exit ramp to State Street. at 3rd light, L on Elm. It will become Grove, then Strawberry Hill, then Newfield. AAA is on right in Newfield Green Shopping Center.

TIP: ART ON THE AVENUE

www.greenwicharts.org/arttotheavenue.asp

If you want to enjoy Greenwich Avenue at its best, do not miss a stroll down the Avenue on the opening night of this festival. The Greenwich Arts Council sponsors this event in early May. Over 150 artists, retailers and restaurants take part. Call the Council at 622.3998 for the details.

See also: AUTOMOBILES

Travel Information

Local commuters can untangle their morning commutes by consulting the following commuter transportation websites:

Metro-North Railroad: www.mta.nyc.ny.us/mnr/index.html
Offers the latest schedule information for all CT/NY/NJ MTA Metro North lines.

MetroPool: www.metropool.com
The site offers news and information on commuting in and around Fairfield and Westchester counties.

New York City traffic cams www.nyc.gov
Click on link to traffic cams for real time traffic cameras focused on trouble spots.

Tappan Zee bridge webcams
www.thruway.ny.us/webcams

Interstate 95 webcams
www.ct.gov/dot
www.i95coalition.org

foreign currency

Greenwich Bank & Trust

115 East Putnam Avenue, 618.8900

This branch has a Travelex foreign currency ATM, www.Travelex.com. Whether you will need Euros or Yen when you arrive, you can get it here.

TIP: PAUL TUDOR JONES CHRISTMAS LIGHTS

The unbelievable display of Christmas lights by Paul Tudor Jones at his waterfront home in Belle Haven, has become so popular that the Greenwich Police are assigned to direct traffic.

passports

Connecticut Passport Agency
50 Washington Street, Norwalk, CT 06854
Automated Appointment Number: 1.877.487.2778
www.Travel.state.gov
The Connecticut Passport Agency serves only customers who are traveling within 2 weeks (14 days), or who need foreign visas for travel. An appointment is required.
Hours: weekdays, 9:00 a.m. - 4:00 p.m., excluding Federal holidays

Ferguson Library
One Public Library Plaza, Bedford & Broad Streets, Stamford, CT
964.1000
www.fergusonlibrary.org/about_us/passport_office/passport_office.html
You may be able expedite it by paying an additional fee, but the normal wait time can be as long as 6 weeks.
Hours: Monday - Thursday: 9 a.m. - 2 p.m. & 5 p.m. - 8 p.m,
Friday & Saturday: 9 a.m. - 2 p.m.

Greenwich Post Offices
You can also apply weekdays from 9 am - 4 pm, through the Greenwich Avenue Post Office; the wait time may be as long as 6 weeks.
Required for a Passport
1. Completed and unsigned DS-11 application. You can download it from
   http://travel.state.gov/passport/about/npic/npic_898.html
2. Proof of Citizenship (previous US Passport or certified birth certificate)
3. Two color photographs (2x2 inches, not from a vending machine)
4. Social Security number (not technically required, but you need it anyway)

Travel Immunizations
The Department of Infectious Diseases at Greenwich Hospital offers many types of immunizations required for foreign travel to less developed countries. Call 863.3270 for an appointment between 8 am & 4 pm. It is best to schedule one at least 6-weeks before your departure.

Ritz Camera Center
82 Greenwich Avenue, Greenwich, 869.0673

Action Arts Photography
242 Sound Beach Ave, Old Greenwich, 637.2685

TIP: UBS STAMFORD PARADE

A spectacular parade is put on every November by UBS; huge balloons and fun for everyone. For informato call 348.5285 or visit www.Stamford-downtown.com

TRAVEL

Liberty Travel
48 West Putnam Ave, 625.8170
www.libertytravel.com
Agents often speak a number of languages. Because Liberty is a large operation with over 189 stores, they have big buying power for packages in the Caribbean and Florida. They are a good place to go to get a packaged tour for just about any purpose, intimate hotels, adventure trips, etc. If you don't quite know what you want, this could be a good bet. They are open every day, a real benefit if you are on a trip and need help immediately.
Hours: Monday - Thursday, 9 am - 7:30 pm; Friday, 9 am - 7 pm; Saturday, 10 am - 5 pm; Sunday, noon - 4 pm.

Putnam Travel
1171 East Putnam Avenue, Riverside, 637.3171
For corporate or personal travel, they still provide personalized service.
Hours: weekdays, 8:30 am - 6 pm.

Unleashed Adventures of Greenwich
17 Intervale Place, 914.967.6941
www.unleashedadventures.com
This Greenwich business, founded by Diane Terry, is for women only. They provide one-week adventure trips to exotic places. They cater to the civilized who will enjoy and benefit from an uncivilized experience. Returnees give their experience rave reviews.

Valerie Wilson Travel
1171 East Putnam Avenue, Riverside, CT, 637.5436
Hours: weekdays, 9 am - 5 pm.

TRAVEL

public transportation

See SENIORS for free Transportation Sources.

bus

Connecticut Transit (CTtransit)
203.327.7433
www.cttransit.com
CT Transit provides frequent bus service from Greenwich and Old Greenwich to Port Chester, Stamford and Norwalk. They also operate one route in Greenwich.
• K-Bus starts at the Stamford RR station and goes through Greenwich to Port Chester.
• L-Bus goes from Sound Beach Avenue & East Putnam Avenue to the Stamford RR station and to North Stamford.
• I-Bus is an express connecting Greenwich and White Plains RR stations.

Greenwich Commuter Connection
800.982.8420
www.NorwalkTransit.com
Norwalk Transit provides commuter bus routes linking the Greenwich RR station and the central business district. Service is during the morning and late afternoon rush hours.

Amtrak

800.USA.RAIL

www.amtrak.com

Operates from Stamford Station and connects to cities throughout the US and Canada.

Metro-North Commuter Railroad

800.638.7646

www.mnr.org

Offers frequent service to Grand Central Station, New York City, weekdays. Check the schedule for weekend and holiday times. Greenwich has four stations.

- Cos Cob Station
  Sound Shore Drive, off Exit 4 of I-95

- Greenwich Station
  Railroad Ave, off Exit 3 of I-95

- Old Greenwich Station
  Sound Beach Ave, off Exit 5 of I-95

- Riverside Station
  Between exits 4 & 5 off I-95

VOLUNTEER OPPORTUNITIES

Greenwich has a wealth of volunteers committed to helping our town. Volunteering in Greenwich is not new. Our Town was originally governed by a town meeting. All interested citizens gathered to make the decisions. Now we have a Representative Town Meeting and many boards and commissions, yet they are all made up of volunteers. Read the history of many of the organizations serving our Town and discover that they have been helping for 20, 30, 50 or more than 100 years. Caring about our neighbors, sharing our time and our talents is our Town's strength and bond.

The Anderson Guide to Volunteers

www.GreenwichVolunteerGuide.com
When asked, "What makes Greenwich special?" the answer: Volunteers! Greenwich has a wealth of volunteers committed to making life in our Town the best it can be. Volunteers are the heart and soul of Greenwich. We wrote a special booklet, The Anderson Guide to Volunteers, listing over 120 Greenwich volunteer organizations. It is designed around interest groups. Joining one of these organizations is a wonderful way to contribute to the Town and to make friends. If you would like a copy please call our main office at 203.629.4519 or e-mail Carolyn@GreenwichLiving.net. This guide is our gift to Greenwich.

The Volunteer Center of Southwestern Fairfield County

62 Palmer's Hill Road, Stamford, 348.7714
www.ucanhelp.org
Many, many volunteer opportunities are available in our surrounding areas. Check with The Volunteer Center for a comprehensive list of volunteer needs. They include Greenwich organizations as well as many other organizations in neighboring towns.

The Greenwich Citizen

41 West Putnam Avenue, 203.422.5230
www.greenwichcitizen.com
Check the "Living" section in this weekly Greenwich newspaper to find local organizatons seeking assistance. In a recent issue, the Bruce Museum was looking for docents, literacy volunteers were seeking readers and Neighbor to Neighbor wanted help sorting donations.

The Greenwich Time

20 East Elm Street, Greenwich, 625.4400

www.greenwichtime.com

Highly recommended are two columns that appear every Sunday in the Greenwich Time, entitled "Caring and Sharing" and "Volunteers Needed". Non-profit community groups seeking goods or services often send their requests to be printed in these columns. Because they provide a list of current needs, these are must-read columns.

The Greenwich Post

22 West Putnam Avenue, 861.9191

www.acorn-online.com/news/publish/greenwich.shtml

This weekly Greenwich paper features many of the volunteer organizations in Town. Be sure to check the column "Postings" for a list of current events for the week including the many benefits and events supporting the volunteer groups.

INDEX

INDEX

D

F

H

INDEX

INDEX

K

INDEX

INDEX

INDEX

T

V

W

INDEX

Z

Carolyn and Jerry Anderson

At what age does one discover that the ordinary is extraordinary? For Jerry and Carolyn Anderson, it was when they returned to Greenwich. Jerry had been away at Harvard as an undergraduate, and then as a graduate at Columbia where he received his Masters in Business and Doctorate in Law. Carolyn had been at Boston University as an undergraduate and then at Columbia where she received her Masters. Jerry and Carolyn were introduced by a Greenwich friend, married, and in 1968 they bought their home on Clapboard Ridge Road in Greenwich. No other town was ever considered.

Jerry grew up in Deer Park and went to Brunswick. His youth was filled with sailing on the sound, playing tennis in the Town tournaments and working on homework in the Greenwich Library. He learned to drive when Greenwich Avenue was a two-way street and dance lessons still required white gloves for boys as well as girls.

Carolyn is a Realtor the President of Anderson Associates, a real estate firm specializing in Greenwich residential properties. Carolyn is also President of the Greenwich Association of Realtors and of the Greenwich Multiple Listing Service. She is a licensed appraiser and a professional member of the American Society of Interior Designers. Prior to opening Anderson Associates, she designed and renovated many restaurants and residences in Greenwich. In her spare time she writes cookbooks. Jerry and Carolyn rarely miss a new restaurant.

Their children, Clifford and Cheryl, were born in Greenwich Hospital. They thrived in the public school system, which launched them to successful academic careers at Harvard and Princeton. Cheryl and Clifford enjoyed the benefits of Greenwich's many resources: water babies at the Y, scouting, running in town races, camping on Great Captain's Island and visiting the wonderful exhibits at Bruce Museum.

However, this book is not just the work of Carolyn and Jerry. It is the product of all of the Anderson Associates. The Anderson Associates are a diverse group. They are all ages and lifestyles, with one interest in common—Greenwich. They live in, work in and love Greenwich. Most grew up and went to school in Greenwich. Each in their own way, has come to the realization that Greenwich is extraordinary.

Amy Zeeve

Amy is Vice President of Anderson Associates. Amy was the inspiration for and the original author of most of the first edition of the Anderson Guide. She is extremely well liked and admired in the real estate community. Because of the extraordinary real estate help she gives her clients, Amy is one of the few people we know whose clients regularly send her flowers.

Amy grew up in Colorado and graduated from the University of Colorado. She moved to Greenwich in 1993. Both Amy and her husband John live in and love Greenwich. They have two young children, Charlie and Stephanie. Charlie is a student at Glenville School. Stephanie is in kindergarten. Under the tutelage of Amy and John, both excellent golfers, Charlie already has a good golf swing. Tiger Woods, watch out. This active youthful family has helped us keep the sections on children's activities and shops current.

ABOUT OUR ILLUSTRATOR

Vanessa Chow

Vanessa, a Greenwich resident, created the maps and drawings. She graduated from Greenwich High School, where she was one of their top art students and won awards at the Old Greenwich Art Society. Vanessa graduated magna cum laude from Connecticut College. She has studied art at Parsons School of Design, Silvermine, New York University, The Art Students League, The Chinese Academy of Fine Arts and Oxford University. She received her Masters Degree from the Rhode Island School of Design.

ORDER FORM

Please send me _____ copies of The Anderson Guide to Enjoying Greenwich Connecticut 7th Edition

Total number of copies   __________ @ 20.00
Price includes postage and sales tax.

Amount due $__________

I wish to pay by [ ] check or [ ] Credit Card

Name: ________________________________

Address: ________________________________

City: ____________________

State: _____ Zip: _________

Telephone: ____________________________

Credit Card Number ______ ______ ______ ______

Expiration Date: ___/___ Security Code _______

Name on Card: ____________________________

Signature: ________________________________

You can fax, mail, email or phone your order to
Avocet Press Inc
19 Paul Court
Pearl River, NY 10965-1539
Toll free phone: 877-4-AVOCET
Fax number: 845-735-6807
Email books@avocetpress.com